LOCKED OUT:
A Texas Legal Guide to Reentry

Last Revised June 2019

4th Edition

Copyright © 2019 Beacon Law, Texas Community Building with Attorney Resources (TEXAS C-BAR) and Texas RioGrande Legal Aid (TRLA). All Rights Reserved.

3rd Edition Copyright © 2018 Beacon Law, Texas Community Building with Attorney Resources (TEXAS C-BAR) and Texas RioGrande Legal Aid (TRLA). All Rights Reserved.

2nd Edition Copyright © 2017 Beacon Law, Texas Community Building with Attorney Resources (TEXAS C-BAR) and Texas RioGrande Legal Aid (TRLA). All Rights Reserved.

First published in 2012 by Texas Community Building with Attorney Resources (TEXAS C-BAR) and Texas RioGrande Legal Aid (TRLA). All Rights Reserved.

ACKNOWLEDGMENTS

Locked Out: A Texas Legal Guide to Reentry is a project of Beacon Law, Texas RioGrande Legal Aid and Texas C-BAR (Community Building with Attorney Resources).

This Guide is intended to assist advocates and others who help people experiencing the often difficult transition from incarceration to mainstream society. It summarizes a few of the most burdensome legal obstacles caused by a criminal record and provides guidance on how to effectively manage these barriers to reentry. The resources referenced in this Guide are publicly available and can be accessed from any public library that offers internet service. We hope that the guidance and resources provided will be of use to practitioners in legal service and their clients, as well as criminal attorneys who hope to provide a more holistic defense and support for their clients.

Beacon Law gratefully acknowledges all of the work accomplished by Texas RioGrande Legal Aid and Texas C-Bar in the creation of the original Guide published in 2012 and especially the privilege they have generously given us to build on their work and produce these successive editions.

We welcome your comments and suggestions for improvements to this Guide.

Leslie E. Ginzel
Beacon Law, A program of The Beacon
lsginzel@beaconlaw.org

Legal Materials Disclaimer

This guide is for informational purposes only. It is not intended to substitute for the services of an attorney, and is distributed with the understanding that the contributors to its content are not rendering legal or other professional services. For legal advice, contact an attorney or your local legal aid office.

INTRODUCTION

The United States has the highest documented incarceration rate in the world, housing nearly one-quarter of the world's prisoners.[1] Nearly one in every 100 adults in the United States is behind bars. One in 5 incarcerated people are locked up for a drug related offense.[2] When probation and parole are included, the number of adults under some form of correction supervision rises to one in 31.[3]

On any given day, Texas' massive state corrections system houses a daily average of 163,000 inmates in 110 state correctional facilities.[4] Texas' 246 county lockups house an additional 41,000 prisoners each day. Over half of the people in the county jails (63%) are not serving a sentence and are being detained for other reasons. There are nearly four times as many prisons and jails in Texas (360) as there are university campuses statewide (94).

This represents an increase over data from 2010 but the count is not reflective of the landscape as a whole. Other reforms afforded courts more sentencing options for new offenders that permitted non prison-based sanctions for parole violations. In recent years, more inmates have been granted parole and for shorter terms.[5] Fewer people are returning to prison for minor infractions and are suffering fewer sanctions for violating conditions of release.[6]

A positive trend is emerging.

The newly released are expected to return to their communities, contribute to the tax base and participate constructively in society. For many, successful reentry - meaningful participation in society – remains a myth. All too often, people with a criminal record find themselves locked out of employment, shelter, public benefits, access to health care – everything that might contribute to a successful transition

Notes

[1] The incarceration *rate* is the number of people under correctional supervision per 100,000 population. International Centre for Prison Studies, Entire World – Prison Population Rates per 100,000 of the National Population (last updated 12.31.2016). The United States' incarceration rate is 655 per 100,000 people. The US represents 5% of the world's population, yet incarcerates almost a quarter of the world's prisoners.

[2] https://www.prisonpolicy.org/reports/pie2019.html

[3] 2012 - http://www.justicepolicy.org/uploads/justicepolicy/documents/fbi_ucr2011jpifactsheet.pdf;

[4] Jacob Kang-Brown, Eital Schattner-Elmaleh, Oliver Hinds. People in Prison in 2018. New York: Vera Institute of Justice, 2019.

[5] Pew Research Center on the States, Prison Count 2010.

[6] Tex. Code Crim. Proc. Art. 42A.702 entitles defendants to time credits toward the completion of their community supervision if certain conditions are met. Time credits can be awarded for participation in programs such as earning a high school diploma or equivalent, payment of fines and fees, and successful completion of anger management programs.

into society. Outmoded laws and policies continue to penalize people who have served time.

Collateral consequences of criminal convictions continue to thwart the efforts of individuals to join society. In recent years, legal initiatives to remove or lessen the impact of these collateral consequences have been gaining momentum on both state and federal levels.[7] In 2015, the Texas Legislature approved sweeping changes to criminal record sealing laws proactively and in 2017 made those changes retroactive. This increased eligibility drastically increases the likelihood that an individual who commits a crime of poverty will not be punished for the rest of their lives.

This publication addresses some of the current barriers faced by previously incarcerated people.[8] It is intended to be a resource guide for advocates that assist previously incarcerated people who find themselves locked out of meaningful participation in society.

---

[7] One such initiative is the proposed Uniform Collateral Consequences Act (UCCA), approved by American Bar Association in 2010. At this writing, the Act has been adopted by North Carolina, and is under legislative consideration in Minnesota, New York, Vermont, West Virginia, and Wisconsin. Key provisions include a collection of collateral consequences for each state compiled in a single document to include both collateral sanctions (automatic bars) and disqualifications (discretionary penalties); notice provisions to Defendants of these consequences at important points in a criminal case and at sentencing; uniform court orders to lift automatic bars, and a certificate of restoration of rights for an individual under consideration for an opportunity or benefit. Uniform Law Commission, Collateral Consequences of Conviction Act.

[8] It excludes consequences of conviction as it relates to immigration status.

Locked Out: A Texas Legal Guide to Reentry, 4th Edition - 2019

1 TABLE OF CONTENTS

1 CONTENTS

Acknowledgments 3
Introduction 4
1. Identification 18
   1.1 Legal Name 18
   1.2 Driver's License or Identity Card 18
      1.2.1 Status of License 19
      1.2.2 Expired License 19
      1.2.3 Securing ID Prior to Release 19
      1.2.4 Proof of Identity 20
   Table 1- Proof of Identity Documents Accepted by DPS 20
      1.2.5 Texas Inmate ID Card 22
      1.2.6 Green Card 23
      1.2.7 Out of State License 23
      1.2.8 New ID or Expired Over 2 Years 23
      1.2.9 "In Person" Requirement 24
      1.2.10 Applicants Under Supervision 24
      1.2.11 Proof of Social Security Number 24
      1.2.12 Proof of Lawful Presence 25
      1.2.13 Exemption for Disabled Veterans 26
   Appendix A: Steps to Obtain a Texas Driver's License or Identity Card. 26
   1.3 Commercial Driver's Licenses (CDL) 26
      1.3.1 Eligibility for CDL 26
      1.3.2 Application Requirements for CDL 27
      1.3.3 CDL from another State 28
      1.3.4 Nonresident CDL – Requirements 28
   Table 2: Driver's License, Identification Card and CDL Fees 29
   1.4 Birth Certificates 30

1.4.1 Information Required for Certified Copy 30

1.4.2 Ordering a Certified Copy of Birth Certificate 30

Table 3 : BVS Order Information 31

1.4.3 Birth Certificate from Another State 32

1.4.4 Amending or Correcting Birth Certificate 32

Table 4: Requirements to Amend or Correct Birth Certificate 33

Appendix B: Steps to Obtain Certified Copy of Texas Birth Certificate 34

1.5 Social Security Identification 34

1.5.1 Original Social Security Card 34

Table 5: SSA Proof of Identity 34

1.5.2 Replacement Card 35

1.5.3 Card for Non-Citizen 36

1.5.4 Change of Name 36

Appendix C: Steps to Apply for or Replace Social Security Card 36

1.6 Passports 36

Table 6: Grounds for Revocation, Application or Renewal of Passport 37

1.6.1 Amending or Correcting Passport Information 37

1.7 Adult Name Change 37

Appendix D: Sample Petition & Order - Name Change of Adult 38

1.7.1 Felony Conviction 38

1.8 Name Change With Existing Criminal History 39

1.8.1 Exception for Sex Offenders 39

1.8.2 2019 New Legislation allowing for Name Change consistent with Primary Criminal Record Name. 39

1.8.3 Declaratory Judgment 39

F E: Sample Declaratory Judgment for Name - Petition and Order 40

2. Transportation and Driving Privileges 41

2.1 Suspension of Driver's License 41

2.1.2 Refusing or Failing Blood or Breath Test 41

2.1.3 Drug Offenses 42

2.1.4 Traffic Violations 42

2.1.5 License Suspended or Invalid 42

2.1.6 Violation of License Restriction 43

2.2   Out-of-State Driving Offenses 43
  2.2.1   Suspended in another State 43
  2.2.2   Unpaid Traffic Fines in another State 43
  2.2.3   Offense from another State 44
  Table 7: Offenses Resulting in Suspension of Driver's License 44
2.3   Driver Surcharges 46
  Table 8: Driver Fines (AKA Surcharges) 46
  2.3.1   Waiver Based on Indigence 47
2.4   Occupational Driver's License 47
  2.4.2   Minimum Liability Amounts in Texas 48
  2.4.3   Court Order Required 48
  2.4.4   Application to DPS for Occupational License 48
  2.4.5   Waiting Periods 49
  2.4.6   Exception to Essential Need Requirement 49
  Appendix F: Petition and Order for Occupational Driver's License 49

3. Offense – Related Debt 50
  3.1   CONSEQUENCES OF FAILURE TO PAY 50
  3.2.1   Judicial Discretion 50
  Table 9: Court's Authority to Waive Debt 51
  3.3   Offense- Related Debt and Child Support 51
  3.4   Court Order Waiving Surcharges 52
  Appendix G: Motion and Order to Waive Surcharge 52
  3.5   Outstanding Tickets and Citations 52
  Appendix H: Motion and Order to Waive Fines and Fees 53
  3.6   Excessive Fines and the 8th Amendment 53

4. Criminal History Records 55
  4.1   Sources of Criminal Records 55
  4.1.1   NCIC 55
  4.1.2   TCIC 56
  4.1.3   Release of Criminal History Records 56
  Appendix I: Steps to Order Criminal History Records 57
  4.2   Dissemination of Records by Private Entities 57

    4.2.1 Consumer Reporting Agencies 57
    4.2.2 Liability for Wrongful Dissemination 57
    4.2.3 DPS and Texas Public Information Act 58
    4.2.4 Enforcement 59
4.3 Contents of Criminal Records 59
4.4 Case Dispositions and Sentencing Alternatives 59
    4.4.1 Pretrial Diversion 60
    4.4.2 Deferred Adjudication 60
    4.4.3 Deferred Disposition 61
    4.4.4 Felony Pretrial Diversion 62
    4.4.5 Deferred Prosecution - Juveniles Only 62
4.5 Protective Orders 62
    4.5.1 Protective Order - Texas Family Code 63
    4.5.2 Emergency Protective Order (Magistrate's Order) 64
    4.5.3 Protective Orders - Sexual Assault, Trafficking and Stalking 64

5. Expunction, Nondisclosure, and Pardon 65
5.1 Difference Between Expunction and Nondisclosure 65
    5.1.1 About Deferred Adjudications 65
5.2 Expunction 66
Table 10: Eligibility for Expunction 66
    5.2.1 Order Directing Expunction 67
    5.2.2 Effect of Expunction 67
Appendix J: Instructions, Petition, Verification and Order for Expunction of Criminal Records 68
5.3 Nondisclosure 68
    5.3.1 Automatic Nondisclosures – Deferred in Certain Misdemeanors: §411.072 68
    5.3.2 Standard Deferred Nondisclosures: Tex. Gov't Code §411.0725 68
    5.3.3 Nondisclosure after Straight Probation Tex. Gov't Code §411.073 69
    5.3.4 Misdemeanor Jail Time Served: Tex. Gov't Code §411.0735 69
    5.3.5 Human Trafficking Victims: Tex. Gov't Code § 411.0728 69
    5.3.6 Limitations on Nondisclosure 70
Table 11: Nondisclosure - Eligible and Ineligible Offenses 70

- 5.3.7 Deferred Adjudication and Nondisclosure 72
- 5.3.8 Nondisclosure Process 72
- 5.3.9 Order of *Nondisclosure* 72
- 5.3.10 Effect of Order of Nondisclosure 73
- Appendix K-1: Office of Court Administration – An Overview of Orders of Nondisclosure 74
- Appendix K-2: Instructions and Letter Requesting an Order of Nondisclosure under Section 411.072, Government Code and Order 74
- Appendix K-3: Instructions and Petition and Order of Nondisclosure under Section 411.0725, Government Code 74
- Appendix K-4: Instructions and Petition and Order of Nondisclosure under Section 411.0727, Government Code 74
- Appendix K-5: Instructions and Petition and Order of Nondisclosure under Section 411.0728, Government Code 74
- Appendix K-6: Instructions and Petition and Order of Nondisclosure under Section 411.073, Government Code 74
- Appendix K-7: Instructions and Petition and Order of Nondisclosure under Section 411.0731, Government Code 74
- Appendix K-8: Instructions and Petition and Order of Nondisclosure under Section 411.0735, Government Code 74
- Appendix K-9: Instructions and Petition and Order of Nondisclosure under Section 411.0736, Government Code 74
- 5.4 Pardon 74
  - 5.4.1 Offenses NOT Eligible for Pardon 74
  - 5.4.2 Pardon Process 75
6. Employment 76
  - 6.1 Civil Rights 76
    - 6.1.1 Bars to Hiring 76
    - 6.1.2 EEOC 2012 Enforcement Guidance 77
    - 6.1.3 "Ban the Box" 79
  - 6.2 Occupational Outlook Handbook 80
  - 6.3 Work Authorization Documents 80
    - 6.3.1 I-9 Employment Verification Form Requirements 80
    - Table 12: I-9 Employment Verification Documents 80
    - 6.3.2 No I-9 Verification Documents 81

6.3.3 E Verify	81
6.4 Job Search with Criminal Record	82
6.4.1 Tips on Conducting a Job Search with a Criminal Record	83
6.4.2 Crimes of "Moral Turpitude"	84
Table 13: Crimes of Moral Turpitude	84
6.4.3 Sex Offenders - Special Issues	86
6.4.4 Internet Use	87
6.4.5 Texas Sex Offender Registration Database	87
Appendix L - Texas Sex Offenses Tiered under Federal Law	88
6.5 Wage and Hour Laws	88
6.5.1 Federal Minimum Wage Law	88
6.5.2 Texas Minimum Wage Law	88
6.5.3 Earnings Statement	88
6.5.4 Wages Paid in Cash	89
6.5.5 Payment Intervals	89
6.5.6 Form and Method of Payment	89
6.5.7 Releases and Vouchers	89
6.5.8 Late Pay	90
6.5.9 Wage Dispute No Excuse	90
6.6 Illegal Deductions from Wages	90
6.6.1 Written Agreement Required	90
6.6.2 Written Agreement Required	91
6.7 "No Match" Letters	91
6.8 Federal Bonding Program	93
6.9 Work Opportunity Tax Credit (WOTC)	94
Table 14: Work Opportunity Tax Credit Target Groups	94
6.10 Starting a Business	95
6.10.1 Child Care	95
6.10.2 Forming a Child Care Co-Op	95
6.11 Leasing	95
6.11.1 Considerations for Job Placement Firms	96
6.12 Day Labor	96

6.12.1	Day Laborers' Rights Regarding Wages and Hours	97
6.12.2	Fees for Transport	98
6.12.3	Essential Tools and Safety Equipment	99
6.12.4	Meals	99
6.12.5	Check Cashing	99
6.12.6	Compliance with other Labor Laws	99
6.13	Employment and Social Media	100
6.14	Job Scams	101
6.14.1	Work at Home Schemes	101
7.	Vocational Licenses	102
7.1	Texas Department of Licensing and Regulation	103
7.1.1	Occupations Regulated by the TDLR	103
7.1.2	Incarceration - Automatic Revocation	104
7.2	TDLR Application Process	105
7.2.1	First Time License	105
7.2.2	License Renewal	105
7.2.3	Criminal Background Check	105
7.2.4	Request for Criminal History Evaluation Letter	106
7.2.5	Consideration of Deferred Adjudication	106
7.2.6	TDLR Evaluation of Application	107
7.2.7	TDLR Grounds for Denial	107
7.2.8	"Directly Related"	108
7.2.9	Appeal	108
7.3	TWIC	109
7.3.1	People Who Must Get a TWIC	109
8.	Public Benefits	110
8.1	Denial of Federal Benefits (DFB)	110
8.2	Temporary Assistance for Needy Families (TANF)	110
8.2.1	TANF for Families	111
8.2.2	Personal Responsibility Agreement	111
8.2.3	"One-Time TANF"	111
8.2.4	One-Time TANF Grandparent Payment	112

8.2.5 Felony Drug Offenses – Lifetime Ban 112
8.3 Food Stamps (SNAP) 112
8.3.1 Emergency SNAP 112
8.3.2 Felony Drug Offenses –Changes to Lifetime Ban 113
8.4 Medicaid and Chip 113
8.5 Social Security and SSI 113
8.5.1 Social Security 113
8.5.2 Social Security Supplemental Income (SSI) 113
8.5.3 Outstanding Warrants 114
8.5.4 "Overpayments" 114
8.6 Unemployment Benefits 114
8.7 Education Assistance 114

9. Shelter and Housing 116
9.1 Homelessness 116
9.1.1 Shelter Resources 116
9.2 Release to Supervision 116
9.2.1 Halfway Houses 116
9.2.2 THAP Program 117
9.2.3 Not Eligible for THAP 117
9.2.4 Living with Family Members 117
9.3 Affordable Housing 118
9.3.1 No Automatic Disqualification 118
9.3.2 Waiting Period 118
9.3.3 Types of Supportive Housing 118
9.3.4 Eligibility for Public Housing 118
9.3.5 Application for Public Housing 119
9.3.6 Criminal Background Check 119
9.3.7 Documents Required 119
9.3.8 Selection Preferences 120
9.3.9 Decision on Application 120
9.3.10 PHA as Landlord 120
9.4 Evictions, Restrictions and Bans 120

Table 14: Bans and Restrictions on Federally Subsidized Housing ... 120
   9.4.1   Evidence Required For Denial ... 121
   9.4.2   Opportunity to Dispute ... 122
   9.4.3   Grievance Procedure ... 122
   9.4.4   Right to Review. ... 122
   9.4.5   Mitigating Circumstances ... 123
   9.4.6   Domestic Violence ... 123
9.5   Housing Discrimination ... 124
   9.5.1   Refusing to Rent or Sell ... 124
   9.5.2   Applying Different Terms and Conditions ... 125
   9.5.3   False Information about Availability ... 125
   9.5.4   Reporting Discrimination ... 125
9.6   Renting with a Record ... 126
   9.6.1   Roommate or Sublet ... 126
   9.6.2   Group Homes or Boarding Houses ... 126
   9.6.3   Renting from Private Owner ... 126
   9.6.4   Selection Criteria and Acknowledgment ... 127
   9.6.5   Consumer Reporting Agencies ... 127
   9.6.6   Criminal History Records ... 128
   9.6.7   Correcting Inaccurate or Stale Information ... 128
   9.6.8   Disclosure and Investigation ... 128
   9.6.9   Damages and Enforcement ... 128
   9.6.10   Application Fee ... 129
   9.6.11   Deposit ... 129
   9.6.12   Forfeiture of Deposit ... 129
   9.6.13   Rejection Deadline ... 129

10 . Rights of Parents ... 131
10.1   Equal Rights to Child ... 131
10.2   Locating Children ... 131
10.3   Custody ... 132
   10.3.1   Nonparent Caregivers ... 132
   10.3.2   Authorization Agreement for Nonparent Relative ... 133

Appendix M: Authorization Agreement for Non Parent Relative 133
10.4 Paternity 133
10.5 Termination of Parental Rights 133
10.6 Child Protective Services (CPS) 134
    10.6.1 Access to CPS Records 134
10.7 Child Support and Modification 135
10.8 Child Support and Previously Incarcerated Parents 135
    Table 15: Other State Laws - Child Support and Incarceration 137
10.9 Duty to Support 138
    10.9.1 Leaving Texas to Avoid Payment 138
    10.9.2 Payments Continue after Child Reaches Adulthood 139
10.10 Consequences of Failure to Support 139
10.11 Conservatorship and Child Support 139
    10.11.1 Orders without "Primary Residence" 140
    10.11.2 Nonparent Custodians 140
10.12 Calculating Child Support 140
    10.12.1 Child Support Guidelines 140
    10.12.2 Multiple Family Guidelines 141
    10.12.3 Maximum Withholding 141
    10.12.4 Duration of Support 141
10.13 Medical Support 142
    10.13.1 Private Health Insurance 142
    10.13.2 CHIP and Medicaid 142
    10.13.3 Cash Medical Support 142
10.14 Retroactive Support and Arrearages 143
    10.14.1 Retroactive Support 143
    10.14.2 Child Support Arrearages 143
10.15 Employer Withholding and Disbursement 144
10.16 Setting Child Support - Additional Factors 144
    10.16.1 Resources of CP 144
    10.16.2 Unemployment and Underemployment 144
10.17 Modifying Child Support 145

10.17.1	Grounds for Modification	145
10.17.2	Incarceration and Release as Grounds to Modify	146

Appendix N: Child Support Information for Incarcerated Parents and Parents Returning to the Community and Inquiry Form 146

10.18	The Modification Process	146
10.18.1	Continuing Jurisdiction	146

Appendix O: OAG Form to Request Child Support Review 146

10.19	Texas Attorney General (OAG) Cases	146
10.19.1	IV-D Cases	146

Table 16: Options for Child Support Modification 147

10.19.2	Steps to Modify Child Support (Non-OAG):	148

Appendix P: Sample Petition to Modify and Order (Non- OAG) 148

10.20	Child Support Enforcement	148
10.20.1	Sources of Unpaid Support	148
10.20.2	License Suspension	149
10.20.3	Enforcement Hearing	149
10.20.4	Contempt of Court	149
10.20.5	Defenses to Nonpayment	149
10.20.6	Criminal Nonsupport	150
11 . Education		151
11.1	Eligibility for Texas Financial Aid	151
11.1.1	Drug Related Offenses	151

Table 17: Length of Ineligibility for Federal Financial Aid - Drug Convictions ... 151

11.1.2	Conviction after Scholarship	152
11.1.3	Eligibility for Texas Grants	152
11.1.4	Zero Tolerance Policies	152
11.2	NonProfit Community Colleges	153
11.3	Proprietary/for-Profit Colleges and Universities	153
12 . Voting and Selective Service		155
12.1	Voting	155
12.1.1	Eligibility to Register to Vote	156
12.1.2	Voting Rights and Deferred Adjudication	156
12.1.3	Voter Registration	156

Appendix Q: Application for Voter Registration 157
    12.1.4   Deadline for Application 157
    12.1.5   Identification Required to Register to Vote 157
    12.1.6   Voter Registration Certificate 157
    12.1.7   Change of Address 158
    12.1.8   Where to Vote 158
12.2   Selective Service Registration 158
    12.2.1   Consequences for Failure to Register 158
    12.2.2   Fines and Penalties 159
    12.2.3   Government Programs and Education 159
    12.2.4   Registration Methods 159
12.3   Status Information Letter 159
    12.3.1   First-Time Registration if Over 25 159
    Appendix R: Request for Status Information Letter 160
    12.3.2   Status Information Letter Not Required 160
    Table 18: Documents in Lieu of Status Information Letter - Categories 160
12.4   Jury Service 160
13 . Collateral Consequences of Conviction 162
    Table 19: Collateral Consequences of Conviction 162
    13.1.1   Uniform Collateral Consequences Act 173
    Table 20: Uniform Collateral Consequences Act - Key Provisions 173
14. Table of Appendices 176

1. IDENTIFICATION

Unlike many countries, America has no true national identity card and no federal mandate that each citizen carry one. Valid proof of identity can be the key that unlocks the doors to housing, employment, education, medical care, benefits, transportation, driving privileges, voting, banking and other financial transactions, vocational and professional licensure -- in short, all services an individual requires to fully participate in society.

For individuals recently released from incarceration, key identification documents can be difficult to acquire because each may require proof of the other. For example, a certified copy of a birth certificate may be required to get a driver's license. A copy of a valid photo ID (usually a driver's license) may be needed to order a certified copy of a birth certificate, driver's license or state identity card, and a social security card. Of these, a driver's license or state ID is the most widely accepted form of identification. This section provides information on how to obtain a Texas driver's license, commercial driver's license and Texas identification card, as well as other important proofs of identity, including a certified copy of a birth certificate, social security card, and a passport.

1.1 LEGAL NAME

Valid identification must include a "legal" name. A legal name is the name given at birth that appears on a person's birth certificate. A nickname is not a legal name. With the exception of marriage, an adult cannot change his or her legal name without a court order.[9] Though newer initiatives exist to provide releasees with state-issued identification, a person newly released from prison may not have any item of identification except their prison identification card. Others may have identification that conflicts with the name that appears on their birth certificate, which can create problems when applying for a driver's license or state identity card.

Accurate proof of identity is required in order to obtain a state-issued driver's license or identity card. In addition to being the most commonly accepted form of identification, a valid state-issued ID *must be carried* by anyone released to parole or mandatory supervision as a condition of release. According to the Texas Board of Pardons and Paroles, this requirement is to be "strictly enforced."[10]

1.2 DRIVER'S LICENSE OR IDENTITY CARD

---

[9] The change of name can be a stand-alone order, or incorporated into another order, such as a divorce decree.
[10] 37 Tex. Admin. Code § 145.27.

In Texas, the Texas Department of Public Safety (DPS) is the state agency responsible for promulgating rules for and issuing driver's licenses and identification cards.

1.2.1 Status of License

The application process depends upon the current status of the license: unexpired, expired less than two years ago, expired more than two years ago, or never applied.

Unexpired DL or ID	**DL or ID Expired less than 2 years**	**No DL or ID, or expired over 2 years**
Must notify DPS of change of address within 30 days of the change.	If expired less than two years before the application, the expired driver's license or ID card may be used as proof of identity to renew.	If license or ID expired over two years before applying, must complete new application and submit proofs of identity accepted by the DPS.

1.2.2 Expired License

Note that an expired Texas driver's license can be used as primary ID without the necessity of other documents IF it expired less than two years before the application date. An expired driver's license or identity card from a state other than Texas is useful only as supporting documentation.

1.2.3 Securing ID Prior to Release

The Texas Department of Criminal Justice (TDCJ) is required to obtain electronic verification of the prisoner's birth record from the Department of Health and Human Services (DHHS). Once verified, TDCJ is to forward the information to DPS along with a request to issue a legal identification card for the inmate prisoner, who can be charged for the actual cost.[11] The law, to be implemented through the Texas Department of Criminal Justice Reentry and Reintegration Division's (RID) Program, can help an inmate secure ID in the following situations:

- If an offender's driver license is eligible for renewal after release, they will be sent a letter noting their eligibility status. An application for a birth certificate will not be completed for them since the driver license is eligible for renewal.

- If the driver license is not eligible for renewal due to expiration or infraction issues, a birth certificate application will be prepared and

---
[11] Tex. Gov't Code § 501.0165;

submitted. If the offender was born in Texas, the agency will cover the cost of the birth certificate. For offenders born outside of Texas, the offender or family will be responsible for covering the cost.

- An application for a replacement social security card will be prepared and submitted for any offender meeting the eligibility criteria.

- For offenders who will be released with no supervision requirements, a state jail or flat discharge, the identification documents will be provided to the offender at time of release from incarceration. Offenders being released on supervision will receive their documents during their initial visit with a parole officer.[12]

1.2.4 Proof of Identity

Each applicant must submit proof of identity accepted by DPS before a license or photo ID may be issued. DPS categorizes acceptable proof of identity as "primary", "secondary", or "supporting". The applicant who lacks "primary" identification must submit either two items of "secondary" identification or one secondary and at least two other "supporting" proofs of identification. The following chart lists the items currently accepted by DPS as proof of identity required to obtain Texas driver's license or Texas identity card:

Table 1- Proof of Identity Documents Accepted by DPS

PRIMARY	SECONDARY	SUPPORTING
MUST INCLUDE PHOTO, FULL NAME AND DOB	**RECORDED US GOVERNMENTAL DOCUMENTS (INCLUDES NAME & DOB)**	**ADDITIONAL RECORDS AND DOCUMENTS THAT AID IN ESTABLISHING IDENTITY**
Accepted for Identification without additional documentation	Applicant must present one secondary and two supporting or two secondary documents to establish identity	
• Texas driver license or Texas identification card not expired more than 2 years	• Original or certified copy of a birth certificate issued by a State Bureau of Vital Statistics or equivalent agency from a U.S. state, U.S. territory, the District of Columbia or a Canadian	• Social security card • Form W-2 or 1099 • Driver license or ID card issued by another U.S. state, U.S. territory, the District of Columbia or Canadian

---

[12] If the documents are not provided to the offender at release or at their first parole visit, they should contact RID by calling them toll free at 1-877-887-6151 or by mail to Reentry and Integration Division 8712 Shoal Creek Blvd. Ste. 280 Austin, Texas 78757.

• Proof of citizenship will be required if not previously established
 	
• Unexpired U.S. passport book or card
 	
• U.S. Certificate of Citizenship or Certificate of Naturalization (N-560, N-561, N-645, N-550, N-55G, N-570 or N-578)
 	
• Unexpired Department of Homeland Security or U.S. Citizenship and Immigration Services document with verifiable data and identifiable photo, such as one of the following:
 	
• U.S. Citizen Identification Card (I-179 or I-197)
 	
• Permanent Resident Card (I-551)
 	
• Foreign passport with attached temporary I-551 (immigrant visa endorsed with ADIT stamp)
 	
• Temporary Resident Identification Card (I-688)
 	
• Employment Authorization Card (I-766)
	province. Laminated copies are not accepted.
	• Birth certificate must:
	  o Be issued by the city, county, or state of birth
	  o List the applicant's full name, date of birth, and place of birth
	  o List the parent(s)' full name
	  o Have the signature of the city, county, or state registrar
	  o Have the date filed with registrar's office within one year of birth
	
	• NOTE: Because Puerto Rican statute provides that Puerto Rican birth certificates issued before July 1, 2010 are no longer valid, the Department cannot recognize these birth certificates as proof of identification or lawful presence. For more information, please select the following link. http://prfaa.pr.gov/birthcertificatesnd2.asp
	• For U.S. citizens born abroad—Certificate of Report of Birth (DS-1350 or FS-545) or Consular Report of Birth (FS-240) issued by the U.S. Department of State
	
	• Original or certified copy of a court order with name and date of birth indicating a name and/or gender change from a U.S. state, U.S. territory, the District of
		province (unexpired or expired less than two years)*
		• Texas driver license or ID card that has been expired more than two years
		• Temporary Texas driver license or ID card
		• School records* (e.g., report cards, photo ID cards)
		• Unexpired U.S. military dependent identification card
		• Original or certified copy of marriage license or divorce decree (if the document is not in English, a certified translation must accompany it)
		• Voter registration card*
		• Pilot license*
		• Concealed handgun license or License to Carry*
		• Professional license issued by a Texas state agency
		• ID card issued by a government agency*
		• Consular document issued by a state or national government
		• Texas Inmate ID card or similar form of ID issued by Texas Department of Criminal Justice
		• Texas Department of Criminal Justice parole or mandatory release certificate
		• Federal inmate identification card
		• Federal parole or release certificate
		• Medicare or Medicaid card

• U.S. Travel Document (I-327 or I-571) • Advance Parole Document (I-512 or I-512L) • I-94 stamped Sec. 208 Asylee with photo • I-94 stamped Sec. 207 Refugee with photo • Refugee Travel Letter with photo, stamped by Customs and Border Protection • American Indian Card (I-872) • Northern Mariana card (I-873) • Foreign passport with attached visa and Form I-94 • Unexpired U.S. military ID card for active duty, reserve or retired personnel with identifiable photo	Columbia or a Canadian province	• Selective Service card • Immunization records* • Tribal membership card from federally-recognized tribe • Certificate of Degree of Indian Blood • Unexpired foreign passport • Unexpired insurance policy valid for the past two years (e.g., auto, home or life insurance) • Current Texas vehicle registration or title • Current Texas boat registration or title • Veteran's ID card issued by the U.S. Department of Veteran Affairs • Abstract (shortened) birth certificate • Hospital-issued birth record* • Military records (e.g., Form DD-214, DD-215, NGB-22) • *The document must be issued by an institution, entity or government from a U.S. state, a U.S. territory, the District of Columbia or a Canadian province. LIST IS NOT EXCLUSIVE; DPS may accept other forms of supporting documentation.

1.2.5 Texas Inmate ID Card

A Texas Inmate ID Card falls within the "supporting" classification of items that may be used to establish proof of identity for the purpose of obtaining a Texas driver's license or identity card. The card is not considered reliable proof of identity because it reflects the name given at the time of arrest, which may not match the inmate's legal name. Documents that fall within the "supporting" category cannot be used as proof of identity unless accompanied by another "supporting" item plus one "secondary" item (usually a birth certificate).

1.2.6 Green Card

A Green Card holder (permanent resident) is someone who has been granted authorization to live and work in the United States on a permanent basis. The government designation for a permanent resident card is US Customs and Immigration Services Form I-551. A valid permanent resident card is primary identification, and is therefore the only proof of identity that DPS requires for a Texas driver's license.

1.2.7 Out of State License

A person holding an unexpired driver's license from another state must apply for a Texas driver's license within 90 days of arrival in Texas by appearing in person at a Texas Driver License office. If the out-of-state license is valid and unexpired, the applicant must surrender it to DPS in order to get a Texas Driver's license. A written test or driving test is not required; only vision will be tested. If the license from another state is expired, the person must produce other acceptable forms of ID (see chart above), surrender the expired license, and pass the written, driving and vision exams.

1.2.8 New ID or Expired Over 2 Years

DPS provides the following instructions for first time applicants and for those whose Texas license expired more than two years from the date of application:[13]

1. Apply in person at a Texas driver license office.
2. Present documents that verify your identity.
3. Present documents that verify you are a U.S. citizen or have lawful presence. The information on each document **must match**. Additional documentation may be required to verify conflicting information, incomplete names, and date of birth.
4. Present proof of Social Security Number. If you do not have a Social Security Number, you must complete a Social Security Affidavit form available at the driver license office.
5. Present proof of your Texas residency.
6. Present proof of Texas vehicle registration and liability insurance on all vehicles you own.
7. Complete the application for driver license or identification card (PDF). You may type your information on the form, print it, and bring it with you

---

[13]From www.txdps.state.tx.us/DriverLicense/ApplyforLicense.htm

to the office. If you don't have a printer, the form is also available at the office.
8. Consent to be photographed, fingerprinted, and provide your signature at the time of application.
9. Pass the written, driving, and vision examinations. (Read more about foreign language examinations.)
10. Pay the required fee with a credit card, cash, money order, or a non-temporary check.
11. Provide a vehicle for the driving exam and present current liability insurance, Texas vehicle registration, and inspection for the vehicle.

1.2.9 "In Person" Requirement

New applicants, or those whose Texas driver's license or ID expired more than two years from the date of application must apply in person at a DPS office to be photographed.

This requirement can present enormous challenges to formerly incarcerated people. Almost a third of Texas' 254 counties do not have a DPS office.[14] Of those that do, less than a fourth has extended hours and none are open on weekends.[15] In a state as large as Texas, ex-offenders with limited access to transportation, who must travel a long distance to get to an office, or are unable to appear at DPS during hours of operation may find appearing in person at DPS more difficult than expected.

1.2.10 Applicants Under Supervision

Parolees who need a license but reside in a county without a DPS office must violate one term of release to comply with another. The Texas Board of Pardons and Paroles "strictly enforces"[16] the requirement that those released to parole or mandatory supervision carry a valid state-issued ID, but to get to the nearest DPS office may violate geographic and travel restrictions. If on parole, the applicant is required to carry DPS-issued photo ID while under supervision. If the parolee resides in a county that lacks a DPS office, he may not be able to travel to a county that does.

1.2.11 Proof of Social Security Number

Every applicant commercial driver's license must submit proof of a social security number (SSN). Proof of a SSN is *not* required to obtain a Texas ID card or a Texas driver's license, though this information is encouraged to be provided. The SSN will remain a part of the driver's record, and later applications for a duplicate license or

---

[14] Eighty-one (81) of Texas' 254 counties do not have a DPS office. US Dept. of Justice letter to Texas Election Commission, March 12, 2012.
[15] Only 49 of Texas' 221 DPS offices across the state have extended hours. *Id.*
[16] 37 Tex. Admin. Code § 145.27.

license renewal will be verified against the SSN on file. If DPS cannot verify the SSN, it can deny issuance or renewal.

Any of the following documents will be accepted to verify a SSN. The document presented can be expired or unexpired but must have the individual's full SSN printed on it.

Documentation must be unaltered originals, not copies.
- Social Security card
- Pilot license
- Military identification (active, reserve, retired or dependent status)
- Texas Commission on Law Enforcement (TCOLE).
- DD-214
- Medicare or Medicaid card
- Health insurance card
- Certified college or university transcript
- IRS form W-2 Wage and Tax Statement
- Form 1099-MISC
- Pay stub (stub must include name and SSN)

To apply for a SSN, visit the Social Security Administration website. Individuals who do not have a SSN, have never been issued a SSN, or are not eligible for a SSN can visit any driver license office and complete an affidavit attesting to such. Providing a false statement in connection with this affidavit will result in the cancellation of the driver license or ID card and may result in criminal charges. An affidavit is not acceptable for the issuance of a commercial driver's license (CDL).

If an SSN has never been assigned, the applicant must complete a Social Security Affidavit (DL-13) provide by DPS and swear to it before a DPS officer. Non-U.S. citizens will need to submit proof of lawful status in the country for a period longer than six months.

NOTE: If you are not eligible for a SSN, then you are not eligible for a commercial drivers license (CDL).

1.2.12 Proof of Lawful Presence

DPS requires applicants who are not U.S. citizens, U.S. nationals, lawful permanent residents, refugees, or asylees to present proof of lawful presence in the U.S. before being issued an original, renewal, or duplicate Texas driver license or identification card. Border Crossing cards alone are *not* accepted by DPS for the purpose of establishing a lawful temporary admission. Proof of lawful presence includes documentation issued by the:
- U.S. Dept. of Justice,
- U.S. Dept. of State,
- U.S. Dept. of Homeland Security, or
- U.S. Citizenship and Immigration Services.

The document(s) must show *lawful temporary admission* to the U.S. For a list of acceptable documents, see DPS's Temporary Visitor Issuance Guide (PDF).

If proof of lawful presence is verified, DPS will issue a license or ID with a "Limited Term" designation that will expire when the period of lawful presence (as shown in the accepted document) expires. If the applicant's lawful presence is indefinite, driver licenses and IDs must be renewed every year.

The holder of a temporary visitor card must provide documents to update the driver license or ID within 45 days after the visitor status date expires. Failure to do so will result in cancellation of the card and a ban on driving.

1.2.13 Exemption for Disabled Veterans

A Texas driver license or ID card may be provided free of charge to a veteran of the United States Armed Forces if the veteran meets the following criteria:
1. Was honorably discharged,
2. Has a service-related disability of at least 60 percent
3. Receives compensation from the United States because of the disability, and
4. Is not subject to sex offender registration requirements

The driver license fee exemption *does not apply* to commercial driver licenses.
For guidance on how to apply, please refer to

Appendix A: Steps to Obtain a Texas Driver's License or Identity Card.

1.3 COMMERCIAL DRIVER'S LICENSES (CDL)

Texas law does not allow residents of Texas to drive commercial vehicles with a personal driver's license. Residents who want to become commercial drivers must have a commercial driver's license, or CDL.

1.3.1 Eligibility for CDL

To get a commercial driver's license, the applicant must be:
- At least 21 years old
- Be domiciled in Texas. A "domicile" is a true, fixed, and permanent home. Domicile can be proved by showing two acceptable documents with name and proof of domicile.[17] The applicant who cannot provide documents with proof of domicile may complete a Texas Residency Affidavit.
- Have a regular driver's license that is at least one-year-old

---

[17] From http://www.txdps.state.tx.us/DriverLicense/domicileReq.htm

- Pass a commercial driver's license test.

All applicants whose driver's license is currently suspended, cancelled, or revoked in Texas or any other state are not eligible for a commercial driver's license (CDL). Domicile can be proved by showing two acceptable documents with name and proof of domicile.[18] The applicant who cannot provide documents with proof of domicile may complete a Texas Residency Affidavit.

1.3.2 Application Requirements for CDL

All first time applicants and applicants who previously held a Texas CDL that has since expired must:

1. Apply in-person at any driver license office and complete the appropriate application.
2. Present documents to verify identity.
    1. Different documents are required if an individual is a U.S. citizen or has lawful presence.
    2. Individuals may be required to present more than one document to verify identity, and the information on all documents must match each other.
    3. Additional documentation may be required to verify conflicting information such as incomplete names or date of birth.
3. Present documents to verify Texas residency.
4. Present evidence of a Social Security Number (a CDL cannot be issued to individuals who do not have a Social Security Number).
5. Meet the self-certification of medical status. Depending on the type of certification, an individual may need to present a medical examiner's certificate.
6. Meet the nonresident commercial requirements (in some states this is also referred to as "non-domicile commercial resident") if they are from a foreign jurisdiction other than Canada or Mexico.
7. Present proof of Texas vehicle registration and liability insurance on all vehicles registered in the individual's name.
8. Complete the Supplement Application Texas Commercial Driver License Certifications and Record of CDL Examination. (CDL-1)
9. Consent to be photographed, fingerprinted and provide your signature.
10. Pass the vision test.
11. Pass the knowledge and skills tests for the appropriate driver license including endorsements.
12. Pay the required fee with a credit card, cash, money order or a non-temporary check.
13. Provide a commercial motor vehicle (CMV) for the driving test. The CMV must be representative of the type of license in which the individual is applying for.
    1. Driving tests may be scheduled online.

---

[18] From http://www.txdps.state.tx.us/DriverLicense/domicileReq.htm

2. Not every driver license office is able to accommodate a CDL road test.

There are additional requirements for school bus drivers.

1.3.3 CDL from another State

A new Texas resident who has a CDL from another state has 30 days to get a Texas CDL. The applicant must:
1. Complete the requirements for an original CDL applicant. (see requirements listed above).
2. Surrender the VALID out-of-state CDL at the driver license office. The written and driving examinations are waived, but the applicant must still pass a vision exam.

OR

3. In the case of an expired CDL, the applicant must surrender their EXPIRED CDL at the driver license office and pass the written, driving and vision exams.

1.3.4 Nonresident CDL – Requirements

A non-resident can obtain a nonresident commercial driver's license (CDL) with proof of a valid social security number. If the applicant does not have a social security number, DPS can issue a temporary non-resident CDL. For a nonresident commercial driver's license, the applicant must:

- Meet all CDL requirements.
- Be a resident of a country whose licensing standards do not meet standards established by US law.[19] (Applicants from Mexico or Canada are ineligible).

Present the following:

- A valid social security number.
- A valid passport issued to the applicant by the country of which the applicant is a resident.
- A valid temporary worker visa.
- A valid Form I-94 Arrival/Departure record, or a successor document.
- Pay a fee of $121.00.

Expiration - A non-resident CDL must expire on the earlier of:

- The expiration date of the visa.

---

[19] 49 CFR 383.

- The expiration date of the Form I-94 Arrival/Departure record, or a successor document.

Table 2: Driver's License, Identification Card and CDL Fees[20]

Driver's License and Identity Card	Fee	Information
Driver's License 18 and older	$25	Expiration 6 years
Driver's license Renewal	$25	Expiration 6 years
Driver's license examination	$11	Does not affect current expiration date
DL/CDL or ID renewal for registered sex offenders (Tex. Code Crim. P Ch. 62)	$21	Annually
Original Commercial Driver's License (CDL)	$61	Expiration 5 years
Original Nonresident CDL	$121	Expires on the earlier of the expiration date of the visa presented or the expiration date of the Form I-94 or a successor document
Original Temporary Non-Resident CDL	$21	Expires on the earlier of the 60th day after the date the license is issued, the expiration date of the visa presented or the expiration date of the Form I-94 or a successor document
CDL Renewal	$61	Expiration 5 years
CDL Examination, Duplicate	$11	Does not affect current expiration date
Original / Renewal ID Card Under age 60 60+	$16 $6	Expiration 6 years Indefinite expiration
ID Duplicates	$11	Does not affect current expiration date

---

[20] For the complete listing, visit the DPS website at https://www.dps.texas.gov/DriverLicense/fees.htm

Occupational License (Essential need)	$10	All reinstatement fees must be paid prior to issuance. (Occupational may be issued up to 2 yrs. at $10.00 per year).
Restricted Interlock License	$10	All reinstatement fees must be paid prior to issuance

1.4 BIRTH CERTIFICATES

A birth certificate is a key form of proof of identity accepted by DPS. People without a "primary" form of identification must submit two "secondary" forms, or one secondary and two "supporting" forms of identification. The "secondary" category is limited to government-issued documents proving that the applicant was born in a U.S. state, territory, the District of Columbia, or a Canadian province, (birth certificate); a U.S. Department of State certificate of birth abroad (born abroad to parents who are citizens), or a certified copy of a court order showing a change of name.

A Texas birth certificate can be ordered online, by mail, or in person. If ordered online or in person, the cost is $22. If ordering by mail, add $8 for certified delivery.

1.4.1 Information Required for Certified Copy

The following information is required of all applicants for certified copy of a Texas birth certificate:

- Full name of the individual on the Birth Certificate
- Date of birth
- City or county where the birth took place
- Full name of the father on the Birth Certificate (if listed)
- Full maiden name of the mother on the Birth Certificate, (if listed)

1.4.2 Ordering a Certified Copy of Birth Certificate

Ordering Online:

Applicants who have a valid state-issued driver's license or government issued ID card can order a certified copy of their birth certificate online through the portal Texas Online, the official eGovernment site for the State of Texas. An applicant who resides in Texas can order his or her own record or the records of immediate family members. A person who resides outside of Texas can order his or her own record, or the record of child, if the person is listed as a parent on the child's record. For online ordering, the applicant must have a:

- Current driver's license or state-issued identification card *and*
- Social Security number

The order will take estimated 10-15 business days to process.

Ordering by Mail:

For applicants who do not have a current state-issued ID, a certified copy can be ordered by mail. To order a birth certificate by mail, the applicant must:

1. Complete an application for a certified copy of a birth certificate, available from the Texas Bureau of Vital Statistics (BVS).

2. Include copy of a photo ID. Acceptable photo ID can be a:

- Texas inmate card or prison ID
- State-issued driver's license
- State/city/county ID card
- Student ID
- Government employment badge or card
- Military ID

If the applicant does not have a photo ID, the applicant may:

- send a copy of the photo ID of an immediate family member, or
- send copies of two documents showing applicant's name (examples: utility bill and Social Security card).
- One of the documents must have applicant's signature.

Mail the application with photocopy of ID and $30 check or money order for payment. BVS cannot process the application for birth certificate without a photo ID or the alternate IDs listed above.

Ordering in Person:

The application can be made in person at BVS offices in Austin, Texas, 1100 W. 49th St., Monday through Friday, 8:00 am - 5:00 pm. Proof of ID is required

Table 3 : BVS Order Information

Additional ordering information is listed in the table below (from BVS website):

Offline application methods	Instructions	Cost	Payment methods accepted	Processing time for most requests
In person at the Texas Vital	Appear in person at 1100 West	$22–Certified copy	Cash Check	Short form birth certificates - 30

Statistics Office in Austin	49th St, Austin, TX 78756 Monday-Friday, 8 am - 5 pm	$60–Heirloom	Money order	minutes to 2 hours. Long form birth certificates - may take several days to process.
Expedited - express mail Send orders to Texas Vital Statistics through overnight mail (Fedex, Lone Star, UPS, etc.) NOT USPS Priority Mail.	Application-pdf (28K)	$22–Certified copy $60–Heirloom + $5 if expedited; + $8 return delivery cost for Lonestar or $18.50 express mail	Check or Money order	10-15 business days Please note: this estimate applies only to complete and acceptable applications. Incomplete or unacceptable applications will require additional processing time.
U.S. Postal Service regular mail	Application-Word (58K) Application-pdf (28K)	$22–Certified copy $60–Heirloom + return delivery cost of $8 for UPS or $18.50 express mail (optional)	Check or Money order	6-8 weeks

1.4.3 Birth Certificate from Another State

Each state has its own agency or office that retains birth records. Contact and ordering information for birth certificates for all 50 states may be found on the Center for Disease Control's state-by-state list.

1.4.4 Amending or Correcting Birth Certificate

If the name on a person's birth certificate needs to be corrected because it is in accurate or does not conform with other forms of identification, the person can file an amendment or correction with the Texas Bureau of Vital Statistics (BVS). The application to amend or correct a Texas birth certificate can be found here.

Every application to amend must include:
- An affidavit from the person(s) specified; and

- One or more of listed documents accepted by BVS.

The form for the affidavit is included in the application to amend.

Table 4: Requirements to Amend or Correct Birth Certificate

The table below lists the source of affidavits and list of required documents:

TYPE OF CHANGE	AFFIDAVIT	DOCUMENTS
Adding Information (Items left blank on original certificate)	children 17 and under - affidavit signed by both parents adults, 18 and over affidavit by older relative	document must show the correct information re: item(s) to be corrected • Hospital record of birth • Baptismal certificate • School record (must be signed by custodian of school records based on earliest attendance) • Birth certificate of older brother or sister • Insurance policy application • Armed forces discharge papers • Social security application (official transcript issued by Social Security administration, Department of Health, Education, and Welfare, • Record of immigration from Immigration and Naturalization Service, US Department of Justice • Passport • Marriage record of parents (copy of certificate, license, or application, whichever supplies the required facts) • Birth or death certificate of registrant's parents
Corrections in Spelling (Names having the same sound)	affidavit by parent(s) or older relative	
First or Middle Name (change or add)	affidavit and one document	
Significant Change in Last Name	a certified court order	
Sex	certification by medical attendant or affidavit and one document	
Name of Father	a paternity determination; application to amend *cannot* be used to add father's name; contact BVS	

		<ul><li>Divorce decree</li><li>Judicial actions (certified copy of any court action affecting information shown on birth certificate.</li></ul>

For step by step instructions on how to order a birth certificate, please review:

Appendix B: Steps to Obtain Certified Copy of Texas Birth Certificate

1.5 SOCIAL SECURITY IDENTIFICATION

Although not initially intended to serve this purpose, a social security number has become another important form of identification. Most of the time, the cardholder need only know his or her own social security number without providing proof of the actual card.

1.5.1 Original Social Security Card

To apply for an original or replacement social security card for a U.S. born citizen, the Social Security Administration requires supporting evidence of identification.

Table 5: SSA Proof of Identity

Evidence of Age	Birth certificate - If no birth certificate, may accept another document showing age, such as: <ul><li>U.S. hospital record of birth (created at the time of birth)</li><li>Religious record established before age five showing age or date of birth</li><li>Passport</li><li>Final Adoption Decree (the adoption decree must show that the birth information was taken from the original birth certificate)</li></ul>

Evidence of Identity	Current, evidence of identity in legal name that will appear on the Social Security card:
	- U.S. driver's license; or
	- U.S. State-issued non-driver identity card; or
	- U.S. passport
	Documents must show legal name AND biographical information (date of birth, age, or parents' names) and/or physical information (photograph, or physical description - height, eye and hair color, etc.).
	NOT ACCEPTED as evidence of identity:
	- birth certificate
	- hospital souvenir birth certificate, social security card stub or a social security record
	SSA may accept other documents that show legal name and biographical information: U.S. military identity card, Certificate of Naturalization, employee identity card, certified copy of medical record (clinic, doctor or hospital), health insurance card, Medicaid card, or school identity card/record. For young children, we may accept medical records (clinic, doctor, or hospital) maintained by the medical provider. We may also accept a final adoption decree, or a school identity card, or other school record maintained by the school.
Evidence of U.S. Citizenship	U.S. birth certificate, U.S. Passport, Consular Report of Birth, Certificate of Citizenship, Certificate of Naturalization.
Evidence of Immigration Status	Current unexpired Department of Homeland Security (DHS) document showing immigration status (e.g., Form I-551, I-94, or I-766). International students and exchange visitors also need e.g., Form I-20, DS-2019, or a letter authorizing employment from F-1 or J-1 sponsor
	NOT ACCEPTED: receipt showing application document. If no work authorization, will issue card for valid non-work reason. Card marked to show not work authorized.

Complete and print <u>Application for a Social Security Card, Form SS-5</u> then deliver or mail it *with supporting documents* to the SSA. For the nearest office, use the SSA's online <u>local office locator</u> or call 2-1-1 for information.

1.5.2 Replacement Card

A Social Security card can be replaced for free if it is lost or stolen. Cardholders are limited to three replacement cards in a year and 10 during in a lifetime. The applicant who needs a replacement card must complete the <u>Application for a Social Security Card, Form SS-5</u>.

1.5.3 Card for Non-Citizen

In general, only noncitizens who have permission to work from the Department of Homeland Security (DHS) can apply for a Social Security number. If a noncitizen does not have permission to work in the United States but needs a social security number for other purposes, see "If you do not have permission to work" for further information.

1.5.4 Change of Name

To change the name on a Social Security card, the applicant must show a recently issued document as proof of legal name change. These include:
- Marriage document;
- Divorce decree;
- Certificate of Naturalization showing a new name; or
- Court order for a name change.

For step by step instructions on securing a social security card, please refer to

Appendix C: Steps to Apply for or Replace Social Security Card

1.6 PASSPORTS

A passport is a document that certifies a person's citizenship and identity. Generally, a criminal conviction will not act as a bar to issuance of a passport unless it was for a drug-related offense or unless issuance would violate the terms of the applicant's parole, probation or sentencing.

The U.S. Department of State (DOS) passport application, does not include any questions about an applicant's criminal history. It does require the applicant to swear under oath that contents of the application are true and that the applicant has not met any of the forbidden "acts and conditions" listed in the application.[21] The applicant must swear to the following:

> "I have not been convicted for a federal or state drug offense or been convicted for "sex tourism" crimes statute and I am not the subject of an outstanding federal, state or local warrant of arrest for a felony; a criminal court order forbidding my departure from the United States; a subpoena received form the United States in a matter involving prosecution for, or grand jury investigation of, a felony."

---

[21] If an act or condition applies, the applicant may submit an explanatory statement with the application.

Depending on the circumstances of the applicant or passport holder, the Department of State can revoke or deny a passport.

Table 6: Grounds for Revocation, Application or Renewal of Passport

Mandatory Denial or Revocation	Discretionary Denial of Application or Renewal
a passport will be denied or revoked if the applicant crossed an international boundary or used the passport in committing the offense[22]	Being in default on repatriation or medical assistance loans while abroad, or behind $2500.00 or more on child support payments;
An issued passport may be revoked, even for misdemeanor drug offenses, if the government finds that the offense should give rise to such disqualification[23]	Having been committed to a mental institution, or was legally declared incompetent by a court; or
	Having been denied previously, had their previous passport revoked, or been issued a temporary passport for specific reasons.[24]

1.6.1 Amending or Correcting Passport Information

Information from the US State Department on how to amend or correct passport information can be found here.

1.7 ADULT NAME CHANGE

It is not uncommon for a single person to have conflicting names on identification documents. If the Department of Public Safety cannot verify conflicting or incomplete names between two or more documents, they may not accept either as proof of identity. One way to resolve the discrepancy is to petition the court for a change of name. This option is not available to felons released or discharged for less than two years.

A request for an adult name change must be made in a petition filed with the court. A certified copy of the court order granting the change of name can then be used to establish legal identity as to one name.

---

[22] 22 USC 2714(a)(1), (b)(1) (2000).

[23] 22 USC 2714 (b) (2) (2000).

[24] 22 CFR 51.60

Appendix D: Sample Petition & Order - Name Change of Adult

1.7.1 Felony Conviction

The name change can be granted at the court's discretion to a person with a final felony conviction only if:
- the person has been pardoned, discharged from TDCJ or completed probation ordered by a court and

- *Not less than two years* have passed from the date of the receipt of discharge or completion of probation. [25]

Certain legal requirements that must be met before the court will issue an Order granting the change of name. All adult petitions for a name change must:
- Be verified; that is, all of the information it contains must be sworn to as true.
- Include a Fingerprint Card - "a legible and complete set of the petitioner's fingerprints on a fingerprint card format acceptable to the Department of Public Safety and the Federal Bureau of Investigation."

- State the full name and place of residence of the petitioner;
- State the full name requested and the reason for the request, and
- State whether the petitioner has been the subject of a final felony conviction, or was convicted under Tex. Code Crim. P Ch. 62 (sex offender).

In addition to the above, the petition must include each of the following, or, if not available, a reason for the omission:
- the petitioner's full name, sex, race, date of birth, and social security number;

- driver's license number for any driver's license issued in the 10 years preceding the date of the petition;

---

[25] The decision of whether to granting a name change for a person with a final felony conviction is within the court's discretion. "(a)[I]f the change is in the interest or to the benefit of the petitioner and in the interest of the public.
(b)A court may order a change of name under this subchapter for a person with a final felony conviction if:
   (1) in addition to the requirements of Subsection (a), the person has:
   (A) received a certificate of discharge by the Texas Department of Criminal Justice or completed a period of community supervision or juvenile probation ordered by a court and not less than two years have passed from the date of the receipt of discharge or completion of community supervision or juvenile probation; or
   (B) been pardoned; or
(2) The person is requesting to change the person's name to the primary name used in the person's criminal history record information.
   (1) (c)A court may order a change of name under this subchapter for a person subject to the registration requirements of Chapter 62, Code of Criminal Procedure, if the person:the requirements of Subsection (a) or is requesting to change the person's name to the primary name used in the [person's criminal history record information; andthe person provides the court with proof that the person has notified the appropriate local law enforcement authority of the proposed name change.
   (1) (d)In this section:"Local law enforcement authority" has the meaning assigned by Article 62.001, Code of Criminal Procedure. Tex. Fam. Code §45.103

- assigned FBI number, state identification number, if known, or any other reference number in a criminal history record system that identifies the petitioner, and

- any offense above the grade of Class C misdemeanor for which the petitioner has been charged and the case number and the court if a warrant was issued or charges filed for the offense.

A Name Change Kit with do-it-yourself forms is available for download from Texas Law Help. More information and instructions can be found in the Texas Young Lawyer's Association Publication "Name Changes in Texas."

1.8 NAME CHANGE WITH EXISTING CRIMINAL HISTORY

A name change is available to previously incarcerated individuals with a felony conviction only if over two years have passed from the date of discharge or release from supervision and the date the petition is filed. Like a Petition for Change of Name, the Petition for Declaratory Judgment should be filed with the district clerk of the county where the person requesting the name change (the Petitioner), resides.

1.8.1 Exception for Sex Offenders

An exception to the two-year waiting period to apply for a legal name change exists for those required to register as a sex offender for the purpose of obtaining identification consistent with their registry requirement. Service of the petition and order the registry agency is required.

1.8.2 2019 New Legislation allowing for Name Change consistent with Primary Criminal Record Name.

It is not uncommon for someone to live their entire life and find out at the least opportune time that their legal name according to their birth record has been incorrect their entire life. In 2019, a bill successfully passed the Texas House and Senate, that expanded eligibility for a legal name change for individuals who have been convicted of a felony. The new law, going into effect September 1, 2019 allows for a legal name change for the purpose of correcting inconsistent records and obtaining identification in ones primary criminal record name without a waiting period.

1.8.3 Declaratory Judgment

The purpose of the Texas Uniform Declaratory Judgments Act[26] is to settle and afford relief from uncertainty and insecurity with respect to rights, status and other

---

[26] Tex. Civ. Prac. & Rem. Code Section 37.002.

legal relations. A person who has a legal interest in a *writing* (such as a birth certificate or other document) and "whose rights, status or other legal relations are affected [may] have determined any question of construction or validity [of the writing] and obtain a declaration of rights, status or other legal relations thereunder."[27] The act is to be "liberally construed and administered."[28] While the new laws allowing for exceptions of the waiting periods greatly reduce the need for a declaratory judgment. There are still cases where this tool can be useful, i.e. when no birth certificate has ever been recorded or name history is more complex.

For a sample Petition for Declaratory Judgment and Order, please refer to

F E: Sample Declaratory Judgment for Name - Petition and Order[29]

---

[27] Tex. Civ. Prac. & Rem. Code §37.004(a).
[28] Tex. Civ. Prac. & Rem. Code § 37.002(a).
[29] Other legal forms are available from county law libraries throughout Texas. For a list of Texas Law Libraries, click here.

2. Transportation and Driving Privileges

Access to transportation is another important aspect of successful re-entry. Transportation is essential to maintaining a job outside of the home. Without an effective network of public transportation, formerly incarcerated Texans, especially those outside of the major cities, are seriously disadvantaged if they have lost driving privileges.

The Texas 2-1-1 website has a searchable database by city and county of local social services and faith based organizations that offer assistance with basic needs, including transportation. For some previously incarcerated people, the ability to access transportation depends upon restoring their driving privileges. Texas law imposes driver license suspensions of varying duration depending on the offense for which the person was convicted.

This section addresses driver's license suspensions, the Texas Driver Responsibility surcharge program, and the process to obtain an occupational driver's license to allow limited driving privileges for a particular purpose.

2.1 Suspension of Driver's License

The Texas Department of Public Safety's website enables drivers to check the status of their driver's license online. Visit http://www.texas.gov, click on the driver's services button, then the driver's license reinstatement and status button and enter the information.

2.1.1 Texas License Eligibility Program

The Texas Department of Public Safety maintains an online License Eligibility system that can be accessed to determine eligibility, pay reinstatement fees, view compliance restrictions and track information related to eligibility. To access this system all you need is your Texas Driver's License or ID Number, Date of Birth and the Last 4 digits of your Social Security Number.[30]

2.1.2 Refusing or Failing Blood or Breath Test

If a person refuses or fails a blood or breath test following an arrest for driving while intoxicated, his license can be suspended for 90 days up to 2 years. A reinstatement fee of $125 will be required prior to the renewal/issuance of a driver license. The license suspension period varies by court order not to exceed two years. A conviction for driving while intoxicated under the age of 21 will result in an

---

[30] https://txapps.texas.gov/txapp/txdps/dleligibility/login.do

automatic suspension for one year. A reinstatement fee of $100 will be required prior to the renewal/issuance of a driver license. Other requirements include:

Proof of insurance (form SR-22) from insurance company. The SR-22 is required for two years from date of conviction.

Certificate of completion of DWI education program, if required by the convicting court, which must be forwarded to DPS before the suspension period expires to avoid a revocation.

2.1.3 Drug Offenses

A person's license is automatically suspended upon final conviction of a drug offense (which does NOT have to occur while operating a motor vehicle). The suspension period is 180 days. In addition, a drug education program is automatically required and must be completed within the 180-day suspension period or the license remains suspended until the certificate of completion is received by the Texas Department of Public Safety. Proof of insurance (Form SR-22) is required, along with a $100 fee to have the driver's license reinstated.

2.1.4 Traffic Violations

A person's driver's license is subject to suspension for excessive traffic violations, depending on the number of violations within a one or two-year period. Suspension can occur if, within:

12 months - driver has 4 or more moving violations

12 months - if under 18, 2-4 moving violations

24 months - driver 7 or more moving violations.

Payment of a $100 fee is required to reinstate, renew, or issue a driver's license following suspension.

2.1.5 License Suspended or Invalid

The offense of "Driving While license Invalid (Suspended)"--except if the person has been previously convicted for this, was operating a motor vehicle in violation of Section 601.191, was intoxicated while committing this offense, or caused/was at fault in a serious motor vehicle accident--is a Class C misdemeanor carrying a fine of up to $500 and confinement of up to six months in the county jail.[31] A person who drives while his license is under suspension, revocation, or cancellation is subject to an additional license suspension for the same period of time as the original suspension. The suspended license cannot be renewed or reissued until the

---

[31] Tex. Transportation Code §521.457

required $100 reinstatement fee paid. A person convicted for this offense must also obtain and file proof of insurance (form SR-22), and maintain the insurance for two years from date of conviction.

The Legislature has delegated certain rulemaking authority to governmental agencies. Reinstatement Fees and the rules relating to their potential waiver or reduction are created and enforced by the Department of Public Safety. While these types of fees were not eligible for waiver or reduction at the time this guide was last updated, DPS reserves the right to change rules and policies.

2.1.6 Violation of License Restriction

A person who has been convicted of two or more violations of a driver license restriction/endorsement is subject to license suspension. A $100 reinstatement fee is required prior to the renewal/issuance of a driver's license. However, a court may waive payment of all or part of a fine or costs imposed on a defendant if the court finds that defendant was either a child at the time of the offense, or indigent or otherwise does not have sufficient resources or income to pay all or part of the fine or costs, was a child at the time of the offense, and alternative methods of discharging the fine or cost under Tex. Code Crim. Proc. Article 43.09 or Article 42.15 would impose and undue hardship on the defendant.

2.2 OUT-OF-STATE DRIVING OFFENSES

2.2.1 Suspended in another State

A person who has a suspended driving status in another state cannot obtain a Texas driver's license. If the Texas Department of Public Safety issues a Texas license and later learns of an adverse driving status in another state, the Texas license is subject to cancellation. The driver must obtain a clear status from that state's driver licensing agency. Once the driving record is cleared in the other state, the person seeking to clear his driving record must contact Texas DPS Headquarters to have the clearance applied to the Texas driver record. The documents must be from the driver licensing agency in the other state. Court documents from another state will not be accepted as proof of compliance.

2.2.2 Unpaid Traffic Fines in another State

The Texas Department of Public Safety may revoke a person's license if the person has not complied with the terms of a traffic citation received in another state. To have your license reinstated, proof of payment for the out of state citation must be submitted to DPS. Proof of payment includes receipt from court, copy of money order or cashier's check, or copy of cancelled check (front and back). A reinstatement fee will also be required prior to the renewal/issuance of a driver license.

2.2.3 Offense from another State

Texas DPS may suspend a person's license upon receipt of a notice of conviction of an offense committed in another state that, if committed in this state, would be grounds for suspension. Examples of offenses that result in suspension of a Texas driver's license are listed in the table below:[32]

Table 7: Offenses Resulting in Suspension of Driver's License

The table below sets forth specific offenses that result in suspension of the offender's driver's license.

Offense	Restriction
Graffiti Tex. Penal Code §28.08	Discretionary one year suspension for conviction or probation Tex. Transp. Code §521.320
Racing Tex. Transp. Code §545.420(a)	Mandatory one year suspension. If under 18 must perform 10 hours of community supervision and can have an occupational license only for attendance to school. Tex. Transp. Code §521.350
Acquiring motor fuel without payment-theft, Tex. Penal Code §31.03	Coupled with an affirmative finding pursuant to Art. 42.019 Tex Code Crim. Proc.-automatic 180 suspension first offense, 1 year for second offense. Tex. Transp. Code. §521.349
Furnishing alcohol to a minor, Tex. Alco. Bev. Code §106.06 (West 2017)	Automatic 180 day suspension first offense, 1 year second offense.Tex. Transp. Code §521.351 (West 2005)
Possession of fake driver's license, allowing another to use one's driver's license, possessing more than one driver's license, falsifying information on an application for a driver's license, or use of a driver's license to represent one is over 21 when they are not, Tex. Transp. Code §§521.451, 521.453	Mandatory but duration determined by the court, suspension for not less than 90 days nor more than 1 year. Tex. Transp. Code §521.346
Fake license plate or Safety inspection certificate, Tex. Transp. Code §§ 502.409 (a)(4), 548.603(a)(1)	Automatic 180 days suspension. Tex. Transp. Code § 521.3466

---

[32] Adapted in part from "Collateral Consequences of Criminal Convictions", Leavitt, Randy T., for the 35th Annual Advanced Criminal Law Course, July 20-23, 2009, in Dallas, Texas.

Criminally negligent homicide (with a motor vehicle), Tex. Penal Code § 19.05, and any state jail felony with a motor vehicle offense involving personal injury or death	Automatic one year suspension. Tex. Transp. Code § 521.341
Evading arrest or detention Tex. Penal Code § 38.04	Automatic one year suspension. Tex. Transp. Code § 521.341
Intoxication assault Tex. Penal Code § 49.07	Automatic one year suspension. Tex. Transp. Code § 521.341; 90 day to one year suspension if set by the court. Tex. Code Crim. Proc. art. 42.12 § 13(n)(1)
DWI with a child passenger Tex. Penal Code § 49.045	Automatic one year suspension. Tex. Transp. Code § 521.341; 90 day to one year suspension if set by the court. Tex. Transp. Code. § 521.344 and Tex. Code Crim. Proc. art. 42.12 § 13(n)(1)
Intoxication manslaughter Tex. Penal Code § 49.08	Automatic one year suspension. Tex. Transp. Code § 521.341; 180 day to two year suspension if set by the court. Tex. Transp. Code. § 521.344; one year suspension for those under 21. Tex. Transp. Code Tex. Transp. Code. § 521.342(b)
Tampering with a government record-motor vehicle registration or license plate Tex. Penal Code § 37.10	Automatic two year suspension. Tex. Transp. Code § 521.3466
DWI Tex. Penal Code § 49.04	Automatic 1 year suspension Tex. Penal Code § 521.341; 90 day to one year suspension if set by the court. Tex. Transp. Code. § 521.344 and Tex. Code Crim. Proc. art. 42.12 § 13(n)(1) Note: DPS automatically suspends for one year, unless vehicle equipped with an ignition interlock device; Tex. Transp. Code § 521.342
Purchase or attempt to purchase, possession or consumption of alcohol by a minor Tex. Alco. Bev. Code § 106.071	Automatic 30 days suspension on the first offense unless deferred, 60 days on the second offense, and 180 days beyond the second offense. Prior order of deferred disposition is considered a conviction for enhancement purposes. Tex. Alco. Bev. Code § 106.071(f)(2)

Offenses under the Texas Controlled Substance Act, non-drug offense felonies under Chapter 481 of the Tex. Health & Safety Code, and other drug offenses.	Automatic 180 days minimum suspension, must complete drug education program before suspension lifted. Tex. Transp. Code § 521.372; Offenders under 21 - suspension from 180 days up to 1 year. Tex. Transp. Code § 521.342 Offenders under 21 - suspension from 180 days up to 1 year Tex. Transp. Code § 521.342
Multiple traffic violations, Tex. Transp. Code § 521.292; 37 Tex. Admin. Code § 15.89	90 day Suspension if no hearing is requested. Tex. Transp. Code § 521.293
Offenses involving a commercial driver's license, Tex. Transp. Code § 522.081; 37 Tex. Admin. Code § 15.82	Disqualification. Tex. Transp. Code § 522.081
Certain Sex Offenses, Tex. Transp. Code § 521.348	If required to register per Tex. Code Crim. Proc. Ch. 62 and fails to apply for a renewal per Tex. Code Crim. Proc. art. 62.060 or art. 62.2021, license revoked until driver comes into compliance.

2.3 DRIVER SURCHARGES

As of September 1, 2019, the Driver Responsibility Program is repealed, and all pending surcharges must be dismissed. The DPS must reinstate all driver's licenses that were only suspended for those pending surcharges. [TX 86(R) HB 2048]

Under the law effective September 1, 2019, new fines are to be accessed at the sentencing phase of prosecution for certain intoxication offenses.

Table 8: Driver Fines (AKA Surcharges)

Type of Conviction	Surcharge *1 time fine to be paid within 36 months.*
1st Driving While Intoxicated (DWI) Offense Texas or out-of state conviction	$3,000
Subsequent DWI Texas or out-of state conviction	$4,500

| DWI with blood alcohol concentration of 0.15 or more. | $6,000 |

2.3.1 Waiver Based on Indigence

A court having jurisdiction over an offense that is the basis of a surcharge/fine shall waive all fines and costs if the court makes a finding of indigence.

2.4 OCCUPATIONAL DRIVER'S LICENSE

An occupational license is a special restricted license issued to persons whose license has been suspended or revoked for certain offenses (other than medical reasons or delinquent child support). It does not apply to commercial driver's licenses. The occupational license authorizes driving privileges to a person whose license has been suspended if driving is necessary for the person's occupation, educational purposes or in the performance of "essential household duties." This means that the individual requesting the license must be able to demonstrate that they need to drive to and from a job, school, or for some other compelling reason, also known as "the essential need requirement."

2.4.1 **Form SR-22** - Proof of Financial Responsibility

The individual must have the SR-22 before the hearing on the occupational license. Tex. Transp. Code § 521.244(c) requires the petitioner for an occupational license to present to the Judge proof of financial responsibility. The proof of financial responsibility is commonly known as form SR-22. The occupational license holder is required to file and maintain a Form SR-22 with DPS. Some features of the SR-22:

- An insurance card or policy IS NOT accepted in place of the Form SR-22.

- Form SR-22 insurance is mandatory for a period of two (2) years from the date of conviction.

- Form SR-22 is a 'certificate of insurance' that shows DPS proof of insurance for the future. It is motor vehicle liability insurance that requires the insurance company to certify coverage to DPS. The insurance company must notify DPS anytime the policy is cancelled, terminated or lapses.

- The form SR-22 must be purchased from an insurance agent. The driver does not need to own a vehicle to buy this type of insurance. If the driver does not own a vehicle, they can obtain a non-owner Form SR-22.

2.4.2 Minimum Liability Amounts in Texas

Minimum liability coverage amounts in Texas are

- $30,000 for bodily injury to or death of one person in one accident,
- $60,000 for bodily injury to or death of two or more persons in one accident,
- $25,000 for damage to or destruction of property of others in one accident.

The Texas Department of Insurance has more information about minimum liability insurance laws.

2.4.3 Court Order Required

The request for an occupational license is made to the county or district court in county where the person resides, or the court where the offense occurred. If approved, the request will result in a court order granting the license. Note that the court order itself is not the actual occupational license. The order granting the license is the part that must be submitted to DPS in order to get an occupational license issued.

The driver must present a *certified* copy of the court order granting the occupational license to DPS. A certified copy bears the court's stamp on every page to certify that the paper is identical to the original. Certified copies can be obtained from the clerk's office where order was filed, and typically run about $1 per page, payable to the clerk of the court. Depending on the court, the judge may grant the order authorizing the issuance of an occupational license on its own motion, without a petition or request from the person seeking the occupational license. While the waiting for DPS to process the application for an occupational license, the driver may use the court order in lieu of the license for thirty (30) days from the date the order was signed without violating the law.

Even after the license is issued, however, the driver must keep a copy of the order on his person while driving because it is the order which advises law enforcement when it is ok for the driver to drive. Tex. Transp. Code §521.250.

2.4.4 Application to DPS for Occupational License

Once the order on the occupational license has been granted and applicant has obtained a certified copy, the applicant must:

1. Submit an original Form SR-22 certificate of insurance. This is the only proof of insurance acceptable.
2. Pay an occupational license fee for a one-year license or less. If the license needs to be extended, the applicant must seek court authorization. The maximum duration of an occupational license, with extensions, is 2 years.

3. Payment of all required reinstatement fees. A <u>reinstatement fee</u> will be required prior to the renewal/issuance of a driver license.

2.4.5 Waiting Periods

An occupational license is issued once the request is processed unless one of the following situations applies:

- The individual's driver license was previously suspended as a result of an alcohol- or drug-related offense then there is a 90-day waiting period.
- The individual's driver license was in suspension as a result of an intoxication-related conviction then there is a 180-day waiting period.
- There are at least two administrative license revocations on the individual's driver record then a mandatory one-year waiting period applies.

2.4.6 Exception to Essential Need Requirement

Texas Transportation Code §521.244(e) provides that "A person convicted of an offense under Sections 49.04-49.08, Penal Code, who is restricted to the operation of a motor vehicle equipped with an ignition interlock device is entitled to receive an occupational license without a finding that an essential need exists for that person, provided that the person shows:

1. evidence of financial responsibility under Chapter 601; and
2. proof the person has had an ignition interlock device installed on each motor vehicle owned or operated by the person."

Resources
Self-help court forms and instructions for Occupational License - see Texas Law Help <u>Getting an Occupational Driver's License in Texas</u>

Appendix F: Petition and Order for Occupational Driver's License

3. OFFENSE – RELATED DEBT

Criminal debt can be a serious financial roadblock for a person experiencing reentry following a period of incarceration. Individuals with a criminal history are already at a disadvantage in the employment arena. One study showed that defendants placed on felony probation owe between $4000 and $5000 in offense-related debt, not including child support, and that the same group had an unemployment rate of around 40%.[33] There are at least three dozen fees and costs that can be assessed depending on the crime and the jurisdiction.[34] Because one in three dollars raised through these costs and fees is spent on projects outside of the court system, some have argued that they are an undeclared general tax that is unconstitutional.[35]

3.1 CONSEQUENCES OF FAILURE TO PAY

There are numerous negative consequences resulting from a person's failure or inability to pay debt related to an offense. Some include:

- Suspension of Driver's Licenses
- Texas is among the handful of states that suspends driver's licenses as punishment for missed payments.
- Extending Probation Terms
- Texas is among many states that can extend probation for failure to pay a criminal justice debt.
- Jail Time
- Unpaid fines can result in the issuance of arrest warrants and resulting jail time.

3.2.1 JUDICIAL DISCRETION

In Texas, sentencing judges do have some discretion to set payment priorities for offenders placed on community supervision[36]

---

[33] "A Framework to Improve How Fines, Fees Restitution and Child Support are Assessed and Collected from People Convicted of Crimes", Texas Office of Court Administration, 2009.

[34] Id.

[35] See "Court Costs Go to Other Uses", an investigative report by Eric Dexheimer in the Austin American Statesman, Austin Texas, March 4, 2012.

[36] See AG Opinion DM-407 (1996).

Table 9: Court's Authority to Waive Debt[37]

Obligation Type	Individual Placed on Probation	
	Can Judge Waive Debt?	*Relevant Authority*
Offense Fine	Yes	Fines are a form of "punishment which is the right of the judge to set. See AG Opinion GA-0220 (2004)
Restitution	Yes	Tex. Code Crim. App. Art. 42.037 allows a judge to forego restitution. Restitution is not "punishment", making the justification of the judicial discretion different from that of other fines. See AG Opinion GA-0220 (2004)
Court Costs/Fees	Yes	Payments of assessed obligations falls under a judge's right to 'set terms of supervision' pursuant to Tex. Crim. Proc. Art. 42A.053 (taking precedence over other statutes) See AG Opinion DM-407 (1996)
Supervision Fees	Yes	"The judge may waive or reduce the fee or suspend a monthly payment of the fee if the judge determines that payment of the fee would cause the defendant financial hardship" Tex. Code Crim. Proc. Art.42A.652(b)
Attorney Fees	Yes	Tex. Code Crim. P. Art. 26.05(g) requires that a judge make an affirmative finding of 'ability to pay' in order to require repayment of attorney fees.

3.3 OFFENSE- RELATED DEBT AND CHILD SUPPORT

Federal law prioritizes child support obligations over all other debts owed to the state, including criminal justice debt, which conflict with child support commitments. Incarcerated people under obligation to pay child support may discover that the support has continued to accrue, with interest, during their period of confinement. An individual reentering society following incarceration is expected to pay current child support, current medical support, and the child support arrearages that accrued during confinement. While not "offense-related" many individuals experiencing re-entry find it difficult if not impossible to fulfill competing court orders.

---

[37] Texas Office of Court Administration, 2009.

Sentencing courts lack the authority to alter a child support child support orders, and may be unaware that the offender has a continuing child support obligation. Some jurisdictions are beginning to address the disconnection between the fines, fees, and costs imposed by the sentencing court and the child support obligation ordered by the family court. Upon motion and order, the child support court can reduce child support payments based on the obligor's lack of financial resources, including poverty brought on by offense-related debt. By law, child support cannot exceed 50% of the obligor's disposable earnings.[38] Court fines, fees, costs and surcharges should first be deducted from the obligor's net income to arrive at a more realistic starting number for disposable earnings from which to deduct child support and medical support.

Some jurisdictions are trying to develop solutions to these problems. For example, judges in the District of Columbia criminal courts are required to inform individuals with a child support order who are sentenced to prison for more than 30 days that they may petition for modification or suspension of payments during incarceration. D. C. Official Code, title 23, Ch. 1.

3.4 COURT ORDER WAIVING SURCHARGES

Effective September 1, 2019, the Driver Responsibility Program, aka Surcharges, will be repealed, so surcharges in their current form will cease to exist. All Texas Driver's Licenses originally suspended under Tex. Transp. Code Section 708.152 should be reinstated by DPS if surcharges were the sole reason for suspension and all surcharges will be waived.[39]

Under the new provisions of Chapter 709 of the Texas Transportation Code additional fines will be assessed by the sentencing court upon conviction for alcohol-related offenses, and failure to pay them results in an automatic suspension of the person's driver's license. Once assessed, an individual has 36 months to pay the additional fine. The new law allows for the individual to prove up the defendant's indigence to the sentencing court and request that all fines/surcharges be waived at the outset. A motion to waive surcharges can be made orally or through written motion, but the Order must be in writing to prove to DPS that the court has waived the surcharges completely.

For a sample Motion to Waive Surcharge and Order, please refer to:

Appendix G: Motion and Order to Waive Surcharge

3.5 OUTSTANDING TICKETS AND CITATIONS

---

[38] Tex. Fam. Code §8.106 and §158.009

[39] TX HB2048 86th Legislature

Unpaid traffic citations can prevent previously incarcerated people from renewing their driver's license. Tickets may have been issued in several different jurisdictions and run into hundreds of dollars in fines. If the fees are not paid before the appearance date, additional charges are added, including the cost of collection. Many local governments outsource the ticket collection process to collection agencies. The stale tickets may go to warrant for failure to appear,

DPS maintains a site with information on violators who have been reported by Texas cities and counties in accordance with Chapter 706 of the Texas Transportation Code. Those that appear on the database cannot renew their Texas driver license until the violation is resolved with the reporting court. Entering a Texas Driver's license number and date of birth, will result in a listing of the reporting court, docket number and contact information for each court. Those who cannot pay the fines can then write to the court and explain why they are unable to pay and ask that they be reduced or waived. Whether to do so is completely within the court's discretion. Once the fees are paid and the violation resolved, the court has five business days to forward the clearance once to DPS. The Failure to Appear Program does not have information on warrants, however, advises the driver to check with the court to confirm whether a warrant has been issued.

The Code of Criminal Procedure [40]authorizes Justice and Municipal Courts to make a finding of indigence and then either waive fines and fees or convert them to community service.

For a sample Motion to Waive Fines and Fees and Order please refer to:

Appendix H: Motion and Order to Waive Fines and Fees

3.6 *EXCESSIVE FINES AND THE 8TH AMENDMENT*

The 8th Amendment to the United States Constitution prevents the imposition of excessive fines and imprisoning those who cannot pay them (thereby abolishing "debtor's prisons"). Yet there the increasing trend to use fines as a revenue stream for municipalities have led to some aggressive collection tactics and jail time for those unable to pay them, possibly without being informed of their right to counsel.[41] Jailing the misdemeanant who cannot pay a traffic fine arguably violates the 8th Amendment's Excessive Fines clause:

> "The touchstone of the constitutional inquiry under the Excessive Fines Clause is the principle of proportionality: The amount of the forfeiture must bear some relationship to the gravity of the offense that it is designed to punish." *United States v. Bajakajian*, 524 U.S. 321, 334 (1998).

---

[40] Tex. Code Crim. Proc. Art. 45.049
[41] "Bronner, Ethan, "Poor Land in Jail as Companies Add Huge Fees for Probation", New York Times, 7.3.2012

In *Bajakajian,* the government violated the Excessive Fines Clause because the amount forfeited was "grossly disproportionate to the gravity of defendant's offense." The court also considered the particular facts of the case, the character of the defendant, and the harm caused by the offense. Surely it could be argued that hundreds of dollars in fines owed by a person without the ability or means to pay is disproportionate to the harm caused by minor traffic violations.

4. CRIMINAL HISTORY RECORDS

A criminal record ("rap" sheet) is a record of an offender's arrests and convictions. Any time the police fingerprint an offender, the information is added to the offender's criminal history. The history will list the date of arrest, the charges, and the final disposition or outcome. Every person who has intersected with the criminal justice system--through arrest, deferred adjudication, dismissal, conviction or any other interaction--should have a copy of their criminal record and carefully review its contents. There are several good reasons to do so:

1. It provides the subject of the record a look at the kind of information that is available to the general public.

2. It allows the subject an opportunity to review the record for errors, explore record entries that may be removed (expunged), and request nondisclosure or pardon for eligible offenses.

3. Entries that are incorrect can be corrected.

4. It presents a shorter criminal history record to a prospective employer, credit reporting agency, government agency, or licensing authority that runs a background check.[42]

4.1 SOURCES OF CRIMINAL RECORDS

"Official" criminal records are maintained by the Federal Bureau of Investigation (FBI) and the Texas Department of Public Safety (DPS). The FBI is responsible for collecting and distributing criminal history information through the National Crime Information Center (NCIC). DPS performs the same function on the state level for the Texas Crime Information Center (TCIC).

4.1.1 NCIC

The National Crime Information Center (NCIC)[43] is a computerized index of criminal justice information that includes criminal record history information as well as information on fugitives, stolen property, and missing persons. NCIC records are not accessible to the general public. Data contained in NCIC is contributed by the FBI, federal, state, local and foreign criminal justice agencies, and authorized courts.

---

[42] For more information about how to obtain criminal records, visit the DPS website, or call, write, or email: Texas Department of Public Safety Crime Records Service CJIS Field Representatives P.O. Box 4143 Austin, Texas 78765 Phone: (512) 424-2478 Email: afis_cjis@dps.texas.gov

[43] National Crime Information Center (NCIC) Criminal Justice Information Services (CJIS) Division
1000 Custer Hollow Road, Clarksburg, West Virginia 26306. Telephone: (304) 625-2000; Hours of Service: 9:00 a.m. - 5:00 p.m.

4.1.2 TCIC

Much like the NCIC, the Texas Crime Information Center (TCIC) is a computerized searchable database that contains criminal history records, information on stolen property, missing persons, and the status of domestic violence protective orders issued under Chapter 71 of the Texas Family Code. Like the NCIC access to the TCIC is available 24 hours a day, 7 days a week. The TCIC is also linked to NCIC, effectively linking Texas to federal offense information and criminal history reported by every state.

4.1.3 Release of Criminal History Records

DPS, the state agency that maintains the TCIC, is authorized to release a person's *full* criminal history record only to criminal justice agencies for criminal justice purposes, and to certain other legally authorized entities identified in the Government Code and a handful of other statutes.

The search is fingerprint-based, and requires a fingerprint card from the person whose records are being sought that is less than 6 months old. DPS has outsourced its fingerprint service through an exclusive contract with a private vendor, L-1 Enrollment Services.

The information can be released to screen applicants for:

1. Certain governmental licenses (such as medical, law, educator);
2. Certain jobs serving vulnerable populations, especially children, the elderly and the disabled (such as day care centers, nursing homes, hospitals, mental health workers)
3. Authorized researchers,
4. Certain security sensitive jobs, such as nuclear power plants, financial institutions, etc.
5. Brady firearm sales
6. An individual or an agency that has a specific agreement with a criminal justice agency; county or district clerk's office;
7. The Office of Court Administration of the Texas Judicial System;
8. To the person himself or herself[44]

    For step by step instructions on how to order criminal history records, please review the next section

---

[44] Tex. Gov't Code §§411.082(2); 411.082(3); 411.083(b).

Appendix I: Steps to Order Criminal History Records

4.2 DISSEMINATION OF RECORDS BY PRIVATE ENTITIES

A third-party vendor can acquire criminal history information directly from state, county, or city court records and make it available to the public, usually for a fee. [45] Under federal law,[46] users must have a legitimate purpose for conducting background research on websites that contain public data of all kinds. What qualifies as a "legitimate purpose" is so broad however, that nearly every background check falls within those broad parameters. If the records were reported inaccurately, the mistake can be replicated over and over again with each vendor's database.

4.2.1 Consumer Reporting Agencies

Private companies that provide criminal background checks combined with a credit report are restricted from reporting certain kinds of adverse information indefinitely. Under federal law,

> (a) no consumer reporting agency may make any consumer report containing...
>
>> (5) Any other adverse items of information, other than records of convictions of crimes which antedates the report by more than *seven years.*

Fair Credit Reporting Act (FCRA), 15 USCS Sec. 1681c(a)(5)

Arrests that do not result in conviction cannot be reported if they are more than 7 years old. There is also a strong argument to be made under FCRA that in Texas, Deferred adjudication offenses that are discharged and dismissed and are more than 7 years old cannot be reported either because they are not convictions.

4.2.2 Liability for Wrongful Dissemination

Private entities that compile and disseminate criminal history information for compensation face potential civil liability for violations. By law, private entities "shall destroy and may not disseminate any information in the possession of the entity with respect to which the entity has received notice that:

---

[45] For example, Public Data (www.publicdata.com) currently offers the following "lookup" categories: Criminal - Federal, State and Area, Most Wanted, Sex Offenders, Terrorists, Department of Motor Vehicles, Professional License, Property Tax, Driver's License, Secretary of State (business filings) and Civil Court Records.
[46] The Gramm-Leach-Bliley Act of 1999.

(1) an order of expunction has been issued under [Tex. Code Crim. Proc. Article 55.02]; or

(2) an order of nondisclosure has been issued under Subchapter E-1.

(b) Unless the entity is regulated by the federal Fair Credit Reporting Act (15 U.S.C. Section 1681 et seq.) or the Gramm-Leach-Bliley Act (15 U.S.C. Sections 6801 to 6809), a private entity described by Subsection (a) that purchases criminal history record information from the department or from another governmental agency or entity in this state:

(1) may disseminate that information only if, within the 90-day period preceding the date of dissemination, the entity:

(A) originally obtains that information; or

(B) receives that information as updated record information to its database; and

(2) shall notify the department if the entity sells any compilation of the information to another similar entity.

(c) The private entity is "liable for any damages that are sustained as a result of the violation by the person who is the subject of that information," as well as the person's court costs and attorney's fees.[47]

4.2.3 DPS and Texas Public Information Act

A private entity that purchases records from DPS and wrongfully releases information that is under an order of expunction or nondisclosure can be banned from access to DPS records for up to one year – but only upon a *court order* showing that *three or more* violations have occurred:

> "If the department receives information indicating that a private entity that purchases criminal history record information from the department has been found by a court to have committed three or more violations of Section 552.1425 [of the Texas Public Information Act] by compiling or disseminating information with respect to which an order of expunction or an order of nondisclosure has been issued under Article 55.02, Code of Criminal Procedure, or an order of nondisclosure of criminal history record information has been issued under Subchapter E-1, the department may not release any criminal history record information to that entity until the first anniversary of the date of the most recent violation."[48]

---

[47] Tex. Gov't Code § 411.0851. Duty of Private Entity to Update Criminal History Record Information; Civil Liability

[48] Tex. Gov't Code §411.0835, Prohibition against Dissemination to Certain Private Entities

4.2.4 Enforcement

Enforcement is through a lawsuit in district court brought by "the attorney general or an appropriate prosecuting attorney." The district court may issue a warning to a private entity for a first violation, after which the entity is liable to the state for a civil penalty not to exceed $500 for each subsequent violation. Once the penalties are collected, they "shall be deposited in the state treasury to the credit of the general revenue fund. [49]

4.3 CONTENTS OF CRIMINAL RECORDS

Generally, every intersection with law enforcement that starts with an arrest, regardless of outcome, will be recorded in a person's criminal history. Arrests not leading to conviction are subject to expunction (removal from the record). Convictions will remain in an adult's criminal history record indefinitely. There are four main components to each offense: arrest, prosecution, conviction and disposition. There are several common misconceptions about the contents and availability of criminal history information. For example:

- If the arrest did not result in a final conviction, it will not appear on a person's criminal history record.

False. Arrests are part of a criminal record regardless of the outcome.

- A deferred adjudication in which the offender has successfully completed its terms will not appear on a criminal history record because there was no conviction or jail time.

False. A deferred adjudication is part of a person's criminal history, but may be subject to an order of nondisclosure.

4.4 CASE DISPOSITIONS AND SENTENCING ALTERNATIVES

Many criminal case dispositions and alternative sentencing options that appear on a person's criminal history record can blur the line leading from arrest to final conviction. These dispositions can cause confusion among employers reviewing criminal background check and the offenders themselves. All of these alternatives are the outcome of plea negotiations (plea bargains) in which the defendant is presumed to be aware of the consequences of agreement. In reality, many who enter into a plea agreement do not fully understand the quality and quantity of information that will later be included in their criminal history records, including a finding of guilt, the length of time the offense will remain on their record (forever); the negotiated charge, classification, punishment and finality of the proceeding. The

---

[49] Tex. Gov't Code §552.1425.

kind and quality of sentencing alternatives vary widely among Texas's 254 counties. The availability of alternatives and the extent to which they are offered depends upon each local prosecutor's office.

Some of the more common alternatives include pretrial diversion, deferred disposition, deferred adjudication and deferred prosecution.

4.4.1 Pretrial Diversion

Pretrial diversion applies only to certain misdemeanors, usually committed by first-time offenders. It is not available for offenses involving intoxication. Other features of pretrial diversion:
- diversion is granted usually before the case is filed.
- The accused does not admit guilt, but agrees to follow the terms of the diversion agreement, which can include attending classes, rehabilitation and other recommendations.
- If the terms of the diversion agreement are met, the case is never filed.
- If the defendant fails to meet the terms or violates the agreement, the case will be filed and proceed in the usual manner and will (unless another plea is entered or the charges are dismissed) appear as a conviction in a person's criminal history.[50]
- A successful diversion, will NOT appear as a conviction or as a dismissal because charges were never filed.
- A successful pretrial diversion WILL be included in a criminal history record, as well as a record of the arrest leading to the diversion.

4.4.2 Deferred Adjudication

The only specific limitations on granting deferred adjudication are as follows:
"A judge may place on community supervision under this section a defendant charged with an offense under Section 21.11, 22.011, or 22.021, Penal Code [all of which are felonies and assaultive offenses], regardless of the age of the victim... only if the Judge makes a finding in open court that placing the defendant on community supervision is in the best interest of the victim."

Tex. Code Crim. Proc. Art. 42A.102(a). See also Tex. Code. Crim. Pro. Art. 42A.102(b) which include other specific limitations.

Unlike a pretrial diversion, the charges are filed but the prosecution is delayed ("deferred") in exchange for the defendant's plea of guilty or no contest. Other features:
- Deferred adjudication is offered only after charges are filed.

---

[50] Tex. Code Crim. Proc. Art. 102.012 and Tex. Gov't Code §76.011.

- Deferred adjudication resembles a type of probation in which the defendant agrees to certain terms and conditions in exchange for freedom.

- Like probation or other forms of community supervision, deferred adjudication involves payment of fines and costs, monthly reporting to an officer and payment of a monthly fee.

- If the defendant successfully completes the terms and conditions, the case will be dismissed, and the individual will be discharged from probation.

- If the terms are not met, the prosecutor may re-file the case and prosecute it. There is no requirement to re-file the case, however. The defendant is only entitled to a hearing limited to the determination by the Court of whether it is going to proceed to adjudication of guilt. See Tex. Code Crim. Pro. Art. 42.12 Sec 5 (b).

- A successful deferred adjudication WILL appear in a criminal history record as dismissal of charges.

- A deferred adjudication [Tex. Gov't Code Sec. 411.0715] above a class C misdemeanor cannot be expunged or removed from a person's record even if it is later dismissed following a period of community supervision.[51] It may, however, be amenable to nondisclosure, depending on the offense. Tex. Gov't Code 411.0725

Many organizations and agencies have internal hiring policies that exclude consideration of a record of a deferred adjudication as a conviction for employment-related purposes. The Texas Department of Licensing and Regulation (TDLR), for example, will not consider the record of a deferred adjudication a "conviction" for the purpose of applying for or maintaining a vocational license.

4.4.3 Deferred Disposition

Unlike deferred adjudication, which covers Class A and B misdemeanors, deferred disposition is limited to Class C misdemeanors only. Deferred dispositions are often mistakenly referred to as deferred adjudications, but the requirements and outcome for each are quite different. Other features:

- There is no monthly reporting to a probation officer.
- Failure to comply with the terms will result in the imposition of a judgment and conviction that will be reported to DPS.
- If the defendant does not re-offend during the deferral period and complies with the terms, the charges will be dismissed.

---

[51] Tex. Code Crim. Proc. Art. 55.01(a)(2)(B).

- If the deferred disposition is successfully completed, the defendant may seek an expunction and have the disposition removed from his or her criminal history record.

4.4.4 Felony Pretrial Diversion

At least one Texas prosecutor's office offers a felony pretrial diversion program for eligible offenses as determined by the district attorney. In Travis County, the District Attorney's Office will consider an application for felony pretrial diversion by an offender charged with a third degree or state jail felony non-violent offense if the defendant is a first time offender. The program allows the offender to avoid prosecution if there are no new arrests during the term and all the requirements of the term are completed. The offender may be required to attend counseling, make restitution, and perform community service and other conditions. If the term is completed successfully, the offender can apply for an expunction of the arrest record.[52]

4.4.5 Deferred Prosecution - Juveniles Only

Deferred adjudication refers to adult proceedings, while deferred prosecution applies only to juveniles. In Texas only juveniles under the age of 17 that are alleged to have committed crimes may be considered for "Deferred Prosecution"[53] In a deferred prosecution, the juvenile completes an informal probation with the county. If successful, the charges are dismissed and the juvenile is not prosecuted. Unlike adult deferred adjudication, a juvenile has the absolute right to request deferred prosecution. If the probationary period is unsuccessful, the juvenile retains the ability to fight the charges.

4.5 PROTECTIVE ORDERS

Protective Orders are orders issued by a court to prevent continuing acts of family, dating or sexual violence. They can be part of a person's criminal history record and are reported to federal, state and local authorities. Protective orders are typically of limited duration and expire on the date specified in the Order or by statute, if the order does not specify an end date.

Protective orders issued under the Texas Family Code may not involve an arrest or conviction, but can still appear in a person's criminal history record or in the database of law enforcement agencies. The agency may enter protective orders in the computer records of outstanding warrants as notice that the order has been issued and is currently in effect. The clerk of the court where the order was issued

---

[52] Travis County Felony Pretrial Diversion Program

[53] Tex. Fam. Code § 53.03.

must notify the agency when the order has been vacated or dismissed, so that the protective order may be removed from the list of outstanding warrants.[54]

A law enforcement agency may enter a protective order in the agency's computer records of outstanding warrants as notice that the order has been issued and is currently in effect. On receipt of notification by a clerk of court that the court has vacated or dismissed an order, the law enforcement agency shall remove the order from the agency's computer record of outstanding warrants People who have had a protective order issued against them at any time in the past, even if the order is expired, should review their criminal history record to ensure that the status of the protective order is accurately reported.

There are several different kinds of protective orders and each varies in duration.

4.5.1 Protective Order - Texas Family Code

A protective order under Chapter 71 of the Texas Family Code is a civil court order issued to prevent continuing acts of family violence, dating violence, or child abuse. By law, the TCIC is required to maintain information about "active" domestic violence protective orders.[55] Features:
- Civil order that is criminally enforceable
- Can be enforced in any state. A protective order issued in another state may be enforced in Texas; a protective order issued by a Texas court is enforceable in all other states.
- Can be issued without an arrest or corresponding criminal charges.[56]
- Has a maximum duration of 2 years:
    - If the order is violated, it *may* be extended or renewed for up to two additional years;
    - Court has discretion to exceed two years in cases of serious bodily injury or perpetrator was the subject of two or more previous protective orders.
    - If the order expires while the person against whom it is directed is incarcerated for more than five years, the order is automatically extended for one year from the date the person is released from incarceration. *However, if the person was incarcerated for five or less years, the order is automatically extended for two years from the date the person is released from incarceration.*[57]

---

[54] Tex. Fam. Code §86.001(b)

[55] 37 Texas Admin. Code Rule 27.72, "Reporting of Information Related to the Protective Order File."

[56] "A prosecuting attorney's decision to file an application for a protective order under Chapter 71, Family Code, should be made without regard to whether a criminal complaint has been filed by the applicant. Tex. Code Crim. Proc. Art. 5.06(b), Family Violence Prevention.

[57] Tex. Fam. Code § 85.025(c)

After one year, the Respondent may file a motion to vacate the protective order upon showing that there is no continuing need for Protective Order.[58]

4.5.2 Emergency *Protective Order (Magistrate's Order)*

A Magistrate's Order for Emergency Protection (Emergency Protective Order, or "EPO") is authorized by the Texas Code of Criminal Procedure,[59] and is issued by a magistrate following an arrest for an offense involving family violence or a sexual assault.

Features:
- Requires an arrest for stalking, sexual assault or an offense involving family or dating violence
- Issued for 31–61 days or for up to 91 days if a weapon is involved.
- Arrest often results in charges against perpetrator (e.g., assault with family violence) Law enforcement is notified of the EPO.

4.5.3 Protective Orders - Sexual Assault, Trafficking and Stalking[60]

The Sexual Assault Protective Order is designed to protect survivors of sexual assault, sex trafficking and stalking from the ongoing threat of further harm from the alleged offender.
Features:
- Can be issued regardless of relationship between applicant and offender;
- Applicant must be a victim of sexual assault, sex trafficking or stalking
- Does not require an accompanying police report, arrest, or charges against the offending person
- May last a lifetime, depending on circumstances

---

[58] Tex. Fam. Code 85.025

[59] Tex. Code Crim. Proc. Art. 17.292

[60] Tex. Code Crim. P. Ch.7A

5. Expunction, Nondisclosure, and Pardon

A criminal record can create barriers to employment, housing, credit, and other life necessities. Once the ex-offender obtains a copy of her criminal history record, it may be possible to remove arrest records not resulting in conviction, or restrict information depending on the offense. Petitions for nondisclosure and for expunctions are two methods by which Texas criminal records can be mitigated. This section is about the availability of these methods and information on how to proceed with each.

5.1 Difference Between Expunction and Nondisclosure

The expunction of criminal records is an aspect of criminal law that most people do not understand.[61] An expunction[62] authorizes the actual destruction of the information surrounding the arrest. A non-disclosure[63] can limit public access to an arrest record but cannot destroy the record information.

Another difference between expunction and nondisclosure is that expunction prohibits any dissemination or use of the information relating to the offense to anyone, whereas nondisclosure shields it from the public but not from law enforcement agencies and other entities named in the statute, such as the State Board for Educator Certification and the Texas Department of Licensing and Regulation.[64]

5.1.1 About Deferred Adjudications

Many believe that by accepting a deferred adjudication or disposition that their criminal record will not reflect that offense, and no evidence of it will be part of their criminal history record.[65] While it is true that a person who successfully completes a term of deferred adjudication *will not show a final conviction* on their criminal record, the records will still include details of the *arrest*. Expunction is not

---

[61] The explanatory paragraphs regarding expunction and nondisclosure of deferred adjudications is adapted in part from a brief article appearing in the Texas Young Lawyer's Association news posting June 29, 2007: Expunction vs. Deferred Adjudication Nondisclosure, by Heath Poole, Hoelscher, Lipsey, Elmore & Benn, P.C. in College Station, Texas ; used with permission.
[62] Tex. Code Crim. P. Ch. 55.

[63] Tex. Gov't Code Ch. 481.

[64] Tex. Gov't. Code 411.0765

[65] Tex. Code Crim. P. Art. 55.01(a)(1)(B) and (c). Juvenile records may be sealed unless there are pending criminal proceedings or the offender has been adjudicated a habitual felon. Tex. Fam. Code §58.003. If sealed, the ex-offender may deny the existence of the record. Tex. Fam. Code §58.003.

available as a remedy to remove deferred adjudication offenses *above* a class C misdemeanor."

5.2 EXPUNCTION

In Texas, expunction is available only under very narrow circumstances. Because it is a limited remedy, anyone with a criminal history record should be especially wary of services that claim to clean up the records for a fee. Expunction cannot remove the record of an adult criminal conviction except in the rare case where the offender has been pardoned, where the conviction was thrown out on appeal, or where the defendant was granted relief on the basis of actual innocence if the court order so states. Tex. Code Crim. P. Art. 55.01(a)(1)(B)(ii)[66]

Table 10: Eligibility for Expunction

EXPUNCTION	
ELIGIBLE	**INELIGIBLE**
Class C misdemeanors where charges were dismissed following a period of deferred adjudication.[67]	Deferred adjudication sentences for Class B, Class A, or felony offenses.
Pardons restoring civil rights and pardons predicated upon a finding of innocence.[68] Or court order indicating that the individual was released based on actual innocence.	Acquittals, dismissals, and arrests arising out of a "criminal episode" or conviction for another offense for which the person was convicted, or is pending prosecution

---

[66] The "actual innocence" provision, added by the Legislature in 2011, was intended to apply to those wrongfully convicted and exonerated. Prior to this language they had to obtain a pardon and then get an expunction to have the wrongful conviction removed from their record.

[67] Tex. Code Crim. P Art. 55.01(a)(2)(B).

[68] See *Ex parte Hernandez*, 165 SW3d 760, 763 (Tex. App.-Eastland, 2005)

Felonies or Misdemeanors where the person is released and the charge has not resulted in a final conviction and is no longer pending and no court ordered supervision under Tex. Crim. Pro. Art 42A, regardless of statute of limitation, provided that the following period has elapsed: • 180 Days for Class C • 1 year for Class A & B Misdemeanor • 3 years for a Felony	A person may not expunge records and files relating to an arrest that occurs pursuant to a probation revocation warrant issued under Tex. Code Crim. Proc. Article 42A.751(b).
Offenses eligible for dismissal or quashed because of the persons successful completion of a pretrial intervention program authorized under Tex. Gov. Code Sec. 76.011.	A person who intentionally or knowingly absconds from the jurisdiction after being released from jail on bond.

5.2.1 Order Directing Expunction

Unlike nondisclosure, where the court has discretion to grant "in the best interest of justice," a petition for expunction must be granted if the offense and resulting arrest or adjudication are eligible under the statute. The court must grant the request to expunge if all of the other legal criteria are met.

5.2.2 Effect of Expunction

After the expunction is ordered, "the release, maintenance, dissemination, or use of the expunged records and files for any purpose is prohibited" and "the person arrested may deny the occurrence of the arrest and the existence of the expunction order."[69] The Order applies to "all records and files relating to the arrest" in the district court in the county where the arrest occurred.[70] If the offense is eligible for expunction, the judge cannot dismiss or deny the request for expunction.[71] Once the order of expunction is entered, the person may deny that the arrest occurred, and deny the existence of the associated expunction order.[72]

For forms and step by step instructions for expunction of criminal history records, please refer to:

---

[69] Tex. Code Crim. Proc. Art. 55.03(1) and (2)

[70] Tex. Code Crim. Proc. Ann. Art. 55.01(a)(1)(B).

[71] *Perdue v. Texas Dept. of Public Safety*, 32 SW3d 333, 334-35 (Tex. App. 2000).

[72] Tex. Code Crim. P Art. 55.03(1),(2)(3), "When questioned under oath in a criminal proceeding about an arrest for which the records have been expunged, [the person] may state only that the matter in question has been expunged."

Appendix J: Instructions, Petition, Verification and Order for Expunction of Criminal Records

5.3 NONDISCLOSURE

The 84th legislature created much greater access to nondisclosure for first time offenders. Unlike expunction, the nondisclosure process does not remove an offense from a person's criminal history record; rather, it shields the record from public disclosure. To restrict access to criminal history through nondisclosure, the following conditions must be met:

5.3.1 Automatic Nondisclosures – Deferred in Certain Misdemeanors: §411.072

- The offense must be among those eligible for nondisclosure, AND
  - excludes all misdemeanors under Penal Code Chapters 20 (kidnapping and unlawful restraint), 21 (indecent exposure and unlawful photography), 22 (assault, deadly conduct, terroristic threat), 25 (bigamy, enticing a child, criminal nonsupport, violation of protective order), 42 (disorderly conduct, harassment, animal cruelty), 43 (prostitution, sexting), 46 (unlawful carrying of a weapon, prohibited weapons), and 71 (engaging in organized criminal activity)
- The offender must have completed deferred adjudication AND
- The offender must have received a discharge and dismissal, AND
- It must be a first offense for the offender, AND
- A period of 180 days must have elapsed from the date that the offender was placed on deferred AND
- Offender is not required to file a petition (though it is recommended) but is required to pay a fee and "present" to the court.

5.3.2 Standard Deferred Nondisclosures: Tex. Gov't Code §411.0725

- The offense must be a Misdemeanor or Felony among those eligible for nondisclosure, AND
- The offender must have received a discharge and dismissal, AND
- The applicable waiting period must have elapsed
  - Most Misdemeanors: No waiting period.
  - Some Misdemeanors: 2 years from dismissal
- All those excluded from automatic nondisclosure above.
  - Felonies: 5 years from dismissal
- Must file a petition and must show that nondisclosure is in the best interest of the public

5.3.3 *Nondisclosure after Straight Probation Tex. Gov't Code §411.073*

- Allows for nondisclosure after a term of straight probation for certain misdemeanors is served, AND
    - Excludes misdemeanors under Alcoholic Beverage Code §106.041 (possession and/or consumption of or selling alcohol to minors); Penal Code §§49.04 (driving while intoxicated), 49.05 (flying while intoxicated), 49.06 (boating while intoxicated), or 49.065 (operating an amusement park ride while intoxicated); AND any conviction under Penal Code Chapter 71 (engaging in organized criminal activity).
- It must be a first offense for the offender, AND
- 2 Year Waiting period for some misdemeanors still applies.
- Must file a petition and show that nondisclosure is in the best interest of the public.

5.3.4 *Misdemeanor Jail Time Served: Tex. Gov't Code §411.0735*

- Allows for nondisclosure after a term of jail time is served for certain misdemeanors is served, AND
    - Excludes misdemeanors under Alcoholic Beverage Code §106.041 (possession and/or consumption of or selling alcohol to minors), Penal Code §§49.04 (driving while intoxicated), 49.05 (flying while intoxicated), 49.06 (boating while intoxicated), 49.065 (operating an amusement park ride while intoxicated), AND any conviction under Penal Code Chapter 71 (engaging in organized criminal activity).
- It must be a first offense for the offender, AND
- 2 Year Waiting period for some misdemeanors still applies.
- Must file a petition and show that nondisclosure is in the best interest of the public.

5.3.5 *Human Trafficking Victims*: Tex. Gov't Code § 411.0728

- Eligibility under this code section was greatly expanded in 2019.
- Applies to persons convicted of prostitution, theft and possession and/or delivery of marihuana, regardless of the sentence.
- Must file a petition and show that they only committed the offenses as a victim of human trafficking and that nondisclosure is in the best interest of the public.
    - Petitioner should show that they either cooperated with the prosecution if called to do so or were unable to do so based on physical or mental disability.
- A request to consolidate all eligible matters should be filed to aggregate all matters under one order.

5.3.6 Limitations on Nondisclosure

As with expunctions, it is important to understand the legal limitations on nondisclosure. Anyone who has *ever* committed any of the offenses appearing in the second column ("Ineligible Offenses") of the following table, regardless of the outcome (including successful deferred adjudication) are NOT eligible to petition for nondisclosure.[73]

It is also important to remember that the Nondisclosure Order only restricts *public* access. Criminal justice agencies can still release the records subject to nondisclosure to other criminal justice agencies, for criminal justice or regulatory licensing purposes, other entities authorized by statute (such as schools, hospitals, public licensing boards, and certain government agencies), to the person who is the subject of the criminal history record, and for the purpose of complying with a requirement under federal law or if federal law requires the disclosure as a condition of receiving federal highway funds.[74]

A person who is currently on deferred adjudication may seek nondisclosure of a previous deferred adjudication that resulted in dismissal and discharge.[75] A person who commits another offense while on deferred adjudication is not eligible to seek nondisclosure of the previous deferred adjudication.

Table 11: Nondisclosure - Eligible and Ineligible Offenses

NONDISCLOSURE	
ELIGIBLE OFFENSES All misdemeanors NOT listed below - no waiting period; for those listed - 2 year waiting period	**INELIGIBLE OFFENSES** Never eligible regardless of the outcome (even completion of deferred adjudication)
Abuse of corpse	Aggravated sexual assault
Advertising for placement of child	Sexual assault
Aiding suicide	Prohibited sexual conduct (incest)
Assault	Aggravated kidnapping
Bigamy	Burglary of a habitation with intent to commit any of the above offenses

---

[73] Tex. Gov't Code §411.074

[74] Tex. Gov't Code §411.0765

[75] Tex. Gov't Code §411.074(a);

Cruelty to animals	Indecency with a child
Deadly conduct	Compelling prostitution
Destruction of flag	Sexual performance by a child
Discharge of firearm	Possession or promotion of child pornography
Disorderly conduct	Unlawful restraint, kidnapping, or aggravated kidnapping of a person younger than 17 years of age
Disrupting meeting or procession	Attempt, conspiracy, or solicitation to commit any of the above offenses
Dog fighting	Capital murder
False alarm or report	Murder
Harassment	Injury to a child, elderly individual, or disabled individual
Harboring runaway child	Abandoning or endangering a child
Hoax bombs	Violation of protective order or magistrate's order
Indecent exposure	Stalking
Interference with emergency telephone call	Any other offense involving family violence
Leaving a child in a vehicle	Trafficking, single offense or continuous.
Making a firearm accessible to a child	
Obstructing highway or other passageway	
Possession, manufacture, transport, repair or sale of switchblade knife or knuckles	
Public lewdness	
Riot	
Silent or abusive calls to 9-1-1 service	
Terroristic threat	

Unlawful carrying of handgun by license holder	
Unlawful carrying weapons	
Unlawful possession of firearm	
Unlawful restraint	
Unlawful transfer of certain weapons	

5.3.7 Deferred Adjudication and Nondisclosure

A person who is currently on deferred adjudication may seek nondisclosure of a previous deferred adjudication that resulted in dismissal and discharge.[76] A person who commits another offense while on deferred adjudication or during the applicable waiting period is not eligible to seek nondisclosure of the previous deferred adjudication.

5.3.8 Nondisclosure Process

The nondisclosure process is a civil court proceeding filed in the criminal court that entered the original adjudication. The person seeking nondisclosure must file a petition for requesting nondisclosure, notify the prosecutor, and appear at a court hearing before a judge.

5.3.9   Order of Nondisclosure

Unlike an expunction, which is mandatory if the expunction criteria are met, the court makes the decision if nondisclosure is "in the best interest of justice", except in the case of automatic nondisclosures for certain misdemeanors. If the court finds that it is, it "shall issue an order prohibiting criminal justice agencies from disclosing to the public criminal history record information related to the offense giving rise to the deferred adjudication."[77]

The order is then sent to DPS, who in turn forwards it to "all law enforcement agencies, jails or other detention facilities, magistrates, courts, prosecuting attorneys, correctional facilities, central state depositories of criminal records, and other officials or agencies or other entities of this state or of any political subdivision of this state, to all central federal depositories of criminal records that there is reason to believe have criminal history record information that is the subject of the order,

---

[76] Tex. Gov't Code §411.074;

[77] Tex. Gov't Code §411.0725(d).

and private entities that purchase criminal history record information from the department or that otherwise are likely to have criminal history record information that is subject to the order."[78]

5.3.10 Effect of Order of Nondisclosure

If granted, the order prohibits criminal justice agencies from disclosing criminal history record information about the deferred adjudication to the public. If access to a criminal record that is covered by a nondisclosure order is requested by someone not authorized to view it, the agency may inform the requestor that it has "no record."[79] A person who releases criminal history information under an order of nondisclosure can be subject to criminal penalties.[80]

For Steps for Nondisclosure and sample forms, please refer to:

---

[78] Tex. Gov't Code §411.075.

[79] Tex. Gov't. Code §411.085; Op.Atty.Gen.2004, No. GA-0255.

[80] Tex. Gov't Code Ann. § 411.085.

Appendix K-1: Office of Court Administration – An Overview of Orders of Nondisclosure

Appendix K-2: Instructions and Letter Requesting an Order of Nondisclosure under Section 411.072, Government Code and Order

Appendix K-3: Instructions and Petition and Order of Nondisclosure under Section 411.0725, Government Code

Appendix K-4: Instructions and Petition and Order of Nondisclosure under Section 411.0727, Government Code

Appendix K-5: Instructions and Petition and Order of Nondisclosure under Section 411.0728, Government Code

Appendix K-6: Instructions and Petition and Order of Nondisclosure under Section 411.073, Government Code

Appendix K-7: Instructions and Petition and Order of Nondisclosure under Section 411.0731, Government Code

Appendix K-8: Instructions and Petition and Order of Nondisclosure under Section 411.0735, Government Code

Appendix K-9: Instructions and Petition and Order of Nondisclosure under Section 411.0736, Government Code

5.4 PARDON

Pardons, or executive clemency, are very rare because the criterion for granting them is narrow and each must be approved by the governor. Clemency includes full pardons, conditional pardons, pardons based on innocence, commutations of sentence, and emergency medical reprieves. Unlike the expunction and nondisclosure process, which are court proceedings, an application for a pardon must be made to the Texas Board of Pardons and Paroles. Pardons are granted by the governor following the Board's recommendation.

5.4.1 Offenses NOT Eligible for Pardon

The following offenses and situations are not eligible for a pardon request:

- treason

- arrests with no conviction
- early dismissals from probation
- Class C misdemeanor
- out-of-state felony conviction
- federal conviction
- applicants who were denied a full pardon less than one year prior to the present application

5.4.2 Pardon Process

The clemency process begins with a lengthy application. Before beginning, the Board of Pardons and Paroles recommends that the applicant obtain all of the following documents:

- offense reports for any arrests;
- certified court documents for these arrests, including complaints, indictments, judgments, and orders of dismissal;
- an official criminal history statement, and
- three current letters of recommendation from persons other than family members who are familiar with the applicant.

The Board has discretion to recommend clemency based on the information provided.[81] As of January 1, 2012, the Texas Constitution was amended and the Governor was given the authority to pardon deferred adjudication offenses. Tex. Code Crim. Proc. Art. 48.01.

For additional information about pardons of deferred adjudication offenses visit http://www.tdcj.state.tx.us/bpp/exec_clem/Deferred_Adjudication.html.

---

[81] The official Texas Board of Pardons and Paroles application form for pardon and pardon checklist may be downloaded from their website.

6. EMPLOYMENT

Seventy-three percent of human resources professionals said their company, or an agency hired by their company, conducted criminal background checks for all job candidates, according to a 2010 survey by the Society for Human Resource Management.

According another study, nearly one in three adults (31.7 percent) in the United States is estimated to have a criminal record on file with the states that will show up on a routine criminal-background check. African-American and Latino workers are the most negatively impacted by the criminal-justice system. Latinos are incarcerated at a rate more than twice that of whites, while African Americans are incarcerated at a rate six times that of whites.[82]

Finding employment may one of the greatest challenges facing previously incarcerated persons. Employers may legally refuse to hire a person based on a criminal record. Depending on the occupation, state licensing boards can restrict access to vocational licenses based on a person's criminal history. Other challenges can include finding access to child care during work hours and transportation to and from the job.

This section addresses general employment issues commonly encountered by previously incarcerated people. Vocational and occupational license restrictions are addressed in Chapters 2 and 7 of this guide.

6.1 CIVIL RIGHTS[83]

6.1.1 Bars to Hiring

A handful of states that protect job applicants from discrimination based on criminal history, but Texas is not among them.[84] A Texas employer can refuse to hire a job applicant for nearly any reason, including a criminal history record, unless the refusal violates federal antidiscrimination laws. Texas law allows employers to terminate an employee for any reason that doesn't violate federal civil rights laws.

---

[82] 99 Pew Center on the States, *One in 100: Behind Bars in America 2008*. (Feb.2008). See also, Devah Pager and Bruce Western, *Race at Work: Realities of Race and Criminal Record in the NYC Job Market* (Princeton University, 2005). as cited in the Excluded Workers Congress 2010 publication Unity for Dignity: Expanding the Right to Organize to Win Human Rights at Work, December 2010

[83] Civil Rights subsection adapted from Unity for Dignity: Expanding the Right to Organize to Win Human Rights at Work, December 2010 (used with permission from the Excluded Workers Congress, https://www.reimaginerpe.org/node/5948).

[84] New York, Connecticut, Minnesota, Hawaii, Illinois, Massachusetts, Pennsylvania, and Wisconsin have laws that protect convicted criminals from discrimination on the basis of their conviction.

Title VII of the Civil Rights Act of 1964 prohibits both disparate treatment and disparate impact. However, because of the disparate impact of the criminal-justice system on communities of color, the EEOC has found that "an employer's policy or practice of excluding individuals from employment on the basis of their conviction records has an adverse impact on [African-Americans and Latinos]."[85] Because of the adverse impact on minorities, EEOC policy prohibits employers from imposing blanket-hiring prohibitions on job seekers based on criminal records.

Despite this important federal protection, more than 60 percent of large employers reported that they would "probably not" or "definitely not" consider a job applicant once aware of the individual's criminal record.[86] African-American and Latino men with a criminal record are less likely to be offered employment than similarly situated whites.[87]

An employer's use of criminal history information may violate civil rights laws if the offense for which they were convicted is not "job related." As a practical matter, proving that a person was unfairly denied employment based on criminal history is more difficult to prove than making a case that the person was discriminated against on the basis on race, color or national origin.[88] If 66% of Texas ex-offenders reentering are classified as Black or Hispanic, the applicant who is rejected for employment may be better able to prove that employer's underlying reason was based on the person's race, not record., [89]Civil rights laws interpreting racial discrimination are more clearly settled than those involving criminal history discrimination, and may provide a clearer legal path to relief.

6.1.2 EEOC 2012 Enforcement Guidance

In April 2012 the U.S. Equal Employment Opportunity Commission (EEOC) issued a formal document on Enforcement Guidance for employers, employment agencies, applicants and employees on the consideration of arrest and conviction records in employment decisions under Title VII of the Civil Rights Act of 1964.[90] Excerpts

---

[85] U.S. Equal Employment Opportunity Commission, *EEOC Policy Statement on the Issue of Conviction Records under Title VII of the Civil Rights Act of 1964, as amended*, 42 U.S.C. § 2000e et seq., 1982, Feb 4, 1987, https://www.eeoc.gov/policy/docs/convict1.html, as cited in the Excluded Workers Congress 2010 publication Unity for Dignity: Expanding the Right to Organize to Win Human Rights at Work, December 2010

[86] Harry Holzer, Steven Raphael &Michael Stoll, *Perceived Criminality, Criminal Background Checks and the Racial Hiring Practices of Employers*, University of Chicago Journal of Law and Economics, 2006. as cited in the Excluded Workers Congress 2010 publication Unity for Dignity: Expanding the Right to Organize to Win Human Rights at Work, December 2010

[87] Devah Pager, *The Mark of a Criminal Record*, 108 AmJSoc. 937 (2003), as cited in the Excluded Workers Congress 2010 publication Unity for Dignity: Expanding the Right to Organize to Win Human Rights at Work, December 2010

[88] Title VII of the Civil Rights Act of 1964, 42 USC §2000e et seq.

[89] Jamie Watson, et.al., A Portrait of Prisoner Reentry in Texas 15 (2004); Equal Employment Opportunity Commission, Policy Statement on the Issue of Conviction Records under Title VII of the Civil Rights Act of 1964, as amended, 42 USC §2000e et seq. (1982) ("Where there is evidence of an adverse impact on blacks or Hispanics, an absolute bar to employment based on the mere fact that an individual has a conviction record is unlawful."),

[90] As amended, 42 U.S.C. § 2000e

from the "Frequently Asked Questions" accompanying the EEOC's release of the guidelines are worth including here:

> *1. How is Title VII relevant to the use of criminal history information?*
>
> There are two ways in which an employer's use of criminal history information may violate Title VII. First, Title VII prohibits employers from treating job applicants with the same criminal records differently because of their race, color, religion, sex, or national origin ("disparate treatment discrimination").
>
> Second, even where employers apply criminal record exclusions uniformly, the exclusions may still operate to disproportionately and unjustifiably exclude people of a particular race or national origin ("disparate impact discrimination"). If the employer does not show that such exclusion is "job related and consistent with business necessity" for the position in question, the exclusion is unlawful under Title VII.
>
> *2. Does Title VII prohibit employers from obtaining criminal background reports about job applicants or employees?*
>
> No. Title VII does not regulate the acquisition of criminal history information. However, another federal law, the Fair Credit Reporting Act, 15 U.S.C. § 1681 et seq. (FCRA), does establish several procedures for employers to follow when they obtain criminal history information from third-party consumer reporting agencies. In addition, some state laws provide protections to individuals related to criminal history inquiries by employers.
>
> *3. Is it a new idea to apply Title VII to the use of criminal history information?*
>
> No. The Commission has investigated and decided Title VII charges from individuals challenging the discriminatory use of criminal history information since at least 1969, thus, applying Title VII analysis to the use of criminal history information in employment decisions is well-established.
>
> ✻✻✻
>
> *6. Is the Commission changing its fundamental positions on Title VII and criminal record exclusions with this Enforcement Guidance?*
>
> No. The Commission will continue its longstanding policy approach in this area: The fact of an arrest does not establish that criminal conduct has occurred. Arrest records are not probative of criminal conduct[.] However, an employer may act based on evidence of conduct that disqualifies an individual for a particular position.

Convictions are considered reliable evidence that the underlying criminal conduct occurred[.] National data supports a finding that criminal record exclusions have a disparate impact based on race and national origin. The national data provides a basis for the Commission to investigate Title VII disparate impact charges challenging criminal record exclusions. A policy or practice that excludes everyone with a criminal record from employment will not be job related and consistent with business necessity and therefore will violate Title VII, unless it is required by federal law.

The Enforcement Guidance also provides best practices for employers to consider when making employment decisions based on criminal records.[91]

6.1.3 "Ban the Box"

"Ban the Box" is an international campaign by civil rights groups and advocates for ex-offenders, aimed at persuading employers to remove from their hiring applications the check *box* that asks if applicants have a criminal record. In addition to employment applications the movement extends to housing and other social services.

By April 2019, a total of 34 states and the District of Columbia have adopted ban the box policies for employment applications. These states are: Arizona, California, Colorado, Connecticut, Delaware, Georgia, Hawaii, Illinois, Indiana, Kansas Kentucky, Louisiana, Maryland, Massachusetts, Michigan, Minnesota, Missouri, Nebraska, Nevada, New Jersey, New Mexico, New York, North Dakota, Ohio, Oklahoma, Oregon, Pennsylvania, Rhode Island, Tennessee, Utah, Vermont, Virginia, Washington, and Wisconsin. In some jurisdictions, ban the box laws apply mostly to public or government jobs. Some apply to private companies, or to businesses of at least a certain size.[92]

The intended goal of ban the box policies are to promote stable employment and increased public safety. Access to employment has a significant impact on reduction in recidivating and success after incarceration. Those who are able to find a job have a better likelihood of being productive members of society and contributing economically.

Unfortunately, in 2016 two new working papers suggest that these policies are actually increasing racial disparities in employment outcomes. When employers are restricted from asking applicants about criminal history they often make assumptions about criminality based on the applicant' race. A recent study found that white applicants received 23% more callbacks than black applicants with similar applications. This white advantage was observed at much higher levels in neighborhoods with higher white populations. Prior to ban the box policies being implemented this gap in callbacks was only 7%.[93]

---

[91] See http://www.eeoc.gov/laws/guidance/qa_arrest_conviction.cfm

[92] From https://www.jobsforfelonshub.com/ban-the-box-states/#ixzz4dmydjDWn

[93] Amanda Y. Agan and Sonja B. Starr, Ban the Box, Criminal Records and Statistical Discrimination: A Field Experiment, University of Michigan Law and Economics Research Paper No. 16-012.

6.2 OCCUPATIONAL OUTLOOK HANDBOOK

The Occupational Outlook Handbook is an annual publication of the U.S. Department of Labor (DOL), Bureau of Labor Statistics (BLS). It covers hundreds of occupations and breaks down information on each, including a description of the job duties, working conditions, training and education required for specific occupations, expected earnings, and the anticipated job market for a specific occupation, the Handbook also provides links to the job market in each state.[94]

6.3 WORK AUTHORIZATION DOCUMENTS

Before applying for a job, job seekers should be aware of the employment eligibility verification required by federal law and be prepared to produce the required documents. When hired, employees are required to prove that they are legally entitled to work in the United States. Employers are required to verify the identity and eligibility to work for all new employees and to keep the verification form on file. All employees, citizens and noncitizens, hired after November 6, 1986 and working in the U.S. must complete United States Citizenship and Immigration Services (USCIS) Form I-9 , Employment Eligibility Verification, to prove authorization to work in the U.S. Failure to provide the verification within 3 days of hire can result in termination of the new employee.

6.3.1 I-9 Employment Verification Form Requirements

A variety of documents are acceptable to prove work authorization. The employee must provide to his employer, within three days of hire, the following:
- One document that establishes both identity and employment eligibility (on List A on the I-9) OR
- One document that establishes identity (on List B), and another document establishing employment eligibility (on List C).

By law, the employer *does not* get to choose which documents the employee must submit, and is not permitted to *retain* the original identification presented. The employer may only photocopy the ID and must return it to the employee.

Table 12: I-9 Employment Verification Documents

I-9 EMPLOYMENT VERIFICATION DOCUMENTS				
LIST A (Documents that establish both identity	O R	**LIST B** (Documents that establish identity only)	A N D	**LIST C**

---

[94] Occupational Outlook Handbook, occupationaloutlookhandbook.txt http://www.bls.gov/ooh/

U.S. Department of Labor (DOL), Bureau of Labor Statistics (BLS) – Occupational Outlook Handbook, 2010-2011 Edition

and employment eligibility)		(Documents that establish employment eligibility only)
• United States Passport • Permanent Resident Card or Alien Registration Receipt Card (I-551) • Temporary Resident Card (I-688) • Employment Authorization Document (I-766, I-688B, or I-688A) • Foreign Passport with temporary I-551 stamp • For aliens authorized to work only for a specific employer, foreign passport with Form I-94 authorizing employment with this employer	• Driver's license issued by a state or outlying possession • ID card issued by a state or outlying possession • Native American tribal document • Canadian driver's license or ID card with a photograph (for Canadian aliens authorized to work only for a specific employer) • School ID card with a photography • Voter's registration card • U.S. Military card or draft record • Military dependent's ID Card	• Social Security account number card without employment restrictions • Original or certified copy of a birth certificate with an official seal issued by a state or local government agency • Certification of Birth Abroad • US Citizen ID Card • Native American tribal document • Form I-94 authorizing employment with this employer (for aliens authorized to work only for a specific employer)

Note that a *current voter registration card* in List B is as valid a form of documentation for the I-9 as is a driver's license or identity card.

6.3.2 No I-9 Verification Documents

An employee who fails to produce the required document, or a receipt for a replacement document if the original is lost, stolen or destroyed within three business days of the date employment begins can be terminated. An employee who shows a receipt to replace a document has ninety days to present the original documents.

6.3.3 E Verify

E-Verify is an Internet-based system run by the United States Citizenship and Immigration Services (USCIS) that allows companies to verify an employee's authorization to work in the United States.

Though all employers must verify their employees' employment eligibility with Form I-9, participation in E-Verify is usually voluntary unless required by state law. Twenty-six states require employer use of e-Verify, including Texas for public employees and contractors. [95]

E-Verify compares Form I-9 information to data from U.S. Department of Homeland Security and Social Security Administration. The following "Know Your Rights" list is adapted from the USCIS e-Verify information site.

- Employers must inform prospective employees that they use e-Verify by posting a notice, or by "electronic notification."
- E-Verify can be used for new hires only, not current employees.
- If an employer uses e-Verify, the employer must use it for all new hires regardless of national origin or citizenship.
- E-Verify must be used only *after* an employee has been hired and accepted employment. The I-9 must be completed first.
- Employers may not prescreen applicants through E-Verify.
- An employer who receives an information mismatch, or Tentative Nonconfirmation (TNC), in E-Verify, the employer must promptly provide the employee with information about how to contest the TNC, including a written notice provided by E-Verify. Note: the employee has 8 workdays to contest the TNC.
- If an employee decides to contest the TNC, the employer must provide the employee with a referral letter provided by E-Verify that contains specific instructions and contact information.
- Employers may not take any adverse action against an employee because he or she contests a TNC. Adverse actions include firing, suspending, withholding pay or training, or otherwise infringing upon his or her employment.
- The employee must be given eight federal government work days to contact the appropriate federal agency to resolve the TNC.

An employee who receives a Tentative Nonconfirmation (TNC) can contest it by contacting the "the appropriate agency "to resolve the mismatch within *eight federal government work days* from receiving the TNC. To resolve an "SSA TNC," the employee must visit an SSA office and bring the TNC referral letter and required documentation. To resolve a "DHS TNC," the employee must call the number listed on the referral letter.

6.4 JOB SEARCH WITH CRIMINAL RECORD

---

[95] For a list of state's laws on e-verify, see the National Council of State Legislatures, information page on e-Verify, last updated September 2015. http://www.ncsl.org/research/immigration/state-e-verify-action.aspx

For a current listing of all states requiring use of e-verify, see https://www.lawlogix.com/e-verify-map/

It is important for a person with a criminal history to be upfront about their experience and explain the circumstances of the arrest. The employer should assess whether the conduct is closely enough related to the job to justify denial of employment. Before going in to an interview, the applicant should be prepared to point out that the past offense(s) are not closely related to the job to which she is applying, after considering

- the nature of the job,
- the nature and seriousness of the offense, and
- the length of time since it occurred.

6.4.1 Tips on Conducting a Job Search with a Criminal Record

A job seeker with a criminal history knows that a background check is coming. Employers want to know if the applicant has the skills to succeed in the position. Here are some tips for previously incarcerated job seekers from employment and human resource professionals:[96]

Know everything about your conviction

It's important to know exactly what you've been convicted of and whether the record was expunged. Many have no idea about the actual charges that they were convicted of. It makes a difference. Applicants should know enough about their criminal record to explain the details. If not, an employer may think that the applicant doesn't care enough about it to explain it to them.

Explore volunteer opportunities

Find at least two civic organizations to volunteer at in order to obtain solid references to back up their application. Six to 18 months of volunteer work volunteer work will go a long way in getting a usable reference."

Consider the type of company to which you're applying

Depending on the type, size or management style of a company, it may or may not conduct a criminal background check or be more lenient in accepting applicants with a criminal past. Most applications ask whether you have been arrested or convicted of a crime. Some will ask for felony convictions only, which means conviction of a misdemeanor might be allowed. A convicted felon may have better opportunities in small businesses where he may have an opportunity to explain what happened directly to the owner."

Participate in a re-entry program

---

[96] Adapted from an article, "How to Conduct a Job Search With a Criminal Record", Auerbach, Debra, April 27, 2012, used with permission.

Programs are available to help job seekers with a criminal record re-enter society and secure employment. One such initiative is the Prison Entrepreneurship Program, a Houston-based nonprofit whose mission is to "stimulate positive life transformation for executives and inmates, uniting them through entrepreneurial passion, education and mentoring." The program connects convicted felons with top executives, MBA students and politicians, and provides education, training and support. This is just one example; search the Web for local organizations that offer similar services.

Be honest

This may be the most important advice. Be honest about references, employment history and criminal records. Failing to disclose when asked can also cause the employer to fire the employee later for failing to disclose it at the time of hire.

A job seeker with a felony record who has 'paid his or her debt' should be transparent about it. Mention it after real interest has been expressed but before the job offer is made. Always answer questions about it truthfully, and never act as if you are hiding something, as it is worse to have it exposed in a background check."

6.4.2 Crimes of "Moral Turpitude"

A common question on job applications is whether the applicant has ever been charged or convicted of a crime involving "moral turpitude." Convictions for crimes of moral turpitude can affect a person's ability to obtain a vocation a license, security clearance, or employment. However, many applicants have little idea what might constitute a crime of "moral turpitude" because the crimes are defined in case law, not in the criminal statutes. Moral turpitude is:

- The quality of a crime involving grave infringement of the moral sentiment of the community,
- Conduct that is base, vile, or depraved, and
- Something that is inherently immoral or dishonest.[97]

Table 13: Crimes of Moral Turpitude
The following is a list of crimes involving moral turpitude as defined by case law:[98]

---

[97] See *Ludwig v. State*, 969 SW2d 22, 28 (Tex. App. – Forth Worth 1998, pet. ref'd).

[98] This chart is adapted from one created by attorney Randy Leavitt, used here with permission. We gratefully acknowledge his contribution.

CRIMES OF MORAL TURPITUDE

Offense	Moral Turpitude As Defined In Case Law	NOT Moral Turpitude As Defined In Case Law
Driving While Intoxicated		*Stephens v. State,* 417 SW2d 286 (Tex.Crim.App. 1967).
Possession of Marijuana (misdemeanor)		*Hernandez v. State,* 976 SW2d 753, 756 (Tex.App. – Houston [1st Dist.], pet denied, 980 SW2d 652 (Tex.Crim.App. 1998). **(1 Warning)**
Issuance of Bad Check		No, unless it was done with intent to defraud. *Dallas County Bail Bond Board v. Danny Mason,* 773 SW2d 586 (Tex.App. – Dallas, 1989). *Caveat*: employers often automatically deny employment because this offense is under the "Fraud" section of the Penal Code.
Criminally Negligent Homicide		*Arnold v. State,* 36 SW 3-D 542, 546-547 (Tex.App. – Tyler 2000).
Prostitution	*Holgin v. State,* 480 SW2d 405 (Tex.Crim.App. 1972).	
Theft	*Benshaw v. State,* 88 SW2d 495 (1935).	
Swindling	*Sherman v. State,* 62 SW2d 146 (1933).	
Assault by a man against a woman	*Hardeman v. State,* 868 SW2d 404, 405 (Tex.App. – Austin 1993, pet. dism'd).	
Making a False Report	*Lape v. State,* 893 SW2d 949, 958 (Tex.App. – Houston [14th Dist.] 1994, pet ref'd).	
Indecent Exposure	"his intent to sexually arouse either himself or another, acts upon motives of baseness, vileness, and depravity." *Polk v. State,* 865 SW2d 627 (Tex.App. – Fort Worth 1993).	
Bigamy		*Ruhe v. State Bar,* 1994 Tex.App. Lexis 3948, 1994 WL 649395

		(Tex.App.—Dallas 1994) (unreported).
Failure to Identify	*Lape v. State,* 893 SW2d 949, 958 (Tex.App. – Houston [14th Dist.] 1994, pet. ref'd).	
Unlawfully Carrying Weapon		*Thomas v. State,* 482 SW2d 218, 219 (Tex.Crim.App. 1972).
Resisting Arrest		*Williams v. State,* 449 SW2d 264, 265 (Tex.Crim.App. 1970).
Criminal Mischief		*Gonzalez v. State,* 648 SW2d 740, 742 (Tex.App. – Beaumont 1983, no pet.).
Criminal Trespass		*Hutson v. State,* 843 SW2d 106, 107 (Tex.App. – Texarkana 1992, no pet.).
Use of abusive language to police officer		*Hartford Accident & Indem. Co. v. Williams,* 516 SW2d 425, 428 (Tex.Civ.App. – Amarillo 1974, writ ref'd n.r.e.).
Delivery of a Simulated Controlled Substance	*United States v. Ekpin,* 214 F. Supp. 2d 707, 714-715 (U.S. Dist., 2002).	
Violation of a protective order (misdemeanor)	If the underlying, uncharged offense is one of family violence or the direct threat of family violence. *Polk v. State,* 865 SW2d 627, 630 (Tex App. – Fort Worth 1993).	

6.4.3 Sex Offenders - Special Issues

Texas - and the nation - have sweeping registration laws for sex offenders. Sex offenders face special issues when it comes to finding a job. First, Texas laws have the effect of restricting registered sex offenders ("registrants") access to the Internet, perhaps the most common method of searching for employment. Second, the Texas Sex Offender Database makes information about these offenses available to everyone, not just larger employers who pay third parties to collect criminal history record information about an applicant.

6.4.4 Internet Use

There is no outright prohibition under Texas law preventing registrant's access to the Internet, creating accounts, on web pages on social networking or photo-sharing websites. However, offenders who are on probation or parole often have access to the Internet monitored or restricted as a condition of supervision. Registrants are required to notify DPS of any "online identifiers" within 7 days of creation, and failure to do so is a felony violation. While the registrants "online identifiers" are not publicly disclosed, DPS is permitted by law to forward the "on-line identifiers" to social networking and other approved sites for monitoring.[99]

6.4.5 Texas Sex Offender Registration Database

The federal law known as the Adam Walsh Child Protection and Safety Act[100] passed in July, 2006, organizes sex offenders into three Tiers defining the minimum registration periods for sex offenders, with Tier 3, the highest, requiring lifetime registration. Texas law mandates that the registration period *exceed* federal law.[101]

The Sex Offender Registration and Notification Act ("SORNA"), created as part of the Adam Walsh Act requires that this information be made public. Free public access to Texas' database of registered sex offenders is maintained by the Texas DPS. The database information is supplied by local criminal justice agencies, and cannot be verified as accurate without a cross-fingerprint check. DPS disclaims any inaccuracies:

> "Extreme care should be exercised in using any information obtained from this website. Neither DPS nor the State of Texas shall be responsible for any errors or omissions produced by secondary dissemination of this information."[102]

It is unlikely that an employer who spots their applicant on the database will go out of their way to request a cross-fingerprint check to verify the accuracy of the database information.

Texas' current (April 2012) list of "reportable conviction or adjudication" sex offenses requiring registration is available from DPS. For a list of registration periods by Texas offense, please refer to

---

[99] Texas Dept. of Public Safety, Public Sex Offender Registry Download - Sex offender registrants: Internet access, Online Identifiers, and Social Networking Sites

[100] 34 U.S.C. Sec 20911 et seq.

[101] The Department shall "determine the minimum required registration period under federal law for each reportable conviction or adjudication"..., then "compile and publish a list of reportable convictions or adjudications... for a period that exceeds the minimum required registration period under federal law." Tex. Code Crim. Proc. Art. 62.402

[102] See Important Caveats

Appendix L - Texas Sex Offenses Tiered under Federal Law

6.5 WAGE AND HOUR LAWS

6.5.1 Federal Minimum Wage Law

The Fair Labor Standards Act (FLSA) establishes minimum wage, overtime pay, recordkeeping, and youth employment standards for private sector workers. Workers covered under the FLSA are entitled to federal minimum wage, currently $7.25 per hour.[103] Overtime pay (for work in excess of 40 hours per week) must be paid at a rate of at least one and one half times the federal minimum wage.[104] The current federal minimum overtime rate is $10.88 per hour.[105]

6.5.2 Texas Minimum Wage Law

All workers covered under the FLSA have the right to be paid minimum wage or higher. *The right to minimum wage is a legal right. It cannot be waived by the worker or employer.* Any agreement to be paid less than minimum wage is legally void and unenforceable. Texas has adopted the federal minimum wage rate by reference.[106] If the federal minimum wage rate changes, Texas' minimum wage changes along with it.

6.5.3 Earnings Statement

Texas law requires employers to provide a written earnings statement to each employee with specific information.[107] An earnings statement can be included on check stub or as a separate written statement. It can also be emailed to the worker to coincide with a direct deposit of wages into the worker's bank account.

The earnings statement must include
- Deductions from pay
- Net wages
- Beginning and ending dates of the pay period.

---

[103] 29 USC § 206(a)(1)(C).

[104] 29 USC § 207(a)(2)(C).

[105] A state minimum wage can exceed the current federal rate of $7.25 per hour. Workers in Washington State are paid a minimum of $8.67 per hour, (the highest in the nation). Federal law supersedes states like Georgia, with a minimum wage of $5.15 per hour but workers must be paid the federal minimum of $7.25.

Local governments may set their own wage rate above the state or federal minimum through a local living wage or minimum wage ordinance. California's minimum wage is $8.00 per hour, but workers in San Francisco benefit from a living wage ordinance that mandates a minimum $9.79 per hour.

[106] Tex. Lab. Code § 62.051 "[A]n employer shall pay to each employee the federal minimum wage under Section 6, Fair Labor Standards Act of 1938 (29 USC Section 206)." Texas is among the twenty-four states whose minimum wage coincides with the federal minimum. A breakdown by state may be found at the Department of Labor's website, https://www.dol.gov/general/topic/wages/minimumwage

[107] Tex. Lab. Code § 62.003.

- Employee name
- Employer's name and address.

6.5.4 Wages Paid in Cash

A *written earnings statement is required* by law to be provided to the worker every time she is paid, *regardless of the form of payment.* There is no exception for wages paid in cash. Workers should be advised to keep earnings statements and check stubs in a safe place, in case pay or deductions from pay are disputed.

6.5.5 Payment Intervals

An employer must set regular paydays and pay employees on that day. Workers are entitled to be paid at least twice a month, with each pay period being as near as possible to an equal number of days.[108] An employer may pay more than twice a month, but neither the worker nor employer can agree to payment *less* than twice a month.

If the employer doesn't designate the two-week intervals, Texas law presumes that the employer must pay wages on the first and 15th day of every month.[109] All work done from the 1st to the 15th of the month must be paid no later than the 26th, and work done from the 16th to the last day of the month must be paid no later than the 10th of the following month.

If entitled to overtime, overtime wages must be paid on the regular payday for the period in which that workweek ends.[110] If overtime cannot be calculated in time for the next pay period, it must be paid no later than the following regular payday.[111]

6.5.6 Form and Method of Payment

Texas law requires employers to pay the worker in dollars by cash, check or by electronic funds transfer. An employee may agree, but only in writing, to have all or part of her wages paid in kind or in another form.[112]

6.5.7 Releases and Vouchers

It is illegal for an employer to agree to pay any employee on the condition that she signs an agreement releasing the employer from liability for unpaid wages. Any release signed by the worker for this purpose is void on its face, and does not preclude a claim for wages owed. Similarly, an employer cannot pay a worker with

---

[108] Tex. Labor Code § 61.011.

[109] Tex. Labor Code § 61.012(b).

[110] 29 CFR § 778.106.

[111] *Id.*

[112] Tex. Labor Code § 61.016.

a "voucher" or by any means that may be subject to a service charge. Payment must be made in U.S. currency for the amount stated in the written earnings statement.

6.5.8 Late Pay

There is no grace period or "late pay" for an employer to pay regular wages. "Late pay" is the same as "no pay" under the FLSA. The law requires payment of wages "when due," which normally means at the next regularly scheduled payday. For overtime pay, an employer can wait until the next payday to pay overtime accrued during the preceding pay period.

6.5.9 Wage Dispute No Excuse

If there is a disagreement about the amount of wages owed, the employer still must pay the undisputed amount (the wages the employer acknowledges are due). A worker's claim that more is owed does not give the employer the right to delay the entire paycheck; only the amount in dispute.

6.6 ILLEGAL DEDUCTIONS FROM WAGES

6.6.1 Written Agreement Required

Both Texas and federal law allow deductions from wages only if there is a *written* agreement with the employee to do so.[113] The deductions must also be:
- Reasonable,
- Customarily furnished by the employer to the workers, and
- Separately stated and identified on the worker's earnings statement or paycheck.[114]

An employer may not withhold or divert any part of an employee's wages unless the employer:
- is ordered to do so by a court of competent jurisdiction;
- is authorized to do so by state or federal law; or
- has written authorization

An employer may deduct for the following items only if the employee has *consented to it in writing:*
- cash shortages,
- breakage, damage, or loss of the employer's property,
- required uniforms,
- required tools or other items necessary for employment, or

---

[113] Tex. Labor Code §§ 61.018, 61.016.

[114] Tex. Labor Code § 62.053.

- loans.[115]

A deduction can be illegal even if the worker *has* agreed to it in writing, including agreed deductions for:
- food or lodging in lieu of wages.[116]
- anything that is primarily for the employer's own benefit, such as safety equipment, tools, or uniforms.[117]
- The cost of housing if the housing violates health or safety regulations.[118]
- Funds to make up for paying overtime.[119]
- Cost of work-related travel.

If an employer uses a handbook or policy manual instead of a separate writing, the worker's signed acknowledgment that she has received a copy of the company policies can be authorization to withhold from wages if it meets the above consent requirements. The signed acknowledgment must also include language stating that the worker agrees to the authorization for deduction.[120]

6.6.2 Written Agreement Required

Generally, if the use of facilities, equipment and uniforms benefit the employer, the employee does not have to pay for them.[121] The cost of uniforms cannot be deducted from wages if the uniform is required by the employer.[122] Other common employer deductions are illegal if they take an employee's pay below minimum wage. These include deductions to cover the cost of tools, safety equipment, and uniforms that do not fall within the definition of "facilities" under the FLSA; disciplinary deductions (such as "fines" for tardiness), and deductions to cover the cost of items lost or damaged by the employee.[123] Texas law additionally requires all deductions to be authorized in writing by the employee.

6.7 "NO MATCH" LETTERS

---

[115] Tex. Admin. Code § 821.27.

[116] 29 CFR § 531.30.

[117] 29 CFR § 531.3(d).

[118] 29 CFR § 531.31.

[119] 29 CFR § 531.37(a)

[120] Tex. Admin Code § 821.28.

[121] 29 CFR § 531.3(d). More information on legal and illegal deductions mat be found on the Texas Workforce Commission website at http://www.twc.state.tx.us/news/efte/deduction_problems_under_tpl.html

[122] 29 CFR § 531.3(d)(1-2).

[123] 29 CFR § 778.304, 778.306, 778.307.

The Social Security Administration may inform employers by letter that there is "discrepancy" between the social security number provided by the employer to the SSA and the one the SSA has on file for the employee. The letters is sometimes referred to as a "no match" letter. Its stated purpose is to ensure that the worker receives credit for earnings and benefits administered by SSA. Such "mismatches" could occur from typographical errors, name changes or incomplete information. The "no match" letters specifically instruct employers that the fact that a current or former employee's name appeared in the letter is not any indication of work authorization status, and that the letter alone is insufficient to take adverse action against (i.e. terminate) the employee. Despite these caveats, employers have fired employees on the assumption that the mismatch meant that the employee was not unauthorized to work, exposing them to legal consequences for unlawful termination.

The US Department of Justice, Office of Special Counsel for Immigration Related Unfair Employment Practices (OSC) provides the following tips for employees who have been notified by their employer of the discrepancy:

What Employees Should Know:

- Name/SSN no-matches can result from simple administrative errors.
- Contact the Social Security Administration (SSA) as soon as possible to update your records following a name change due to marriage, divorce or some other reason.
- Double-check your name and SSN on your Social Security card for errors.
- If you receive a no-match notice or discover an error on your Social Security card, an SSA representative can review it with you.
- Your employer may periodically ask for information on the status of your efforts to address and resolve the no match.

Employees Should Request:

- Notice from their employer of the nature and source of any reported name/SSN no-match.
- An opportunity to review and correct name/SSN errors in employer records.
- Continued employment while addressing and resolving a reported name/SSN no-match.
- A reasonable period of time to gather documents and resolve a reported name/SSN no-match with SSA

- Equal treatment under the employer's policies regarding name/SSN no-matches regardless of citizenship status or national origin.

Employees Should Call OSC's Hotline If An Employer:

- Attempts to immediately re-verify an employee's employment eligibility by requesting the completion of a new Form I-9 based solely on receipt of a no-match notice.

- Terminates, suspends or takes any other adverse action affecting an employee's employment based only on the notice of name/SSN no-match.

- Fails to provide a reasonable period of time for an employee to address and resolve the reported no-match.

- Follows different procedures for different classes of employees based on national origin or citizenship status.

- Requires an employee to produce specific documents to address the no-match.

- Requires an employee to produce specific written evidence from the SSA or any other governmental entity that the no-match has been resolved.

6.8 FEDERAL BONDING PROGRAM

Job seekers who committed a fraudulent or dishonest act (crime of moral turpitude), or who have served time are often rejected for employment. The Federal Bonding Program (FBP) is an employer hiring incentive that guarantees employers of persons who have been convicted of a crime involving moral turpitude.[124] The Department of Labor (DOL) provides the Texas Workforce Commission with bonds to provide employers with incentives to hire people with a criminal record.
- Employers receive bonded employees free-of-charge which serves as an incentive to hire hard-to-place job applicants.

- The FBP bond insurance was designed to reimburse the employer for any loss due to employee theft of money or property with no employer deductible.

Additional bonds may be purchased from the bonding agent by organizations providing reentry services. For information on employer participants in the federal

---

[124] See Re-Entry Mythbusters, a project of the Federal Interagency Reentry Council.

bonding program, contact the Texas Workforce Commission, www.twc.state.tx.us.[125]

6.9 WORK OPPORTUNITY TAX CREDIT (WOTC)

The Work Opportunity Tax Credit (WOTC) is a Federal tax credit incentive provided to employers for hiring certain groups who face significant barriers to employment. The disadvantaged person is hired and the employer is compensated by being able to reduce their federal income tax liability.

The program used to cover some recipients of public benefits (TANF, SNAP, SSI) recipients, the disabled, and ex-felons (defined as an individual who has been convicted of a felony and has a hiring date which is not more than one year after the last date on which he was so convicted or released from prison.). At present, WOTC credit is *only* available for hiring within the following.

Table 14: Work Opportunity Tax Credit Target Groups

WOTC Target Groups	Maximum Tax Credit*	Age**
Designated Community Resident	$2,400	18-39
Disconnected Youth (expired 12/31/2010)	$2,400	16-24
Ex-Felon	$2,400	None
SNAP† (Food Stamp) Recipient	$2,400	18-39
Summer Youth	$1,200	16-17
Supplemental Security Income (SSI) Recipient	$2,400	None
TANF†† Recipient—Long-Term Family Assistance *(This target group has a possible combined 2-year maximum tax credit of $9,000.)*	*Year 1: $4,000* *Year 2: $5,000*	None
TANF†† Recipient—Short-Term IV-A	$2,400	None
Veteran: -SNAP† (Food Stamp) Recipient	$2,400	None
-Service-Connected Disabled Veteran	$4,800	None
Unemployed Veteran (expired 12/31/2010)	$2,400	None
Vocational Rehabilitation Referral	$2,400	None

---

[125] Information for employers wishing to participate in the Federal Bonding Program should contact the Texas Workforce Commission, Fidelity Bonding Services, at www.twc.state.tx.us/svcs/rio/fidelitybonding.html.

Locked Out: A Texas Legal Guide to Reentry, 4th Edition - 2019

For more information, contact the Texas Workforce Commission.

6.10 STARTING A BUSINESS

For people who cannot find work because of their criminal record, another option is to start a business. Composing a business plan, opening a business bank account, and starting with some working capital are all parts of starting a business. The amount of funds (capital) required depends on the type of business. Some businesses require materials and equipment, and others may require a vocational license. Examples of businesses that do not require a vocational license include painting services, lawn care, and carpentry. Others, such as plumbing, may require vocational licenses, whose validity may be affected as a result of conviction. Vocational and occupational licenses are discussed in the next section.

Excellent guidance and information for ex-offenders who wish to start their own business can be found in the publication Hire Yourself: A Guide to Starting a Small Business for Ex Offenders,[126].

6.10.1 Child Care

Many parents find it impossible to get a job because they lack child care. Texas offers childcare subsidy (http://www.twc.state.tx.us/svcs/childcare/) through local Workforce Development Boards to allow those in need of child care while they work, attend school, or get training for their job. The income-based subsidy covers children age 13 and under.

6.10.2 Forming a Child Care Co-Op

Temporary Employment and Staff An alternative to seeking a government childcare subsidy or imposing on relatives and friends for child care is to form a child care cooperative. A child care cooperative is made up of a number of families in a community who share child care among the group. No money is exchanged. Points are earned by providing care for children of a member family. Points are spent by having a member parent care for another member family's children. A secretary who keeps track of the points or credits could be "paid" for this task by extra credits or points. The co-op members can "pay" a member in points to act as secretary and record- keeper, or to arrange the childcare scheduling among the co-op members.[127]

6.11 LEASING

---

[126] A publication of Legal Assistance to Microenterprises Program, Texas C-BAR, and Texas RioGrande Legal Aid

[127] For a short summary of how a child care co-op is organized, go to http://www.extension.iastate.edu/publications/pm1808.pdf, a publication of Iowa State University.

Individuals with a criminal history who find it difficult to secure employment often turn to temporary staffing agencies. These agencies can be a good place to start, but the job seeker should be sure to ask about fees and hidden costs associated with placement, and compare their wages with what the agency charges to the employer. Some job placement agencies misrepresent their services, promote outdated or fake job offerings, or charge high fees for services that may not lead to a job.

6.11.1 Considerations for Job Placement Firms

Before spending money on a job placement service or signing a contract, the Federal Trade Commission (FTC) recommends the following:[128]

- Reject any company that promises a job.

- Be skeptical of any employment-service firm that charges first, even if it guarantees refunds.

- Get a copy of the firm's contract and read it carefully before paying any money. Understand the terms and conditions of the firm's refund policy. Understand what services the firm will provide and what you'll be responsible for doing.

- Take time to read the contract and avoid high-pressure sales pitches that require payment immediately or risk losing out on an opportunity.

- Avoid purchasing services or products from a firm that's reluctant to answer questions.

- Note that listing services and "consultants" can write ads to sound like a job when they are selling general information about getting a job.

- Follow up with the offices of any company or organization mentioned in an ad or an interview by an employment service to find out if the company is really hiring.

- Be wary of firms promoting "previously undisclosed" federal government jobs. All federal positions are announced to the public on www.usajobs.gov.

6.12 DAY LABOR[129]

---

[128] Adapted from Job Hunting/Job Scams from the Money Matters section of the FTC's website.

[129] This section adapted from National Employment Law Project, www.NELP.org fact sheet for organizers, 2002: Day Laborers' Rights under Federal Law: Waiting Time and Deductions from Wages. http://nelp.3cdn.net/c348fa1fdf4b2bca59_2im6b5yha.pdf

"Day laborers" are people employed on a temporary, day-to-day basis, normally working in construction, light manufacturing, landscaping and other similar jobs. Day laborers find work either through a temporary day labor agency (or labor hall) or by waiting on a designated street for an employer to arrive and hire workers as needed. Workers often do not know from day to day whether they will get work.

Day laborers have problems that are unique to the nature of the short term temporary work they perform. Among them:
- Employers wishing to minimize costs and increase flexibility

- One "employer" (the day labor agent) hiring and paying the worker and another "employer" (at the work site) directing the work

- Lack of union representation

- Workers' immigration status and lack of work authorization

Despite the non-standard nature of the day labor employment relationship, day laborers are entitled to the benefit of minimum wage and overtime laws. In summary,
- If workers are **waiting** at a designated place at the employer's request, they should generally be paid for the waiting time.

- Generally, **deductions** that that do not bring the hourly wage below the federal minimum wage are permissible.

- Deduction of fees for **transportation** to the work site is generally allowed. However, if the transportation is part of and necessary to the employment, deductions may not bring the hourly wage below the federal minimum.

- The cost of **safety equipment** or **tools** required for a job generally should not be deducted from wages if the deduction reduces the wage below the minimum level.

- If accepting **meals** is voluntary, the meals are generally considered to be for the benefit or convenience of the employee and the reasonable cost can therefore be deducted from the employee's wage whether or not it reduces the wage below the minimum.

- If a **check cashing** service is voluntary, it could be considered primarily for the benefit of employees and therefore a fee could be deducted from the wages even if that deduction reduces the wage below the minimum.

6.12.1 *Day Laborers' Rights Regarding Wages and Hours*

Two areas where day laborers are vulnerable to employers' wage and hour violations involve waiting time and wage deductions.

Waiting Time

Employers take advantage of day laborers in numerous ways, including payment of low wages and requiring workers to wait without any promise of work at all. Because workers are usually free to stay or go as they wish prior to getting an assignment, courts typically do not find an employment relationship before a job is assigned. It is therefore more difficult to get wages paid for the period between arriving at the labor hall, or job pick-up site, and the time the job is assigned.

But, if a worker is required to report for work at a specified time, either at the day labor agency or at the worksite, the workday commences at that point even if the worker has to wait until a later time for the actual work activities to begin. If the worker has to report and wait each day for the same job over a number of days, it is easier to recover waiting-time pay.

Deductions from Wages

A worker's pay can be made up of a combination of wages and other benefits. In some circumstances, an employer can legally make deductions from a worker's wages. The general rule under federal law is that deductions are generally permitted as long as they do not bring the hourly cash pay below the federal minimum wage. Federal law only regulates deductions that bring the "cash" component of a worker's wages below the minimum wage.

Federal law allows deductions that *do* cut into the minimum wage, provided the following six requirements are met:

1. the employee actually and voluntarily received the benefit;
2. the benefit was not furnished primarily for the benefit or convenience of the employer;
3. the benefit was not furnished in violation of any federal or state law;
4. the deduction is provided at a reasonable cost;
5. the payment of non-cash wages is not prohibited by a union agreement;
6. the benefit is customarily provided to employees. That is, the items must be provided regularly or similar items must be provided by other employers in similar businesses in comparable geographic locations.

6.12.2   *Fees for Transport*

Day laborers are often provided with transportation between the work hall, or pick-up location, and the work site. Employers frequently deduct an amount from the employees' wages for providing transportation. If the transportation is part of and necessary to the employment, transportation deductions cannot bring workers' wages below the minimum. In federal courts, travel by day haul workers in a contractor's bus from a recruitment site to the fields is normally not compensable time, in the absence of some work-related activity at the recruitment site or during the trip.

6.12.3 Essential Tools and Safety Equipment

These items should generally not be deducted from wages, if the deduction reduces the wage below the minimum level, for the following reasons:

1. such deductions should be regarded as primarily for the benefit or convenience of the employer;

2. uniforms are not deductible if they are required by law, by the employer, or by the nature of the work performed. Examples of safety equipment include gloves, hard hats and boots. These items should be regarded as necessary for the benefit or convenience of the employer if they are required to safely perform the work asked of the worker. The use of such safety items might also be required by law and could then be considered uniforms.

6.12.4 Meals

If accepting meals is voluntary, the meals are generally considered to be for the benefit or convenience of the employee and therefore the cost can be deducted from the employee's wage whether or not it reduces the wage below the minimum. The amount deducted is restricted to the reasonable cost of the meal (the lesser of the actual cost and the market value of the meal).

6.12.5 Check Cashing

If the service is voluntary, it could be considered primarily for the benefit of employees and therefore a fee could be deducted from the wages. Federal law requires that wages (up to the minimum wage) be paid "free and clear."

6.12.6 Compliance with other Labor Laws

Employer abuse can take other forms. One survey showed that almost half of all day laborers experienced at least one instance of wage theft in the two months prior to being surveyed. Forty-four percent were denied food, water or breaks while on the job. One third of the day laborers surveyed had been abandoned on the job, and one-quarter of the workers had suffered violence at work.[130] Redress for these and other day labor grievances depend on state and local laws.[131]

6.13 EMPLOYMENT AND SOCIAL MEDIA

In addition to criminal history background checks, employers routinely check the social media sites (like Facebook) of prospective or current employees. Anyone applying for a job should consider the likelihood that an employer has already read - or will read - the applicant's Facebook page or conduct a Google search of the person's name.

Job hunters with social media accounts should

- review their social media page and delete any information they think might be prejudicial in an employment setting.

- Make sure that appropriate privacy settings are in place. Unless the privacy options are selected, the page defaults to public access. Privacy requires action from the holder of the account.

Even applicants who have been careful enough to use Facebook's privacy settings are vulnerable to uninvited observers. Companies like Social Intelligence Corporation (SocialIntel)[132] are hired by employers to do a "credit check" of an applicant's or employee's social-media activity, collect information and provide it to potential employers.

A disturbing trend among some employers is to ask prospective job applicants for their passwords to social media sites like Facebook. An employer may even ask a prospective employee for access during the job interview. An interviewee should not be required to "voluntarily" turn over their passwords in order to be considered for a job, or as a condition of maintaining a job. If an employer asks for this information, the applicant can

- Ask the employer if revealing the password is something that is required to move forward with this job interview

---

[130] "The only national survey of day laborers ever performed in the United States was released in 2006. These statistics come from that survey. Abel Valenzuela, Nik Theodore, Edwin Melendez & Ana Luz Gonzalez, On the Corner: Day Labor in the United States, Jan 2006, <http://www.sscnet.

http://portlandvoz.org/wp-content/uploads/images/2009/04/national-study.pdf as cited in a 2010 publication by the Excluded Worker's Congress.

[131] State and local laws can provide more rights for day laborers. For more information, see Drafting Day Labor Legislation: A Guide for Organizers and Advocates. https://www.nelp.org/publication/drafting-day-labor-legislation-a-guide-for-organizers-and-advocate/.

[132] SocialIntel is subject to the federal Fair Credit Reporting Act, but as a result, it can keep an archive of a person's social-media activities for seven years. The information stored is to be used only for background checks but can be captured even if the information has been deleted from the account by the user.

- Tell the employer that he is careful with his personal, private online information and does not feel comfortable giving out any passwords

An employer's demand for access to a prospective employee's private medial pages may violate existing anti-eavesdropping and privacy laws, as well as federal statutes relating to unauthorized access to computers and electronically-stored information[133] Because the law in this area is still in flux, the best course for the job seeker is to clear up his media page(s), apply the privacy settings, and refrain from posting anything that he would not want the employer to see.

6.14 JOB SCAMS

6.14.1 Work at Home Schemes

Fraudulent promoters use classifieds and the Internet sites to advertise of work-at-home offers, from medical billing and envelope stuffing to assembly and craft work. The ads make promises about earnings, merchandise, or marketability that are not always accurate. According to the Federal Trade Commission, here are some work-at-home jobs to avoid:[134]

Envelope Stuffing. The job promises work stuffing envelopes at home for a "small" fee. Once the fee is paid the promoter will not have work but try to get the worker to recruit friends and relatives to buy the same envelope-stuffing "opportunity."

Assembly or Craft Work. Ads promise money for assembling crafts or other products at home. Often these require the worker to invest in equipment or supplies, like a sewing or sign-making machine, or other materials. Once the materials are purchased and the product is made, the company will not pay for the product.

Rebate Processing. Promises to generate income by helping to process rebates. The work involves payment of a fee for training, certification or registration materials and no rebates to process.

Online Searches. Income is generated by running Internet searches on prominent search engines and filling out forms in exchange for a small handling fee paid online. These scams use financial information to charge recurring fees.

Medical Billing. This scam usually in involves an investment by the worker of hundreds of dollars to launch a medical billing business, along with software and technical support. The work is often not available. Many doctors' offices process

---

[133] The Stored Communications Act (SCA), or the Computer Fraud and Abuse Act (CFAA). Those two acts, respectively, prohibit intentional access to electronic information without authorization, and prohibit intentional access to a computer, without authorization, to obtain information.

[134] Federal Trade Commission Work at Home Schemes

their own medical claims, and doctors who contract their billing use well-established firms, not someone working from home.

1.1.1.1 *Resources*
- Ready4Work - coalition of faith-based and community nonprofit organizations and corrections officials working for sustainable ex-offender reentry and employment.
- To check for complaints about a specific company or business:
- Companies can be screened through a local consumer protection agency, state Attorney General's Office, and the Better Business Bureau to see if any complaints are on file.
- U.S. Department of Labor, Employment Information Handbook for Ex-Offenders, available at: http://www.doc.state.nc.us/Publications/DOL.Exoffender.Handbook.pdf.
- The National H.I.R.E. Network is a resource for formerly incarcerated people seeking to re-enter the workforce: http://www.hirenetwork.org.
- U.S. Department of Labor Civil Rights Guidelines Governing Background Checks and Federally-Funded Workforce Development Programs http://wdr.doleta.gov/directives/corr_doc.cfm?DOCN=9230
- U.S. Equal Employment Opportunity Commission Guidelines on Use of Arrest and Conviction Records for Employment http://eeoc.gov/laws/guidance/upload/arrest_conviction.pdf
- U.S. Reentry Council, National Reentry Resource Center http://www.nationalreentryresourcecenter.org/
- No Match Letters and discrimination based on nationality Office of Special Counsel: 1-800-255-7688/1-800-237-2525 (Hearing Impaired/TDD)
- Excluded Worker's Congress: national networks of organizations that represent workers excluded from the right to organize in the United States. Each network represents a different industry, sector, or kind of work.
- Texas Voices For Reason and Justice Statewide non-profit promoting a more balanced, effective, and rational criminal justice system for persons required to register for sex related offenses and their families.

7 . VOCATIONAL LICENSES

Renewing, maintaining, or applying for a vocational license[135] is important for formerly incarcerated workers because it shows employers that they have received specialized training in a particular field. The training typically culminates in an examination, which, if passed, results in the award of a vocational license. A vocational license usually results in better employment opportunities and better pay. Prison-based programs include training to become an electrician, truck driver, or cosmetologists (which require licenses) to welder and carpenter (which do not).

---

[135] As distinguished from an "occupational" license, this is a type of restricted driver's license allowing for limited driving privileges during a period of driver's license suspension.

State law governs some areas of the licensing process as it relates to criminal convictions, but each licensing authority is generally free to create its own rules and standards for the profession it regulates. This includes internal rules for license application, renewal, disqualification and revocation. Whether a criminal background will bar an applicant from obtaining a license depends to a large extent on the profession.

This section addresses the effect of a criminal conviction on a person's ability to apply or renew a vocational license for an occupation that falls under the jurisdiction of the Texas Department of Licensing and Regulation (TDLR). [136] Professions such as law and medicine are not regulated by the TDLR but have their own licensing entities and rules regarding applicants with a criminal history.

A criminal conviction does not automatically prohibit a previously incarcerated person from obtaining an occupational license. The TDLR reported that 14% of all applicants for an electrician's license had criminal convictions, but only a third of those were denied a license based on a prior conviction. [137]

7.1 Texas Department of Licensing and Regulation

The Texas Department of Licensing and Regulation (TDLR) is the state's umbrella agency responsible for overseeing most licensed occupations. It regulates businesses, industries, general trades, and occupations that are regulated by the state and assigned to the TDLR for oversight. The TDLR is also responsible for deciding if the rules of a licensing authority unlawfully restrict or bar people who have been convicted of a crime from obtaining a license.

7.1.1   Occupations Regulated by the TDLR

The ability of ex-offenders to hold occupational licenses is restricted by the TDLR in over 100 different licensed occupations, ranging from plumber to electrician to dietician. [138]

Lawyers, doctors, accountants and other professions are governed by other state agencies and laws. The Texas Medical Board controls licensing of most health care

---

[136] Some of the material in this section is adapted from the guide, "Occupational Licenses in Texas" prepared by the Texas Young Lawyers Association and available under "publications" at www.texasbar.com.

[137] "Working with Conviction - Criminal Offenses as Barriers to Entering Licensed Occupations in Texas"

(citing Texas Department of Licensing and Regulation). In 2006, TDLR opposed the application for a master electrician's license submitted by a man convicted of four counts of felony indecency with a child. After considering the applicant's good conduct in the years since his offense, and the fact that licensure posed little danger of future criminal activity involving the public or the applicant's customers, an administrative law judge ruled in favor of licensure. Texas Department of Licensing and Regulation v. Clark, SOAH Docket No. 452-05-6493.ELC, 2006 WL 4488807 (Mar. 24, 2006).

[138] https://www.texaspolicy.com/library/doclib/2007-11-PP28-licensing-ml.pdf For a complete list of occupations with license restrictions on ex-offenders, see Statutory Restrictions on Employment of Convicted Felons in Texas

related occupations; pharmacists, veterinarians, peace officers, and emergency medical services personnel each have separate licensing agencies. The TDLR regulates the following occupations and industries:

**OCCUPATIONS AND INDUSTRIES REGULATED BY
TEXAS DEPT. OF LICENSING AND REGULATION**

Air Conditioning and Refrigeration	Personnel Employment Services
Architectural Barriers	Polygraph Examiners
Auctioneers	Property Tax Consultants
Barbers	Property Tax Professionals
Boiler Safety	Service Contract Providers
Combative Sports	Vehicle Protection Product Warrantors
Court Interpreters	Staff Leasing Services
Cosmetologists	Talent Agencies
Electricians	Temporary common Worker Providers
Elevator/Elevator Safety	Tow Truck Operators
For-Profit Legal Services	Vehicle Storage Employees
Identity Recovery Service Contract	Used Auto Parts Recyclers
Providers	Weather Modification
Industrialized Housing and Buildings	Water Well Drillers and Pump Installers
Loss Damage Waivers	

***7.1.2** Incarceration - Automatic Revocation*

Automatic revocation is a matter of state law and cannot be appealed to the TDLR. A person who is incarcerated because of a felony conviction is not eligible to obtain or renew a license from the TDLR. If a person already has a license, it will be automatically revoked under two circumstances:
- If the person is convicted of a felony *followed by imprisonment*.

- When the person's parole or mandatory supervision is revoked.[139]

The automatic revocation is not a lifetime ban. If a license is revoked by operation of law[140] the person must wait until release from imprisonment before applying for a new license.

Aside from automatic revocation, any person with a criminal record can apply to the TDLR for a license. The TDLR has discretion to deny or accept the application, but certain rules apply to the application process and how it will be considered once submitted.

7.2 TDLR APPLICATION PROCESS

7.2.1 First Time License

Each occupation has its own application requirements and fees.[141] A person seeking a license for the first time must complete the TDLR's application form, pay the application fee, and complete all requirements for the occupation within one year of applying. If the license requirements are not completed within a year, the person must reapply.

7.2.2 License Renewal

To renew a license, a person must apply for renewal before the current license expires. The TDLR may run a criminal background check at the time of renewal to reveal offenses that may have occurred since the license was issued or that were not reported at the time of the original application. If the license has been expired for more than one year, it cannot be renewed, and a new application must be submitted.

7.2.3 Criminal Background Check

Depending on the license sought, the TDLR's Licensing Division will run a criminal background check through the Department of Public Safety (DPS) on each application for a license or application for renewal. If a person's criminal history is an issue, the application is referred to TDLR staff for further review. If the recommendation is to grant the license, the file is returned to the Licensing Division.

If the application is denied, the TDLR will send the applicant a letter that identifies the offenses that form the basis of the denial. The applicant has a right to appeal the decision. Criminal background checks are part of the licensing process. People

---

[139] Tex. Occ. Code §53.021.

[140] Tex. Occ. Code §53.021(b).

[141] Since requirements differ by occupation, a potential licensee should contact the TDLR at to verify the requirements for a particular license.

with criminal histories should review their criminal records *before* starting the license application process with the TDLR.

A seemingly extensive criminal history can be considerably shortened if entries unrelated to conviction are eliminated. Errors should be corrected, if possible; arrests that did not result in conviction may be expunged, and nondisclosure may be requested for eligible offenses.

For information on expunction and nondisclosure of criminal history records, please refer to Part 4: Expunction, Nondisclosure, and Pardon.

7.2.4 Request for Criminal History Evaluation Letter

Anyone applying for a license through TDLR can request a "criminal history evaluation letter." The TDLR will perform a preliminary criminal history evaluation and provide the results before the individual applies for a license. The letter offers some insight into how the TDLR might evaluate a person's criminal history if an application were filed. By obtaining an evaluation first, an applicant can make an informed decision about whether to apply for a license before devoting time and resources to training for that occupation.[142] To request a criminal history evaluation letter, the applicant must:

- submit a determination of eligibility <u>request form</u>. There is a different form for each occupation.

- complete a <u>criminal history questionnaire</u> for each conviction or placed on deferred adjudication, and

- pay a $25.00 fee.

The TDLR will issue a criminal history evaluation letter within 90 days of receiving a complete request. The letter will state whether the TDLR would or would not recommend granting a license based on the information provided by the requestor. The letter is a recommendation only, and only for a specific occupation. It is not binding or final, and regardless of the results, a person can proceed with a formal license application at any time.

7.2.5 Consideration of Deferred Adjudication

Although an offense resulting in deferred adjudication is not a conviction, the TDLR is permitted to consider it when making a decision on a licensing application.[143] Applicants must include all offenses in the licensing application, including those that resulted in deferred adjudication. Omitting them from an application can hurt an applicant's prospects, because the TDLR has the ability to run the applicant's criminal history record to verify the information provided.

---

[142] For more information, go to TDLJ's Criminal History Evaluation Letter page, See <u>Section 51.4012</u> and <u>Chapter 53, Subchapter D, of the Occupations Code</u>, permit individuals to request a criminal history evaluation letter from the Department before formally applying for a license.

[143] <u>Chapters 51</u> and <u>53</u>, Tex. Occ. Code

The TDLR cannot consider a deferred adjudication as the sole basis for rejection or renewal of a license, unless the TDLR decides that:
1. the person may pose a continued threat to public safety; or
2. employing the person in the licensed occupation would create a situation in which the person could repeat the prohibited conduct.

A rejected applicant can appeal if the rejection appeared to be based on grounds unrelated to public safety or repeated prohibited conduct.

7.2.6 TDLR Evaluation of Application

In deciding whether the license should be granted, the TDLR is supposed to consider:
- the nature and seriousness of the crime;
- the relationship of the crime to the purposes for requiring a license to engage in the occupation;
- the extent to which a license might offer an opportunity to engage in the same type of criminal activity in which the applicant was previously involved; and
- the relationship of the crime to the ability, capacity, or fitness required to perform the duties and discharge the responsibilities of the licensed occupation.

The TDLR will also evaluate the applicant's fitness to perform the duties and discharge the responsibilities of the licensed occupation by considering:
- the extent and nature of the applicant's past criminal activity;
- the applicant's age when the crime was committed;
- the amount of time that has elapsed since the applicant's last criminal activity;
- the applicant's conduct and work history before and after the criminal activity;
- evidence of the applicant's rehabilitation or rehabilitative effort while imprisoned or after release; and
- other evidence of the applicant's fitness, including letters of recommendation from prosecutors and law enforcement and correctional officers who prosecuted, arrested, or had custodial responsibility for the applicant; the sheriff or chief of police in the community where the applicant resides; and any other person who has had contact with the applicant.

7.2.7 TDLR Grounds for Denial

By law, [144] the TDLR is permitted to deny, suspend or revoke a license if the crime is:

1. an offense that directly relates to the duties and responsibilities of the licensed occupation;

2. until September 1, 2019, an offense that does not directly relate to the duties and responsibilities of the licensed occupation but was committed fewer than five years before the person applies for the license;

3. an offense for which a person is not eligible for probation or community supervision; or

4. sexually violent offenses, as defined by Article 62.001 of the Code of Criminal Procedure.[145]

7.2.8 "Directly Related"

A potential applicant cannot be disqualified unless the TDLR can show that the applicant's offense is "directly related" to the duties and responsibilities of that occupation. The term "directly related" can be so broadly defined that it can be made to include virtually all offenses. Persons convicted of theft or burglary, for example, may be prevented from holding an electrician's license because electricians "have access to private residences and businesses, where they may come into direct contact with unattended property." The disqualification decision based on "direct relationship" grounds can be appealed to the TDLR.

Regardless of whether there is a "direct relationship" between the offense and the occupation, the TDLR may deny an applicant if it has been less than five years since the commission of the offense. The time runs from the date the offense was *committed*, not from the date of conviction.

7.2.9 Appeal

If an application is denied, it can be appealed to an administrative law judge in the State Office of Administrative Hearings (SOAH).[146] The TDLR will schedule a hearing and send a notice of the hearing date and time to the applicant. It is helpful to have attorney assistance at the hearing; contact an attorney or the local legal aid office for help.

---

[144] Tex. Occ. Code §53.021(a).

[145] Tex. Code Crim. P. § 62.001(6). "Sexually violent offense" is defined to include the following offenses under the Texas Penal Code: §21.02 (Continuous sexual abuse of young child or children), §21.11(a)(1) (Indecency with a child), §22.011 (Sexual assault), or §22.021 (Aggravated sexual assault), §43.25 (Sexual performance by a child), §20.04(a)(4)(Aggravated kidnapping, if the defendant committed the offense with intent to violate or abuse the victim sexually; §30.02 (Burglary, if with intent to commit certain crimes involving children).

[146] "The [SOAH] shall conduct all hearings in contested cases under Chapter 2001 that are before the Texas Department of Licensing and Regulation under Chapter 51, Occupations Code

At the hearing, the applicant can offer testimony and written evidence to an administrative law judge to support why the license should be granted. Following the hearing, SOAH will issue a proposal for decision. The decision is not binding on the agency unless the board rules state that they will be bound by SOAH's decisions. If licensing board decides not to adopt a favorable decision from SOAH, the adverse decision can be appealed to state court.[147]

The process is the same where an offense is revealed after the license is granted. In the case of renewal, the decision will be whether the license should be suspended or revoked instead of whether to grant or deny.

Evidence for the hearing can be anything that might help alter the decision to deny. This can include information probation or parole officials but should also show that the applicant has:
1. been steadily employed;
2. supported his or her dependents;
3. maintained a record of good conduct; and
4. paid all outstanding court costs, supervision fees, fines, and restitution ordered in any criminal case.

7.3 TWIC

TWIC is the identification credential for anyone that requires unescorted access to secure areas of Maritime Transportation Security Act (MTSA). Individuals who meet TWIC eligibility are issued a credential based on fingerprint information.

7.3.1 People Who Must Get a TWIC

Coast Guard-credentialed merchant mariners, port facility employees, longshore workers, truck drivers, and others requiring unescorted access to secure areas of maritime facilities and vessels regulated by the MTSA. More information and resources are available on the official TWIC Program website (www.tsa.gov/twic) and through the TWIC help desk (1-866-DHS-TWIC).

---

[147] "The occupational licensing agency and any other party to the contested case is entitled to obtain judicial review of the final decision in accordance with this chapter." Tex. Gov't. Code §2001.058(f)(5).

8 . PUBLIC BENEFITS

Public benefits are the common term for a variety of state and federal programs designed to help those in need of assistance. Food stamps (SNAP), Temporary Assistance for Needy Families (TANF) often called cash assistance; Social Security Supplemental Income (SSI) and Medicaid are all examples of public benefits. A criminal conviction or prison sentence can restrict eligibility for various federal benefits, depending on the type and grade of offense and the specific benefit.

8.1 DENIAL OF FEDERAL BENEFITS (DFB)

The Denial of Federal Benefits (DFB) Program[148] gives state and federal courts- as part of the sentencing process- the ability to deny all or selected federal benefits to individuals who are convicted of drug trafficking or drug possession. Examples of benefits denied include:
- Owners of small businesses losing Small Business Administration loans, or the right to make contracts with the federal government.

- Researchers who lose eligibility to apply for grants.

- Broadcasters and airline pilots losing their Federal Communications Commission or Federal Aviation Administration licenses.

- Doctors who cannot authority to prescribe medicine.

The DFB sanction can be part or combined with of other criminal sanctions. Courts have the option to deny all or some benefits, and to determine the duration of the period of denial, depending on the crime. If benefits are denied as part of a sentence, the sentencing court must notify a government agency that in turn notifies the U.S. General Services Administration (GSA). The GSA publishes a list of the names of individuals who are denied benefits (referred to as the "Debarment List.")

8.2 TEMPORARY ASSISTANCE FOR NEEDY FAMILIES (TANF)

The 1996 Personal Responsibility and Work Opportunity Reconciliation Act (PRWORA) ended the individual entitlement to welfare and replaced it with a block grant to States (Temporary Assistance for Needy Families, or TANF), set a five-year lifetime limit on benefits, required adults to work to receive benefits and strengthened child support enforcement requirements for non-custodial parents.

---

[148] See Denial of Federal Benefits Program, § 5301 of the Anti-Drug Abuse Act of 1988 (P.L. 100-690); https://www.ncjrs.gov/pdffiles1/bja/193770.pdf.

Temporary Assistance for Needy Families (TANF) provides financial help for children and their parents or relatives who are living with them. Monthly cash payments help pay for food, clothing, housing, utilities, furniture, transportation, telephone, laundry, household equipment, medical supplies not paid for by Medicaid and other basic needs. The amount of the TANF payments depend family size and income.[149]

8.2.1 TANF for Families

To be eligible, a family must be below income and resource limits as determined by Texas HHSC, including cash on hand, money in the bank and number and type of vehicles. Some features of TANF:

- Families approved for TANF will receive payments for six months.

- Families who receive TANF benefits can also get Medicaid benefits.

- TANF is paid through the Lone Star Card, an electronic debit card.

- TANF payments range from 12 to 36 months for adults, depending on the situation. There are no time limits for children under age 18. If the child is a full time student expected to graduate before age 19, benefits can be paid through the child's graduation.

- A child's parent or relative cannot be approved for TANF unless he or she signs a Personal Responsibility Agreement.

8.2.2 Personal Responsibility Agreement

The agreement requires adult TANF recipients to:
- Train for a job or look for employment if capable.[150]
- Cooperate with the Office of Attorney General - Child Support Division and take parenting skills classes if required.
- Not voluntarily quit a job, or abuse alcohol or drugs.
- Make sure the children are attending school and are up-to-date on medical screenings and required immunizations (usually through Medicaid).

8.2.3 "One-Time TANF"

People leaving prison may qualify for short-term, nonrecurring TANF benefits to meet immediate personal and family needs following release. Families who already get TANF cannot get a one-time TANF payment. Unlike regular TANF, this benefit is not considered "assistance." One-time TANF is designed to help with short-term crisis such as:

---

[149] HHSC TANF (www.hhsc.state.tx.us/Help/Financial/temporary-assistance.shtml#TANFpayment). Follow link to Apply for TANF

[150] Employment assistance provided by the Texas Workforce Commission.

- Loss of a job, loss of a home, or other sudden financial loss, such as loss of financial support for a child or help paying living expenses like rent, utilities and food.
- Unemployment following graduation from an institution of higher learning (university, college, junior college, technical training school).
- Loss of employment income because vehicle is not working.
- A Medical emergency.

8.2.4 One-Time TANF Grandparent Payment

The One-Time TANF Grandparent Payment is $1,000 cash assistance given to a grandparent who cares for a child receiving TANF. A grandparent can only receive this payment once, even though other grandchildren may move in at a later time.

8.2.5 Felony Drug Offenses – Lifetime Ban

A person is disqualified from receiving benefits if the Texas Health and Human Services Commission (HHSC) determines the person is a fugitive (a person fleeing to avoid prosecution or confinement for a felony criminal conviction, or found by a court to be violating federal or state probation or parole) or is convicted of a felony drug offense (not deferred adjudication) in Texas or another state committed on or after April 1, 2002.[151]

8.3 FOOD STAMPS (SNAP)

SNAP food benefits "food stamps" are available for eligible single persons or families. The benefits periods last for 6 months, but can as short as 1 month or as long as 3 years. Adults between the ages of 18 and 50 who do not have children at home can only receive SNAP for up to 3 months in a 3-year period. The period can be longer than three months for a single person if he or she works at least 20 hours a week or is in job training. Like TANF, SNAP benefits are through the Lone Star Card.

As with TANF, in order to obtain benefits, formerly incarcerated people on probation or parole are required to attend welfare-to-work programs, have no outstanding warrants and be compliant with the terms and conditions of probation or parole to maintain eligibility for SNAP.

8.3.1 Emergency SNAP

Emergency SNAP benefits are for those in an emergency situation who need immediate food assistance, including families with less than $35 combined income

---

[151] Texas Admin Code §372.501(a)

and resources, whose existing resources cannot cover rent and utilities, or migrant or seasonal workers with very low income and resources.

8.3.2 Felony Drug Offenses –Changes to Lifetime Ban

Effective September 1, 2015 persons with a final felony conviction will be able to obtain food stamps so long as they successfully complete their sentence. Violating terms of their parole or probation could trigger a two-year disqualification and a new offense will trigger a lifetime ban.[152]

8.4 MEDICAID AND CHIP

Low income families can apply to the state's Medicaid Program for health care. Families who qualify for Medicaid also qualify for TANF. Families who fall outside of Medicaid resource and income guidelines might qualify for CHIP, or the Children's Health Insurance Program. This program covers medical and dental care as well as eye examinations.

A family can receive Medicaid benefits as long as income and resource requirements are met. Before the end of each six month period of coverage, a renewal application is sent to the family.

8.5 SOCIAL SECURITY AND SSI

8.5.1 Social Security

Generally, the term social security describes a program that provides elderly or disabled people old age, disability, and survivors insurance, as well as supplemental security income. The money raised from social security taxes goes to providing benefits for those who have reached retirement age or are otherwise currently eligible. Social Security benefits are based on the amount of Social Security taxes paid based on individual income.

The SSA expects offenders to inform them (and if a Veteran, the Department of Veterans Affairs) when convicted of a felony involving incarceration. Benefits will be suspended for the offender during the period of incarceration. Family members who are eligible for benefits based on the offender's work history can continue to receive benefits.

8.5.2 Social Security Supplemental Income (SSI)

Supplemental Security Income is funded by general tax revenues (not Social Security taxes). SSI benefits can be paid to people who are 65 or older, or blind or disabled people who have little or no income. No SSI benefits are payable for any

---

[152] Texas Admin Code §372.501(b)

month that an offender is in jail or prison, and payments are halted during the period of incarceration.

A jail or prison sentence of twelve months or more terminates eligibility for SSI benefits. If incarcerated for one month, benefits will be suspended but not terminated; there is no need to reapply. The correctional facility is supposed to notify the Social Security Administration when the offender is released, so that eligibility for SSI can be restored. People recently released from incarceration should follow up with the Social Security Administration to make sure that the agency has been notified of the release.

8.5.3 Outstanding Warrants

Criminal warrants can affect eligibility for SSI. People with outstanding felony warrants are ineligible. Violations of the conditions of probation or parole that are imposed as part of a federal or state sentence will also trigger ineligibility.[153] A warrant, even for an unpaid fine, must be resolved in order to restore eligibility for benefits.

8.5.4 "Overpayments"

Whether in prison or under warrant, SSI may consider any benefits paid during the period of ineligibility to be an "overpayment." If this is the case, the SSI recipient will receive an overpayment notice, which can be appealed. For help with the appealing the denial of benefits, contact an attorney or local legal aid office.

8.6 UNEMPLOYMENT BENEFITS

Texas offers temporary financial help to people who are unemployed or partially unemployed through no fault their own. Job loss because of a criminal conviction would not likely qualify that person for unemployment benefits, because the loss is attributable to fault of the applicant.[154] In a right-to-work state, the employee is at a disadvantage if criminal history is a reason for termination. Regardless of a criminal conviction, a person finds a job and subsequently loses it through no fault of their own might qualify for unemployment.[155]

8.7 EDUCATION ASSISTANCE

Effective July 1, 2000, Congress placed restrictions on student financial aid for students who have been convicted of certain drug-related offenses. A conviction prior to July 1, 2000 might affect financial aid eligibility.

---

[153] For more information or to apply for benefits, contact the Social Security Administration's SSI page or call 2-1-1 for information on where to apply in person.

[154] Texas Workforce Commission, Unemployment Insurance Benefits Handbook at 8, *available at* http://www.twc.state.tx.us/ui/bnfts/bi-99.pdf.

[155] More information about qualifying for unemployment is available from the Texas Workforce Commission's Unemployment Insurance Benefits Handbook.

Students who are ineligible can regain eligibility early by either having the conviction invalidated or by successfully completing an approved drug rehabilitation program, which includes two unannounced drug tests. The Department of Education uses the FAFSA (Free Application for Federal Student Aid) to enforce these restrictions.

A non-drug related conviction does not automatically render a person ineligible for federal financial aid. People barred from federal financial aid because of a drug conviction may still be eligible for non-federal aid from states and private institutions. Every student should therefore complete the FAFSA.

Resources
- Texas 2-1-1 - Office of Eligibility Services: For questions, information or assistance with Food Stamps, (SNAP), Medicaid (adult or children), Children's Health insurance Program (CHIP) or Temporary Assistance for Needy Families (TANF), dial 2-1-1 or visit YourTexasBenefits.com.
- Texas Law Help: Free Legal Information on Public Benefits and other topics: www.texaslawhelp.org
- Social Security: www.socialsecurity.gov

9 . SHELTER AND HOUSING

For people newly released from prison, stable housing is pivotal to successful reentry. This section addresses housing options, the effect a person's criminal history plays in obtaining housing, and legal rights as they pertain to housing.

9.1 HOMELESSNESS

Ideally, offenders close to release will have been counseled on housing options and made a reentry plan that addresses shelter and housing issues.[156] Far too many people facing reentry have no place to call home and no family members willing to take them in. For these individuals, immediate housing options may be limited to homeless shelters or charities.[157]

This problem is especially acute for people under a "serve-all," or day-for-day sentence. Once released, they are no longer under the jurisdiction of the corrections system or the Board of Pardons and Paroles. Those directly released from incarceration leave with nothing more than with their personal belongings, $100, and a bus ticket. With nowhere to go, a homeless shelter might be the only alternative to sleeping on the streets.

9.1.1 Shelter Resources

The availability of shelter resources for the homeless vary by location. To search shelters by Texas County, see the Homeless Shelter Directory website.

9.2 RELEASE TO SUPERVISION

Individuals released on parole are still under the jurisdiction of the TDCJ. By law, they must be paroled to the county where they resided at the time the offense was committed, or to the county of conviction, sometimes called the Legal County of Residence (LCOR).[158] Exceptions to release to the LCOR depend on circumstances such as the availability of employment and location of family members.[159] Other restrictions apply to the release of persons convicted of certain sex crimes.

9.2.1 Halfway Houses

---

[156] The Texas Department of Criminal Justice's (TDCJ) Re-Entry and Integration Division (RID) addresses housing issues as part of its voluntary re-entry plan.

[157] For a comprehensive list of Texas housing resources for formerly incarcerated people, please refer to the Texas Criminal Justice Coalition's free publication, A New Start – A Re-Entry Guide for Texas.

[158] Tex. Govt. Code §508.181(a).

[159] Tex. Govt. Code §508.181(b).

The terms and conditions of a person's release from prison may require living in a halfway house.[160] Halfway houses are intended to provide transitional housing for the formerly incarcerated people in the process of reintegration, while still providing monitoring and support. Regardless of the offense, bed space available in TDCJ-approved halfway houses severely limited, so that people who otherwise qualify for early release sometimes remain in prison until space is available.[161]

9.2.2 THAP Program

The Temporary Housing Assistance Program (THAP) was created to provide temporary housing for those who have approved for parole and are approaching their mandatory release date.[162] THAP site providers receive payments directly from TDCJ. THAP payments cannot exceed the cost that TDCJ would pay to incarcerate the person for the same time period for which the payment is issued.

There is no application for THAP. Candidates are screened for THAP before release for eligibility. If accepted, the THAP recipient must to actively seek employment, adhere to the housing provider's rules and be able to secure a more stable work and housing situation when the three month term has expired. THAP housing continues to be limited due to the availability of THAP providers.

9.2.3 Not Eligible for THAP
- People released under a "serve-all" sentence
- People who have housing provided by family or friends
- People whose county of return has a TDCJ-funded halfway house (Dallas, El Paso, Jefferson, Harris, Tarrant, and Travis Counties).

9.2.4 Living with Family Members

Those who are not awaiting placement to a halfway house may have other housing options, like moving in with a family or friend during the transition period. Family members can often provide shelter and social support for a successful reentry. If the family is living in federally subsidized housing, all household members should be aware that:
- The reentering person will not be counted as a household member for purposes of getting a larger housing subsidy or living accommodation.

---

[160] Special rules apply to sex offenders. §508.181(g). By law, there is a limit to the number of sex offenders that can be released to the county of conviction or residence. When this number (based on a percentage of the total number of sex offenders released to supervision) is exceeded, they must be released to a different county.

[161] Currently, there are only six TDCJ-approved halfway houses in Texas, located in the major population centers of Beaumont, Ft. Worth, Austin, Dallas, El Paso and Houston. TDCJ- Parole Division, Halfway House Directory (last reviewed November 21, 2011). Five of the six are managed by private for-profit companies under contract with TDCJ. The GEO Group, a multinational corporation headquartered in Boca Raton, Florida, manages the TDCJ halfway houses in Beaumont, Ft. Worth and Houston. Avalon Correctional Services, Inc., headquartered in Oklahoma City, Oklahoma, manages houses in Austin and El Paso. The sixth, Wayback House in Dallas, is operated by a nonprofit. Only three of the six halfway houses – in Beaumont, El Paso and Houston – accept sex offenders and parolees from other counties.

[162] Tex. Gov. Code §508.157.

- If the re-entering person disrupts or violates the public housing rules, the entire household could be evicted, regardless of regardless of whether the behavior is a criminal offense.

9.3 AFFORDABLE HOUSING

9.3.1 No Automatic Disqualification

There is no federal "ban" or automatic disqualification on either type of housing for people with criminal convictions, but each program is locally managed and has wide discretion to develop local policies governing admission and occupancy.

9.3.2 Waiting Period

People who may not have access to affordable housing may qualify for subsidized housing, but the wait for affordable housing can take months, even years. Each housing authority maintains its own waiting list(s).

9.3.3 Types of Supportive Housing

There are two types of federally supported housing: Public Housing and the Housing Choice Voucher Program. With public housing, local government agencies both provide and regulate housing units. With the housing choice voucher program (or "Section 8"), the government provides a subsidy (voucher) to private landlords in exchange for renting to a qualifying tenant at a reduced rate.

The federal government, through the U.S. Department of Housing and Urban Development (HUD) provides support to local Public Housing Authorities (PHA's). PHA's are responsible for providing and regulating affordable housing within their communities.[163]

9.3.4 Eligibility for Public Housing

Public housing is limited to low-income families and individuals. A PHA determines eligibility based on:
- annual gross income;
- whether the applicant qualifies as elderly, a person with a disability, or as a family;
- U.S. citizenship or eligible immigration status;
- preferences that may give some families preference over others on the waiting list depending on the needs in its own community, and
- other tenant selection factors that the local PHA may establish as long as they do not violate federal antidiscrimination laws.

---

[163] There are 424 PHA's in the state of Texas that collectively manage over 66,000 public housing units. The San Antonio Housing Authority is the largest with 6,611 units, followed by El Paso (6,028), Dallas (4,667) and Houston (3,485). A full list of the PHA's in Texas and their contact information is available on the HUD website.

PHA's have the authority to:

- access criminal records of the applicant or current tenant, and
- access records from drug treatment facilities where that information is *solely* related to whether the applicant is currently engaging in the illegal use of a controlled substance.[164]

9.3.5 Application for Public Housing

A person seeking public housing must apply through their local PHA. As part of the application, the PHA will need the following information:

1. Names, sex, date of birth and relationship to the applicant of all who are expected to live in the unit;

2. The applicant's present address and telephone number;

3. Other family circumstances that might qualify the family for a tenant selection preference, such as veteran status, current housing situation;

4. Contact information on current and previous landlords so that they can be contacted about the family's suitability as a tenant;

5. The family's estimated anticipated income for the next twelve months and its sources;

6. Contact information for the applicant's employers, banks and any other information needed to verify income and the family composition; and

7. The applicant's acknowledgement that the PHA has the right to visit the home to interview the applicant and family members to check on upkeep of the home.

9.3.6 Criminal Background Check

Federal law requires criminal background checks to be run on adult household members applying to live in public housing. Because criminal records can contain errors, PHA's must give applicants an opportunity to dispute the accuracy of their criminal records.[165]

9.3.7 Documents Required

---

[164] The Housing Opportunity Program Extension Act of 1996, codified at 42 USCA §§1437d(s);1437d(t)

[165] Tran-Leung, Marie Claire, When Discretion Means Denial for People With Criminal Records in Federally Subsidized Housing, Shriver Center 2015

The applicant may need to provide certain documents to verify the information in the application, such as a birth certificate or tax returns. The PHA can also ask the applicant to sign a release enabling the PHA to get information from third parties, like an employer, to verify employment status.

9.3.8 Selection Preferences

Each local PHA can set its own preferences as long as they are nondiscriminatory. A PHA may have a preference for a family over a single person, or for a disabled person over a single family. Applicants should ask the PHA what preferences they may apply. The PHA can close the waiting list if there are more families on the list than they can place in the near future.

9.3.9 Decision on Application

The PHA must send written notice of its decision. If accepted, the PHA will usually add the applicant's name to a waiting list and contact the applicant when housing is available. Once housing is available, the applicant will sign a lease with the PHA. The PHA is the landlord. If the application is denied, the PHA is required to state why and provide information on how to appeal the decision.

9.3.10 PHA as Landlord

Rent is referred to as the Total Tenant Payment (TTP). It is based on the family's anticipated gross annual income less deductions. As the landlord, they are responsible for ensuring that the tenant follows the lease, maintenance and repairs, move tenants to another unit if required and terminate the lease if the tenants are in violation.

If the tenants comply with the lease and remain income-eligible, they can usually stay in public housing indefinitely. The PHA is permitted to re-examine the family income at least once every 12 months to make sure the family remains eligible for public housing.

9.4 EVICTIONS, RESTRICTIONS AND BANS

Federal laws govern both admission and eviction standards for federally subsidized housing. These laws give the PHA's broad discretion to craft eviction policies for their individual communities. Access to public housing can be restricted or banned based on some of the following:

Table 14: Bans and Restrictions on Federally Subsidized Housing

Type of Restriction	Reason	Duration	Authority
Mandatory Permanent	Ban on current people who are current illegal users or pattern that demonstrates	Permanent	42 USC § 1437n. 1.

	ongoing use and threat to others		
	Lifetime ban for conviction for Methamphetamine manufacture in federally assisted housing		
	Lifetime ban on sex offenders subject to lifetime registration		
	Any tenant evicted from federally assisted housing by reason of drug-related criminal activity in the last three years.		
Mandatory Temporary	Any household member currently engaging in illegal use of a controlled substance. Regulations define "currently engaged in" as "if the person has engaged in the behavior recently enough to justify a reasonable belief that the behavior is current." PHA's are advised to define "recently" as a specific period of time, such as the past month or six months.	3 years from date of eviction unless: shortened with evidence successful rehab or circumstances of eviction no longer exist	42 USC § 13661 24 CFR § 982.553; 24 CFR § 960.204.
	Drug related criminal activity		
	Violent criminal activity		
Discretionary	Criminal activity poses a threat to the owner, residents or PHA staff on or off premises; eviction must comply with due process	Can be accepted if criminal activity occurred a "reasonable"# The definition of "reasonable" is left to local PHA.# time before the person seeks admission.	42 USCA §13661 (c). 42 USC §1437d. See 42 USC §1437d(k); 24 CFR §966.51.

9.4.1 *Evidence Required For Denial*

PHA and Section 8 housing can be denied or terminated for criminal activity based on a preponderance of evidence.[166] Preponderance of evidence is defined as evidence which as a whole shows that a fact is more probable than not. The intent is to prove that the act(s) occurred, not that a crime took place. Evidence from police and court records, testimony from neighbors, documentation of drug raids or arrest warrants can all be credible evidence. HUD states that examples of evidence of illegal activities "may include a conviction record, former landlord references, etc."[167] This applies to both public housing and Section 8 housing.[168]

9.4.2 Opportunity to Dispute

If the housing authority chooses to terminate the lease, it must notify the tenant, provide copies of the criminal record information and an opportunity to dispute the information. The opportunity to dispute must be offered before the housing authority can take any action against the tenant based on the information.[169]

9.4.3 Grievance Procedure

HUD requires housing authorities to have an administrative grievance procedure under which tenants will:

- be advised of the specific grounds of any proposed adverse public housing agency action;

- have an opportunity for a hearing before an impartial party upon timely request within any period applicable under subsection (l) of this section;

- have an opportunity to examine any documents or records or regulations related to the proposed action;

- be entitled to be represented by another person of their choice at any hearing;

- be entitled to ask questions of witnesses and have others make statements on their behalf; and

- be entitled to receive a written decision by the public housing agency on the proposed action. 42 USCA § 1437d(k).

9.4.4 Right to Review.

---

[166] See, e.g., FY 2014 Administrative Plan, Housing Authority of the City of Arlington at 186, available at, http://www.arlington-tx.gov/cdp-housing/wp-content/uploads/sites/30/2014/10/Admin-Plan-FY2014-AHA.pdf

[167] HUD Notice H 2002-22, at 5.

[168] 42 USC 1437d(1)(6).

[169] 24 CFR §5.903(f)

A person who is denied housing assistance must be provided an opportunity to review the adverse decision.[170] The review process must be included with the notice of denial or termination.[171]

9.4.5 Mitigating Circumstances

The PHA "is required" to consider mitigating circumstances for applicants such as evidence of rehabilitation or willingness to participate in counseling or social services.[172]

The PHA "may" consider mitigating circumstances for Section 8 Applicants.[173]

Applicants can bring positive letters or other documents to show evidence of rehabilitation. Some examples include:

- School: transcript or letter from teacher or school administrator detailing length of attendance, grades, punctuality, etc.
- Job Training: letter from a program supervisor or administrator
- Employment: letter for a supervisor detailing length of employment and job performance (include any employment during incarceration)
- Counseling or social service program: letters describing attendance, positive drug tests, etc.
- Certificate of Relief from Disabilities or Certificate of Good Conduct
- Other, such as certificates from programs such as anger management, drug/alcohol treatment; letter from Parole Officer with positive information; letters from clergy; letters from landlords or building superintendents; letters from neighbors; proof of your children's successes; letters from family.

9.4.6 Domestic Violence

---

[170] 24 CFR § 982.554.

[171] At minimum, the review procedure must comply with the following:

- The review may be conducted by anyone designated by the PHA except the person that made the decision to deny housing assistance.
- The applicant must be given an opportunity to present written or oral objections to the PHA decision.
- The PHA must notify the applicant of the PHA final decision after the informal review, including a brief statement of the reasons for the final decision.

[172] 24 CFR §960.203(d)

[173] 24 CFR §982.552(c)(2)(I)

Public housing and Section 8 tenants must comply with the Violence Against Women Act, and cannot exclude or deny housing to victims of family or dating violence.[174]

9.5 HOUSING DISCRIMINATION

If the real reason housing is denied is illegal discrimination, not offender status, an applicant can pursue certain legal remedies to challenge the denial. Under federal law, a housing provider may not discriminate based on a person's race, sex, national origin, religion, family status or disability.[175] This is true for all housing, regardless of whether it is private, federally subsidized, or publicly owned.

Discriminatory practices can range from flagrant abuses to more subtle forms. Part of the challenge in combating illegal discrimination is in identifying when it occurs and recognizing housing practices that have a discriminatory effect. [176]

9.5.1 Refusing to Rent or Sell

An obvious violation of civil rights laws occurs when an apartment manager, leasing agent, landlord or owner simply refuses to rent or sell to a member of a protected class.[177] For example, a landlord's refusal to rent an apartment to a single black woman who otherwise qualifies might constitute discrimination based on race, sex, or family status. A leasing agent who refuses to show a property to an applicant from Pakistan may be discriminating on the basis of national origin, religion, or both. Disability-based discrimination may be obvious where a landlord refuses to rent to a blind or deaf person.[178] It is less obvious where the disability is addiction or alcoholism. Denying housing to an alcoholic or former addict who is not currently abusing alcohol or engaged in the current use of illegal drugs is illegal discrimination based on disability. Sexual discrimination can also take more subtle forms. For example, a manager of an apartment complex who demands sexual favors from a woman in return for renting to her is sexual harassment, which is a form of sexual discrimination. [179]

---

[174] Act CFR Tit. 24, Subt. A, Pt. 5, Subpt. L.

[175] The source of legal protection is the federal Fair Housing Act. Title VIII of the Civil Rights Act of 1968, as amended in 1988 (42 USC §3601 et seq.), also known as the Fair Housing Act, and the Civil Rights Act of 1866 (Title 42 of the United States Code sections 1981 and 1982) both prohibit discrimination in a wide array of real estate practices, including housing sale and rental, provision of homeowner's insurance and mortgage lending.

[176] For more information, see The Legal Action Center publication "Making a Claim of Racial Discrimination Under the Federal Fair Housing Act".

[177] 42 USC §3604(a) Refusals to sell or rent:

"To refuse to sell or rent after the making of a bona fide offer, or to refuse to negotiate for the sale or rental of, or otherwise make unavailable or deny a dwelling to any person because of.." membership in a protected class.

[178] A "handicap" or disability is a physical or mental impairment, or a record of having an impairment, which substantially limits a person's major life activities.

[179] Sexual harassment includes verbal comments, gestures, or physical contact that creates an offensive environment.

9.5.2 Applying Different Terms and Conditions [180]

Discrimination may be present when an owner or landlord applies different terms and conditions surrounding the lease or sale of housing to some people but not to others. Uneven treatment can be illegal discrimination when, for example, a landlord demands a higher security deposit from a family with children (discrimination based on family status) or where a leasing agent charges an exorbitant rental application fee to a minority (racial discrimination).[181]

9.5.3 False Information about Availability[182]

Other owners, managers or leasing agents might lie about the availability of housing to some applicants but not to others; as for, example, an apartment complex with "now leasing" signage claims tells an applicant in a wheelchair user that all units are full. Providing false information about the availability of a property can be evidence of discrimination.

9.5.4 Reporting Discrimination

People who believe that they have been denied housing because of discrimination based on their race, color, national origin, religion, sex, family status or disability can file a fair housing complaint. The Texas Workforce Commission Civil Rights Division will accept a housing complaint
- In person: by coming to the Division office located at 1117 Trinity St., Room 144-T in Austin, Texas, or
- By telephone: toll free number: 1-888-452-4778, between 8:00 AM and 5:00 PM.
- By letter: addressed to:
Texas Workforce Commission
Civil Rights Division
1117 Trinity Street, Rm. 144-T
Austin, Texas 78701

After the complaint is received, the applicant will be assigned an investigator who discuss the process for filing the complaint, how it will be investigated, and help with preparing the complaint. A complaint may also be filed through the U.S. Department of Housing and Urban Development (HUD), by calling 1-888-560-8913, or in writing to:

---

[180] 42 USC §3604(b) Discrimination in terms, conditions or privileges of rental or sale:

"To discriminate against any person in the terms, conditions, or privileges of sale or rental of a dwelling, or in the provision of services or facilities in connection therewith, because of.." membership in a protected class.

[181] Under federal fair housing laws, "family status" includes families of one adult parent or guardian, and at least one child under 18. A pregnant woman is also defined as "family."

[182] 42 USC §3604(d) Denying availability:

"To represent to any person because of..." membership in a protected class "...that any dwelling is not available for inspection, sale, or rental when such dwelling is in fact so available."

U.S. Department of Housing and Urban Development,
Southwest Office of Fair Housing and Equal Opportunity,
801 Cherry Street, P.O. Box 2905, Fort Worth, Texas 76113-2905

9.6 RENTING WITH A RECORD

Most larger apartment complexes order both credit and criminal history records on prospective tenants from private vendors of this information. Many private noncommercial rentals, however, do not require a criminal background or even a credit screening as a prerequisite to renting. Accordingly, avoiding properties offered through a commercial leasing agency in favor those managed by a local, private owner might provide an ex-offender with a better opportunity to explain his criminal history directly to the person that he will be renting from, rather than a leasing agent employed by a commercial property management company.

The local owner or landlord can also be more flexible and perhaps willing to negotiate the lease terms.

Establishing credit is important in order to build a credit history that will enable the renter to upgrade based on a positive payment history. Settling for a rental property that is not ideal may be worth signing the lease in the short term in order to build a credit history that may lead to an upgrade to better housing.

9.6.1 Roommate or Sublet

Seeking a roommate situation or a sublet might resolve an immediate need for a place to stay. Renting a room as a sublet has the advantage of not requiring a criminal background check that would normally be part of a lease.

9.6.2 Group Homes or Boarding Houses

This type of housing is generally unregulated, but may violate zoning restrictions if there are too many unrelated people reside in the same house. Other occupants may have criminal convictions that may or may not be known to the other household members. A renter on probation or parole could therefore unwittingly violate the terms and conditions of release that prohibit association with other ex-offenders.

9.6.3 Renting from Private Owner

In housing that is not federally subsidized, factors such as credit history and criminal history can be used by a private owner to refuse to rent to a prospective tenant. Private or corporate owners and landlords have the legal right to deny housing to any person for any reason, unless the landlord is engaged in illegal housing discrimination.

9.6.4 Selection Criteria and Acknowledgment

Along with the rental application, the landlord must provide written notice of the criteria used to accept or deny the application, such as the applicant's:

- Criminal history;
- Previous rental history;
- Current income;
- Credit history; or
- Failure to provide accurate or complete information on the application form.

Selection criteria are not limited to the items listed above. The written notice can appear in the body of rental application or in a separate document. If it is in the rental application, it must be underlined or appear in bold-faced type. It must also state that the application fee will not be refunded if the application is rejected. A typical notice may state:

> "Signing this acknowledgment indicates that you have had the opportunity to review the landlord's tenant selection criteria. The tenant selection criteria may include factors such as criminal history, credit history, current income, and rental history. If you do not meet the selection criteria, or if you provide inaccurate or incomplete information, your application may be rejected and your application fee will not be refunded."

The applicant's written acknowledgment indicates only that she had an *opportunity* to review the landlord's selection criteria. The landlord's selection criteria are not limited to the criteria listed on the notice, and applicant is entitled to review the selection criteria used by that particular landlord. The law prevents both the landlord and prospective tenant from waiving the notice. Any attempt to waive the application notice will render the application void.

9.6.5 Consumer Reporting Agencies

Most landlords hire consumer reporting agencies (CRAs), such as ChoicePoint or First Advantage Safe Rent to provide background checks background checks on a consumer's criminal history and credit history. When landlords use CRAs the Fair Credit Reporting Act (FCRA) applies.[183] The FCRA does not protect prospective tenants from being denied admission on the basis of a criminal record, but can add transparency to the process.

---

[183] See 15 USC §1681 *et seq*.

9.6.6 Criminal History Records

CRA's cannot report "other adverse items of information, other than records of convictions of crimes which antedates the report by more than *seven years.* [emphasis supplied]. Fair Credit Reporting Act (FCRA), 15 USCS 1681c(a)(5).

In sum, under the FCRA, CRA's

- Can report offenses resulting in criminal convictions indefinitely.

- Cannot report arrests not resulting in conviction if they are more than 7 years old. [184]

- Although not specifically addressed under the FCRA, offenses resulting deferred adjudication that are discharged and dismissed and are more than 7 years old should not be reported either, because they are not convictions.

9.6.7 Correcting Inaccurate or Stale Information

CRAs must maintain "reasonable procedures to assure maximum possible accuracy of the information" in the report.[185] To claim a violation, a prospective tenant must show that:
1. The report included inaccurate information;
2. The report included the inaccurate information because the CRA did not maintain reasonable procedures;
3. The suffered injury; and
4. The inaccurate information caused the injury.[186]

9.6.8 Disclosure and Investigation

Upon request, CRAs must give a prospective tenant a copy of his or her file, disclose the sources of the information in the file, and identify each landlord that procured a report within the past year. If a person notifies a CRA that the report is inaccurate or incomplete, the CRA must, free of charge, conduct a reasonable reinvestigation to determine if the information is inaccurate or incomplete and update the file within 30 days.[187]

9.6.9 Damages and Enforcement

---

[184] 15 USC §1681c(a)(2)

[185] 15 USC § 1681e(b).

[186] *Philbin v. Trans Union Corp.,* 101 F.3d 957, 963 (3rd Cir. 1996).

[187] § 1681i(a)(1).

The Federal Trade Commission enforces most of the provisions of the FCRA.[188] The FTC is entitled to file suit to recover civil penalties from a CRA or a landlord for a knowing violation that constitutes a pattern or practice[189]

9.6.10 Application Fee

A landlord may require two initial payments to secure rental housing: an application fee and an application deposit. The application fee is paid by the prospective renter at the time the application is made. Not all landlords require an application fee. The purpose of the application fee is to reimburse the landlord for the cost of obtaining a background check, which normally includes the applicant's credit history, rental history, current income, criminal history, and similar information. Although there is no legal limit on the amount that can be charged for an application fee, most run under $50.00. Application fees are nonrefundable except in cases where the landlord rejected the applicant without stating the reason. If the application is accepted, a security deposit may also be required.

9.6.11 Deposit

In addition to the application fee, the landlord may also require a deposit to hold the property while the application is being processed. This application deposit is the prospective tenant's assurance to the landlord that he will move into the unit if approved.

9.6.12 Forfeiture of Deposit

There is no grace period to back out of a signed rental application. If the application is approved, the application deposit may be applied to the security deposit when the lease is signed. If the application is approved but the applicant changes her mind – even later the same day – she risks forfeiting the application deposit. Some rental applications require that the lease be signed within three days of approval or the deposit will not be returned. The Texas Tenant Advisor suggests in case of a change of mind after the deposit is made to wait until at least seven days have passed before seeking return of the deposit. If the application is rejected, or the applicant doesn't' hear back within seven days (no decision is considered a rejection) the landlord is expected to refund the application deposit.

9.6.13 Rejection Deadline

Some landlords don't use an application at all, and may or may not ask the prospective tenant to make a deposit. If a deposit is made to hold the property, the landlord has seven days from the date of the deposit to decide whether to rent. If within seven days no action is taken, the application is considered rejected and the deposit must be refunded.

---

[188] §1681s(a)-(b).

[189] §1681s(a)(2)

However, there is no legal deadline by which the landlord must refund it. If the landlord does not refund it, a lawsuit may be the only way to get the application deposit returned. For this reason, a prospective tenant should never pay an application deposit or sign the application unless absolutely sure that he will move into the unit if approved. If the renter can show that the landlord acted in bad faith by failing to refund the application deposit, the landlord can be liable for $100, three times the amount of the deposit, and attorney's fees.

Resources

Texas

- Call 2-1-1 for contact information on local shelters and food pantries, and other social services. 2-1-1 is answered every day, 24 hours a day, 7 days a week.
- Texas State Bar Tenants' Rights Handbook
- Texas Workforce Commission Civil Rights Division
- Texas Low Income Housing Information Service Affordable housing and tenant/landlord information
- Texas Department of Housing and Community Affairs State Housing Agency

Tenant Organizations

- Texas Tenant Advisor
- Texas Tenants Union (Dallas based)
- Housing Crisis Center (Dallas based)
- Austin Tenants' Council Austin Tenants' Council
-

National

- National Alliance of HUD Tenants
- National Housing Law Project
- National Housing Trust
- National Low Income Housing Coalition
- U.S. Department of Housing and Urban Development
- Huduser Housing data

10. Rights of Parents

This section describes some of the most common legal barriers faced by parents who have been apart from their children due to incarceration, including rights of parents, locating children, and court proceedings that affect the rights of parents and children.

10.1 Equal Rights to Child

Parents are the natural custodians of their children, and their rights are superior to all others. Both parents have equal rights to their child. Absent a court order limiting or defining custody, access and possession, either parent can take the child from the other parent, collect the child from school, attend all school activities, authorize medical and psychiatric care for the child and all of the other rights and duties to which parents are legally entitled. This is true regardless of time a parent may have spent away from the child, such as period of absence due to incarceration. Incarceration alone does not alter the natural rights of the parent. The only way the relationship can be altered, or custody determined, is by a court that has issued an order signed by a judge.

10.2 Locating Children

Regardless of whether there is a court order for custody and visitation, the law does not require a parent or caregiver to take children to visit an incarcerated parent. Without regular contact during a period of incarceration, it is easy for some parents lose track of their children's whereabouts.

Most Texas court orders involving children require both parents to keep each other and the court informed about their current residence and place of employment. If there is a court order in place for custody child support, the address of both parents must be listed in the Order. Both parties are required to keep the court updated on their addresses as well as those of the children.[190] A copy of the court order can be obtained from the district court clerk in the county where a decree was issued or paternity was established.

Check with the school district they last attended and request copies of the child's school records, which may list the child's current address or the address of the school to which they were transferred. The school may require a copy of the current custody order before the records are released. If there is no court order in place, the formerly incarcerated parent is as entitled to contact the children through their school as the other parent, but may need to show proof of parentage.

---

[190] Tex. Fam. Code 105.006. As a practical matter, few comply with the requirement to update this information, but it must be included in the order unless there is a compelling reason (e.g., family violence) to exclude it.

A parent who is not currently paying court-ordered child support might consider contacting the Office of Attorney General - Child Support Division (OAG) and volunteer to pay support. If the other parent is receiving public benefits, the OAG is entitled to seek child support in behalf of the children. By volunteering to pay, the OAG may then be able to initiate a proceeding that would match the custodial parent currently receiving benefits to the parent who wishes to pay child support and as a result of the court order, be entitled to access and possession ("visitation") of the children.

10.3 CUSTODY

Regardless of whether the parents are married, the court can decide (often as part of a child support proceeding) which parent should be named the child's primary conservator, or custodial parent. In making this decision, a court is required to consider the "best interest of the child" over the wishes of either parent. If the child is 12 or older, upon request the court must interview the child to determine the child's wishes as to which parent the child wants to live with most of the time. For children under 12, the court may interview the child but does not have to. In determining possession and access, the court will consider, among others, the following factors[191]:
- the desires of the child;

- the emotional and physical needs of the child now and in the future
- the emotional and physical danger to the child now and in the future;
- the parental abilities of the individuals seeking custody;
- the programs available to assist these individuals to promote the best interest of the child;
- the plans for the child by these individuals or by the agency seeking custody;
- the stability of the home or proposed placement;
- the acts or omissions of the parent which may indicate that the relationship is not a proper one; and any excuse for the acts or omissions of the parent.

10.3.1   Nonparent Caregivers

Nonparents can also be awarded custody of children. A nonparent caring for a child in behalf of a parent or parents, whether by agreement with the parent(s) or as a result of a CPS placement, may decide to file suit to get legal custody of the child.

Regardless of the circumstances, Texas law allows a custody suit by:
"a person, other than a foster parent, who has had actual care, control, and possession of the child *for at least six months ending not more than 90 days preceding the date of the filing of the petition.*[192]

---

[191] *Holly v. Adams*, 544 Sewed 367 (Tex. 1976).

[192] Tex. Fam. Code §102.003

This provision confers legal standing on anyone who has been caring for a child longer than six months to file for custody. For a previously incarcerated parent who wants to retain custody of her child who is currently in the care of a friend or relative, it is important to assert parental rights and take the child back before the caregiver can legally sue for custody. A criminal history record can affect a parent's right to retain custody, depending on the nature of the offense(s) and if the court can be persuaded that awarding a nonparent custody would be in the child's best interest.

10.3.2 *Authorization Agreement for Nonparent Relative*

Previously incarcerated parents experiencing reentry may not be in the best position to immediately care for their children. A parent who is temporarily unable to care for her child can execute an Authorization Agreement for Nonparent Relative. This agreement authorizes a third party to care for a child temporarily, but also carries an expiration date which shows the parent's intent to remain the child's conservator. Completing the authorization agreement will not bar a custody suit by the nonparent, but can be introduced as evidence in a custody suit to show that the intent of the agreement with the nonparent to care for the child was temporary.

For a blank Authorization Agreement, please refer to

Appendix M: Authorization Agreement for Non Parent Relative

10.4 PATERNITY

Under Texas law, when a father and mother sign an Acknowledgment of Paternity and the court accepts these documents, the father becomes the "legal" father. Paternity means that fatherhood has been legally established and the father may be ordered to pay child support. A registry of paternity is established in the bureau of Vital Statistics. A man who wants to acknowledge paternity voluntarily may register with Paternity Registry
- Before the birth of the child, but
- Not later that the 31st day after the date of the birth of the child.

If the relationship between the father and the child has been established under another law, or if a man begins a proceeding to adjudicate his paternity before the court has terminated his parental rights, then he is entitled to notice of the proceeding regardless of whether he registers with the registry of paternity.

10.5 TERMINATION OF PARENTAL RIGHTS

Termination lawsuits are broadly divided into two categories, voluntary terminations and involuntary terminations.

Voluntary termination cases are cases in which the parent whose rights are to be terminated consents to the termination. It is unlikely that a court will terminate the parental rights of a person obligated to pay child support. The exception is where there is another person willing to adopt the children affected by the termination and therefore assume financial responsibility.

Involuntary termination cases are brought without the consent of the parent whose rights are to be terminated. The majority of these cases are brought by CPS following an investigation of child abuse or neglect. While there are two dozen or so specific statutory grounds for involuntary terminations, most fall under general categories of abandoning parental responsibilities, endangering the child, engaging in serious criminal conduct or cases in which the parent has exposed the children to harm, abuse or neglect

In either type of termination case, the court must reach the conclusion that the termination is in the child's best interest. The parent whose rights are to be terminated must be notified of the termination lawsuit after it has been filed and they can contest the lawsuit if they choose. Assuming a court does order a termination of parental rights, the parent whose rights are terminated will lose all parental rights, becoming a "legal stranger" to the child and will no longer have a duty to pay child support.

10.6 CHILD PROTECTIVE SERVICES (CPS)

If CPS is or has been involved with the children, the newly released parent should confirm whether the CPS case is still active. In an active CPS case where the children have been removed from a parent or caregiver based on allegations of abuse or neglect, parents have the following rights:
- The right to an attorney, if CPS is seeking to terminate parental rights.
- The right to admit or deny the allegations that prompted the investigation.
- The right to be notified of all court hearings.
- The right to attend all court hearings and meetings.
- The right to an interpreter in court if you do not understand English or are hearing impaired.
- The right to talk to the CPS caseworker and attorney.

10.6.1 Access to CPS Records

Agency case records of children and adults are only releasable to certain parties and not to the general public. Whether CPS records are released depends upon the requestor's relationship to a case. The requestor may or may not be entitled to the information sought.

CPS records are confidential under Section 261.201(a) of the Texas Family Code. Most records will not be released unless there is a court order to release the records. Those entitled to a copy of CPS records without a court order include:

- The parent or other legally responsible adult of the child who is the subject of the case,
- An adult who was, as a child, the subject of the case, including adoptions,
- A person alleged or designated to be the perpetrator in the case, or
- Other individuals identified in the Texas Administrative Code.[193]

Resources
- To request CPS records: http://www.dfps.state.tx.us/policies/Case_Records/default.asp
- Texas Law Help This website is an online resource for free and low-cost civil legal assistance for those who cannot afford legal help. http://texaslawhelp.org/TX/index.cfm
- Women's Law.org: This website provides easy-to-understand legal information and resources to women. http://www.womenslaw.org/index.php

10.7 CHILD SUPPORT AND MODIFICATION

Texas law does not permit an exemption, automatic suspension, or reduction in child support payments for incarcerated persons who are under court order to provide support.

If the offender was under a child support order going in to prison, the support obligation remains the same and child support debt continues to accrue, with interest on the unpaid balance. Child support obligations take priority over all other obligations that the inmate may have.

This section provides some basic information about child support:

- How it is calculated,
- The factors a court may consider when setting or modifying support,
- Medical child support orders, and
- Other matters relating to support of minor children.

10.8 CHILD SUPPORT AND PREVIOUSLY INCARCERATED PARENTS

In Texas, a previously incarcerated parent may have accrued a staggering amount child support debt during the period of incarceration. The order establishing the child support may not have been enforced during incarceration because the incarcerated parent may have lacked the ability to pay. Once released, the expectation is that the individual will secure employment and continue to pay on the current obligation as well as catch up on missed payments that have been accruing statutory interest.

For currently or previously incarcerated parents who owe court-ordered child support, it is important to be aware that

---

[193] 40 Texas Admin. Code. §700.203. DFPS must comply with all statutes and rules pertaining to confidentiality of CPS records. 40 Texas Adm. Code § 700.201- 700.207.

- Child support can be ordered for the first time, or the previous order modified, while the offender is in prison.
- Texas law authorizes withdrawals from an inmate's trust account to pay child support.[194]
- Court-ordered child support payments remain in effect until changed by a subsequent court order.
- Child support and medical support payments are not cancelled or suspended due to incarceration.
- Child support arrearages are not automatically reduced or discounted for ex-offenders, although the court may take into account the fact of incarceration.

Competing financial demands, problems finding employment because of a criminal history, lack of stable housing, and other factors can make it difficult for a person newly released from incarceration to turn his or her attention to the child support debt. Yet ignoring the child support debt and allowing it to accrue can land the person who owes it back in prison. Ignoring the court's order can cause the parent to be held in contempt of court or worse, be prosecuted for criminal nonsupport. That's why regardless of how much is owed it is important to act on the child support matter before the courts take action against the person who owes it.

In setting or adjusting support, the court can take into account factors that may have made it difficult to make the payments as well as any other information that is relevant to the child support issues. Missed payments due to incarceration, unstable income on release, the total number of children the parent must support and whether there are multiple child support orders in place for children in different households - all of these factors can influence the amount the person who owes support might have to pay.

The law also limits the amount child support that can be deducted from a person's disposable earnings, regardless of how much is owed. A person owing thousands of dollars in back child support can often work out payment plan on the arrearages that will be financially adjusted to reflect a parent's lack of resources and meager income. A parent's voluntary contribution of some nominal amount towards back child support not only shows good faith, it may forestall enforcement action for collection of the entire amount.

---

[194] Tex. Gov't. Code §501.014

Table 15: Other State Laws - Child Support and Incarceration

OTHER STATE LAWS - SUSPENSION OR MODIFICATION OF CHILD SUPPORT DURING INCARCERATION	
CONNECTICUT	The court must establish or modify orders for incarcerated or institutionalized noncustodial parents that are based upon their present income in accordance with the state's child support guidelines (2003 Conn. Gen. Acts 258, §2 (2003)).
MICHIGAN	Suspension of child support charges during incarceration is an administrative process. Upon notification of a payer's incarceration the Friend of the Court verifies the payer's minimum sentence is at least one year and submits an order to the court stopping support. Upon the payer's release from incarceration, the Friend of the Court verifies the release date and submits another order to reinstate the child support charges. See, e.g. modification information for Barry County, MI. -
DISTRICT OF COLUMBIA	Criminal court judges are required to inform individuals with a support order who are sentenced to prison for more than 30 days that they may petition for modification or suspension of payments during incarceration. (Official Code, title 23, chapter 1.)
COLORADO	As of 2003, new child support orders and motions for modification in Colorado were set at $ 50 per month where parents' monthly gross income is less than $ 850. Parents who earn more than $ 850 but less than $ 1,850 per month receive a low-income adjustment calculation that will be added to minimum child support amounts of $ 75 for one child and $ 150 for two (14-10-115 C.R.S.).* Note - amounts may have changed.
OREGON	Rebuttable presumption that an incarcerated parent with income of less than $200 per month is unable to pay any support. The state will reduce an order to zero if the parent requests modification and is expected to be in prison for at least six more months. Or. Admin. R. 461-200-3300 (2002). By statute, 60 days after the inmate is released, the order automatically reverts to its pre-incarceration level Or. Rev. Stat. §416.425 (2003)

MASSACHUSETTS	Inmates meet with child support staff at intake, file a modification request, and suspend enforcement. After release, a court hearing reviews order. Massachusetts has the <u>discretionary authority</u> to settle arrears accumulated during periods of unemployment or incarceration: Terms or conditions of settlement might include regular payments of current support, active participation in job search, community service, or a responsible parenthood program.
NORTH CAROLINA	North Carolina allows a child support order to be suspended with no arrears accruing "during any period when the supporting party is incarcerated, is not on work release, and has no resources with which to make the payment" (N.C. Gen. Stat. §50-15.10 (2004)).
CALIFORNIA	Under California law, child support of the incarcerated person is suspended for any period exceeding 90 consecutive days in which the person ordered to pay support is incarcerated, unless the obligor has the means to pay support while incarcerated. The suspension remains in effect until release, then the payment obligation "shall immediately resume in the amount otherwise specified in the child support order." Upon release from incarceration the obligor may petition the court for an adjustment of the arrears pursuant to the suspension of the support obligation. Family Code: 4007.5: Title IV-D cases (IV-D of the Social Security Act, 42 U.S.C. Sec. 651 et seq.)

10.9 DUTY TO SUPPORT

In the legal sense, "child support" refers to court-ordered financial support for the child. The obligation to pay child support carries with it the duty to provide medical support, either through private insurance or by cash payment in addition to child support. The amount of child support and medical support are then added together to arrive at the total current monthly support obligation.

Unless parental rights have been terminated by a court order, parents have a legal duty to support their children. The duty to support exists even if:
- The parents were never married or never lived together
- The father's name does not appear on the birth certificate
- The child does not have the father's last name
- The father has little or no contact with the child

10.9.1 Leaving Texas to Avoid Payment

Moving from the state where the child lives or the order was entered will not stop a court from enforcing a child support order, because an order issued in one state can be enforced in all others. Every state has adopted a law that gives full faith and credit to child support orders from any other state.[195] Texas, like most states,

---
[195] Uniform Interstate Family Support Act (UIFSA), codified under <u>Tex. Fam. Code Ch. 159</u>.

aggressively pursues child support and child support arrearages, even across state lines.

10.9.2 *Payments Continue after Child Reaches Adulthood*

Even after the child subject to the support order reaches adulthood, the back child support debt will remain, and unpaid interest on the balance will continue to accumulate. The obligor is under a continuing obligation to pay down the child support arrearages or be subject to a enforcement proceeding which may include a finding of contempt of court, arrest, jail time and other remedies for enforcement.

10.10 CONSEQUENCES OF FAILURE TO SUPPORT

The consequences attached to ignoring a court order for child support can be dire. Below is a partial list.

- Violating Conditions of Release

Previously incarcerated parents released to mandatory supervision are in danger of violating the conditions of release by failing to maintain child support payments.

- State Jail Felony

Although child support orders are issued by the civil court, failure to pay pursuant to the order can have criminal consequences. In Texas, it is a state jail felony for a person to intentionally or knowingly fail to provide court-ordered child support.[196]

- License Revocation

A continued failure to pay can result in loss of nearly every license issued by the State of Texas, including vocational licenses and driver's licenses.

- Asset Forfeiture

Income tax returns can and often are garnished by the State and applied to the child support deficiency. Bank accounts and other assets may be seized to satisfy the debt. The child support debt also cannot be discharged in bankruptcy.

10.11 CONSERVATORSHIP AND CHILD SUPPORT

Texas law favors the term "conservatorship" over "custody." It is most commonly understood to mean the parent that cares for the child more than half the time. Usually both parents are appointed "joint managing conservators" of the children, which means that parents share in decision making. Nearly all custody orders carry with them the obligation to pay child support. In court orders, the joint managing conservator is typically the parent awarded the "right to determine the child's

---
[196] Texas Penal Code §25.05

primary physical residence" (custody) and the "right to receive periodic payments for support of the child" (child support). The joint managing conservator who pays child support and has the right of "access and possession" (visitation) of the child is the noncustodial parent (NCP).

10.11.1 Orders without "Primary Residence"

Some recent custody orders do not give either parent the right to determine the child's residence, ordering instead that the child reside within a certain geographical area (e.g. Travis and surrounding counties). Even if no custodial parent is appointed, one parent will usually be required to pay support to the other.

10.11.2 Nonparent Custodians

A person who is not the parent of a child, but who has assumed parental responsibilities and duties can be named the "CP" for purposes of custody and child support. For example, a grandmother who has been the primary caregiver of her grandchild for at least six months can become the CP. In this situation, both parents would probably be named as NCP's, and both would have a duty to pay child support to the CP grandmother.

10.12 CALCULATING CHILD SUPPORT

Basic child support is calculated based on the NCP'S net monthly income from any and all sources, including:
- severance pay
- retirement benefits and pensions
- social security benefits other than supplemental security income (SSI), unemployment benefits
- disability and workers' compensation benefits[197]

10.12.1 Child Support Guidelines

Texas has adopted child support guidelines as the legal threshold for calculating support. "Guideline" child support is considered the legal *minimum*. The NCP can always pay more than guideline support, but must have a compelling reason to pay less.

The guidelines are a percentage of net monthly income. For purposes of child support, net income is referred to as "disposable earnings." Only the standard payroll deductions may be taken to calculate disposable earnings: federal income tax, social security and Medicare.[198]

Guideline child support is based on the following percentage of disposable earnings:

---

[197] Tex. Fam. Code §154.062

[198] Tax tables with gross and corresponding net income after standard deductions are available on the Texas Attorney General's office, www.oag.state.tx.us/cs/attorneys.

- 20% for one child
- 25% for two children
- 30% for three children
- 35% for four children
- 40% for five children
- For six or more children, the amount must be at least 40%.

10.12.2 Multiple Family Guidelines

The Family Code's multiple family guidelines can significantly reduce the percentage of child support the NCP must pay. The multiple family guidelines take into account children in other households, including his own, that an NCP may have a duty to support, and reduce the percentage he must pay accordingly.

If the court is not aware of the NCP's duty to support other children, then it cannot apply the guidelines, so it is up to the NCP to inform the court of any additional children. If the multiple family guidelines apply, the NCP has a right to have his child support reduced. For example, typical guideline support for one child is 20% of the NCP's disposable earnings. If the NCP has a duty to support a second child in a different household, his support obligation is 17.50% of his disposable earnings.[199] The Multiple Family Adjusted Guidelines are set forth in table form in Tex. Fam. Code Sec. 154.129.

10.12.3 Maximum Withholding

Texas law provides that cash withholding for child support exceed 50% of disposable earnings.[200] Again, the change is not automatic, so if an NCP suffers a reduction in income and more than 50% is being withheld, he has the legal right to modify the child support withholding so that it does not exceed the 50% limit.

10.12.4 Duration of Support

Generally, the obligation to pay support lasts until the child turns 18 or graduates from high school, whichever is later. Payments can continue after the child turns 18 or graduates if:

- The "adult" child is disabled and in need of continued support
- There is unpaid "back" child support (arrearages)

---

[199] In this scenario, based on a net income of $2000 a month, application of the multiple family guidelines would reduce his monthly support obligation by $50 monthly (from $400 at 20% to $350 at 17.5%).

[200] Tex. Fam. Code §8.106 and §158.009

- The child is now over age 18 and successfully sues for retroactive support.[201]

10.13 MEDICAL SUPPORT

Parents also have a duty to provide medical support for minor children. A court can order the NCP to:
- Add the children to her health insurance plan
- Reimburse the CP for the cost of carrying the children on her health insurance plan.
- Pay the cost of insuring the children through CHIP
- If the children receive Medicaid, pay cash medical support to the CP in addition to child support.

10.13.1   Private Health Insurance

If private health insurance is available to either parent, the court can issue an order to direct the parent's employer to provide health insurance coverage for the employee's child.[202] Most people exiting the prison system following a period of incarceration do not have access to private health insurance. In fact, regardless of offender status, less than 50% of Texans have access to employer-based health insurance. [203]

10.13.2   CHIP and Medicaid

If neither parent has private health insurance, the court can order a parent to enroll the child in either CHIP (Children's Health Insurance Program) or Medicaid. Eligibility for both programs is based on family income. CHIP provides health insurance for families who cannot qualify for Medicaid, but cannot afford other health insurance. Medicaid is an entitlement program created to pay the medical bills of low-income people and increase access to health care.[204] Every state has a Medicaid program, and everyone who is eligible is entitled to services. Since implementation is left to each state, there are variations in the eligibility, benefits, reimbursements and other details of the program among states.

10.13.3   Cash Medical Support

---

[201] Tex. Fam. Code §154.009. The court retains jurisdiction to render an order for retroactive child support in a suit if a petition requesting retroactive child support is filed not later than the fourth anniversary of the date of the child's 18th birthday. **Tex. Fam. Code Sec. 154.131**

[202] Tex. Fam. Code §154.187

[203] In 2007, Texas ranked 50th in the nation, with only 46.7 percent of Texans having employment-based health insurance coverage. Source: Texas Medical Association.

[204] Medicaid is a federal-state matching program established by Congress under Title XIX of the Social Security Act (SSA) of 1965 and administered by the Centers for Medicare and Medicaid Services (CMS) within the U.S. Department of Health and Human Services (HHS).

Unlike child support, cash medical support is calculated based on a percentage of gross monthly income. The percentage of gross income applied to medical support payments is periodically adjusted, but is usually between 5% and 9% of the NCP's gross income.[205]

10.14 RETROACTIVE SUPPORT AND ARREARAGES

10.14.1 Retroactive Support

In addition to basic child support and medical support, a court can order an NCP to pay retroactive support and/or child support arrearages (back child support).
Retroactive child support:
- may be ordered in cases where there is no prior order establishing child support;
- may be ordered in cases where the parent did not provide voluntary support;
- Is not required but left to the judge's discretion;
- can date back to the separation of the child's parents;[206]
- is in addition to and expressed as a separate amount added to current child support
- a *maximum of 4 years'* worth of retroactive support is both reasonable and fair, unless it is in the best interest of the child to order more than four years.

The court may consider factors such as whether the NCP knew the child was his but did not support the child, and whether ordering retroactive support would impose an "undue hardship" on top of the regular support obligation.[207] Retroactive support is expressed in the court's order as a money judgment plus interest, to be paid in installments along with regular child support, until the judgment is paid in full.

10.14.2 Child Support Arrearages

Child support arrearages are also referred to as "back child support" or unpaid child support, represent the amount of support owed that has not been paid. In a typical case, the missed payments are consolidated into a single lump sum, plus interest (usually 6%) and "confirmed" by the court as a money judgment. The NCP is expected to pay some preset amount towards this debt along with the amount ordered for current child and medical support, and sometimes retroactive support. Like retroactive support, it is expressed as a judgment to be paid in installments along with current child support.

Regarding child support arrearages:

---

[205] Tex. Fam. Code §154.181.

[206] Tex. Fam. Code §154.009.

[207] Tex. Fam. Code §154.131(b)

- Statutory interest on child support cannot be waived by either of the parties, by agreement or by the court, or by Domestic Relations.

- Texas law allows for child support arrearages and interest to continue until all amounts are paid in full regardless of the age or marital circumstances of the child(ren).

- Texas law allows income withholding to continue until all arrearages is paid in full, regardless of the age or marital circumstances of the child(ren).

10.15 EMPLOYER WITHHOLDING AND DISBURSEMENT

A court order for child support is usually accompanied by an Order to Withhold Earnings for Child Support (Withholding Order). This is a separate court order to employers ordering them to withhold the amount(s) specified in the order and forward the payments to the Texas State Disbursement Unit (TXSDU) in San Antonio, Texas. The TXSDU will then distribute the child support payment to the CP, usually by direct deposit or debit card. TXSDU maintains an account of all payments. If the NCP is self-employed, child support payments must be made directly to TXSDU.

10.16 SETTING CHILD SUPPORT - ADDITIONAL FACTORS

10.16.1 Resources of CP

Texas law does not require the court to take into account the income or resources of the CP, even if the CP earns much more than the NCP.[208]

10.16.2 Unemployment and Underemployment

If the NCP's income is unknown, or if he or she is able to work but unemployed, guideline child support is usually based on minimum wage (currently $7.25 per hour) for a 40-hour week.[209] As earlier noted, the court is entitled to consider other factors in setting child support or confirming back child support, including a parent's period of incarceration or illness that caused unemployment or underemployment that affected the ability to pay.

Unemployed NCPs owing support can be ordered to participate in state-sponsored work activities and job training.[210] If a NCP does not work up to her earning potential or is *intentionally* underemployed in order to avoid support payments or

---

[208] Tex. Fam. Code §154.069.

[209] Tex. Fam. Code §154.068

[210] Tex. Fam. Code §§157.001; 157.002.

an increase in support, the CP is entitled to base the support on the NCP's earning ability and skills rather than what he or she is currently bringing in as income.[211] The court is also entitled to average the income of the NCP. If the NCP's income changes from month to month or year to year, the court can add the income together and calculate support based on an average monthly income.[212]

10.17 MODIFYING CHILD SUPPORT

Once a child support order is entered, it can only be changed by a subsequent court order. In Texas, the process of changing the order is called a modification. There is no limit on the number of times a child support order can be modified. It is not unusual to have several modifications before a child reaches adulthood, reflecting changes in income and circumstances affecting the child or parents.

The amount of support stated in the child support order, which can include four separate payments of regular child support, cash medical support, arrearages and retroactive support, will continue to accrue until one of the parents or the OAG takes some action to change it. Loss of a job, incarceration, and other life events will not change the order.

10.17.1 Grounds for Modification

Either party to a child support order [213] can modify an existing child support order if it can be shown that:
- It has been three or more years since the order was established or last modified **and** the monthly amount of the child support ordered differs by either 20 percent or $100 from the amount that would be awarded according to child support guidelines, or

- A *material and substantial change in circumstances* has occurred since the child support order was last set.[214]

Examples of a material and substantial change are usually because
- A party's income has either increased or decreased.
- A party is legally responsible for additional child(ren) since the last order.
- The child(ren)'s medical insurance coverage has changed.
- The child(ren)'s living arrangements have changed.

---

[211] Tex. Fam. Code §154.066. For example, if the NCP used to earn $21 an hour as an electrician, but intentionally accepted a lower-paying job to avoid a higher support obligation, the court is authorized to set support based on the higher wage of $21 an hour.

[212] For example, if a self-employed father made $60,000.00 for the two years preceding the divorce and $22,000.00 in the year of divorce, support can be based on his average income for those 3 years (average of $47,333.00 or $3,944.00 monthly).

[213] For purposes of this section, the person ordered to pay support is referred to as the "NCP" (Noncustodial Parent) while the person to whom support is paid is the "CP" (Custodial Parent).

[214] Tex. Fam. Code §156.401 et seq.

10.17.2 Incarceration and Release as Grounds to Modify

Incarceration, and release from incarceration, both qualify as a "material and substantial" change in circumstance that a court can consider in changing the current payments and deciding how much should be paid towards back child support (arrearages).

For instructions on how to request a child support modification from the OAG during incarceration, please refer to

Appendix N: Child Support Information for Incarcerated Parents and Parents Returning to the Community and Inquiry Form

10.18 THE MODIFICATION PROCESS

Generally, a person who wants to modify a Texas child support order has two options: request a "status review" from the OAG or file a lawsuit called a "Petition to Modify in Suit Affecting Parent-Child Relationship" (SAPCR). If the modification is agreed upon by the parties, the papers can be signed without a court hearing. If the modification is contested must be set for hearing before the court.

10.18.1 Continuing Jurisdiction

Once a Texas court enters an order concerning a child, that court becomes the "court of continuing jurisdiction and retains the authority to make subsequent orders concerning the child. If there is already a child support order, the petition to modify it must be filed in the court where the first child support order or decree of divorce was entered.

If the last order was entered as part of an OAG proceeding, or the child is receiving public benefits, the person seeking modification should ask the OAG for a "status review." A change of status review is a form request to the OAG requesting a modification of current support. For a change of status review form, please refer to

Appendix O: OAG Form to Request Child Support Review

The other option is to file a Petition to Modify in Suit Affecting the Parent Child Relationship (SAPCR) in the court of continuing jurisdiction.

10.19 TEXAS ATTORNEY GENERAL (OAG) CASES

The Texas Attorney General – Child Support Division (OAG) is the state agency charged with establishing, enforcing, and reviewing child support orders. The OAG represents the legal interests of the State of Texas, and is not on either "side" of any case.

10.19.1 IV-D Cases

If the CP is receiving public benefits like Medicaid, the right to pursue child support is automatically assigned to the Child Support Division of the Office of the Attorney General.[215] If the CP is not receiving child support, the OAG can step in to enforce the NCP's legal duty to provide it, as well as recoup the part of the cost of public benefits expended on CP. Note that:

- A custodial parent who receives public benefits cannot terminate the OAG's services.

- The OAG can pursue child support against the other parent regardless of the wishes of the custodial parent.

- OAG services are available to anyone who applies, but public assistance cases are given priority.

As with all child support cases, the OAG retains right to enforce unpaid child support until the debt is paid in full, even after NCP's current support obligation ends (usually the child's 18th birthday or graduation from high school, whichever is later).

Below is a comparison modification through the OAG or by filing a petition to modify with the help of an attorney.

Table 16: Options for Child Support Modification

OAG CHILD REVIEW	MODIFICATION
Services are free	Attorney needed unless *pro se* (self-represented)
OAG represents the interests of the State of Texas, not the child or parent	Attorney represents interest of client/parent
Hearing usually in child support (IV-D) court	Hearing usually in district court
If child is on Medicaid, OAG will include cash medical support in addition to child support	Child usually carried on one parent's health insurance and other parent ordered to reimburse cost of coverage for child.
Less flexibility in setting support outside of statutory guidelines	More flexibility in setting non-guideline child support
Will only address child support, not access/possession (visitation) issues	can modify other child-related issues (such as visitation) in addition to child support
Large backlog of cases may delay review for modification	No case backlog, faster path to modification.

---

[215] Tex. Fam. Code §231.104

OAG prioritizes cases where child, parent or both are receiving public benefits	No case priority based on receipt of public benefits

10.19.2 Steps to Modify Child Support (Non-OAG):

If a person does not want to go through the OAG to modify support, or wants to change the terms of access and possession (visitation) he should find an attorney to represent him in the modification proceeding. If attorney services are out of financial reach, he can exercise his Constitutional right of access to the courts by acting as his own attorney (*pro se*). The court process is different in each county, but certain steps must be taken in all non-OAG modification lawsuits.

For a sample Petition to Modify Child Support and Order, please refer to refer to

Appendix P: Sample Petition to Modify and Order (Non- OAG)

10.20 CHILD SUPPORT ENFORCEMENT

There is no predetermined amount of unpaid child support that will trigger a lawsuit to enforce payment. The court can enforce child support regardless of whether the NCP[216] is behind in payments for a month, a year, or a decade. Depending on the frequency of support payments (monthly, bimonthly, weekly or biweekly) a suit to enforce child support can be brought after a single missed payment, usually are not filed until several payments have been missed.

A suit to enforce payment of the unpaid child support can be filed even after the current support obligation ends (usually the child's 18th birthday or graduation from high school, whichever is later).

10.20.1 Sources of Unpaid Support

The following sources can be seized or withheld for unpaid child support:
- Inmate trust account
- Wages and overtime wages
- Income Tax Refunds
- Social Security Payments
- Unemployment Compensation
- Worker's Compensation
- All other sources of income, including overtime wages and self-employment income, (except some types of disability payments)

---

[216] Noncustodial Parent

The court can enforce child support through other means, including filing a lien on property and bank accounts.

10.20.2 License Suspension

Failure to maintain support can result in suspension or revocation of licenses, including:
- Driver's licenses
- Most vocational licenses (check with the TDLR for a specific occupation)
- Professional licenses

10.20.3 Enforcement Hearing

The only issue on the table in a child support enforcement hearing is the NCP's present ability is support. Visitation, parenting skills and other issues are relevant only as they relate to the support of the child. Previously incarcerated people should be up-front about their offender status and inform the court of how this affected their ability to maintain child support payments.

Before the hearing, the person sued for enforcement should gather proof of current income and expenses and have some idea of what to suggest as payment towards current support and arrearages. The court will not expect a person just released from incarceration to come up with the entire balance at the enforcement hearing. The court may reduce the current support obligation or minimize payments on arrearages in order to balance the payment with the parent's life circumstances.

10.20.4 Contempt of Court

A motion for enforcement often carries with it a request to hold the delinquent parent in contempt of court. Contempt is a legal term that means a court order is not being followed. In a child support case, a payer can be held in civil contempt for disobeying a previous order to pay child support. Civil contempt in a child support case carries up to six months of jail time and $500 for each violation, in addition to attorney's fees and court costs. A violation is a missed payment.

Unlike criminal prosecutions, there is no right to counsel in civil matters. Parties must hire lawyers or represent themselves. If a suit to enforce child support alleges contempt of court, the party threatened with contempt may be entitled to a court appointed attorney if:
- The person has little or no income to hire a lawyer, and
- The person will likely be placed in jail as a result of the hearing.

10.20.5 Defenses to Nonpayment

The Family Code recognizes two defenses to nonpayment of child support: when the child lives with the parent owing support and the parent's inability to pay the amount of support ordered. Lack of ability to pay is difficult to prove. The person owing support must prove that he:
- lacked the ability to provide support in the amount ordered;

- had no property that could be sold, mortgaged, or otherwise pledged to raise the funds needed;
- actually attempted to borrow the funds needed but was unsuccessful; AND
- knew of no source at all from which he could have borrowed or obtained the money by ANY legal means.[217]

Partial payments of child support are taken into consideration by the court when considering sanctions for failure to pay support. Payment of some amount towards the child support obligation is always preferable to no payment at all.

It is also a defense to nonpayment if the child has come to live with the parent who is ordered to pay support. This defense is available only if the child is in the payer's possession. If the other parent sent the child to live with someone else other than the payor, this defense cannot be raised.

10.20.6 Criminal Nonsupport

A person can be criminally prosecuted for intentional and knowing failure to pay child support. In a criminal case, including a prosecution for nonpayment of child support, the person being prosecuted is entitled to court-appointed counsel. Criminal nonsupport is a state jail felony.[218] A felony conviction is sufficient to deport someone who is not a citizen of the United States.

---

[217] Tex. Fam. Code §157.008 (c)

[218] Tex. Penal Code §25.05. See the OAG's "Criminal Nonsupport Handbook" for prosecutors.

11 . EDUCATION

Education increases employment opportunities for all people, including those with a criminal record. Federal Student Financial Aid provides the resources that enable those with limited resources to have access to quality higher education. A conviction does not automatically render a person ineligible for federal aid. A person who, because of her criminal history is rendered in eligible for federal student aid may still qualify for federal aid from some states and private institutions. Federal Student Aid consists of:
- Stafford Loans
- Graduate PLUS Loans
- Consolidation Loans
- Federal Supplemental Educational Opportunity Grants (FSEOGs)
- Federal Work-Study
- Federal Perkins Loans
- Pell Grants

11.1 ELIGIBILITY FOR TEXAS FINANCIAL AID

Basic federal education grants are not available to those who are incarcerated in federal or state prisons and to those convicted of certain drug-related offenses. Aside from these limited exceptions there is no lifelong ban on the receipt of federal financial aid because of a person's criminal history.[219] States are free to place limitations on state-based student aid that are more restrictive than the federal law.

11.1.1 Drug Related Offenses

Students who have been convicted of "any offense under any Federal or State law involving the possession or sale of a controlled substance" can become temporarily or permanently ineligible for federal loans or grants.[220] The table below shows ineligibility periods for drug offenses:

Table 17: Length of Ineligibility for Federal Financial Aid - Drug Convictions

	Drug Possession	Drug Sales
First offense	One year	Two years
Second offense	Two years	Indefinite
Third offense	Indefinite	Indefinite

---

[219] Violent Crime Control and Law Enforcement Act of 1994, Pub.L.No. 103-322, 20411, 108 Stat. 1796 (1994).

[220] Drug Free Student Loans Act of 1998, 20 USC 1091(r), 2002.

Exceptions to the above provisions can change a student's eligibility status despite a conviction for drug possession or sale:
- Convictions that have been dismissed or expunged, and juvenile court delinquency findings, do not disqualify a candidate[221]

- The disqualification ends if the conviction is reversed.

- A student whose eligibility has been suspended may resume eligibility before the end of the eligibility period if the student successfully completes a drug rehabilitation program that is approved by the Secretary of Education and includes at least two unannounced drug tests.

11.1.2   Conviction after Scholarship

State education funding can also be lost as a result of a criminal conviction that occurs after the student has been qualified for a higher education scholarship. A person who commits a felony or Class A misdemeanor, or an offense under the Texas Controlled Substances Act, forfeits a prepaid higher education scholarship.[222] The offenses that will result in forfeiture of a scholarship include:
- offenses of possession of marijuana,
- possession or delivery of drug paraphernalia, and
- falsification of drug test results.

11.1.3   Eligibility for Texas Grants

The eligibility for Texas grants mirrors the drug-related offense exclusions under federal law. A person is not eligible to receive a TEXAS grant or TEXAS II grant for two years after completing a sentence for a felony or an offense under Chapter 481 of the Health and Safety Code, per Tex. Educ. Code §§ 56.304 and 56.354. Moreover, Education Code §§ 56.305 and 56.355 render one ineligible to continue to receive a TEXAS grant or a TEXAS II grant if already receiving one when convicted. This apparently would include Class B and C misdemeanors under the Texas Controlled Substance Act.

11.1.4   Zero Tolerance Policies

Many schools have adopted "zero tolerance" policies that cover any type of criminal offense, not just those that occur on campus or at sponsored activities. Any criminal conviction or deferred adjudication could be grounds for disciplinary action or loss of school benefits depending on school policy. Most universities have

---

[221] 20 USC §1091(r)(2)(B).

[222] Tex. Educ. Code §54.633.

disciplinary codes that allow for denial of degrees and expulsion for violations of criminal statutes.[223]

11.2 NONPROFIT COMMUNITY COLLEGES

Nonprofit Community colleges are a good place to start exploring and training for a new trade or profession. Most have open admissions policies, local campuses, and tuition far lower than that of for-profit schools.

11.3 PROPRIETARY/FOR-PROFIT COLLEGES AND UNIVERSITIES

At the time of writing, Proprietary or for-profit colleges and universities continue to come under greater and great scrutiny. The Department of Education no longer recognizes the Accrediting Council for Independent Colleges and Schools, the largest accreditor of for-profit colleges. Many of the mainstays of the for-profit college industry have shuttered their doors leaving 10's of thousands of students in limbo with large amounts of debt.

Formerly incarcerated people have several options for higher education: colleges, universities, community colleges and proprietary (for profit) schools. A senate investigation on released in June 2012 ("For Profit College Investigation") revealed that many for-profit college companies use misleading tactics to lure students into certificate and associate degree programs that cost, on average, *six times* the cost of similar programs in community colleges. Among the 30 colleges identified in the study were the University of Phoenix, DeVry, ITT (now defunct), Bridgepoint, Apollo, and National American University.[224] The study also showed that

- Many used aggressive recruiting tactics, and recruiters often hide the ball on matters of cost, transferability of credits, graduation rates, and employment and salary after graduation.
- Fifty-four percent of students who enrolled in the 2008-2009 school year withdrew by summer 2010.
- Close to one in four students who attends a for-profit school defaults on his or her federal student loans within 3 years of leaving school. These schools reenroll 10 percent of American higher education students but account for nearly 50% of all student loan defaults.
- Colleges claimed that their schools were accredited when they were not. Accreditation can affect whether the graduate can apply for a vocational license in their chosen profession.

---

[223] See, *Institutional Rules on Student Services and Activities*, Chapter II, Student Discipline and Conduct, University of Texas (2008-09)

[224] Earlier studies reached similar conclusions. See "Piling it On: The Growth of Proprietary School Loans And the Consequences for Students" National Consumer Law Center January 2011

Before enrolling in a proprietary school or applying for financial aid, prospective students should do their homework:

- Research the school's accreditation with the Texas Higher Education Coordinating Board.
- Contact the state licensing office for that vocation, or Texas Department of Licensing and Regulation, to find out if the training or diploma will be accepted by the licensing board for that particular profession.
- Find out if credits can be transferred from the college to another college or university
- Get a clear picture on how much tuition and fees will be over the course of the entire degree program, how much of tuition must be borrowed, the interest rate and how long it will take to pay off the loan(s).
- Know in advance if the course have actual classrooms and campus or will be taught through distance learning. If taught online, see if the classes will be taught in real time and are interactive (allowing the student to communicate with the instructor).

Resources

College Grants - The Texas Higher Education Coordinating Board helps students find financial aid, http://www.thecb.state.tx.us/

12 . VOTING AND SELECTIVE SERVICE

Civic participation includes all the ways citizens participate in the democratic process. It includes the right to vote, serve on a jury, and run for elected office. This section addresses eligibility to vote, registration requirements, selective service and jury duty.

12.1 VOTING

The laws governing voting rights of incarcerated and formerly incarcerated persons vary widely from state to state.[225] Previously, felony convictions in Texas resulted in lifetime prohibition against voting. Today, an otherwise qualified voter who has been finally convicted of a felony may vote if he has completely discharged his sentence, including incarceration, parole or probation, or been pardoned. When these requirements have been met, a formerly incarcerated person is once again eligible to vote and may register with the voter registrar in the county of residence.

Texas Voter Identification Law

As of this writing, Texans are required to produce one of seven approved forms of identification at the polls and if they cannot reasonably obtain one, they are allowed additional options at the polls. The Acceptable forms of photo ID are as follows: [226]

- Texas driver license issued by the Texas Department of Public Safety (DPS)
- Texas Election Identification Certificate issued by DPS
- Texas personal identification card issued by DPS
- Texas license to carry a handgun issued by DPS
- United States military identification card containing the person's photograph
- United States citizenship certificate containing the person's photograph
- United States passport

If the voter does not possess one of the foregoing acceptable forms photo ID and cannot obtain one due to a reasonable impediment, the following are supporting documents that can be presented, and along with execution of a Reasonable Impediment Declaration, cast a ballot:

---

[225] Prisoners of the Census: The census counts incarcerated people as "residents" of the prison location, despite the fact that they cannot vote while serving time and often know nothing about the surrounding community. Some argue that that this distorts the population-based voting districts by giving voters who live in a community with a correctional facility more influence in government than other citizens The Texas Election Code specifically excludes prisons from the definition of a "residence" Tex. Elec. Code § 1.015(e)

[226] The United States District Court for the District of Columbia, Pursuant to section 5 of the Voting Rights Act of 1965, Texas was required to show that Senate Bill 14 (SB 14) "neither has the purpose nor will have the effect of denying or abridging the right to vote on account of race[,] color," or "member[ship] [in] a language minority group." 52 U.S.C. §§ 10304(a), 10303(f)(2). State of Texas v. Holder, US Dist. Court - DC Cir., civil action no. 12-cv-128, August 30, 2012.

- Valid voter registration certificate
- Certified birth certificate (must be an original)
- Copy of or original current utility bill
- Copy of or original bank statement
- Copy of or original government check
- Copy of or original paycheck
- Copy of or original government document with your name and an address (original required if it contains a photograph)

12.1.1 *Eligibility to Register to Vote*

To be eligible to register to vote in Texas, a person must be:
- At least 18 years old on Election Day;
- A United States citizen;
- A resident of the Texas county where the voter applied for registration;
- Not determined by a final judgment of a court exercising probate jurisdiction to be (1) totally mentally incapacitated; or (2) partially mentally incapacitated without the right to vote; and
- Not finally convicted of a felony, or, if so convicted must have
  - (1) fully discharged the sentence, including any term of incarceration, parole, or supervision, or completed a period of probation ordered by any court; or
  - (2) been pardoned or otherwise released from the resulting disability to vote.[227]
-

12.1.2 *Voting Rights and Deferred Adjudication*

Texas law recently clarified the law as it relates to the voting eligibility of people who have who have received deferred adjudication. The Texas Election Code described a qualified voter as a person who had not been finally convicted of a felony. <u>A deferred adjudication is not a final conviction for purposes of voting eligibility.</u>[228]

12.1.3 *Voter Registration*

In most Texas counties, the County Tax Assessor-Collector is also the County Voter Registrar. In some counties, the County Clerk or County Elections Administrator registers voters. A person can also register to vote when applying for or renewing a Texas driver's license. Once the form is completed it can be mailed postage-free to the County Voter Registrar, or hand-delivered.
For a voter registration application, please refer to:

---

[227] Tex. Elec. Code §11.002, 13.001(5).

[228] Tex. Elec. Code §§11.002; 13.001

Appendix Q: Application for Voter Registration

12.1.4   *Deadline for Application*

The application must be received in the County Voter Registrar's office or postmarked 30 days before an election in order to vote in that election. The voter registration certificate will arrive by mail for the voter to take to the polls when voting.

12.1.5   *Identification Required to Register to Vote*

As of this writing, photo identification is required to register to vote.
Here is a list of the acceptable forms of photo ID:
- Texas driver license issued by the Texas Department of Public Safety (DPS)
- Texas Election Identification Certificate issued by DPS
- Texas personal identification card issued by DPS
- Texas license to carry a handgun issued by DPS
- United States military identification card containing the person's photograph
- United States citizenship certificate containing the person's photograph
- United States passport

With the exception of the U.S. citizenship certificate, the identification must be current or have expired no more than 4 years before being presented for voter qualification at the polling place.

Here is a list of the supporting forms of ID that can be presented if the voter does not possess one of the forms of acceptable photo ID and cannot obtain one due to a reasonable impediment:
- Valid voter registration certificate
- Certified birth certificate (must be an original)
- Copy of or original current utility bill
- Copy of or original bank statement
- Copy of or original government check
- Copy of or original paycheck
- Copy of or original government document with your name and an address (original required if it contains a photograph)

After presenting a supporting form of ID, the voter must execute a Reasonable Impediment Declaration.[229]

12.1.6   *Voter Registration Certificate*

---

[229] From the Vote Texas website: https://www.votetexas.gov/register-to-vote/ Additional Exceptions for those with Disabilities or religious exemptions from photo identification.

- After applying, a voter registration certificate (proof of registration) will be mailed within 30 days.
- The voter should correct any mistakes on the registration by making corrections to the registration certificate and returning it to the voter registrar immediately.
- If the voter certificate is lost, contact the county voter registrar in writing for a new one.
- The voter will automatically receive a new certificate every two years by mail to the address listed on the previous registration.

12.1.7   Change of Address

If the voter moves within the same county where she is registered to vote, she can:

- change the address online
- complete a new voter registration application form and checking the "change" box
- change the address for voter registration and driver's license at the same time at the driver's license office.

A new certificate with the new address will be mailed to the voter.

12.1.8   Where to Vote

A voter's residence is located in a specific "precinct," which is an area within the county. Polling places are usually listed in local newspapers before an election and are also available online on the website for each county. A voter who moves to another county must re-register by filling out a new application for voter registration. The voter will be registered in the new county 30 days after the application is submitted, and will receive a new voter certificate.

12.2   SELECTIVE SERVICE REGISTRATION

The Selective Service system is how the United States maintains information for a military draft. Almost all males between the ages of 18 and 25 are required by law to register. Incarcerated or hospitalized men must register *within thirty days after their release*.

12.2.1   Consequences for Failure to Register

A young man who fails to register with Selective Service may be ineligible for opportunities that may be important to his future. He must register to be eligible for federal student financial aid, state-funded student financial aid in many states, most federal employment, some state employment, security clearance for contractors, job training under the Workforce Innovation and Opportunity Act (formerly known as the Workforce Investment Act), and U.S. citizenship for immigrant men.[230]

12.2.2 Fines and Penalties

Failure to register carries with it a fine of up to $250,000 and/or up to five years' imprisonment for failure to register. During peacetime, the regular maximum penalty is a $2,500 fine and up to four months imprisonment. Immigrant men are not eligible for citizenship without registering.

12.2.3 Government Programs and Education

Registration for Selective Service is linked to federal programs and benefits, including:
- federal student loans and grant programs
- federal job training under the Workforce Investment Act
- federal jobs or security clearance as a contractor
- U.S. citizenship

12.2.4 Registration Methods

Registration for the selective service may be accomplished:
- Online with the registrant's social security number at www.sss.gov,
- On the application for Federal Student Financial Aid (FAFSA),
- In person when renewing or applying for a driver license or Texas identification card,
- By completing a "mail-back" registration form available at any U.S. Post Office.

12.3 STATUS INFORMATION LETTER

12.3.1 First-Time Registration if Over 25

Males over 26 years old who never registered for Selective Service between the ages 18-25 are not eligible to receive financial aid and other benefits tied to selective service registration unless they can show special circumstances as to why the failed to register during the age window. Incarceration can be a "special circumstance." If failure to register was due to incarceration or for some other reason, the applicant must complete and return a "Request for Status Information Letter." Because the previously incarcerated person is expected to register within thirty days after release, proof of incarceration dates alone may not be sufficient; the individual should consider including reasons why he missed the 30-day post-incarceration window. A Request for Status Information Letter form and instructions, is available at

---

[230] https://www.sss.gov/Registration/Why-Register/Benefits-and-Penalties

Appendix R: Request for Status Information Letter

12.3.2   Status Information Letter Not Required

A status information letter is not required for men who are in the categories in the table below:

Table 18: Documents in Lieu of Status Information Letter - Categories

No Status Information Letter Required	Documents Required in lieu of Status Information
A male born prior to 1960	Official government issued document showing date of birth such as state ID card, driver's license, passport, birth certificate.
A Veteran	DD-214 or current full-time active duty orders, military ID card.[231]
Non-U.S. Male arriving in US for the first time after his 26th birthday	Date of entry stamp in his passport, I-94 with date of entry stamp on it, or a letter from the U.S. Citizenship and Immigration Services (USCIS) indicating the date the man entered the United States. If the men entered the U.S. illegally after his 26th birthday, he must provide proof that he was not living in the U.S. from age 18 through 25. Resident Alien Card (Green Card) is not valid as proof of the date of entry to the United States.
Non-U.S. Male on a valid non-immigrant visa	For example, if the man entered the United States as an F-1 student visa and remained in that status until his 26th birthday, he would need to provide documentation indicating that he was admitted on an F-1 visa and attended school full-time as required. Acceptable documentation for this situation include a copy of his I-20 form or a letter from the school he attended indicating his full-time attendance as a non-immigrant alien. The same thing applies for all non-immigrant statuses.

12.4   JURY SERVICE

A person is *absolutely disqualified* from serving on a Texas jury or grand jury if they have been convicted of misdemeanor theft or a felony; or are under indictment or other legal accusation for misdemeanor theft or a felony.[232] A prospective juror may

---

[231] From the Selective Service website, https://www.sss.gov/Registration/Status-Information-Letter

[232] Tex. Gov't Code §§62.102(8),(9); Tex. Code Crim. Proc. art. 19.08(7), (8).

be challenged "for cause" (may be excluded as a juror at trial by either party) if convicted of "theft or any felony," or under indictment or other legal accusation for misdemeanor theft or a felony.[233]

A person is *not* disqualified as a result of a misdemeanor theft charge or a felony if:
1. the person has successfully completed a deferred adjudication,
2. the person has completed a term of probation and the conviction has been dismissed under Tex. Code Crim. Proc. Ann. art. 42.12, § 20

If the person is *currently serving* a term of deferred adjudication supervision for a felony or misdemeanor theft, they are disqualified because they are still under the legal accusation.

Resources
Registering to Vote:
Texas Secretary of State:
http://www.sos.state.tx.us/elections/voter/reqvr.shtml.
http://www.sos.state.tx.us/elections/voter/votregduties.shtml

---

[233] Tex. Code Crim. Proc. Art. 35.16(a)(2), (a)(3).

13. COLLATERAL CONSEQUENCES OF CONVICTION

Collateral consequences are the legal disabilities that attach as an operation of law when an individual is convicted of a crime, but are not part of the sentence for the crime. Examples include denial of government issued licenses and ineligibility for public services and public programs. Sentencing judges and lawyers may not be aware of the collateral consequences that can hamper efforts towards effective and successful reentry.

Collateral consequences attached to criminal convictions vary widely by state. The table below is a partial listing of collateral consequences of conviction under Texas and federal law:

Table 19: Collateral Consequences of Conviction

	OFFENSE(S)	CONSEQUENCE	SOURCES
VETERANS	Espionage, treason, mutiny, sabotage, rendering assistance to an enemy	Lifetime ineligibility for all benefits	38 USC 6105(a),(b)
	Felonies & misdemeanors	Military Pension – No pension paid after first 60 days incarceration; suspended during incarceration Pension paid to inmate's spouse/ children, if any.	38 USC. 1505(a); 38 USC. 1505(b)
HOUSING	Sex Offender subject to lifetime registration	Federally assisted housing- Ineligible	42 USC 13663
	Any offense - violation of probation or parole.	Federally funded public housing- Eviction	42 USC 1437f(d)(1)(B)(v)(II);

		Lifetime Ineligibility

Subject to eviction for suspicion of drug related or criminal activity - no conviction | 42 USC 1437d(k). |
| **FOOD STAMPS** | Drug offenses (after Aug. 22, 1996) | Supplemental Nutrition - Lifetime Ineligibility

Benefit received by household with ex-offender proportionally reduced. | 21 USC 862a(a).(b),(d)(2) |
| **TANF** | Drug offenses (after Aug. 22, 1996) | Supplemental Income- Lifetime Ineligibility

Benefit received by household with ex-offender proportionally reduced. | 21 USC 862a (a),(b),(d)(2) |
| **VOTE** | Any felony conviction | Constitutionally Ineligible Until fully discharged or pardoned

Subject to any exception the Texas legislature may make. | Tex. Constit. Art. 6 §1;

Tex. Elec. Code Art 11.002 |
| **NAME CHANGE** | Any felony conviction | Not eligible if on parole or under supervision. Fingerprint card and criminal history must accompany Petition; may be denied if not in public interest; effective Sept 1, 2019, may change | Tex. Fam. Code §§ 45.102; 45.103 |

		name to be consistent with criminal records	
VOCATIONAL LICENSE	Felony or misdemeanor directly relating to the duties of the licensed occupation.	Suspend, revoke, or deny licensure; Depends on license and action taken. Applies to a wide variety of licensed occupations	Tex. Occupations Code
DRIVING PRIVILEGES	Intoxication manslaughter Tex. Penal Code §49.08	Automatic one-year suspension.	Tex. Transp. Code §521.341
	DWI with a child passenger	Automatic one year suspension	Tex. Penal Code §49.045 Tex. Transp. Code §521.341
	Drug offenses under the Texas Controlled Substance Act	Automatic 180 days minimum suspension, must complete drug education program before suspension lifted. Offenders under 21 - suspension from 180 days up to 1 year	Tex. Trans. Code §§ 521.372, 521.342
	Intoxication assault	Automatic one-year suspension.	Tex. Penal Code §49.07 Tex. Transp. Code §521.341
	Criminally negligent homicide (with a motor vehicle, and any state jail felony with a motor vehicle offense involving	Automatic one-year suspension.	Tex. Penal Code § 19.05; Tex. Transp. Code § 521.341

	personal injury or death)		
	Graffiti	Discretionary one year suspension for conviction or probation	Tex. Penal Code § 28.08 Tex. Transp. Code § 521.320
	Racing	Mandatory one-year suspension. If under 18 must perform 10 hours of community supervision and can have an occupational license only for attendance to school.	Tex. Transp. Code §§ 545.420(a); Tex. Transp. Code § 521.350
	Acquiring motor fuel without payment- theft	Coupled with an affirmative finding pursuant to Art. 42.019 Tex Code Crim. Proc.- automatic 180 suspension first offense, 1 year for second offense.	Tex. Penal Code § 31.03 Tex Code Crim. P. Art. 42.019 Tex. Transp. Code § 521.349
	Furnishing alcohol to a minor	Automatic 180 day suspension first offense, 1 year second offense.	Alcohol Beverage Code §106.06, Tex. Transp. Code §521.351
	o Possession of fake driver's license o Allowing another to use one's driver's license o Possessing more than one driver's license o Falsifying information on driver's license application	Mandatory but duration determined by the court, suspension for not less than 90 days nor more than 1 year.	Tex. Transp. Code §§521.451; 521.453; §521.346

	o Use of a driver's license to represent one is over 21 when they are not		
	o Fake license plate or Safety inspection certificate,)	Automatic 180 day suspension.	Tex. Transp. Code §§502.475(a)(4); 548.603(a)(1);521.3466
	Evading arrest or detention Tex. Penal Code § 38.04,	Automatic one-year suspension.	Tex. Transp. Code § 521.341
	Tampering with a government record- motor vehicle registration or license plate	Automatic two-year suspension.	Tex. Penal Code §37.10 Tex. Transp. Code §521.3466
	DWI (minor under 21) §49.04 Tex. Penal Code	Automatic 1-year suspension - 90 day to one year suspension if set by the court. Note: DPS automatically suspends for one year, unless vehicle equipped with an ignition interlock device.	Tex. Code Crim. P. art. 42.12 §13(n)(1) Tex. Transp. Code §§521.342 521.344.
	Purchase or attempt to purchase, possession or consumption of alcohol by a minor	Automatic 30 days suspension first offense unless deferred, 60 days for the second offense, and 180 days for third and subsequent offenses. Prior order of deferred disposition is considered a	Tex. Alco. Bev. Code §106.071; §106.071(f)(2)

		conviction for enhancement purposes	
	Multiple traffic violations,	90-day suspension	Tex. Trans. Code §521.292; 37 Tex. Admin. Code §15.82
	Offenses involving commercial driver's license	Suspension	Tex. Transp. Code §522.081; 37 Tex. Admin. Code §15.82
	Certain Sex Offenses	If required to register per Ch. 62 Tex. Code Crim. Proc. and fail to apply for a renewal per Tex. Code Crim. Proc. Art. 62.060, license revoked until driver comes into compliance.	Tex. Trans. Code §521.348
DRIVER SURCHARGES	1st Driving While Intoxicated (DWI) Offense BAC under .15	$3,000 with 36 months of Sentencing	Ch. 708 Tex. Transp. Code.
	Subsequent DWI BAC Under .15		Ch. 708 Tex. Transp. Code.
	DWI with blood alcohol concentration of 0.16 or more Texas or out-of state conviction	$6,000 within 36 Months of Sentencing	Ch. 708 Tex. Transp. Code.

EDUCATION	Students convicted of "any offense under any Federal or State law involving the possession or sale of a controlled substance"	May be temporarily or permanently ineligible for federal loans or grants for one year from first possession offense to indefinite period for a third possession, or second sale, offense. Convictions reversed or rendered useless, successful completion of a drug rehabilitation program, or passing two unannounced drug tests may resume eligibility before the end of the ineligibility period. Findings do not disqualify a candidate	Drug Free Student Loans Act of 1998, 20 USC 1091(r), 2002; 20 USC 1091(r)(2)(B).
	Felony or Class A misdemeanor drug offense.	Includes possession of marijuana, possession or delivery of drug paraphernalia,	Ch. 481 Texas Health & Safety Code (Texas Controlled Substances Act)

	Includes Class B and C

Misdemeanors under Texas Controlled Substance Act if receiving grant when convicted. | falsification of drug test results.

Texas education funding forfeited - prepaid higher education

scholarship. Ineligible to apply or continue to receive TEXAS grant or TEXAS II grant for two years after completing a sentence for a felony or an offense under Chapter 481. | Texas Edu. Code §§54.633

56.304, 56.354.

If convicted when receiving - §§ 56.305 and 56.355 |
| **FIREARMS** | All felony convictions | Texas: Prohibits a convicted felon from possessing a firearm unless discharged from probation with order setting aside conviction

With "early discharge order" pursuant to art. 42.12 §20 not subject to restrictions of §46.04(a) Tex. Penal Code – felon in

Possession offense.

Conviction affects ability to obtain a concealed handgun license.

Can possess gun at residence after 5 years from release from confinement or community supervision, parole or mandatory | § 46.04 Tex. Penal Code;

Art. 42.12 § 20, Tex. Code Crim. Proc.

Tex.Gov. Code § 411.172 et seq.

Tex. Penal Code 46.04

18 USC 922(g) and (n). |

		supervision, whichever is later. Federal: Bans possession, shipping, receiving, or transporting firearm or ammunition by person convicted of offense with a maximum punishment of more than one year in prison.	
	Misdemeanor Assault with Family Violence	Texas: Class A misdemeanor conviction for misdemeanor family violence assault - illegal to possess firearm before the fifth anniversary of the later of: (1) the release from confinement or (2) the date of discharge from probation. Federal: Misdemeanor conviction of domestic violence - prohibited from possessing, shipping, receiving, or transporting a firearm.	22.01 Tex. Penal Code 18 USC 922(g)(9).
FEDERAL OFFICE / EMPLOYMENT	All Felony convictions	Various federal statutes provide that a conviction may result in the loss of or ineligibility for office. For example, conviction of treason renders the defendant incapable of holding any office	18 U.S.C. ' 2381.

		under the United States.	
	extortion, bribery, conspiracy to defraud the United States, making false entries...	dismissal from office or discharge from employment of any officer or employee of the United States acting in connection with any federal revenue law who is guilty of extortion, bribery, conspiracy to defraud the United States, making false entries, or another enumerated offense; fined up to $10,000; and imprisoned for up to 5 years	(26 U.S.C. ' 7214(a)).
ARMED FORCES	Any felony	An individual convicted of a felony is ineligible to enlist in any service of the armed forces. (Unless an exception is made by the Secretary)	10 U.S.C. ' 504.
LABOR ORGANIZATION	robbery, bribery, extortion, embezzlement, grand larceny, burglary, arson, drug violations, murder, assault with intent to kill, rape, and certain offenses relating to a labor organization or employee benefit plan	disqualifies an individual from serving in any of a wide range of capacities relating to a labor organization or an employee benefits plan, including consultant, adviser, officer, director, trustee, business agent, manager, or member of the labor organization=s governing board for 13 years after conviction or until the end of such	29 U.S.C. " 504, 1111

		imprisonment, whichever is later, unless the sentencing court sets a shorter period of no less than three years.	
IMMIGRATION	Crime involving moral turpitude	An undocumented immigrant is ineligible for admission to the United States if he or she has been convicted of (or admits committing) a crime involving moral turpitude (unless the immigrant was younger than 18 when the crime was committed, he committed only one crime, the penalty for which was less than one year's imprisonment and a sentence of six months or less was imposed, and the crime was committed (and the immigrant was released from confinement) more than five years before applying for admission) or multiple offenses for which the aggregate sentences to confinement were five years or more.	8 U.S.C. " 1182(a)(2)(A), (B).
FAMILY	Felony conviction, or/and served one year or more in prison	In addition to no-fault grounds, the court may not grant a divorce in favor of the spouse without the felony conviction	Tex. Fam. Code §6.004

| | | if the convicted spouse was convicted on the testimony of the other spouse. | |

13.1.1 Uniform Collateral Consequences Act

The Uniform Collateral Consequences Act (UCCA) is a proposal of the Uniform Law Commission to encourage States to provide some uniformity and information among the states that would allow previously incarcerated people to gain partial relief from these consequences.

The UCCA was completed by the Uniform Law Commission in 2009 and amended in 2010. The American Bar Association approved the Act in 2010.[234] At this writing, the Act has been adopted by a single state (Vermont), and is under legislative consideration in Minnesota, Nevada, New Mexico and New York. The following is a summary of the key provisions of the key provisions of the UCCA as stated by the Uniform Law Commission are as follows:

Table 20: Uniform Collateral Consequences Act - Key Provisions

UNIFORM COLLATERAL CONSEQUENCES ACT	
Collection	All collateral consequences contained in state laws and regulations, and provisions for avoiding or mitigating them, must be collected in a single document. The compilation must include both collateral sanctions (automatic bars) and disqualifications (discretionary penalties). In fulfilling their obligations under the Uniform Act, jurisdictions will be assisted by the federally-financed effort to compile collateral consequences for each jurisdiction that was authorized by the Court Security Act of 2007.
Notification	Defendants must be notified about collateral consequences at important points in a criminal case: At or before formal notification of charges, so a defendant can make an informed decision about how to proceed; and at sentencing and when leaving custody, so that a defendant can comport his or her conduct to the law. Given that collateral consequences will have been collected in a single document, it will not be difficult to make this information available. The 2010 Supreme Court decision in *Padilla v. Kentucky* has significantly raised the profile of the

---

[234] American Bar Association approval letter, http://www.uniformlaws.org/Shared/Docs/ABA Approval 5-11-2010.pdf

	problem of collateral consequences. Section 5 of the Act instructs trial courts to confirm that the defendant has received and understood notice of collateral consequences and has had an opportunity to discuss them with defense counsel.
	The UCCA facilitates notification of collateral consequences before, during, and after sentencing and aids courts and lawyers in providing the defendant with a constitutionally adequate defense.
Authorization	Collateral sanctions may not be imposed by ordinance, policy or rule, but must be authorized by statute. An ambiguous law will be considered as authorizing only discretionary case-by-case disqualification.
Standards for Disqualification	A decision-maker retains the ability to disqualify a person based on a criminal conviction, but only if it is determined, based on an individual assessment, that the essential elements of the person's crime, or the particular facts and circumstances involved, are substantially related to the benefit or opportunity at issue.
Overturned and Pardoned Convictions; Relief Granted by Other Jurisdictions	Convictions that have been overturned or pardoned, including convictions from other jurisdictions, may not be the basis for imposing collateral consequences. Charges dismissed pursuant to deferred prosecution or diversion programs will not be considered a conviction for purposes of imposing collateral consequences. The Act gives jurisdictions a choice about whether to give effect to other types of relief granted by other jurisdictions based on rehabilitation or good behavior, such as expunction or set-aside.
Relief from Collateral Consequences	The Act creates two different forms of relief, one to be available as early as sentencing to facilitate reentry (Order of Limited Relief) and the other after a period of law-abiding conduct (Certificate of Restoration of Rights).
	• An Order of Limited Relief permits a court or agency to lift the automatic bar of a collateral sanction, leaving a licensing agency or public housing authority, for example, free to consider whether to disqualify a particular individual on the merits.
	• A Certificate of Restoration of Rights offers potential public and private employers, landlords and licensing agencies concrete and objective information about an

	individual under consideration for an opportunity or benefit, and a degree of assurance about that individual's progress toward rehabilitation, and will thereby facilitate the reintegration of individuals whose behavior demonstrates that they are making efforts to conform their conduct to the law.

14. TABLE OF APPENDICES

Appendix A: Steps to Obtain a Texas Driver's License or Identity Card 178

Appendix B: Steps to Obtain Certified Copy of Texas Birth Certificate 183

Appendix C: Steps to Apply for or Replace Social Security Card 186

Appendix D: Sample Petition & Order - Name Change of Adult 188

Appendix E: Sample Declaratory Judgment for Name - Petition and Order ... 193

Appendix F: Petition and Order for Occupational Driver's License 198

Appendix G: Motion and Order to Waive Surcharge 208

Appendix H: Motion and Order to Waive Fines and Fees 214

Appendix I: Steps to Order Criminal History Records 218

Appendix J: Instructions, Petition, Verification and Order for Expunction of Criminal Records 220

Appendix K-1: Office of Court Administration – An Overview of Orders of Nondisclosure 231

Appendix K-2: Instructions and Letter Requesting an Order of Nondisclosure under Section 411.072, Government Code and Order 250

Appendix K-3: Instructions and Petition and Order of Nondisclosure under Section 411.0725, Government Code 260

Appendix K-4: Instructions and Petition and Order of Nondisclosure under Section 411.0727, Government Code 273

Appendix K-5: Instructions and Petition and Order of Nondisclosure under Section 411.0728, Government Code 286

Appendix K-6: Instructions and Petition and Order of Nondisclosure under Section 411.073, Government Code 298

Appendix K-7: Instructions and Petition and Order of Nondisclosure under Section 411.0731, Government Code 311

Appendix K-8: Instructions and Petition and Order of Nondisclosure under Section 411.0735, Government Code 325

Appendix K-9: Instructions and Petition and Order of Nondisclosure under Section 411.0736, Government Code 339

Appendix L - Texas Sex Offenses Tiered under Federal Law 353

Appendix M: Authorization Agreement for Non Parent Relative 358

Appendix N: Child Support Information for Incarcerated Parents and Parents Returning to the Community and Inquiry Form 360

Appendix O: OAG Form to Request Child Support Review..........................371

Appendix P: Sample Petition to Modify and Order (Non- OAG) 375

Appendix Q: Application for Voter Registration...380

Appendix R: Request for Status Information Letter...................................382

14. TABLE OF APPENDICES

Appendix A: Steps to Obtain a Texas Driver's License or Identity Card 178

Appendix B: Steps to Obtain Certified Copy of Texas Birth Certificate 183

Appendix C: Steps to Apply for or Replace Social Security Card 186

Appendix D: Sample Petition & Order - Name Change of Adult 188

Appendix E: Sample Declaratory Judgment for Name - Petition and Order ... 193

Appendix F: Petition and Order for Occupational Driver's License 198

Appendix G: Motion and Order to Waive Surcharge 208

Appendix H: Motion and Order to Waive Fines and Fees 214

Appendix I: Steps to Order Criminal History Records 218

Appendix J: Instructions, Petition, Verification and Order for Expunction of Criminal Records 220

Appendix K-1: Office of Court Administration – An Overview of Orders of Nondisclosure 231

Appendix K-2: Instructions and Letter Requesting an Order of Nondisclosure under Section 411.072, Government Code and Order 250

Appendix K-3: Instructions and Petition and Order of Nondisclosure under Section 411.0725, Government Code 260

Appendix K-4: Instructions and Petition and Order of Nondisclosure under Section 411.0727, Government Code 273

Appendix K-5: Instructions and Petition and Order of Nondisclosure under Section 411.0728, Government Code 286

Appendix K-6: Instructions and Petition and Order of Nondisclosure under Section 411.073, Government Code 298

Appendix K-7: Instructions and Petition and Order of Nondisclosure under Section 411.0731, Government Code 311

Appendix K-8: Instructions and Petition and Order of Nondisclosure under Section 411.0735, Government Code 325

Appendix K-9: Instructions and Petition and Order of Nondisclosure under Section 411.0736, Government Code 339

Appendix L - Texas Sex Offenses Tiered under Federal Law 353

Appendix M: Authorization Agreement for Non Parent Relative 358

Appendix N: Child Support Information for Incarcerated Parents and Parents Returning to the Community and Inquiry Form 360

Appendix O: OAG Form to Request Child Support Review 371

Appendix P: Sample Petition to Modify and Order (Non- OAG) 375

Appendix Q: Application for Voter Registration 380

Appendix R: Request for Status Information Letter 382

APPENDIX A:
STEPS TO OBTAIN TEXAS DRIVER'S LICENSE OR TEXAS IDENTITY CARD[1]

Start here. Check each as it applies and it will lead you to the next step(s).

☐ I am a US Citizen. → go to STEP 1

☐ I am a Non-Citizen. DPS has special application requirements for non-citizens. They are available at any Texas driver license office, or from the DPS website.[2]

STEP 1: CHECK STATUS OF DRIVER'S LICENSE OR ID

☐ I have an UNEXPIRED Texas DL or ID:

____ In my physical possession AND

____ It shows my current address and legal name. STOP. *No further action needed.*
  or
____ It *does not* show my current address or legal name. → Go to STEP 2.

☐ I have an EXPIRED Texas DL or ID that:

____ Expired less than 2 years ago. → Go to STEP 3A

  OR

____ Expired more than 2 years ago. → Go to STEP 3

☐ I DO NOT HAVE a Texas DL or ID because:

____ It is lost or missing. → Go to STEP 4

____ I have never applied for one. → Go to STEP 3.

____ I have an unexpired (or expired within the last 2 years) Out of State License.[3] → Go to STEP 3.

____ I am leaving Texas *within the next 30 days* to reside elsewhere. STOP. *No further action needed.*[4] Apply for or renew your DL or ID in the state or country where you plan to live.

---

[1] For information on office locations, fees, and the required identification documents, visit the DPS at www.txdps.state.tx.us/DriverLicense.
[2] https://www.dps.texas.gov/DriverLicense/LawfulStatusDLID.htm
[3] "Out of state" also applies to licenses from US territories and Canada.
[4] Each state has different laws for issuing and renewing driver's licenses and identity card. Check with the driver's license agency in the state where you plan to live.

STEP 2: CHANGE OF ADDRESS OR NAME

☐ Address: I need to change my address on my DL or ID.[5]

____ In writing: Complete and return DPS form DL-64. Form DL-64 can be obtained from any Texas driver's license office, the DPS website,[6] or your local post office.

____ Online:[7] DPS accepts online address changes if ALL the following requirements are met:
- You are a US citizen over 18 years of age
- Your license is not currently suspended
- You have no outstanding traffic tickets or warrants
- DL or ID is current (unexpired) and in your possession
- DL or ID is not Class A or B non-commercial or commercial
- You can provide the last 4 digits of your social security number
- You have use of a valid credit card (MasterCard, Visa, Discover, or American Express).

☐ Name: I need to change my name on my DL or ID.[8]

In person only, at any Texas driver license office:[9]
____ Pay the $11 fee, and
____ Show proof of name change. DPS will accept the following as proof:
- Marriage license,
- Divorce decree,
- Certified court order granting a change of name or
- Amended birth certificate.[10]

STEP 3: APPLY FOR TEXAS DRIVER'S LICENSE OR ID

☐ I need a Texas *identity card* and have *never* applied for one.

____ I do not have a social security number. A social security number is not required for an ID card (it is for a driver's license). → Go to STEP 3A

☐ I need a Texas *driver's license* and have *never applied* for one OR my driver's license has been expired for more than two years. Proof of a social security number is required for a Texas Driver's license.[11]

____ I have a social security *card* in my possession → Go to STEP 3A

____ I have a social security *number* but no card. You must show proof of your SSN before you can get a driver's license. The social security number must be stated on the document.

☐ I have at least one of the documents listed below as proof of my SSN (if yes, go to) → STEP 3A. If no, STOP. Acceptable documentation of SSN must be obtained before applying for a Texas Driver's License.

- Federally issued Social Security Card. (Metal Social Security cards or types sold at flea markets will NOT be accepted).
- Health Card (if member number represents Social Security Number).
- Pilot's license

---

[5] Texas law requires that DPS be notified within 30 days of any change of address.
[6] http://www.txdps.state.tx.us/InternetForms/Forms/DL-64.pdf
[7] An address change can be made online at http://www.txdps.state.tx.us/DriverLicense/dlfork.aspx?action=change,
[8] Holders of a Texas DL or ID are required to notify DPS within 30 days of any name change.
[9] http://www.txdps.state.tx.us/administration/driver_licensing_control/rolodex/search.asp,
[10] Foreign marriage licenses or divorce decrees are accepted if written in English or accompanied by a certified English translation. Same sex marriage licenses are not accepted for name changes.
[11] Note that DPS *may* request proof of a social security number for license renewals and duplicate licenses at any time, even if they already have an SSN on file.

- Military identification (Applies to active, reserve and dependent status).
- Peace officer's license - Texas Commission on Law Enforcement Officer Standard and Education.
- DD-214
- Medicare/Medicaid Cards
- Certified college/university transcript (designating number as SSN).
- Veteran's administration card (with social security number preprinted)

STEP 3A: PROOF OF IDENTITY

DPS divides acceptable proof of identity into three groups: Primary, Secondary and Supporting.

PRIMARY

Primary documents must have a name, birthdate and *identifiable photo*. Check at least ONE original item from the primary list below you have with you or that you can easily locate.

☐ I have at least one original (not a copy) of the primary items listed below. STOP. *If you have 1 primary, you do not need other proof.*

- Texas Driver's License or Texas Identity Card within two years of expiration date.
- Unexpired passport book or passport card
- US Citizenship or Naturalization Certificate (N-560, N-561, N-645, N-550, N-55G, N-570 or N-578) with photo
- Unexpired DHS or USCIS document, which can be any of the following:
    - US Citizen Identification Card (I-179 or I-197)
    - Permanent Resident Card (I-551)
    - Temporary Resident Identification Card (I-688)
    - Employment Authorization Card (I-766)
    - U.S. Travel Document (I-327 or I-571)
    - Advance Parole Document (I-512 or I-512L) (these are immigration documents).
    - I-94 stamped Sec. 208 Asylee or stamped Sec. 207 Refugee, with photo
    - American Indian Card (I-872) or Northern Mariana card (I-873)
    - Transportation Workers Identification Card
    - Foreign Passport or visa (valid or expired) and I-94 with a defined or undefined expiration date (e.g., duration of status)
- US Military ID – Unexpired, for active duty, reserve, or retired, with photo

☐ I do NOT have any primary proof of ID → Go to SECONDARY list.

SECONDARY

Secondary documents are *recorded government documents*. They must include your full name and date of birth. Check *all original* items from secondary list below that you have with you or that you can easily locate.

☐ I have at least TWO secondary items from the list below. STOP. *If you have two secondary, you do not need other proof.*

- Birth Certificate - Original or certified copy of birth certificate issued by the Texas bureau of vital statistics or equivalent agency in any other U.S. state, U.S. territory, the District of Columbia, or a Canadian province. (Note: A hospital birth record is not a birth certificate and cannot be used as proof).

- Certification of Birth Abroad - This is a birth certificate issued to you by the US Department of State if you are US citizen born abroad (State Department Form FS-240, DS-1350, or FS-545).

- Court Order for Change of Name - Original or certified copy of court order from any US State or territory, District of Columbia or Canada. It must show the name and date of birth with the official change of name.

☐ I have only ONE secondary item in the list above. *If you have one secondary, you also need two supporting items.* → Go to SUPPORTING list.

☐ I do NOT have any of the secondary items listed above. STOP. *You must have either primary or secondary proof before you can proceed with your DPS application.* Go to BIRTH CERTIFICATES.

SUPPORTING

Supporting documents are additional proofs of identity that cannot be used as the only kind of proof. You need at least one secondary and two supporting documents (3 pieces of identification). The list below show examples of supporting documents. *Note: A TDJC-ID counts as a supporting document.* Check at least two *original* supporting documents from the list below that you have with you, or that you can easily locate.

☐ I have TWO OR MORE supporting items listed below, AND ONE secondary item.

- Social security card
- Form W-2 or 1099
- Driver license or ID card issued by another U.S. state, U.S. territory, the District of Columbia or Canadian province (unexpired or expired less than two years)*
- Texas driver license or ID card that has been expired more than two years
- Temporary Texas driver license or ID card
- School records* (e.g., report cards, photo ID cards)
- Unexpired U.S. military dependent identification card
- Original or certified copy of marriage license or divorce decree (if the document is not in English, a certified translation must accompany it)
- Voter registration card*
- Pilot license*
- Concealed handgun license or License to Carry*
- Professional license issued by a Texas state agency
- ID card issued by a government agency*
- Consular document issued by a state or national government
- Texas Inmate ID card or similar form of ID issued by Texas Department of Criminal Justice
- Texas Department of Criminal Justice parole or mandatory release certificate
- Federal inmate identification card
- Federal parole or release certificate
- Medicare or Medicaid card
- Selective Service card
- Immunization records*
- Tribal membership card from federally-recognized tribe
- Certificate of Degree of Indian Blood
- Unexpired foreign passport
- Unexpired insurance policy valid for the past two years (e.g., auto, home or life insurance)
- Current Texas vehicle registration or title
- Current Texas boat registration or title
- Veteran's ID card issued by the U.S. Department of Veteran Affairs
- Abstract (shortened) birth certificate
- Hospital-issued birth record*
- Military records (e.g., Form DD-214, DD-215, NGB-22)

*The document must be issued by an institution, entity or government from a U.S. state, a U.S. territory, the District of Columbia or a Canadian province.

☐ I do NOT have two or more supporting items (and one secondary item). STOP. *You must have at least 2 supporting and one secondary item before you can proceed.* → Go to BIRTH CERTIFICATES.

STEP 4: LOST OR STOLEN

- ☐ LOST – appear in person at any DPS office and give acceptable:

    ___ Proof of Identity → Go to STEP 3A

    ___ Proof of Lawful Presence. DPS has special application requirements for non-citizens. They are available at any Texas driver license office, or from the DPS website.[12]

    ___ Proof of Social Security number (for driver's license only) -> Go to STEP 3

- ☐ STOLEN
    ___ File a police report. Then, appear in person at any driver's license office, and
    - o provide a copy of police report, and
    - o evidence that the DL or ID number is being used fraudulently (identity theft)

---

[12] https://www.dps.texas.gov/DriverLicense/LawfulStatusDLID.htm

APPENDIX B:
STEPS TO OBTAIN CERTIFIED COPY OF TEXAS BIRTH CERTIFICATE[1]

A certified copy of a birth certificate is secondary proof of identity for purposes of getting a Texas Driver's license, ID card, or CDL through the Texas Department of Public Safety.[2]

STEP 1 - BIRTH STATUS

- ☐ I was born in Texas. → go to STEP 2

- ☐ I was NOT born in Texas. STOP. You must contact your birth state or country to obtain your birth certificate.

STEP 2 - PHOTO ID

☐ I have one of the photo IDs listed below: → go to STEP 3

- prison ID or
- state/city/county ID card or
- DPS issued driver's license or ID card or
- student ID or
- government employment badge or card or
- military ID.

☐ I do not have any photo ID. → Go to STEP 4

STEP 3 – COMPLETE AND SUBMIT BVS FORM

☐ Complete application for a certified copy of a birth certificate, available from Texas Bureau of Vital Statistics (BVS).

　_____ submit in person (bring photo ID) and $22 check or money order

　_____ submit by mail (need copy of photo ID) and check or money order for fee[3].

STEP 4 – NO PHOTO ID

- Obtain a copy of the photo ID of an immediate family member, or
- Obtain copies of two documents showing your name (examples: utility bill; Social Security card)

One of the documents submitted must have your signature.

　Complete STEP 3 with above documents instead of photo ID.

---

[1] To AMEND or CORRECT an existing birth certificate, go to www.dshs.state.tx.us/vs/reqproc/faq/amendment.shtm#a1
[2] A birth certificate alone is insufficient proof of identity for a Texas driver's license or ID, but can be used along with other proof of identity acceptable to the Texas Department Public Safety (DPS).
[3] By mail to Texas Vital Records, Department of State Health Services, P.O. Box 12040 Austin, TX 78711-2040; In person: 1100 West 49th Street Austin, TX 78756 during regular business hours.

OFFICE USE ONLY

TEXAS Department of State Health Services

OFFICE USE ONLY
Remit No
By   ZZ 708-153

MAIL APPLICATION FOR BIRTH AND DEATH RECORD

PLEASE PRINT. INCLUDE A PHOTOCOPY OF YOUR VALID ID WHEN SENDING IN THE REQUEST.
Make check or money orders payable to: DSHS - Vital Statistics. All funds are deposited directly to the Texas Comptroller of Public Accounts. For any search of the files where a record is not found, the searching fee is not refundable or transferable.

Birth Certificates				Death Certificates			
Type		Cost X	# of copies=	Total	Type	Cost X	# of copies=	Total
Standard Size ☐ Long form ☐		$22			Certified Copy (1 copy)	$20		
Heirloom Flag ☐ Bassinet ☐		$60			Additional Copies	$3		
Total (Check or money order payable to DSHS)					Total (Check or money order payable to DSHS)			

☐ I wish to make a voluntary contribution of $5.00 to promote healthy early childhood by supporting the Texas Home Visitation Program administered by the Office of Early Childhood Coordination of Health and Human Services.

IDENTIFY BIRTH OR DEATH RECORD INFORMATION (Part I)

Full Name of Person on Record	First Name	Middle Name		Last Name	
Date of Birth/Death	Month	Day	Year	Sex	
Place of Birth/Death	City or Town	County		State	
Full Name of Parent 1	First Name	Middle Name		Maiden Name/Last Name	
Full Name of Parent 2	First Name	Middle Name		Maiden Name/Last Name	

APPLICANT INFORMATION (Part II)

Applicant Name		Telephone #		Email Address		
Full Mailing Address	Street Address		City		State	Zip
Relationship to person listed above			Purpose for obtaining this record:			

☐ I authorize mailing to the address below. I have verified that the address below will receive my order.

Name of Person Receiving Copies, if Different from Applicant		
Mailing Address for Copies, if Different from Applicant		
City	State	Zip

AFFIDAVIT OF PERSONAL KNOWLEDGE (MUST BE SIGNED IN PRESENCE OF A NOTARY PUBLIC) (Part III)

STATE OF _____ COUNTY OF _____ Before me on this day appeared _____
(Applicant name)

now residing at _____
(Address)   (City)   (State)

who is related to the person named on Part I as _____ and who on oath deposes and says that the contents of this affidavit are true and correct.
(Relationship)

The applicant presented the following type and number of identification: _____

Applicant Signature _____

Sworn to and subscribed before me, this ____ day of ____, 20 ____.

(Seal)

Signature of Notary Public and Notary ID Number _____

Typed or Printed Name: _____

Commission Expires: _____

Street Address _____

City, State, Zip: _____

WARNING: IT IS A FELONY TO FALSIFY INFORMATION ON THIS DOCUMENT. THE PENALTY FOR KNOWINGLY MAKING A FALSE STATEMENT ON THIS FORM OR FOR SIGNING A FORM WHICH CONTAINS A FALSE STATEMENT IS 2 TO 10 YEARS IMPRISONMENT AND A FINE OF UP TO $10,000. (HEALTH AND SAFETY CODE, CHAPTER 195, SEC. 195.003.

MAIL THIS APPLICATION, PAYMENT AND A VALID PHOTO ID TO:
Texas Vital Records Department of State Health Services
P.O. Box 12040 Austin, TX 78711-2040

VS-142.3 Rev. 06212016

VITAL STATISTICS
TEXAS DEPARTMENT OF STATE HEALTH
SERVICES AUTHORIZATION FORM

STATE OF _____
COUNTY OF _____

I request that Vital Statistics Unit in Austin, Texas allow

_____ to obtain a certified copy of the birth/death certificate on my behalf.

The qualified applicant's relationship to the **person on the certificate is**:
_____ (spouse, mother, father, son, daughter, sibling, grandparent or legal representative of person on record).

The information on the (birth/death) certificate being requested:

Name: _____

Date of event: _____

Place of event: _____

Mother: _____   Father: _____

_____

A Copy of Qualified Applicants valid ID or the form must be notarized.

Signature of *Qualified Applicant*:

_____

Subscribed and sworn before me on this the _____ day of _____, in the year of _____.

SEAL

_____
Signature of Notary Public

Please note: If the request for a death certificate is for legal reasons, please provide the legal documents that provide you the legal reason for obtaining the certificate, such as co-owner of business, executor or beneficiary of an estate, etc. Genealogy is not a legal reason to obtain a certificate. Death certificates are restricted for 25 years, and birth certificates are restricted for 75 years.

WARNING: IT IS A FELONY TO FALSIFY INFORMATION ON THIS DOCUMENT, THE PENALTY FOR KNOWINGLY MAKING A FALSE STATEMENT ON THIS FORM OR FOR SIGNING A FORM WHICH CONTAINS A FALSE STATEMENT IS 2 TO 10 YEARS IMPRISONMENT AND A FINE OF UP TO $10,000 (HEALTH AND SAFETY CODE, CHAPTER 195, SEC. 195.003)
VS
140 /2013

APPENDIX C:
STEPS TO APPLY FOR OR REPLACE SOCIAL SECURITY CARD

☐ I want to *replace* my lost Social Security card. Contact the Social Security Administration (SSA)

- Complete Application for a Social Security Card, Form SS-5.
- Telephone (toll free) 1-800-772-1213.
- Apply to local office in person – for locations, call 1-800-772-1213 or visit www.ssa.gov/ssnumber.

☐ I want to *apply* for a Social Security Number (SSN). The SSA requires applicants to show evidence of proof of U.S. *citizenship* or immigration status, *age*, and *identity*. Some documents serve as evidence in more than one category. A US birth certificate is evidence of both citizenship and age.

STEP 1: PROOF OF CITIZENSHIP OR IMMIGRATION STATUS

☐ I have one or more of the following Evidence of US Citizenship

- U.S. birth certificate,
- U.S. passport,
- Consular Report of Birth
- Certificate of Naturalization or
- Certificate of Citizenship.

If NO, → go to STEP 2. If YES, go to →STEP 3

STEP 2: EVIDENCE OF IMMIGRATION STATUS

☐ I have Evidence of Immigration Status:

Current unexpired Department of Homeland Security (DHS) document showing immigration status (e.g., Form I-551, I-94, or I-766).[1]

STEP 3: EVIDENCE OF AGE

☐ I have one or more of the following Evidence of Age:

- Birth certificate - If no birth certificate, may accept another document showing age, such as:
  - U.S. hospital record of birth (created at the time of birth)
  - Religious record established before age five showing age or date of birth
  - Passport
  - Final Adoption Decree (the adoption decree must show that the birth information was taken from the original birth certificate)

STEP 4: EVIDENCE OF IDENTITY

☐ I have one or more of the following Evidence of Identity:

- U.S. driver's license; or
- U.S. State-issued non-driver identity card; or
- U.S. passport

*Documents must show legal name AND biographical information (date of birth, age, or parents' names) and/or physical information (photograph, or physical description - height, eye and hair color, etc.).

---

[1] International student and exchange visitors must also have Form I-20, DS-2019, or a letter authorizing employment from F-1 or J-1 sponsor. NOT ACCEPTED: receipt showing application document. If no work authorization, will issue card for valid non-work reason. Card marked to show not work authorized.

SSA may accept *other documents* that show *legal name and biographical information*

- U.S. military identity card,
- Certificate of Naturalization,
- employee identity card,
- certified copy of medical record (clinic, doctor or hospital),
- health insurance card,
- Medicaid card, or school identity card/record.

NOT ACCEPTED as evidence of identity:

- birth certificate
- hospital souvenir birth certificate, social security card stub or a social security record

STEP 5: APPLICATION

Complete and print Application for a Social Security Card, Form SS-5 then deliver or mail it *with supporting documents* to the SSA. For the nearest office, use the SSA's online local office locator or call 2-1-1 for information.

APPENDIX D_____
SAMPLE PETITION, VERIFICATION and ORDER FOR NAME CHANGE OF AN ADULT
Note: These forms are intended only as an example and guide for drafting. Please seek the help of an attorney before seeking a name change.

CAUSE NO: _____

IN RE	§	IN THE DISTRICT COURT
	§	
_____	§	_____ JUDICIAL DISTRICT
	§	
AN ADULT	§	HARRIS COUNTY, TEXAS

ORIGINAL PETITION FOR CHANGE OF NAME

TO THE HONORABLE JUDGE OF THIS COURT:

COMES NOW, _____ **[Petitioner's Old Name] AKA** _____ **[Petitioner's New Name]**, Petitioner, files this Petition for Change of Name and in support thereof respectfully shows the Court the following:

1) This Court has jurisdiction and venue over the subject matter of this action pursuant to Texas Government Code Section 24.008 and Texas Family Code Section 45.101(5), respectively.

2) No discovery is intended.

3) This suit is brought by _____ **[Petitioner's Old Name] AKA** _____ **[Petitioner's New Name]**, Petitioner, who's mailing address is _____. Petitioner is an adult.

4) Petitioner's current true full name is _____

5) Petitioner requests that his name be changed to _____

6) The reason for the requested change is because [reason for name change].

7) Petitioner [has/has not] been the subject of a final felony conviction.

8) Petitioner [is/is not] required to register as a sex offender, under Chapter 62 of the *Texas Code of Criminal Procedure*.

9) A legible and complete set of the petitioner's fingerprints on a fingerprint card format acceptable to the Department of Public Safety and the Federal Bureau of Investigation will be completed and the results returned to the court reviewing this matter.

10) In accordance with Section 45.102 of the *Texas Family Code*, the following information is supplied about Petitioner:

    a) Petitioner is a _____ [Gender]

    b) Petitioner's race is _____

    c) Petitioner's date of birth is _____ and Petitioner was born in the City of _____ County of _____ State of _____.

d) Petitioner's most recent identification was issued by the state of Texas and was Driver's License Card number _____

e) Petitioner's Social Security Number is xxx-xx-_____.

f) Petitioner is unaware of any FBI number.

g) Petitioner [has/has not] been convicted of a crime or charged with any offense above the grade of a Class C misdemeanor, does not have any judgments against him, and is not involved in any pending civil legal actions.

Petitioner prays that the Court issue an order changing his name to _____ and ask that the Court grant any other relief to which Petitioner is entitled, general or specific, legal or equitable.

Respectfully submitted,

_____
[ATTORNEY OR PETITIONER PRO SE]
ADDRESS
PHONE NUMBER

CAUSE NO: _____

IN RE	§	IN THE DISTRICT COURT
	§	
_____	§	_____ JUDICIAL DISTRICT
	§	
AN ADULT	§	HARRIS COUNTY, TEXAS

VERIFICATION OF ORIGINAL PETITION FOR CHANGE OF NAME

BEFORE ME, the undersigned authority, on this day personally appeared _____ **[Petitioner's Old Name] AKA** _____ **[Petitioner's New Name]** Petitioner, known to me to be the person whose name is subscribed to the foregoing instrument, who, after being duly sworn, upon oath stated that he has read the foregoing *Original Petition for Change of Name,* and that the facts stated therein are within his personal knowledge and are true and correct.

_____
[Petitioner]

SWORN TO AND SUBSCRIBED BEFORE ME by the said **[Petitioner's Old Name] AKA [Petitioner's New Name]** on this the _____ day of _____, _____, to certify which witness my hand and seal of office.

_____
NOTARY PUBLIC, STATE OF TEXAS

CAUSE NO: _____

IN RE	§	IN THE DISTRICT COURT
	§	
_____	§	_____ JUDICIAL DISTRICT
	§	
AN ADULT	§	HARRIS COUNTY, TEXAS

ORDER GRANTING CHANGE OF NAME OF ADULT

Pursuant to Section 45.101 of the Texas Family Code, _____, Petitioner, requested this Court to change Petitioner's name to _____.

The Court FINDS:

1) _____ is a resident of Harris County, Texas. Petitioner's Social Security Number is xxx-xx-_____. Petitioner's Texas Driver's License/Identification number is _____. Petitioner's date of birth is _____. Petitioner's SPN number in the Harris County Justice Information Management System is [SPN # (IF APPLICABLE)].

2) The Petitioner was born in _____, _____ County, _____, United States of America.

3) The Petitioner is a United States Citizen.

4) The Petitioner [is/is not] a sex offender and [is/is not] required to register as such.

5) The proposed change of name to _____ is in the interest or to the benefit of the petitioner and is not adverse to the interest of the public.

The Court ORDERS:

1) The legal name of _____, is now changed to _____.

2) ONLY USE #2 IF CLIENT HAS KNOWN CRIMINAL HISTORY The clerk of the Court shall transmit a copy of this Order to the following criminal justice agencies to permit them to update their criminal history records with the petitioner's new name:

   a. _____ County District Attorney's Office
      Attn: General Litigation Division
      [Address]

b. _____ County Sheriff's Office
Attn: Criminal Justice Bureau
[Address]

c. Texas Department of Public Safety
Crime Records Service
P.O. Box 4143
Austin, TX 78765-4143

d. FBI CJIS Division
1000 Custer Hollow Road
Clarksburg, WV 26306
Attn: Special Processing Center

3) Nothing in this Order forecloses any public or private entity from maintaining records of the petitioner's previous name and the petitioner's changed name as identifiers associated with their currently existing records. *See* TEX. FAMILY CODE § 45.104 ("A change of name under this subchapter does not release a person from liability incurred in that person's previous name or defeat any right the person had in the person's previous name.")

4) Any orders requested that do not appear are denied.

Signed this _____ day of _____, _____.

_____
JUDGE PRESIDING

APPENDIX E:
SAMPLE PETITION AND VERIFICATION FOR DECLARATORY JUDGMENT OF NAME

Note:
These forms are for individuals who are ineligible to petition for a change of name.
They are intended only as an example and guide for drafting. Please seek the help of an attorney before seeking a declaratory judgment.

CAUSE NO: _____

IN RE	§	IN THE DISTRICT COURT
[OLD NAME OF PETITIONER]	§	
AKA [NEW NAME OF PETITIONER]	§	_____ JUDICIAL DISTRICT
	§	
AN ADULT	§	HARRIS COUNTY, TEXAS

ORIGINAL PETITION FOR DECLARATORY JUDGMENT

TO THE HONORABLE JUDGE OF THIS COURT:

COMES NOW, [OLD NAME OF PEITIONER] AKA [NEW NAME OF PETITIONER], Petitioner, through undersigned counsel, files this Petition for Declaratory Judgment, pursuant to the *Texas Uniform Declaratory Judgments Act* in Chapter 37 of the *Civil Practice and Remedies Code* and in support thereof respectfully shows the Court the following:

JURISDICTION AND VENUE

1. The subject matter in controversy is within the jurisdictional limits of this Court.
2. This Court has jurisdiction over the parties because all of the parties are Texas residents.
3. Venue in Harris County is proper in this cause.

FACTS

1. This suit is brought by **[OLD NAME OF PETITIONER] AKA [NEW NAME OF PETITIONER]**, Petitioner's mailing address is: [mailing address].
2. Petitioner requests that their name be changed to [NEW NAME OF PETITIONER]. because:
    a. The name on Petitioner's birth certificate conflicts with the name on Petitioner's [driver's license, state ID, other documents]
    b. (Supporting document 1) A copy of _____ is attached hereto as **Exhibit "A"**.
    c. (Supporting document 2) A copy of _____ is attached hereto as **Exhibit "B"**.
    d. (Supporting document 3) A copy of _____ is attached hereto as **Exhibit "C"**.
    e. Petitioner has included with this Petition a legible and complete set of their fingerprints on a fingerprint card in a format acceptable to the Texas Department of Public Safety and the Federal Bureau of Investigation which will be sent to the Texas Department of Public Safety for the purpose of requesting a Criminal History Record Information.
    f. The following information is provided for the courts convenience:
        1) Petitioner is a [Gender].
        2) Petitioner's race is [Race].
        3) Petitioner's date of birth is [Date of Birth] and Petitioner was born in the City of [city of birth], County of [county of birth], State of [state of birth].

4) The last four digits of Petitioner's Social Security Number are xxx-xx-[last 4 of ssn]
5) To the best of their knowledge Petitioner does not have an FBI Number.
6) Petitioner has been convicted of a crime or charged with an offense above the grade of a Class C misdemeanor, does not have any judgments against them, and is not involved in any pending civil legal actions.

STATEMENTS OF LAW

The purpose of the Uniform Declaratory Judgments Act is to settle and to afford relief from uncertainty and insecurity with respect to rights, status, and other legal relations; and it is to be liberally construed and administered. Tex. Civ. Prac. & Rem. Code Ann. § 37.002(a). A person who has an interest in a writing "whose rights, status, or other legal relations are affected by a statute, municipal ordinance, contract, or franchise may have determined any question of construction or validity arising under the instrument, statute, ordinance, contract, or franchise and obtain a declaration of rights, status, or other legal relations thereunder." Tex. Civ. Prac. & Rem. Code Ann. § 37.004(a).

There exists a genuine controversy herein that would be terminated by the granting of declaratory judgment. Petitioner's registered name with the Social Security Administration Texas Department of Public Safety and the Texas Department of Corrections is [NEW NAME OF PETITIONER], while their birth certificate reflects a legal name of [OLD NAME OF PETITIONER] . Unfortunately under *Texas Family Code* Section 45.103, Petitioner is not eligible to apply for a change of name if "not less than two years have passed from the date of the receipt of discharge..." from a felony. In this particular case, Petitioner was given a [length of sentence] of which _____ years were served. Petitioner will not meet that requirement until _____.

Texas law protects the legitimate governmental interest of being able to identify persons sought on warrant and detainer and to preserve the criminal history of felons. *See Matthews v. Morales,* 23 F.3d 118, 119 (5th Cir. 1994). Petitioner's registered name with the Texas Department of Corrections is [NEW NAME OF PETITIONER], and petitioner simply requests the Court to enter a declaratory judgment which conforms their name to the records of the Texas Department of Corrections.

In order to obtain a Texas Identification Card or Driver's License, a person needs to present:

1. One of these documents which are called "secondary documents":
    a. original or certified copy of a birth certificate issued by the appropriate State Bureau of Vital Statistics or equivalent agency;
    b. original or certified copy of United States Department of State Certification of Birth (issued to United States citizens born abroad); or
    c. original or certified copy of court order with name and date of birth (DOB) indicating an official change of name and/or gender.
2. And two of these documents which are called "supporting documents":
    a. school records;
    b. insurance policy (at least two years old);
    c. vehicle title;

d. military records;

e. unexpired military dependent identification card;

f. original or certified copy of marriage license or divorce decree;

g. voter registration card;

h. Social Security card;

i. pilot's license;

j. concealed handgun license;

k. Texas driver's license temporary receipt;

l. unexpired photo DL or photo ID issued by another (United States) state, US territory, the District of Columbia or Canadian province;

m. expired photo DL or photo ID issued by another (United States) state, US territory, the District of Columbia or Canadian province that is within two years of the expiration date;

n. a consular document issued by a state or national government; or

o. an offender identification card or similar form of identification issued by the Texas Department of Criminal Justice. Tex. Admin. Code 15 § 24.

Because the Petitioner's birth certificate states their name is [OLD NAME OF PETITIONER] and any supporting documents Petitioner has controvert the Birth Certificate and state their name is [NEW NAME OF PETITIONER], the Petitioner cannot provide proof of identity with their birth certificate. The only other option is to have a Court Order establishing their name is [NEW NAME OF PETITIONER].

PRAYER

Petitioner prays that the Court issue an order declaring that the Petitioner is one and the same as **[NEW NAME OF PETITIONER]**, whose date of birth is [Date of Birth] and ask that the Court grant any other relief to which Petitioner is entitled, general or specific, legal or equitable.

Respectfully submitted,

_____
[ATTORNEY FOR PETITIONER OR PETITIONER PRO SE]
Address
Telephone

CAUSE NO: _____

IN RE	§	IN THE DISTRICT COURT
[OLD NAME OF PETITIONER]	§	
AKA [N NAME OF PETITIONER]	§	_____ JUDICIAL DISTRICT
	§	
AN ADULT	§	HARRIS COUNTY, TEXAS

VERIFICATION OF ORIGINAL PETITION FOR DECLARATORY JUDGMENT

BEFORE ME, the undersigned authority, on this day personally appeared **[OLD NAME OF PETITIONER] AKA [NEW NAME OF PETITIONER]**, Petitioner, known to me to be the person whose name is subscribed to the foregoing instrument, who, after being duly sworn, upon oath stated that he has read the foregoing *Original Petition for Declaratory Judgment,* and that the facts stated therein are within their personal knowledge and are true and correct.

_____
Signature of Petitioner

SWORN TO AND SUBSCRIBED BEFORE ME by the said **[NAME OF PETITIONER]** on this the _____ day of _____, _____, to certify which witness my hand and seal of office.

_____
NOTARY PUBLIC, STATE OF TEXAS

APPENDIX E:
SAMPLE - DECLARATORY JUDGMENT OF NAME - ORDER

CAUSE NO: _____

IN RE	§	IN THE DISTRICT COURT
	§	
[OLD NAME OF PETITIONER] AKA	§	_____ JUDICIAL DISTRICT
[NEW NAME OF PETITIONER]	§	
	§	
AN ADULT	§	_____COUNTY, TEXAS

ORDER OF DECLARATORY JUDGMENT OF NAME

On _____, the Court heard the *Original Petition Declaratory Judgment* filed by Petitioner, born [OLD NAME OF PETITIONER] and thereafter known only as [NEW NAME OF PETITIONER].

Petitioner appeared in person and through attorney of record and announced ready.

The Court finds that it has jurisdiction of the case and the Petitioner.

The Court finds that Petitioner is a citizen of the United States and was born in [Place of Birth] on [Date of Birth].

The last four digits of the Petitioner's Social Security Number are xxx-xx-[last 4 of ssn].

The record of testimony was duly reported by the court reporter for the _____ Judicial District Court.

IT IS ORDERED that Petitioner's name is **[NEW NAME OF PETITIONER]** and his date of birth is [Date of Birth].

IT IS ORDERED that all relief requested in this case and not expressly granted is denied.

SIGNED this _____ day of _____, _____.

_____
JUDGE PRESIDING

APPENDIX F PETITION AND ORDER FOR OCCUPATIONALS DRIVER'S LICENSE

NOTICE: THIS FORM CONTAINS SENSITIVE DATA

Ex Parte

Cause No: _____ *The clerk fills out below*

Print your name

_____
First   Middle   Last

☐ District ☐ County ☐ Justice Court of:
_____ County, Texas

Petition for Occupational Driver's License

Print your answers:

My name is:_____.
               First   Middle   Last

I am the Petitioner, and I am asking the court for an Occupational Driver's License.

I ask the Court to consider the information I have provided below.

Upon approval of this Petition, I ask the Clerk to send a certified copy of the Petition and the court Order setting out the judge's findings and restrictions to the Texas Department of Public Safety.

I. Petitioner's Personal Information

1. Home address: _____
        Street address   City
   _____, Texas
      County   Zip

2. Mailing address *(if different from above):* _____

3. Phone number: (___) _____

4. Email address: _____

5. Date of birth: _____
                 Month   Day   Year

6. The last four digits of my Social Security Number are _ ___ ___ ___ ___.

7. Jurisdiction:
   (Check all that apply.)

   ☐ Petitioner resides in this County.

   ☐ The offense for which Petitioner's license was suspended happened in this county.

   ☐ This Court convicted Petitioner of an offense under the laws of this state that resulted in the automatic suspension or cancellation of Petitioner's license.

CV-ODL-100 *Petition for Occupational Driver's License* (Rev. 7-2018)
©TexasLawHelp.org

II. Driver's License Information

8. *Check all that apply and provide requested information:*

    ☐ I have never held a Texas Driver's License.

    ☐ My Texas Driver's License # is: _____. Expiration date: ___/___/_____.

    ☐ My Driver's License was issued by the state of _____.
    My Driver's License number is _____. Expiration date: ___/___/_____.

9. Is your license suspended because of a physical or mental disability? ☐ Yes ☐ No

    Is your license suspended for non-payment of child support? ☐ Yes ☐ No

    Have you had 2 or more occupational driver's licenses because of a conviction in the last 10 years? ☐ Yes ☐ No

III. Notice to the State If Applicable

10. If any of the following are applicable, the Clerk of the Court should serve the State with notice of this Petition as required by the Texas Transportation Code section 521.243(a).

    (Check all that apply and fill in the blanks.)

    A. My license is suspended under Transportation Code section 521.342. (Conviction of various offenses of an individual under the age of 21)

    ☐ Yes ☐ No

    _____
    Date of conviction   Court of conviction

    B. My license is suspended because I was convicted of:

    a. ☐ Criminally Negligent Homicide — *Penal Code 19.05*
    b. ☐ Driving While Intoxicated — *Penal Code 49.04*
    c. ☐ Driving While Intoxicated with Child Passenger — *Penal Code 49.045*
    d. ☐ Flying While Intoxicated — *Penal Code 49.05*
    e. ☐ Boating While Intoxicated — *Penal Code 49.06*
    f. ☐ Assembling or Operating an Amusement Ride While Intoxicated — *Penal Code 49.065*
    g. ☐ Intoxication Assault — *Penal Code 49.07*
    h. ☐ Intoxication Manslaughter — *Penal Code 49.08*

    on _____ in _____ _____
    Date of conviction   Court of conviction   County of conviction

IV. Suspensions and Charges

11. Why is your Driver's License suspended? *(Check all that apply and fill in the blanks):*

    A. ☐ I was arrested on ___/___/___ and the breath sample I provided registered above 0.08.
         (date)

    B. ☐ I was arrested on ___/___/___ , and I did not give a breath sample, as requested.
         (date)
    Within the past ten (10) years from the date of the arrest that led to your current suspension, have you had a suspension for refusal to give a breath/blood sample or providing a sample with a blood alcohol content greater than .08 following an arrest for DWI?

    ☐ YES ☐ NO

    C. ☐ This court convicted me of _____ on (date) ___/___/___
    under cause number _____.

    D. ☐ A Texas court determined that I am a "habitual violator of traffic laws."

    E. ☐ A Texas court ordered me to go to a Driver Education Program, and my license, permit, and/or driving privilege is automatically suspended for 365 days.

    F. ☐ Other *(If you did not check any of the above, why is your license suspended or invalid? Be specific.)*

    _____
    _____
    _____
    _____

12. I have the following criminal charges *pending*: *(You do not need to list traffic or Class C charges.)*

    _____
    _____
    _____

V. Petitioner's Essential Need to Drive

If you required to have an interlock device installed on each motor vehicle you own or operate because your license is suspended based on an offense under Penal Code 49.04 - 49.08 or because of a court order or bond requirement, you do not need to complete Numbers 12, 13, and 14 below.

13. Why do you need an Occupational Driver's License? *(Check all that apply):*

    ☐ I need an Occupational Driver's License to drive to and from my place of work.
    <u>Name of Employer #1</u>: _____

    Employer's Address: _____

    Employer's Telephone: _____

    Days and hours you work: _____

    Job title: _____

    <u>Name of Employer #2</u>: _____

    Employer's Address: _____

    Employer's Telephone: _____

    Days and hours you work: _____

    Job title: _____

    ☐ I am self-employed as: _____

    My work address is: _____

    ☐ I need to go to and/or transport family members to school. *(Fill out below):*

    <u>School #1 Name</u>: _____ Telephone: _____

    Address: _____

    <u>School #2 Name</u>: _____ Telephone: _____

    Address: _____

    ☐ Other *(explain):* _____
    _____
    _____
    _____

    ☐ I drive as part of my work or essential needs throughout the following county or counties.
    _____

14. Driving schedule you are requesting:

	Monday	Tuesday	Wednesday	Thursday	Friday	Saturday	Sunday
From:	___ am/pm	___ am/pm	___ am/pm	___ am/pm	___ am/pm	___ am/pm	___ am/pm
To:	___ am/pm	___ am/pm	___ am/pm	___ am/pm	___ am/pm	___ am/pm	___ am/pm

15. If you are asking the Court to allow you to drive for more than 4 hours per day, explain why below:
    _____
    _____
    _____

VI. Petitioner's Request to the Court

16. I ask the Court to order the Texas Department of Public Safety to issue me an Occupational Driver's License to drive for the purposes described above.

    I further ask this Court to order the Texas Department of Public Safety to administer any and all tests required for the issuance of said Occupational License.

_____
Petitioner's name (print)

▶ _____   _____
Petitioner's signature   Date

Unsworn Declaration Made Under Penalty of Perjury
As allowed by Section 132.001 of the Texas Civil Practices and Remedies Code, I am filing this Unsworn Declaration in support of the Petition for Occupational Driver's License in place of a Verified Petition.*

My current legal name is:

_____.
First   *Middle*   *Last*

My date of birth is: _____/_____/_____.
                    Month *Day* *Year*

My address is:

_____
Street Address   *City*   *State*   *Zip Code*   *Country*

I declare under penalty of perjury that all information in this Petition is true and correct. I understand I could be prosecuted for lying on this form.

Formally signed in _____ County, _____
                              County   *State*

on this date: _____/_____/_____.
              Month *Day* *Year*

▶ _____
Signature of Person Asking for Occupational Driver's License

*Pursuant to Texas Civil Practice and Remedies Code Section 132.001, an unsworn declaration may be used in lieu of a written sworn declaration, verification, certification, oath, or affidavit required by statute or required by a rule, order, or requirement adopted as provided by law. This provision does not apply to an oath of office or an oath required to be taken before a specified official other than a notary public. An unsworn declaration made under this section must be 1) in writing, 2) signed by the person making the declaration as true under penalty of perjury and 3) in substantially the form used above.

See below for a list of documents to attach to this Petition:

- ☐ A certified abstract (Type AR) of your driver's license record.
- ☐ An SR22 from your insurance company providing proof of current valid auto liability insurance.
- ☐ Proof of need to drive: Examples of proof: A letter from your employer or immediate supervisor on your employer's letterhead that verifies your work schedule, a current pay stub, school registration with schedule, or your sworn affidavit explaining to the court why you need to drive unless your license is suspended solely based on an intoxication offense under Penal Code 49.04 – 49.08 and any vehicle you own or operate must be equipped with an interlock device.

NOTICE: THIS FORM CONTAINS SENSITIVE DATA

Ex Parte

Print your name

_____
First   Middle   Last

Cause No: [The clerk fills out below.]

☐ District ☐ County ☐ Justice Court of:
_____ County, Texas

Order for Occupational Driver's License

On this date, the Court heard the petitioner's Application for Occupational Driver's License.

The Petitioner named below appeared in person without an attorney.

The Court finds that **notice to the State**: *(Check one.)* [The Court fills out this box.]
☐ was not required.
☐ was given as required by Texas Transportation Code Section 521.243 and: *(Check one.)*
☐ the attorney representing the State did not appear.
☐ the attorney representing the State, _____, also appeared.

I. Findings

1. The Court FINDS that Petitioner's **personal information** is as follows:
   a. Name: _____
          first   middle   last
   b. *(Check all that apply and fill in the blanks)*
      ☐ Petitioner's Texas Driver's License Number is _____.
      ☐ Petitioner's Texas Driver's License expiration date is _____.
      ☐ Petitioner has never had a Texas Driver's License.
      ☐ Petitioner has a Driver's License from _____ with License Number _____.
   c. Home address: _____
          Street address
      _____
      City   County   State   Zip Code
   d. Phone number: (___)_____
   e. Date of birth: ___/___/_____
          Month Day Year

2. The Court FINDS that it has **jurisdiction and venue** over this case and the Petitioner because: *(Check all that apply and fill in the blanks.)*
   ☐ Petitioner resides in this County.
   ☐ The offense for which Petitioner's license was suspended happened in this county.
   ☐ This Court convicted Petitioner of an offense under the laws of this state that resulted in the automatic suspension or cancellation of Petitioner's license.

3. The Court FINDS that Petitioner has provided the Court with the following:
   - a certified abstract (type AR) of Petitioner's driver's license record *and*
   - an SR-22 financial responsibility insurance certificate.

NOTICE: THIS FORM CONTAINS SENSITIVE DATA

4. The Court FINDS that Petitioner's driver's license is **suspended** because: *(Check all that apply and fill in the blanks.)*

    ☐ This Court convicted Petitioner of _____ on (date) __/__/__
    under cause number: _____.

    ☐ Petitioner refused to submit to a breath or blood test or submitted a breath or blood test that registered more than 0.08 following an arrest on __/__/__ for:
    Date

    (Check one.)
    ☐ Driving While Intoxicated
    ☐ Other: _____

    ☐ The Texas Department of Public Safety said Petitioner was a habitual violator of traffic laws.
    ☐ Other: _____
    _____

5. **The Court FINDS that Petitioner's driver's license is not denied, suspended or revoked because of a physical or mental disability or nonpayment of child support.**

    The Court further FINDS that Petitioner has not been issued more than one Occupational Driver's License following a conviction during the past 10 years.

6. *(Check all that apply and fill in the blanks.)*

    ☐ The Court FINDS that the suspension of Petitioner's license **began/begins** on or about __/__/__ and **ends** on or about *(date):* __/__/__.

    ☐ The Court FINDS that the Petitioner's license is invalid for an indefinite period of time.

7. The Court FINDS that Petitioner: *(Check all that apply and fill in the blanks. NOTE: If you are required to have an interlock device installed on each motor vehicle you own or operate, because your license is suspended based on an offense under Penal Code 49.04 - 49.08 or pursuant to a court order or bond requirement, you do not need to complete Number 7.)*

    ☐ works for the following employer(s):

    Employer #1: _____ Work Phone: _____

    Work Address _____

    Employer #2: _____ Work Phone: _____

    Work Address _____

    ☐ works for him/herself. Petitioner's occupation is: _____

    Petitioner's work address is: _____

    ☐ drives as part of his/her work and/or essential needs throughout the following county or counties:
    _____

    ☐ attends school at or transports family members to the following school(s):

    School #1: _____ School Phone: _____

    School Address: _____

    School #2: _____ School Phone: _____

    School Address: _____

    ☐ has other essential needs to drive _____
    _____

CV-ODL-200 *Order for Occupational Driver's License* (Rev. 7-2018)
©TexasLawHelp.org

NOTICE: THIS FORM CONTAINS SENSITIVE DATA

The Court fills out the rest of this form.

(Check applicable.)

☐ The Court FINDS that Petitioner's driver's license is suspended because of an intoxication offense and the Occupational License here Ordered is subject to the restrictions set out below.

☐ The Court FINDS that Petitioner has an **essential need** to drive and the Occupational Driver's License here Ordered is subject to the restrictions set out below.

II. Orders

The Court **ORDERS** that this Petition for Occupational Driver's License is **GRANTED** subject to the following restrictions and **ORDERS** Petitioner to follow all restrictions listed below.

The Court **ORDERS** the Texas Department of Public Safety to issue an Occupational Driver's License to Petitioner subject to the following restrictions. The Court further orders the Texas Department of Public Safety to administer any and all tests required for the issuance said Occupational License, and, if Petitioner passes all required tests, issue an Occupational Driver's License to Petitioner subject to the following restrictions.

Restrictions

- ✓ Petitioner **must not** drive a commercial vehicle with this license.
- ✓ Petitioner **must** maintain in full force and effect an SR-22 automobile liability insurance policy for the entire period the Occupational Driver's License is in effect.
- ✓ Petitioner **must** have in his/her possession a certified copy of this court order while driving and **must** allow a peace officer to examine the order when requested.

The Court also **ORDERS** the restrictions checked below: *(Check all that apply.)*

☐ Any vehicle owned or operated by the Petitioner MUST be equipped with a working ignition interlock device in accordance with Texas Transportation Code Section 521.2465.

☐ Petitioner **must not** refuse any lawful request by law enforcement for a sample of Petitioner's breath or blood if stopped for Driving While Intoxicated.

☐ Petitioner **must** submit to periodic testing for alcohol or controlled substances as follows:
_____

☐ Petitioner **must** attend the alcohol/drug counseling program listed below and give the court clerk proof of attendance within _____ days of this order.
Program:_____

☐ Petitioner **must** submit to community supervision as follows:
_____

☐ Petitioner **may** only drive in the counties listed here:
_____
_____

☐ Petitioner **must** only drive to and from work or school and for essential duties, including medical appointments, court appointments, attorney appointments probation office meetings, and any supervision, education, counseling, or other essential needs authorized by this court.

NOTICE: THIS FORM CONTAINS SENSITIVE DATA

Petitioner **must not** drive more than: *(Check one.)*

☐ **4** hours in any 24 hour period.

☐ **12** hours in any 24 hour period. The Court specifically finds that Petitioner needs to drive more than 4 hours and ORDERS that the 4 hour limitation is waived.

☐ Petitioner **must** only drive on the days and at the times listed below:

	Monday	Tuesday	Wednesday	Thursday	Friday	Saturday	Sunday
From:	___ am/pm	___ am/pm	___ am/pm	___ am/pm	___ am/pm	___ am/pm	___ am/pm
To:	___ am/pm	___ am/pm	___ am/pm	___ am/pm	___ am/pm	___ am/pm	___ am/pm

☐ Petitioner **must** always keep a log book in any car Petitioner drives. Petitioner must correctly record in the log book all dates and times Petitioner drives and the destination and reason for each trip. Petitioner must show this log book to any law enforcement officer upon demand.

☐ Additional Restrictions:

_____
_____
_____
_____
_____
_____
_____

III. Date this Order takes Effect

The Court Clerk shall send a certified copy of the Petition and the court Order setting out this Court's findings and restrictions to the Texas Department of Public Safety.

This Order takes effect on: *(Check one and write in the date, if applicable.)*

☐ the date this Order is signed by the Court.

☐ ___/___/_____ which is 91 days after the date Petitioner's license was suspended.

☐ ___/___/_____ which is 181 days after the date Petitioner's license was suspended.

☐ ___/___/_____ which is 366 days after the date Petitioner's license was suspended.

If all driver testing requirements have been met, Petitioner may use a certified copy of this Order for Occupational Driver's License as a restricted license ONLY for 45 days, beginning on the date this Order takes effect.

NOTICE: THIS FORM CONTAINS SENSITIVE DATA

IV. Date this Order Ends

Unless revoked by the Court, this Order for Occupational Driver's License remains valid until:

(Check one and write in the date, if applicable.)

☐ ___/___/_____.

☐ ___/___/_____ which is the date Petitioner's current driver's license suspension ends.

The reason for Petitioner's current driver's license suspension is listed in 4 above.

V. Warnings to Petitioner

It is a **Class B Misdemeanor** for you to drive in violation of any of the restrictions listed above.

It is a **Class B Misdemeanor** for you to drive without a certified copy of this order in your possession.

The Court may revoke this Order, at any time, for good cause.

This Order and your Occupational Driver's License are automatically revoked if you are convicted of driving in violation of any of the restrictions listed above or convicted of driving without a certified copy of this Order in your possession.

If all driver testing requirements have been met, you may use a certified copy of the Order for Occupational Driver's License to drive for 45 days only, beginning on the date this Order takes effect. **If you do not receive your Occupational Driver's License from the Texas Department of Public Safety (DPS) before the 45th day after the date this Order takes effect, you MUST not drive until you receive your Occupational Driver's License from Texas Department of Public Safety or come back to court to get an Amended Order for Occupational Driver's License that extends the 45-day time period.**

If this ORDER includes a finding of an essential need to drive, and the places, reasons, days or times that you need to drive change, you must come back to Court to get an Amended Order for Occupational Driver's License that reflects those changes.

Signed On: _____   By: _____
                                             Judge's Signature

APPENDIX G
SAMPLE MOTION, AFFIDAVIT OF INABILITY TO PAY AND ORDER TO WAIVE SURCHARGES
Note: These forms are intended only as an example and guide for drafting. Please seek the help of an attorney.

CAUSE NO. _____

THE STATE OF TEXAS	§	IN THE _____ COURT
	§	
V.	§	PRECINCT_____, PLACE _____
	§	
_____	§	_____, TEXAS

DEFENDANT'S MOTION FOR FINDING OF INDIGENCE AND WAIVER OF SURCHARGES

COMES NOW, _____, the Defendant in this case and files this *Motion for Finding of Indigence and Waiver of Surcharges* (the "Motion"), [through counsel _____ (if applicable).]

I. **Indigence**

Defendant moves that this court make a finding of indigence in this matter. Defendant shows the court the following in support of this claim of indigence:

1. Defendant is currently homeless and their income is below the current Federal Poverty Guideline as supported by the attached Sworn Affidavit of Defendant, which is attached hereto as **Exhibit A**.

2. Defendant is unable to obtain a Texas Driver's License because of this outstanding case.

3. Without a Texas Driver's License, Defendant is unable to obtain employment and other services necessary to restabilization, and payment of these fines.

II. **Waiver of Surcharges**

Pursuant to Texas Transportation Code §708.158, the Defendant meets one or more of the qualifications for indigency and is unable to pay the surcharges imposed.

The Defendant humbly requests the court grant this Motion, make a finding of indigence and all of the surcharges assessed but the Texas Department of Public Safety under Chapter 708 of the Texas Transportation Code be waived in their entirety and that the Defendant be discharges from any further financial responsibility to pay any surcharges imposed in connection with this Cause.

Respectfully Submitted,

_____
[Attorney Or Pro Se Petitioner]
Address
Phone Number

CAUSE NO. _____

THE STATE OF TEXAS	§	IN THE _____ COURT
	§	
V.	§	PRECINCT____, PLACE _____
	§	
_____	§	_____, TEXAS

SWORN AFFIDAVIT OF DEFENDANT

On this day, _____, appeared before me, the undersigned notary public, and after I administered an oath, upon their oath, said:

1. "My name is, _____, and I am the Defendant in this case.

2. I am currently Employed/Unemployed and support a family of _____.

3. I receive $_____ per month in income. I have $_____ in cash assets, I do not own real property and I have the following monthly expenses:

4. Necessary monthly living expenses:

House payment or rent	$_____
Utilities including telephone	$_____
Food including school lunches	$_____
Child Care	$_____
Car payment and auto insurance	$_____
Gasoline, oil, parking, bus fares, tolls, repairs	$_____
Attorney's fees	$_____
Health and life insurance premiums	$_____
Uninsured medical related expenses	$_____
Clothing and laundry	$_____
Personal	$_____
Total	$_____

5. I wish to resolve the matters I have pending in this court.

6. I am unable to pay the court cost or any part of or to give security required by the rules and the court because I am unemployed, unable to obtain a Texas Driver's License and cannot afford it. My expenses exceed my income and I am unable to borrow the money.

7. I verify that the statements made in this affidavit are true and correct.

_____
By: [Defendant]

SWORN TO and SUBSCRIBED before me by [Defendant] on the _____ day of _____, _____.

_____
Notary Public in and for the State of Texas

Exhibit A

CAUSE NO. _____

THE STATE OF TEXAS	§ §	IN THE _____ COURT
V.	§	PRECINCT _____, PLACE _____
_____	§ §	_____, TEXAS

ORDER FINDING OF INDIGENCE AND WAIVER OF FINES AND COURT COSTS

I. On this date, the court considered the *Motion for Finding of Indigence and Waiver of Surcharges* of the named Defendant pursuant to Tex. Transp. Code Ann. §708.158 (West).

II. The court finds that the Defendant in this matter is indigent.

IT IS THEREFORE ORDERED that the Texas Department of Public Safety shall waive all surcharges assess under Chapter 708 of the Texas Transportation Code in connection with this Cause.

It is, therefore, ORDERED and ADJUDGED.

_____   _____
Date   Judge Presiding

TEXAS DRIVER RESPONSIBILITY PROGRAM
Indigency/ Incentive Application for Reduction of Surcharges

You are applying to the Indigency/Incentive Programs and the Department or its designee will determine the program you qualify for by the supporting documentation you submit.

Print Full Name: _____

DL/ID/DPS Assigned Number: _____

Date of Birth (MM/DD/YYYY): _____

All questions must be answered in full to be reviewed and considered for acceptance into the program.

****

The following information will be used to determine your eligibility. NOTE: You **will be** required to send supporting documentation with this application. If your application is incomplete, it will be returned to you with a request for the additional information required.

Your Household:
- ☐ I live alone and support myself.
- ☐ I have dependents and support others. _____

Please list their name(s) and relationship to you. You are required to provide proof of dependents.

- ☐ I am a dependent and am supported by someone else. _____

Please list their name(s) and relationship to you. You are required to list their income under "Other Household Income."

- ☐ I reside in housing, either partially or completely funded by government, or private assistance.
- ☐ I am incarcerated _____

Please list TDCJ or County Jail Inmate Number

Employment & Income Information:
(Provide gross income, before taxes, and unemployment benefits, if applicable)

- ☐ I am   ☐ I am not   employed   or   ☐ self employed

If unemployed, when did you file for unemployment? _____
Please explain reason, if you did not file for unemployment: _____

*All Income: $ _____ per week OR $ _____ per month

*Include all of **your** income received within the past 12 months from all employment, business, or income from rent payments, Social Security, Veteran benefits, interest, dividends, retirement, annuity payments, or any other sources. Income from others household members will be included under "Other Household Income". (If you entered zero income above, you **are required** to provide supporting documentation regarding your living status.)

INC-A (V3.03/15)

For Office Use Only:

*Other Household Income: This includes **all** other household income not included previously.

Name	Monthly Amount	Source	Relationship

Cash Assets:
I have the following accounts (please list balances):
Checking: $ _____   Savings: $ _____   Money Market: $ _____   Pre-Paid/Debit: $ _____

Supporting Documentation:

You will be **required to submit** supporting documentation to verify your eligibility for the Indigency/Incentive Programs. Check those you are submitting with your application.

Do not send original documents. They will not be returned.

- ☐ A copy of SSI benefits statement.
- ☐ A copy of the most recent Medicaid benefits statement.
- ☐ A copy of your two (2) most recent and complete bank statements. *(General overview statements will not be accepted.)*
- ☐ Your most recent 1040 and related 1099. *(Please note that additional evidence of income may be requested to determine most current income status.)*
- ☐ Evidence of dependents, if not listed on the previous documents.
- ☐ A copy of your two (2) most recent pay statements.
- ☐ A copy of the two (2) most recent pay statements from Other Household income listed above.
- ☐ A copy of your Unemployment approval or denial letter.
- ☐ A copy of your Veteran Benefits statement.
- ☐ Evidence of housing assistance which may include a Government Housing contract.
- ☐ Other applicable documentation.

TEXAS DRIVER RESPONSIBILITY PROGRAM
Indigency/ Incentive Application for Reduction of Surcharges

You are applying to the Indigency/Incentive programs and the department will determine which program you qualify for by the supporting documentation you submit.

ENTER ADDITIONAL INFORMATION IN THIS SPACE

_____
_____
_____
_____
_____
_____

_____
Signature of Applicant

_____
Date

NOTICE: Additional documentation may be requested. You will be notified in writing of the specific documentation required. Requested documentation must be received within 30 days of the date on the initial notice, to be considered as part of this application. If you are unable to respond within 30 days, you will be required to fill out and submit a new application with new supporting documentation.

Mail the completed form to:

INDIGENCY/INCENTIVE APPLICATION PROCESSING
PO BOX 16733 – AUSTIN, TX 78761-6733

TOLL FREE **(800) 688-6882**
Mon – Thur 8AM–9PM, Fri 8AM – 6PM
Saturday 8AM – 12PM

INC-A (V3.0 03/16)

TEXAS DRIVER RESPONSIBILITY PROGRAM
Indigency/Incentive Application for Reduction of Surcharges

You are applying to the Indigency/Incentive programs and the department will determine which program you qualify for by the supporting documentation you submit.

Indigency/Incentive Programs

These programs provide drivers the ability to comply with surcharges owed under the Driver Responsibility Program and maintain driving privileges. Under the Indigency Program, the surcharges are waived. However, under the Incentive Program, the surcharges *are not waived* but are reduced. The objective is to ensure drivers can become licensed, obtain financial liability insurance, and continue to keep our roads safe. Any surcharge assessed on or after September 1, 2003 are eligible for the Indigency/Incentive Programs.

The **Indigency Program** applies to individuals who are living at or below 125% of the federal poverty level, defined annually by the United States Department of Health and Human Services. For approved applicants, surcharges will be waived with accounts totaling a zero balance.

The **Incentive Program** applies to individuals who are living above 125% but are below 300% federal poverty level, defined annually by the United States Department of Health and Human Services. For approved applicants, the surcharge fees will be reduced by 50% of the total amount assessed (service fees apply).

Once approved for a reduction under the Incentive program, the individual must pay the the reduced balance in full *within six (6) months*. All surcharge suspensions will be lifted during this period. If the individual does not pay the balance in full by the due date, their *driving privileges will be suspended until the reduced balance is paid in full*.

These programs will not remove other suspensions on the driving record. To check the status of your driving record, please visit www.texas.gov/driver, then select Driver License and Reinstatement Status.

To Apply – Complete the application in black or blue ink only. The application must be completed in full prior to submission. Use notes section on page 2 for additional information. You may also apply online at www.txsurchargeonline.com.

PLEASE NOTE: Until your application review is completed, you must continue to remit the minimum monthly payment by the due date to avoid suspension of your driving privileges.

Supporting Documents - Applicants must include supporting documentation based on answers provided on the application. If submitting an online application, you may upload all documents, including your application. *All documents must be complete and accurate*. Your application and any supporting documents you provide may be forwarded to the Texas Department of Public Safety for additional review. If your application is found to be fraudulent, it can result in criminal penalties.

Approved - A written notice will be sent to the applicant and will provide the due date and the reduced balance owed.

Denied - A written notice will be sent to the applicant with the reason for the denial.

Status - If you applied online, you can check the status of your application online. Online notices will be available 10-14 business days after your completed application is submitted. If you applied by mail, written notices take up to 60 days after your completed application is submitted.

Payment-The reduced payment must be received by the due date or driving privileges will be suspended. Available payment methods include: ACE Cash Express, MoneyGram, Western Union, Check, Money Order, or Credit or Debit Card. You can also contact us directly at 1-800-688-6882 or visit www.txsurchargeonline.com.

New Surcharges- If additional surcharges are assessed *within 90 calendar days* of reduction approval, those surcharges will be automatically reduced and a letter sent with the new balance due. The original due date remains the same. If new surcharges are assessed *91 days or more after* the reduction approval, a new application will be required.
All notices will be sent to the address associated with the surcharge account(s).

APPENDIX H
SAMPLE PETITION, AFFIDAVIT OF INABILITY TO PAY AND ORDER FOR CLASS C MISDEMEANORS
Note: These forms are intended only as an example and guide for drafting. Please seek the help of an attorney

CAUSE NO. [DOCKET OR CITATION NUMBERS]

THE STATE OF TEXAS	§	IN THE _____ COURT
	§	
V.	§	PRECINCT _____, PLACE _____
	§	
_____	§	_____, TEXAS

DEFENDANT'S MOTION FOR FINDING OF INDIGENCE AND WAIVER OF FINES AND COURT COSTS

COMES NOW, _____, the Defendant in this case and files this *Motion for Finding of Indigence and Waiver of Fines and Court Costs* (the "Motion"), [through counsel _____ (if applicable).]

I. **Indigence**

Defendant moves that this court make a finding of indigence in this matter. Defendant shows the court the following in support of this claim of indigence:

1. Defendant is currently homeless and their income is below the current Federal Poverty Guideline as supported by the attached Sworn Affidavit of Defendant, which is attached hereto as **Exhibit A**.

2. Defendant is unable to obtain a Texas Driver's License because of this outstanding case.

3. Without a Texas Driver's License, Defendant is unable to obtain employment and other services necessary to restabilization, and payment of these fines.

II. **Waiver of Fines and Court Costs**

Article 45.0491 of the Texas Code of Criminal Procedure confers authority upon the judiciary of municipal and justice courts to waive all fines and court costs upon a finding that a defendant is indigent, Tex. Code Crim. Proc. Ann. art. 45.0491 (West).

As conviction in this case can result in additional barriers to obtaining a Texas Driver's License we humbly request that the court dismiss this cause and waive all fines and costs associated or assess community service to be completed in satisfaction of the fines and court costs.

In the alternative, Defendant waives their right to a jury trial and requests the court accept a plea of No Contest and assess a sentence which will not present an undue burden or hardship on the Defendant.

The Defendant humbly requests the court grant this Motion, make a finding of indigence and waive all fines and court costs in the interest of justice.

Respectfully Submitted,

_____
[ATTORNEY OR PRO SE PETITIONER]
Address
Phone Number

CAUSE NO. [DOCKET OR CITATION NUMBERS]

THE STATE OF TEXAS	§ §	IN THE _____ COURT
V.	§ §	PRECINCT_____, PLACE _____
_____	§	_____, TEXAS

SWORN AFFIDAVIT OF DEFENDANT

On this day, _____, appeared before me, the undersigned notary public, and after I administered an oath, upon their oath, said:

1. "My name is, _____, and I am the Defendant in this case.

2. I am currently Employed/Unemployed and support a family of _____.

3. I receive $_____ per month in income. I have $_____ in cash assets, I do not own real property and I have the following monthly expenses:

4. Necessary monthly living expenses:

House payment or rent	$_____
Utilities including telephone	$_____
Food including school lunches	$_____
Child Care	$_____
Car payment and auto insurance	$_____
Gasoline, oil, parking, bus fares, tolls, repairs	$_____
Attorney's fees	$_____
Health and life insurance premiums	$_____
Uninsured medical related expenses	$_____
Clothing and laundry	$_____
Personal	$_____
Total	$_____

5. I wish to resolve the matters I have pending in this court.

6. I am unable to pay the court cost or any part of or to give security required by the rules and the court because I am unemployed, unable to obtain a Texas Driver's License and cannot afford it. My expenses exceed my income and I am unable to borrow the money.

7. I verify that the statements made in this affidavit are true and correct.

_____
By: [Defendant]

SWORN TO and SUBSCRIBED before me by [Defendant] on the _____ day of _____, ____.

_____
Notary Public in and for the State of Texas

Exhibit A

CAUSE NO. [DOCKET OR CITATION NUMBERS]

THE STATE OF TEXAS	§	IN THE _____ COURT
	§	
V.	§	PRECINCT_____, PLACE _____
	§	
_____	§	_____, TEXAS

ORDER FINDING OF INDIGENCE AND WAIVER OF FINES AND COURT COSTS

I. On this date, the court considered the *Motion for Finding of Indigence and Waiver of Fines and Court Costs* of the named Defendant, through counsel, pursuant to Tex. Code Crim. Proc. Ann. art. 45.0491 (West). Defendant has waived their right to a jury trial and entered a plea of No Contest.

II. The court finds that the Defendant in this matter is indigent and Orders that:

_____ All fines and costs are hereby dismissed.

_____ The Defendant's plea of No Contest is accepted and all fines and court costs are waived.

_____ The Defendant's plea of No Contest is accepted and is ordered _____ hours community service in lieu of all fines and court costs.

III. Any surcharges resulting from this conviction are also waived in accordance with Tex. Transp. Code Ann. §708.158 (West). The Defendant's Texas Driver's License number is _____ and date of birth is _____.

It is, therefore, ORDERED and ADJUDGED.

_____ _____
Date   Judge Presiding

APPENDIX I:

STEPS TO ORDER A TEXAS CRIMINAL HISTORY RECORD

Start here. Check each as it applies and it will lead you to the next step(s).

STEP 1: CHOOSE TYPE OF CRIMINAL HISTORY RECORD

Choose between a name-based search (what the public can see), or a fingerprint search (by law, visible only to you, law enforcement, certain government agencies and other entities).

- ☐ Name-based online search – basic information available to the public. → Go to STEP2

- ☐ Fingerprint-based searched – comprehensive, complete history available to law enforcement, licensing agencies and others authorized by statute to view it. → Go to STEP 3

STEP 2: NAME-BASED SEARCH

- ☐ You will need:
  - Access to a computer
  - Access to a printer or flash drive (to save the results)
  - A credit card (does not have to be yours)

  ___ Search through DPS - Go to the DPS Criminal Record Search public site:
  https://records.txdps.state.tx.us/DpsWebsite/index.aspx
  OR

  ___ Search online private vendor, such as Public Data www.publicdata.com. Cost varies based on the vendor and the records sought.

STEP 3: FINGERPRINT–BASED SEARCH

You will need:

- ☐ DPS Form CR-63, Review of Criminal History Information[1]

- ☐ Fingerprint card less than 6 months old.

- ☐ $25.00 ($15.00 for record check plus $10.00 for fingerprints)

  - *Electronic submission:*
    Fingerprints can be sent to DPS electronically through L-1 Enrollment, a.k.a. Fingerprint Applicant Services of Texas (FAST). The record results will be mailed to you at the address you provided.

    ___ Complete DPS Form CR-63 (FAST pass form).

    ___ Make an appointment to be fingerprinted. Go to www.L1enrollment.com for Texas FAST locations, or call 1-888-467-2080.

    ___ Bring a check or money order for $25.00 to the appointment.

---

[1] From DPS, www.txdps.state.tx.us/internetforms/Forms/CR-63.pdf

- *Mail submission:*

    ___ Complete DPS Form CR-63.

    ___ Make sure your fingerprint card is less than 6 months old.
    If not, make an appointment to be fingerprinted. Go to L1enrollment.com for Texas FAST locations, or call 1-888-467-2080.

    Mail the (FAST) pass form, check or US money order for $25.00 and fingerprint card to:

    L-1 Enrollment Services
    1650 Wabash Avenue, Suite D
    Springfield, IL 62704

The card will be scanned, then sent to DPS. The record will mailed to you or someone designated by you (such as an employer) in about 10 business days.

APPENDIX J:
STEPS FOR EXPUNCTION OF CRIMINAL HISTORY RECORD

STEP 1: DETERMINE ELIGIBILITY FOR EXPUNCTION

Note: Expunction is available only to clear arrests that did not lead to conviction and for Class C misdemeanors resulting in deferred adjudication. Expunction *cannot* remove records of adult criminal convictions except 1) where the person has been pardoned; 2) where the conviction was thrown out on appeal, or 3) where the person was granted relief on the basis of actual innocence in a court order finding the same. Tex. Code Crim. P.Art. 55.01(a)(1)(B)(ii).

You must meet all of these requirements. If you do not, STOP.

- ☐ You were released after your arrest and not charged or convicted of a crime.

- ☐ You have never been under community or court supervision for this arrest. You have not attended any classes, paid any fines, or been placed on any kind of probation for this arrest.

- ☐ Your arrest was not part of a "criminal episode," and you have never been charged for any other crime as a part of a criminal episode.

STEP 2: GATHER INFORMATION FOR EXPUNCTION

You will need:

- ☐ An official criminal history record.[1]
- ☐ Your fingerprint record.
- ☐ Court Filing Fee. Call the clerk of the court where you intend to file for the total cost of filing the Petition for Expunction. If you cannot afford the fee, complete an
    - o Affidavit of Inability to Pay Court Costs

STEP 3: COMPLETE PETITION FOR EXPUNCTION

- ☐ Complete Petition for Expunction of Criminal Records[2]
- ☐ Sign the Petition in front of Notary and make extra copies.

STEP 4: FILE PETITION FOR EXPUNCTION

- ☐ File the original petition (not copy) in the district court for the county where
    - o You were arrested, OR

---

[1] Your criminal history record will usually contain all of the information you must include in the Petition for Expunction required by Tex. Code Crim. P. Art 55.02 Sec. (2): (b) The petition must be verified and shall include the following or an explanation for why one or more of the following is **not** included:
(1) the petitioner's full name; sex; race; date of birth; driver's license number; social security number; and address at the time of the arrest;
(2) the offense charged against the petitioner;
(3) the date the offense charged against the petitioner was alleged to have been committed;
(4) the date the petitioner was arrested;
(5) the name of the county where the petitioner was arrested and if the arrest occurred in a municipality, the name of the municipality;
(6) the name of the agency that arrested the petitioner;
(7) the case number and court of offense.
[2] Self help forms and instructions for Expunction may be downloaded from Texas Law Help, or visit your local law library for other styles of forms. For a list of all county law libraries in Texas, click here.

- - The offense was alleged to have occurred.[3]
- ☐ Ask the clerk to file-stamp your extra copies.
- ☐ Pay the filing fee to the clerk of the court.
- ☐ Ask the clerk to set a hearing on the Petition.[4]

STEP 5: ATTEND THE EXPUNCTION HEARING

You will need:

- ☐ Order Directing Expunction of Criminal Records. Fill in the information in the Order that you used to complete your Petition. Leave the judge's signature bar blank. Take the completed Order to your hearing.
- ☐ If the judge agrees, s/he will sign the Order. The clerk of the court will send a certified copy of the Order to everyone listed on your Petition ordering them to return or destroy all records about this arrest.[5]
- ☐ Get a certified copy of the Order from the clerk's office to keep with our files (usually about $1 a page). This is important in case you need to prove that the Order was granted.

---

[3] Tex. Code Crim. P. Art. 55.02 §(2)(a). Both the criminal history record and fingerprint record are available through the Texas Dept. of Public Safety. The cost for both is about $30.00. To find your local DPS office, go to www.txdps.state.tx.us/administration/driver_licensing_control/rolodex/search.asp or call 2-1-1 o find the location nearest you.

[4] Tex. Code Crim. P. Art. 55.02§ (2)(c) The court shall set a hearing on the matter no sooner than thirty days from the filing of the petition and shall give to each official or agency or other governmental entity named in the petition reasonable notice of the hearing.

[5] Tex. Code Crim. P. Art. 55.02 §5(d).

APPENDIX J
SAMPLE PETITION, VERIFICATION AND ORDER SETTING HEARING FOR EXPUNCTION OF CRIMINAL HISTORY
Note:
These forms are intended only as an example and guide for drafting.[6]

CAUSE NO. _____

EX PARTE	§	IN THE _____ DISTRICT COURT
	§	
[PETITIONER]	§	_____ COUNTY, TEXAS

ORIGINAL PETITION FOR EXPUNCTION OF CRIMINAL RECORDS

TO THE HONORABLE JUDGE OF SAID COURT:

COMES NOW **[PETITIONER]** (hereinafter "Petitioner") and pursuant to Articles 55.01 and 55.02, V.T.C.A., Code of Criminal Procedure, moves the court the expunction of all records relating to or resulting from the offense described more particularly below. The Petitioner would respectfully show the Court the following:

I.

The following information is provided to identify the Petitioner:

NAME:
GENDER:
RACE:
DATE OF BIRTH:
DRIVER'S LICENSE NUMBER:
SOCIAL SECURITY NUMBER:
ADDRESS AT TIME OF ARREST:

II.

The following information is provided to identify the charges the Petitioner is requesting the Court expunge:

ALLEGED OFFENSE:
DATE OF ARREST:
COUNTY WHERE ARRESTED:
MUNICIPALITY WHERE ARREST OCCURRED:
ARRESTING AGENCY:
CAUSE NUMBER:
OFFENSE REPORT NUMBER:
COURT:

III.

The following reason demonstrates the Petitioner's grounds for expunction:

On [DISMISSAL DATE] the court dismissed the [felony/misdemeanor] charge in this cause for the offense of [OFFENSE]. Petitioner has been released, the charge against them has not resulted in a final conviction, and is no longer pending.

---

[6]Visit your county local law library for other styles of forms. For a list of all county law libraries in Texas, click here.

IV.

Issuance of an order expunging the criminal history record information related to the offense which was dismissed is in the best interest of justice.

V.

The Petitioner has reason to believe that the following law enforcement agencies have records or files subject to expunction herein and should be cited to appear and show cause why an expunction order should not be granted:

1. _____ County District Attorney's Office
   [Address]

2. _____ County Attorney's Office
   [Address]

3. _____ County District Clerk's Office
   [Address]

4. _____ County Sheriff's Department
   [Address]

5. _____ Police Department ←(Arresting Agency)
   [Address]

6. Texas Department of Public Safety
   Crime Records Service MSC 0234
   P. O. Box 4143
   Austin, TX 78765-4143

THEREFORE, the Petitioner respectfully requests that the Court set this matter hearing as provided by law and that upon said hearing, that an expunction order be granted, requiring all of the above-named agencies to expunge all of their records relating to the above-described arrest.

Respectfully submitted,

_____
[ATTORNEY FOR PETITIONER OR PETITIONER PRO SE]
[Address and Telephone]

Certificate of Service

I hereby certify that a true and correct copy of the foregoing Petition has been served on the _____ County District Attorney's Office on this ____day of _____ 20___.

_____
[Attorney or Petitioner Pro Se]

CAUSE NO. _____

EX PARTE	§ §	IN THE _____ DISTRICT COURT
[PETITIONER]	§	_____ COUNTY, TEXAS

VERIFICATION OF ORIGINAL PETITION FOR EXPUNCTION OF CRIMINAL RECORD

BEFORE ME, the undersigned authority, on this day personally appeared **[PETITIONER]**, Petitioner, known to me to be the person whose name is subscribed to the foregoing instrument, who, after being duly sworn, upon oath stated as follows:

My name is [PETITIONER]. I have read the foregoing motion, and the facts stated therein are within my personal knowledge and are true and correct.

_____
[PETITIONER]

SWORN TO AND SUBSCRIBED BEFORE ME by [PETITIONER] on this the ____ day of _____ 20___.

_____
NOTARY PUBLIC, STATE OF TEXAS

CAUSE NO. _____

EX PARTE	§	IN THE _____ DISTRICT COURT
	§	
[PETITIONER]	§	_____ COUNTY, TEXAS

ORDER SETTING HEARING DATE

It is ORDERED that a hearing on the petition for expunction of criminal records file in the above-mentioned cause will be held on _____, 20___ at _____ o'clock ___.m in the courtroom of the district court for the _____ Judicial District of Texas in _____, Texas.

Signed this _____ day of _____, 20____.

_____
JUDGE PRESIDING
_____ District Court
_____ County, Texas

NOTICE: THIS DOCUMENT CONTAINS SENSITIVE DATA

Cause Number: _____

Ex Parte:

_____
(Your Initials, example: M.K.S.)

An Adult

In the _____
District Court

of _____ County, Texas

Order Granting Expunction of Criminal Records

Today, the Court considered Petitioner's Petition for Expunction of Criminal Records. The Court finds that it has jurisdiction over this case. The Court further finds and ORDERS as follows:

1. Information about Petitioner

The Court finds that Petitioner's information is as follows:

a. Full Name: _____.

b. Race: _____.

c. Sex: ☐ male. ☐ female.

d. Date of Birth: ___/___/_____.

e. Driver's License Number: _____.
   or ☐ Petitioner does not have a driver's license number.

f. State identification (SID) number is: _____ State: _____
   or ☐ Petitioner does not have a state identification (SID) number.

g. Social Security Number: _____.
   or ☐ Petitioner does not have a social security number.

2. Information about Respondents

The Court finds that the following Respondents have been properly served by the Clerk of this Court as required by law:

Texas Department of Public Safety– Crime Records Service (MSC0234)
For itself and for: the Federal Bureau of Investigation, Identification Section, the National Crime Information Center, the Texas Crime Information Center, the Governor's Division of Emergency Management, the State Operations Center/Preparedness Section, the Texas Fusion Center, ***and*** <u>any entity that purchases Texas Department of Public Safety records</u>.
ATTN: Expunctions
PO Box 4143, Austin, Texas 78765

Name of Agency:	
ATTN: Expunctions	
Physical Address:	
Email Address:	

Name of Agency:	
ATTN: Expunctions	
Physical Address:	
Email Address:	

Name of Agency:	
ATTN: Expunctions	
Physical Address:	
Email Address:	

Name of Agency:	
ATTN: Expunctions	
Physical Address:	
Email Address:	

Name of Agency:	
ATTN: Expunctions	
Physical Address:	
Email Address:	

Name of Agency:	
ATTN: Expunctions	
Physical Address:	
Email Address:	

Name of Agency:	
ATTN: Expunctions	
Physical Address:	
Email Address:	

Name of Agency:	
ATTN: Expunctions	
Physical Address:	

Email Address:	

(Check only if applicable.)

☐ The Court finds that the Respondents listed in the attached *Additional Respondents Exhibit* have been properly served by the Clerk of this Court as required by law and ORDERS that the attached *Additional Respondents Exhibit* is fully incorporated into this Order.

3. Expunction of the following Arrest

The Court finds that Petitioner is entitled to expunction of the following arrest:

a. Petitioner's DPS tracking incident number for this arrest is: _____.

b. Petitioner was arrested on _____/_____/_____.

c. Petitioner was arrested in: _____.
                                 City   County   State

d. Petitioner was arrested by this law enforcement agency:
   _____.

e. Petitioner's address **at the time of this arrest** was:
   _____.
       Street Address   City   State   Zip

The Court finds that no charges arising from this arrest have been filed and the statutory waiting period or statute of limitation expired before Petitioner filed its Petition for Expunction of Criminal Records:

1st Offense: _____
        Date offense allegedly occurred: _____/_____/_____.

2nd Offense: _____
        Date offense allegedly occurred: _____/_____/_____.

3rd Offense : _____
        Date offense allegedly occurred: _____/_____/_____.

4th Offense : _____
        Date offense allegedly occurred: _____/_____/_____.

4. Expunction of Additional Arrest or Arrests

(Check only if applicable.)

☐ The Court finds that Petitioner is entitled to expunction of the arrest or arrests listed in the attached: *(Check all that apply.)*

    ☐ *Additional Arrest Exhibit A* which is fully incorporated into this Order.

    ☐ *Additional Arrest Exhibit B* which is fully incorporated into this Order.

    ☐ *Additional Arrest Exhibit C* which is fully incorporated into this Order.

5. Orders

For purposes of this ORDER, the phrase "all records and files pertaining to the arrest" includes records and files that were generated by Respondents during this expunction proceeding, including the copies of the Petition and of this ORDER that are served on each Respondent.

It is therefore **ORDERED, ADJUDGED AND DECREED** that all records and files pertaining to the arrest or arrests listed in this Order be expunged. Related arrests of the same or similar charge, date, or arresting agency not specifically listed herein are excluded from this ORDER. However, records of such unexpunged arrests that would not have been generated except for the expunged arrest are ORDERED expunged.

Records and files pertaining to the expunged arrest shall be expunged by delivering them to the Clerk of this Court, in a sealed envelope, by hand-delivery or mail to:

District Clerk of _____ **County, Texas**
Address: _____

Each Respondent named above shall attach a certificate to the sealed envelope certifying that the enclosed records are all the records that the Respondent possesses that are subject to the ORDER. If returning records expunged by this ORDER to the Clerk is impractical, records pertaining to the arrest may be expunged by the Respondent by obliterating or destroying said records; and then by deleting from its public records all index references to the records and files that are subject to this ORDER. The Respondent shall then send a certificate to the Clerk certifying that the records have been obliterated or destroyed.

Videotapes and audiotapes shall be expunged by erasure.

Records that pertain both to this arrest and to other arrests that are not included in this ORDER, and which would have been generated even if the expunged arrest(s) had not been made shall be obliterated by covering with tape, liquid paper, or other opaque substance insofar as they pertain to arrests that are the subject of this ORDER.

The Texas Department of Public Safety shall forward this ORDER to any and all central federal depositories of criminal records and request that they return or destroy the records pertaining to the expunged arrest(s). The Texas Department of Public Safety shall also certify that it has requested any and all central federal depositories of criminal records to return all records and files subject to this ORDER.

It is further ORDERED that the Texas Department of Public Safety, by secure electronic mail, electronic transmission, or facsimile transmission, provide notice of this ORDER, together with an explanation of this ORDER and instruction to the entity to destroy all records and information subject to this ORDER, to the following:

1. The current list of all "Customers who have purchased the CCH Database," as maintained by the Texas Department of Public Safety, Crime Records Service, and as currently displayed at the following page of the DPS Website: https://records.txdps.state.tx.us/DpsWebsite/CriminalHistory/Purchases.aspx.
2. All private entities who have purchased criminal history record information from the Department of Public Safety within the ten (10) years preceding the date of this Petition.

3. Each person who applies or has applied for access to criminal history record information maintained by the Department of Public Safety [Texas Govt. Code Sec 411.085(b)(1)].
4. Any private entity which notifies the Department of Public Safety that it sells or has sold any compilation of criminal history record information to another similar entity, and any similar entity as having purchased such information from a private entity [Texas Govt. Code Sec 411.085(b)(2)].
5. All entities listed in the attached "Private Entity List."

All state agencies that sent information concerning the instant arrest to a central federal depository are ORDERED to request that the depository return all records and files subject to this ORDER.

The Clerk of this Court shall certify when the ORDER is final and shall mail certified copies of the certification to: 1) the Travis County District or County Attorney's Office; 2) to Petitioner; and 3) by certified mail, return receipt requested, to all other Respondents.

It is further ORDERED that the Clerk of the Court maintain any and all records returned pursuant to this ORDER in a manner not subject to public view and destroy all records, including the records of this expunction proceeding, on or after one year from the date of this ORDER.

Pursuant to the Code of Criminal Procedure Article 55.03, the maintenance, release, dissemination or use of the records, for any purpose, expunged herein, is prohibited. Petitioner may deny the occurrence of the arrest referred to herein and the existence of this Order of Expunction, unless questioned under oath in a criminal proceeding, in which case the Petitioner may state only that the matter in question has been expunged.

SIGNED on _____.

_____
JUDGE PRESIDING

APPROVED AS TO FORM AND SUBSTANCE:

_____
Petitioner

An Overview of Orders of Nondisclosure
September 1, 2017

What is an Order of Nondisclosure?

An order of nondisclosure is a court order prohibiting public entities, including courts, clerks of the court, law enforcement agencies, and prosecutorial offices, from disclosing certain criminal records. If you have a criminal record, you may benefit from obtaining an order of nondisclosure.

An order of nondisclosure legally frees you from having to disclose certain information about your criminal history in response to questions on job applications. You are not required to disclose information related to an offense that is the subject of an order of nondisclosure.

Please note that an order of nondisclosure applies to a particular criminal offense. The order does not apply to all offenses that may be on your criminal history record, but you may obtain multiple orders of nondisclosure for multiple offenses.

As mentioned above, an order of nondisclosure prohibits entities holding information about a certain offense on your criminal history record from disclosing that information. This is a general rule. There are exceptions. Certain criminal justice and state agencies may still obtain information concerning an offense that is the subject of an order of nondisclosure.

Changes Effective September 1, 2017

Prior to September 1, 2017, the date of the offense determined what law applied and forms to use when petitioning a court for an order of nondisclosure. However, effective September 1, 2017, the current nondisclosure laws, as set forth in Subchapter E-1 of Chapter 411 of the Government Code, will apply to all persons seeking an order of nondisclosure, regardless of the date of the offense, and everyone will choose among the same forms.

The following laws address the types of nondisclosure petitions and orders available:

- Section 411.072, Gov't Code (Deferred Adjudication Community Supervision; Certain Nonviolent Misdemeanors);
- Section 411.0725, Gov't Code (Deferred Adjudication Community Supervision; Felonies and Certain Misdemeanors);
- Section 411.0727, Gov't Code (Procedure Following Successful Completion of Veterans Treatment Court Program);
- Section 411.0728, Gov't Code (Victims of Trafficking of Persons);
- Section 411.073, Gov't Code (Community Supervision Following Conviction; Certain Misdemeanors);
- Section 411.0731 Gov't Code (Procedure for Community Supervision Following Conviction; Certain Driving While Intoxicated Convictions) (*NEW – effective September 1, 2017*);
- Section 411.0735, Gov't Code (Conviction and Confinement; Certain Misdemeanors); and
- Section 411.0736, Gov't Code (Procedure for Conviction; Certain Driving While Intoxicated Convictions) (*NEW – effective September 1, 2017*)

Each of the sections listed above provides specific procedures and requirements that you must satisfy in order to obtain an order of nondisclosure. The procedures and requirements for each section are different. You must determine which section is the correct section for you to use to request an order of nondisclosure.

WHEN A PETITION IS REQUIRED, YOU MUST FILE IT WITH THE CLERK OF THE COURT ("CLERK") THAT SENTENCED YOU OR PLACED YOU ON COMMUNITY SUPERVISION ("PROBATION") OR DEFERRED ADJUDICATION COMMUNITY SUPERVISION ("DEFERRED ADJUDICATION"). THE CLERK WILL SEND THE PETITION TO THE JUDGE, AND EITHER THE JUDGE OR THE CLERK WILL SEND A COPY OF THE PETITION TO THE ATTORNEY REPRESENTING THE STATE.

Documents You Should Gather to Assist You

You may need one or more of the following documents, depending on your case, to help you to determine if you are eligible for an order of nondisclosure:

1) a copy of the judgment in your case;
2) a signed order or document showing that the judge reduced your period of deferred adjudication, probation, or confinement, or granted you an early termination;

3) a signed order or document showing that you completed your deferred adjudication or probation, including any term of confinement imposed and payment of all fines, costs, and restitution imposed;

4) a **discharge** order (an order or document showing that you were discharged from probation or deferred adjudication);

5) a **discharge and dismissal** order (an order showing that the judge set aside the verdict in your case or permitted you to withdraw your plea and dismissed the accusation, complaint, information, or indictment against you in accordance with Section 42A.701, Code of Criminal Procedure (formerly, Section 20(a), Article 42.12); and

6) a signed order or judgment reflecting any affirmative findings made by the judge, including any finding that it is not in the best interest of justice for you to receive an order of nondisclosure, any finding of family violence, and any finding that you have to register as a sex offender.

Basic Eligibility Requirements for All Orders of Nondisclosure

In addition to the specific procedures and requirements of each section listed above, in order to be eligible for an order of nondisclosure under any of them, you **MUST** first satisfy the basic requirements of Section 411.074, Government Code. There are three basic requirements under Section 411.074 (see Nos. 1 thru 3 immediately below). **IF YOU CANNOT SATISFY THESE REQUIREMENTS, YOU ARE NOT ELIGIBLE FOR AN ORDER OF NONDISCLOSURE, and there is no need for you to request an order of nondisclosure because the court does not have the legal authority to grant an order of nondisclosure to you.**

1. You are not eligible for an order of nondisclosure if the offense for which the order of nondisclosure is requested, or any other offense you have ever been convicted of or placed on deferred adjudication for was one of the following:
    (A) an offense requiring registration as a sex offender under Chapter 62, Code of Criminal Procedure;
    (B) an offense under Texas Penal Code Section 20.04 (aggravated kidnapping), regardless of whether the offense is a reportable conviction or adjudication for purposes of Chapter 62, Code of Criminal Procedure;
    (C) an offense under any of the following sections of the Texas Penal Code:
    - 19.02 (murder);
    - 19.03 (capital murder);
    - 20A.02 (trafficking of persons);

- 20A.03 (continuous trafficking of persons);
- 22.04 (injury to a child, elderly individual, or disabled individual);
- 22.041 (abandoning or endangering a child);
- 25.07 (violation of court orders or conditions of bond in a family violence, sexual assault or abuse, stalking, or trafficking case);
- 25.072 (repeated violation of certain court orders or conditions of bond in family violence, sexual assault or abuse, stalking, or trafficking case); or
- 42.072 (stalking); or

(D) any other offense involving family violence, as defined by Section 71.004, Family Code.

2. You are not eligible for an order of nondisclosure if the court made an **affirmative finding** that the offense for which the order of nondisclosure is requested involved family violence, as defined by Section 71.004, Family Code.

3. You are not eligible for an order of nondisclosure if, during the period after you were convicted or placed on probation or deferred adjudication for the offense for which the order of nondisclosure is requested, and during any applicable waiting period following completion of the sentence, probation, or deferred adjudication (*see* **Note** below), you were convicted of or placed on deferred adjudication for another offense other than a traffic offense punishable by fine only.

> **Note:** There are waiting periods for some of the orders of nondisclosure. After determining which nondisclosure law applies to you, confirm that you have not been convicted of or placed on deferred adjudication for another offense other than a traffic offense punishable by fine only during the waiting period.

If you meet the requirements of Section 411.074 discussed above, you can proceed to the next portion of this overview.

Selecting the Appropriate Procedure for Requesting an Order of Nondisclosure

In order to make it simpler for you to determine which type of order of nondisclosure is the correct one for you, this overview will lead you through a series of questions. After answering the questions, you will determine either that you are not eligible for an order of nondisclosure and should proceed no further, or that you are eligible for an order of nondisclosure and should proceed below to a particular section under **Types of Nondisclosure** for additional information and instructions. Each section designated below has requirements that you must satisfy in addition to those listed above for Section 411.074.

The following five questions will assist you in determining which nondisclosure law, if any, applies to your offense.

Question 1:

Is the offense for which the order of nondisclosure is requested an offense under one of the following sections?

Section 43.02, Penal Code (Prostitution);

Section 43.03(a)(2), Penal Code (Promotion of Prostitution), punishable as a Class A misdemeanor;

Section 481.120, Health and Safety Code (Delivery of Marihuana), punishable as a Class B misdemeanor;

Section 481.121, Health and Safety Code (Possession of Marihuana), punishable as a Class B misdemeanor; or

Section 31.03, Penal Code (Theft), punishable as a Class C or B misdemeanor;

- If your answer to Question 1 is "NO," proceed to Question 2.
- If your answer is "YES", you should carefully go through the discussion under Section 411.0728 in the **Types of Nondisclosure** section below and the **Instructions for Completing the Model Petition for an Order of Nondisclosure under Section 411.0728** to determine whether you qualify to file a petition under that section. If you find that you are not eligible for an order of nondisclosure under Section 411.0728, you should return to this point in the overview and continue with Question 2.

Question 2:

Is the offense for which the order of nondisclosure is requested an offense for which you successfully completed a veterans treatment court program, as defined by Chapter 124 of Title 2 of the Government Code, or former law?

- If your answer to Question 2 is "NO," proceed to Question 3.
- If your answer is "YES," you should carefully go through the discussion under Section 411.0727 in the **Types of Nondisclosure** section below and the **Instructions for Completing the Model Petition for an Order of Nondisclosure under Section 411.0727** to determine whether you qualify to file a petition under that section. If you find that you are not eligible for an order of nondisclosure under Section 411.0727, you should return to this point in the overview and continue with Question 3.

Question 3:
Is the offense for which the order of nondisclosure is requested a Class B misdemeanor driving while intoxicated offense under Section 49.04, Penal Code?
- If your answer to Question 3 is "YES," were you placed on probation **following** your conviction for the offense?
    - If your answer is "YES," you should carefully go through the discussion under Section 411.0731 in the **Types of Nondisclosure** section below and the **Instructions for Completing the Model Petition for an Order of Nondisclosure under Section 411.0731** to determine whether you qualify to file a petition under that section. If you find that you are not eligible under Section 411.0731, you may be eligible for an order of nondisclosure under Section 411.0736. You should carefully go through the discussion under 411.0736 in the **Types of Nondisclosure** section below and the **Instructions for Completing the Model Petition for an Order of Nondisclosure under Section 411.0736** to determine whether you qualify to file a petition under that section.
    - If your answer is "NO," you should carefully go through the discussion under Section 411.0736 in the **Types of Nondisclosure** section below and the **Instructions for Completing the Model Petition for an Order of Nondisclosure under Section 411.0736** to determine whether you qualify to file a petition under that section. If you find that you are not eligible for an order of nondisclosure under Section 411.0736, you are not eligible for an order of nondisclosure for your driving while intoxicated offense and none of the other questions apply to you.

- If your answer to Question 3 is "NO," proceed to Question 4.

Question 4:
Is the offense for which the order of nondisclosure is requested a felony?
- If your answer to Question 4 is "NO," proceed to Question 5.
- If your answer is "YES," were you placed on deferred adjudication for that offense?
    - If your answer is "YES," follow the procedure for Section 411.0725.
    - If your answer is "NO," you are **not** eligible for an order of nondisclosure and none of the remaining questions apply to you.

Question 5:
Is the offense for which the order of nondisclosure is requested a misdemeanor for which you were you placed on deferred adjudication?
- If your answer to Question 5 is "YES," other than the offense for which the order of nondisclosure is requested, have you ever been previously convicted of or placed on deferred adjudication for an offense other than a traffic offense that is punishable by fine only?
  - If your answer is "YES," follow the procedure for Section 411.0725.
  - If your answer is "NO," is the offense for which the order of nondisclosure is requested a misdemeanor in which the judge entered an affirmative finding that it is not in the best interest of justice for you to receive an automatic order of nondisclosure and filed a statement of this affirmative finding in the papers of your case?
    - If your answer is "YES," follow the procedure for Section 411.0725.
    - If your answer is "NO," is the offense for which the order of nondisclosure is requested a misdemeanor under Penal Code Chapters 20 (kidnapping, unlawful restraint, or smuggling of persons), 21 (sexual offenses), 22 (assaultive offenses), 25 (offenses against the family), 42 (disorderly conduct and related offenses), 43 (public indecency offenses), 46 (weapons offenses), or 71 (organized crime offenses)?
      - If your answer is "YES," follow the procedure for Section 411.0725.
      - If your answer is "NO," follow the procedure for Section 411.072.
- If your answer to Question 5 is "NO," other than the offense for which the order of nondisclosure is requested, have you ever been previously convicted of or placed on deferred adjudication for an offense other than a traffic offense that is punishable by fine only?
  - If your answer is "YES," you are **not** eligible for an order of nondisclosure. None of the remaining questions apply to you.
  - If your answer is "NO," is the offense for which the order of nondisclosure is requested one of the following: Alcoholic Beverage Code Sec. 106.041 (driving or operating watercraft under the influence of alcohol by minor); Penal Code Secs. 49.04 (driving while intoxicated), 49.05 (flying while intoxicated), 49.06 (boating while

intoxicated), or 49.065 (assembling or operating an amusement ride while intoxicated); or Chapter 71 (organized crime)?

- If your answer is "YES," you are **not** eligible for an order of nondisclosure, and none of the remaining questions apply to you. (This assumes that you do not qualify under Section 411.0731 or 411.0736, Government Code. See Question 3 above.)
- If your answer is "NO," were you placed on probation for the offense for which the order of nondisclosure is requested, including a probation that required you to serve a term of confinement as a condition of the probation or to be placed on probation after you served a term of confinement?
  - If your answer is "YES," follow the procedure for Section 411.073.
  - If your answer is "NO," follow the procedure for Section 411.0735.

Types of Nondisclosure

At this point, it is time to review the **additional** requirements for specific sections of the Government Code to see if you qualify for an order of nondisclosure under the section that applies to you.

THE INFORMATION PROVIDED FOR EACH TYPE OF NONDISCLOSURE LISTED BELOW ASSUMES THAT YOU HAVE DETERMINED THAT YOU MEET THE BASIC ELIGIBILITY REQUIREMENTS SET FORTH IN SECTION 411.074, GOVERNMENT CODE, AS DISCUSSED ABOVE, AND THAT YOU HAVE IDENTIFIED THE TYPE OF NONDISCLOSURE, IF ANY, THAT APPLIES TO YOUR OFFENSE. THE INFORMATION PROVIDED ABOVE IDENTIFIES THE CIRCUMSTANCES AND OFFENSES THAT MAKE YOU INELIGIBLE FOR AN ORDER OF NONDISCLOSURE UNDER SOME OR ALL OF THE SECTIONS LISTED BELOW. IF YOU HAVE NOT REVIEWED THE INFORMATION PROVIDED ABOVE AND ANSWERED THE QUESTIONS TO DETERMINE WHICH ORDER OF NONDISCLOSURE, IF ANY, APPLIES TO YOUR OFFENSE, PLEASE DO SO BEFORE READING THE REMAINING PARTS OF THIS OVERVIEW.

SECTION 411.072 – Procedure for Deferred Adjudication Community Supervision for Certain Nonviolent Misdemeanors

1. You are not eligible for an order of nondisclosure under Section 411.072 if your discharge and dismissal occurred prior to September 1, 2017.

2. You are not eligible for an order of nondisclosure under Section 411.072 if it has not been at least 180 days since the Court placed you on deferred adjudication.

3. You are not eligible for an order of nondisclosure under Section 411.072 if the court entered an affirmative finding that it is not in the best interest of justice that you receive an automatic order of nondisclosure under Section 411.072. If the court entered such a finding, you may still qualify under Section 411.0725.

To obtain an order of nondisclosure under Section 411.072, if you are eligible, the process is as follows:

1) You are not required to file a petition;
2) You are required to present any evidence necessary to establish that you **are** eligible to receive an order of nondisclosure under Section 411.072. You can meet this requirement by completing the **Letter Requesting an Order of Nondisclosure under Section 411.072** available at this link: http://www.txcourts.gov/rules-forms/orders-of-nondisclosure; and
3) You must pay a $28 fee or submit a Statement of Inability to Afford Payment of Court Costs to the clerk before the court will issue the order. The Statement of Inability to Afford Payment of Court Costs is described in Rule 145 of the Texas Rules of Civil Procedure. You may view Rule 145 online at: *http://www.txcourts.gov/media/1435952/trcp-all-updated-with-amendments-effective-912016.pdf.* You may click here to obtain the form for the Statement of Inability to Afford Payment of Court Costs: *http://www.txcourts.gov/media/1435953/statement-final-version.pdf.*

If you received a discharge and dismissal of the proceedings against you, the law requires the court to determine whether you satisfy the requirements of Section 411.074, and if the court finds that you have satisfied the requirements of that section, the court must issue the order of nondisclosure. **However, the court cannot issue the order before the 180th day following the date the court placed on deferred adjudication.**

The court will have access to your criminal history record information and may use it to determine your eligibility for an order of nondisclosure under Section 411.072.

SECTION 411.0725 – Procedure for Deferred Adjudication –for Felonies and Certain Misdemeanors

1. You are not eligible for an order of nondisclosure under Section 411.0725 if you **QUALIFY** for an order of nondisclosure under Section 411.072. You must make sure that you do not qualify under Section 411.072 before proceeding under Section 411.0725.

2. You are not eligible for an order of nondisclosure under Section 411.0725 if you did not receive a discharge and dismissal under Article 42A.111 (or former law), Code of Criminal Procedure, for the offense for which the order of nondisclosure is requested.

3. You are not eligible for an order of nondisclosure under Section 411.0725 if during the period after the court placed you on deferred adjudication for the offense for which the order of nondisclosure is requested, and during any applicable waiting period (described in Number 4 below) following completion of your deferred adjudication, you were convicted of or placed on deferred adjudication for another offense other than a traffic offense punishable by fine only.

4. Waiting Period. You are eligible to file a petition for an order of nondisclosure under Section 411.0725 as follows:
    a) Immediately after discharge and dismissal, if the offense for which you are requesting an order of nondisclosure is a misdemeanor offense other than one of the misdemeanor offenses listed in b) below;
    b) On or after the second anniversary of the date of your discharge and dismissal, if you were placed on deferred adjudication for a misdemeanor offense under Penal Code Chapters 20 (kidnapping, unlawful restraint, or smuggling of persons), 21 (sexual offenses), 22 (assaultive offenses), 25 (offenses against the family), 42 (disorderly conduct and related offenses), 43 (public indecency offenses), or 46 (weapons offenses); or
    c) On or after the fifth anniversary of the date of your discharge and dismissal if the offense for which you are requesting an order of nondisclosure is a felony.

In order to obtain an order of nondisclosure under Section 411.0725, if you are eligible, you must file a petition. The form and instructions for obtaining an order of nondisclosure under Section 411.0725 are available at this link: http://www.txcourts.gov/rules-forms/orders-of-nondisclosure.

You should not have to pay the clerk to notify the prosecutor of your petition. Under Section 411.0745(e), Government Code, the court must notify the prosecutor. Additionally, if the court issues an order of nondisclosure, you should not have to pay the clerk to notify law enforcement. Under Section 411.075, Government Code, the clerk must notify the Crime Records Service Division of the Texas Department of Public Safety (hereinafter "DPS") of the order of nondisclosure, and DPS must notify the law enforcement agencies and entities designated in the statute.

SECTION 411.0727 – Procedure Following Successful Completion of Veterans Treatment Court Program

1. If you did not successfully complete a veterans treatment court program ("program") for the offense for which the order of nondisclosure is requested, you are not eligible for an order of nondisclosure under Section 411.0727.

2. If your entry into the veterans treatment court program arose as a result of a conviction for an offense involving the operation of a motor vehicle while intoxicated, you are not eligible for an order of nondisclosure under Section 411.0727.

3. If you have been previously convicted of an offense listed below, you are not eligible for an order of nondisclosure under Section 411.0727:
   - Section 15.03, Penal Code, if the offense is punishable as a felony of the first degree;
   - Section 19.02, Penal Code (Murder);
   - Section 19.03, Penal Code (Capital Murder);
   - Section 20.04, Penal Code (Aggravated Kidnapping);
   - Section 20A.02, Penal Code (Trafficking of Persons);
   - Section 21.11(a)(1), Penal Code (Indecency with a Child);
   - Section 22.011, Penal Code (Sexual Assault);
   - Section 22.021, Penal Code (Aggravated Sexual Assault)
   - Section 22.04(a)(1), Penal Code (Injury to a Child, Elderly Individual, or Disabled Individual), if the offense is punishable as a felony of the first degree and the victim of the offense is a child;
   - Section 29.03, Penal Code (Aggravated Robbery);

- Section 30.02, Penal Code (Burglary), if the offense is punishable as a first degree felony under Subsection (d) of that section and the actor committed the offense with the intent to commit a felony under Section 21.02, 21.11, 22.011, 22.021, or 25.02, Penal Code;
- Section 43.05, Penal Code (Compelling Prostitution);
- Section 43.25, Penal Code (Sexual Performance by a Child);
- Chapter 481, Health and Safety Code, for which punishment is increased under Section 481.140 of that code (Use of Child in Commission of Offense) or Section 481.134(c), (d), (e), or (f) of that code (Drug-free Zones) if it is shown that the defendant has been previously convicted of an offense for which punishment was increased under any of those subsections; and
- A sexually violent offense, as defined by Article 62.001, Code of Criminal Procedure.

4. If you were convicted of any felony offense during the 2 years following your completion of the veterans treatment court program, you are not eligible for an order of nondisclosure under Section 411.0727.

5. Waiting Period. You must wait **two years** from the date that you successfully completed the veterans treatment court program before you may file a petition for an order of nondisclosure under Section 411.0727.

In order to obtain an order of nondisclosure under Section 411.0727, if you are eligible, you must file a petition. The form and instructions for obtaining an order of nondisclosure under Section 411.0727 are available at this link: http://www.txcourts.gov/rules-forms/orders-of-nondisclosure.

You should not have to pay the clerk to notify the prosecutor of your petition. Under Section 411.0745(e), Government Code, the court must notify the prosecutor. Additionally, if the court issues an order of nondisclosure, you should not have to pay the clerk to notify law enforcement. Under Section 411.075, Government Code, the clerk must notify the Crime Records Service Division of the Texas Department of Public Safety (hereinafter "DPS") of the order of nondisclosure, and DPS must notify the law enforcement agencies and entities designated in the statute.

SECTION 411.0728 – Procedure for Certain Victims of Trafficking of Persons

1. You are not eligible for an order of nondisclosure under Section 411.0728

if you **were not convicted of one or more of the following offenses solely on the ground that you were a victim of trafficking of persons**:
- prostitution (felony or misdemeanor),
- promotion of prostitution (Class A misdemeanor only),
- delivery or possession of marihuana (Class B misdemeanor only), or
- theft (Class C or B misdemeanor only)

2. You are not eligible for an order of nondisclosure under Section 411.0728 if you were not placed on probation following your conviction.

3. You are not eligible for an order of nondisclosure if your conviction was not subsequently set aside.

4. You are not eligible for an order of nondisclosure under Section 411.0728 if the order that set aside your conviction occurred prior to September 1, 2017, unless your conviction was for a prostitution offense under Section 43.02, Penal Code. If your conviction was for a prostitution offense, the order that set aside your conviction must have occurred on or after September 1, 2015.

In order to obtain an order of nondisclosure under Section 411.0728, if you are eligible, you must file a petition, but you cannot file the petition **before** your conviction has been set aside. Additionally, your petition must assert that you have not previously received an order of nondisclosure under Section 411.0728.

The court must determine that you committed the offense solely as a victim of trafficking of persons and issuance of the order of nondisclosure is in the best interest of justice before the court can issue the order. The court must also determine that you have not previously received an order of nondisclosure under Section 411.0728. The forms and instructions for filing a petition under Section 411.0728 are available at this link: http://www.txcourts.gov/rules-forms/orders-of-nondisclosure.

You should not have to pay the clerk to notify the prosecutor of your petition. Under Section 411.0745(e), Government Code, the court must notify the prosecutor. Additionally, you should not have to pay the court to notify law enforcement of the order of nondisclosure, if the court issues an order. Under Section 411.075, Government Code, the clerk must notify the Crime Records Service Division of the Texas Department of Public Safety (hereinafter "DPS") of the order of nondisclosure, and DPS must notify the law enforcement agencies and entities designated in the statute.

SECTION 411.073 – Procedure for Community Supervision Following Conviction for Certain Misdemeanors

1. You are not eligible for an order of nondisclosure under Section 411.073 if your probation was revoked.

2. You are not eligible for an order of nondisclosure under Section 411.073 if you did not successfully complete your period of probation, including any term of confinement imposed and payment of all fines, costs, and restitution imposed.

3. You are not eligible for an order of nondisclosure under Section 411.073 if during the period after the court placed you on probation for the offense for which the order of nondisclosure is requested, and during any applicable waiting period (described in No. 4 below) following completion of your probation, you were convicted of or placed on deferred adjudication for another offense other than a traffic offense punishable by fine only.

4. Waiting Period. You are eligible to file a petition for nondisclosure under Section 411.073 either:

    a) On or after you complete probation, unless the offense for which you are requesting an order of nondisclosure is one of the misdemeanor offenses listed in b) below; or
    b) On or after the second anniversary of the date you completed probation if you were placed on probation for a misdemeanor offense under Chapter 20 (kidnapping, unlawful restraint, or smuggling of persons), 21 (sexual offenses), 22 (assaultive offenses), 25 (offenses against the family), 42 (disorderly conduct and related offenses), 43 (public indecency offenses), or 46 (weapons offenses) of the Penal Code.

In order to obtain an order of nondisclosure under Section 411.073, if you are eligible, you must file a petition. The form and instructions for obtaining an order of nondisclosure under Section 411.073 are available at this link: http://www.txcourts.gov/rules-forms/orders-of-nondisclosure. The court must determine that you are entitled to file the petition and that issuance of the order of nondisclosure is in the best interest of justice before the court can grant your request.

You should not have to pay the clerk to notify the prosecutor of your petition. Under Section 411.0745(e), Government Code, the court must notify the prosecutor. Additionally, you should not have to pay the court to notify law enforcement of the order of nondisclosure, if the court issues an order. Under Section 411.075, Government Code, the clerk must notify the Crime Records Service Division of the Texas Department of Public Safety (hereinafter "DPS") of the order of nondisclosure, and DPS must notify the law enforcement agencies and entities designated in the statute.

SECTION 411.0731 - Procedure for Community Supervision Following Conviction; Certain Driving While Intoxicated Convictions

1. You are not eligible for an order of nondisclosure under Section 411.0731 if your conviction for driving while intoxicated was a Class A misdemeanor or higher category of offense, or if your alcohol concentration level was 0.15 or more. Your offense must have been punishable as a Class B misdemeanor.

2. You are not eligible for an order of nondisclosure under Section 411.0731 if you did not receive probation.

3. You are not eligible for an order of nondisclosure under Section 411.0731 if your probation was revoked or you did not complete probation, including serving any term of confinement imposed and paying all fines, costs, and restitution imposed. You may still be eligible if the court waived all or part of the fine and costs imposed.

4. You are not eligible for an order of nondisclosure under Section 411.0731 if you have been previously convicted of or placed on deferred adjudication for another offense, except for a traffic offense punishable by fine only. In other words, you must be a first time offender, but fine only traffic tickets do not count against you.

5. You are not eligible for an order of nondisclosure under Section 411.0731 if your commission of the driving while intoxicated offense resulted in a motor vehicle accident involving another person, including any passenger in your motor vehicle, even if that person did not suffer death or bodily injury.

6. Waiting Period. You are eligible to file a petition for an order of nondisclosure

under Section 411.0731 either:
- a) Two years after you complete probation, if you successfully complied with a condition of probation that required you to use an ignition interlock device while driving a motor vehicle for at least 6 months; or
- b) Five years after you complete probation, if the court that placed you on probation did not order you to use an ignition interlock device while driving a motor vehicle, or the court ordered you to use one for a period that was less than 6 months.

In order to obtain an order of nondisclosure under Section 411.0731, if you are eligible, you must file a petition. The form and instructions for obtaining an order of nondisclosure under Section 411.0731 are available at this link: http://www.txcourts.gov/rules-forms/orders-of-nondisclosure. **You must file the petition with the court that placed you on probation, and your petition must include evidence that shows you are entitled to file the petition.**

The court must determine that you are entitled to file the petition and that issuance of the order of nondisclosure is in the best interest of justice before the court can grant your request. Also, if the prosecuting attorney presents evidence sufficient to show that your commission of the driving while intoxicated offense resulted in a motor vehicle accident involving another person, including a passenger in your vehicle, the court cannot grant your request.

You should not have to pay the clerk to notify the prosecutor of your petition. Under Section 411.0745(e), Government Code, the court must notify the prosecutor. Additionally, you should not have to pay the court to notify law enforcement of the order of nondisclosure, if the court issues an order. Under Section 411.075, Government Code, the clerk must notify the Crime Records Service Division of the Texas Department of Public Safety (hereinafter "DPS"), and DPS must notify the law enforcement agencies and entities designated in the statute.

SECTION 411.0735 – Procedure for Conviction for Certain Misdemeanors

1. You are not eligible for an order of nondisclosure under Section 411.0735 if you **QUALIFY** for an order of nondisclosure under Section 411.073. You must make sure that you do not qualify for an order of nondisclosure under Section 411.073 before proceeding under Section 411.0735.

2. You are not eligible for an order of nondisclosure under Section 411.0735 if you have not completed your sentence, including any term of confinement

imposed and payment of all fines, costs, and restitution imposed.

3. You are not eligible for an order of nondisclosure under Section 411.0735 if the court determines that the offense for which you are requesting an order of nondisclosure was violent or sexual in nature. However, if you were convicted of an assault under Section 22.01, Penal Code, you are still eligible for an order of nondisclosure under 411.0735.

4. Excluding the offense for which the order of nondisclosure is requested, you are not eligible for an order of nondisclosure if you have ever been convicted of or placed on deferred adjudication for any other offense other than a traffic offense punishable by fine only.

5. Waiting Period. If you were convicted of a misdemeanor punishable by fine only, you are eligible to petition the court for an order of nondisclosure under Section 411.0735 on or after the date that you completed your sentence in the case. Otherwise, you must wait until the second anniversary of the date that you completed your sentence before filing a petition for an order of nondisclosure under 411.0735.

In order to obtain an order of nondisclosure under Section 411.0735, if you are eligible, you must file a petition. The form and instructions for obtaining an order of nondisclosure under Section 411.0735 are available at this link: http://www.txcourts.gov/rules-forms/orders-of-nondisclosure. The court must determine that you are entitled to file the petition and that issuance of the order of nondisclosure is in the best interest of justice before the court can grant your request.

You should not have to pay the clerk to notify the prosecutor of your petition. Under Section 411.0745(e), Government Code, the court must notify the prosecutor. Additionally, you should not have to pay the court to notify law enforcement of the order of nondisclosure, if the court issues an order. Under Section 411.075, Government Code, the clerk must notify the Crime Records Service Division of the Texas Department of Public Safety (hereinafter "DPS") of the order of nondisclosure, and DPS must notify the law enforcement agencies and entities designated in the statute.

SECTION 411.0736 - Procedure for Conviction; Certain Driving While Intoxicated Convictions

1. You are not eligible for an order of nondisclosure under 411.0736 if you QUALIFY for an order of nondisclosure under Section 411.0731. You must be sure that you do not qualify under Section 411.0731 before proceeding under Section 411.0736. **If your probation was revoked, or if you were not placed on probation following your conviction for the DWI, you do not qualify under 411.0731.**

2. You are not eligible for an order of nondisclosure under Section 411.0736 if your conviction for driving while intoxicated was a Class A misdemeanor or higher category, or if your alcohol concentration level was 0.15 or more. You offense must have been punishable as a Class B misdemeanor.

3. You are not eligible for an order of nondisclosure under Section 411.0736 if you did not complete your sentence, including serving any term of confinement imposed and paying all fines, costs, and restitution imposed. You may still be eligible if the court waived all or part of the fine and costs imposed.

4. You are not eligible for an order of nondisclosure under Section 411.0736 if you have been previously convicted of or placed on deferred adjudication for another offense, except for a traffic offense punishable by fine only. In other words, you must be a first time offender, but fine only traffic tickets do not count against you.

5. You are not eligible for an order of nondisclosure if your commission of the driving while intoxicated offense resulted in a motor vehicle accident involving another person, including any passenger in your motor vehicle, regardless of whether any person involved in the accident suffered death or injury.

6. Waiting Period. You are eligible to file a petition for an order of nondisclosure under Section 411.0736 either:
    a) Three years after you complete your sentence, if you successfully complied with a condition of the sentence that restricted your operation of a motor vehicle to a motor vehicle equipped with an ignition interlock device for a period of not less than 6 months; or
    b) Five years after you complete your sentence, if the court that sentenced you did not restrict your operation of a motor vehicle, or the court restricted your operation of a motor vehicle to a vehicle equipped with an ignition interlock device for a period that was less than 6 months.

In order to obtain an order of nondisclosure under Section 411.0736, if you are eligible, you must file a petition. The form and instructions for obtaining an order of nondisclosure under Section 411.0736 are available at this link: http://www.txcourts.gov/rules-forms/orders-of-nondisclosure. **You must file the petition with the court that sentenced you**, and your petition must include evidence that shows you are entitled to file the petition.

The court must determine that you are entitled to file the petition and that issuance of the order of nondisclosure is in the best interest of justice before the court can grant your request. Also, if the prosecuting attorney presents evidence sufficient to show that your commission of the driving while intoxicated offense resulted in a motor vehicle accident involving another person, including a passenger in your vehicle, the court cannot grant your request.

You should not have to pay the clerk to notify the prosecutor of your petition. Under Section 411.0745(e), Government Code, the court must notify the prosecutor. Additionally, you should not have to pay the court to notify law enforcement of the order of nondisclosure, if the court issues an order. Under Section 411.075, Government Code, the clerk must notify the Crime Records Service Division of the Texas Department of Public Safety (hereinafter "DPS"), and DPS must notify the law enforcement agencies and entities designated in the statute.

Procedure after Order of Nondisclosure Issues

If the court grants the order of nondisclosure, no later than 15 business days after the order issues, the clerk will send a copy of the order to DPS. Then, no later than 10 business days after DPS receives the copy of the order, DPS will seal the criminal history record information that is the subject of the order and forward the order to the state and federal agencies listed in 411.075(b), Government Code. See Section 411.075(b) for a complete list of the agencies and entities that DPS must notify.

Office of Court Administration

Instructions and Letter Requesting Court to Issue an Order of Nondisclosure under Section 411.072

BEFORE BEGINNING MAKE SURE YOU ARE ELIGIBLE TO USE THE LETTER PROVIDED BELOW. THE INSTRUCTIONS AND LETTER ARE ONLY FOR PERSONS REQUESTING AN ORDER OF NONDISCLOSURE UNDER SECTION 411.072, GOVERNMENT CODE. DO NOT ATTEMPT TO USE THE LETTER PROVIDED BELOW WITHOUT FIRST REVIEWING THE OVERVIEW OF ORDERS OF NONDISCLOSURE TO DETERMINE IF YOU ARE ELIGIBLE FOR AN ORDER OF NONDISCLOSURE AND TO IDENTIFY THE CORRECT FORM TO USE. THE NONDISCLOSURE OVERVIEW IS AVAILABLE AT THIS LINK: http://www.txcourts.gov/rules-forms/orders-of-nondisclosure.

NOTE: You are not eligible for an order of nondisclosure under Section 411.072, if your discharge and dismissal occurred prior to September 1, 2017. If your discharge and dismissal occurred prior to September 1, 2017, you cannot use this letter. You may be able to file a petition for an order of nondisclosure under Section 411.0725, if you satisfy the requirements of that section. The form and instructions for an order of nondisclosure under Section 411.0725 are available at this link: http://www.txcourts.gov/rules-forms/orders-of-nondisclosure.

Order of Nondisclosure under Sec. 411.072

If you are eligible for an Order of Nondisclosure under Section 411.072, you do not have to file a petition, and you should not have to pay the filing fees that normally accompany the filing of a petition. **The letter that you will complete and submit to the court is not a petition.**

The statute places the responsibility on the court to determine whether you qualify for an order of nondisclosure under this section and to issue the order if you do. However, you must present evidence necessary to establish that you are eligible to receive an order of nondisclosure under Section 411.072 and pay a $28 fee (**this is not a filing fee**) or submit a *Statement of Inability to Afford Payment of Court Costs* to the court before the court issues the order.

As a general rule, you must pay the $28 fee before the court will issue the order. However, you may be eligible to file a Statement of Inability to Afford Payment of Court Costs in lieu of paying the fee. The statement is described in Rule 145 of the Texas Rules of Civil Procedure. You may view Rule 145 online at http://www.txcourts.gov/media/1435952/trcp-all-updated-with-amendments-effective-912016.pdf. The form for the Statement of Inability to Afford Payment of Court Costs is available at this link: http://www.txcourts.gov/media/1435953/statement-final-version.pdf.

To facilitate your ability to present the evidence necessary to establish that you are eligible to receive an order of nondisclosure under Section 411.072, the letter below is provided. However, you must complete the letter before submitting it to the court. The letter will provide the information that the court needs to determine your eligibility for the order of nondisclosure.

A **proposed order** for the order for nondisclosure is provided in these materials as well. You should submit the proposed order with the letter. The court will complete the proposed order if the court determines that an order should issue.

Required Waiting Period

If the court finds that you satisfy the requirements for an order of nondisclosure under Section 411.072, the court is required to issue the order of nondisclosure as follows:

- If the court discharges and dismisses the proceedings against you on or **after** the 180th day after the court placed you on deferred adjudication, the court is required to issue the order of nondisclosure at the same time the court discharges and dismisses the proceedings against you; or

- If the court discharges and dismisses the proceedings against you **prior** to the 180th day after the court placed you on deferred adjudication, the court is required to issue the order of nondisclosure "as soon as practicable" after the 180th day after the court placed you on deferred adjudication.

The court is not permitted to issue the order of nondisclosure until at least 180 days have passed following your placement on deferred adjudication. Also, please note that to satisfy the requirements under Section 411.074 (this is required to qualify for an order of nondisclosure under Section 411.072), the period in which you cannot have been convicted of or placed on deferred adjudication for any offense other than a traffic offense punishable by fine only INCLUDES the "waiting period" outlined above. Therefore, neither you nor the court will know if you qualify until the 180-day waiting period is over.

Summary of Procedure

If you are eligible for an order of nondisclosure under Sec. 411.072, Government Code, you should take the following steps:

1. Complete the letter provided below, and if 180 days have passed since the date that the court placed you on deferred adjudication, submit the letter and proposed order (*Order of Nondisclosure under Section 411.072*) to the clerk of the court (hereinafter "clerk"); and

2. Pay $28 or submit a *Statement of Inability to Afford Payment of Court Costs*. Ask the clerk about their procedures for paying the fee or submitting the statement.

If the court has not already issued an order of nondisclosure, the court will review your letter and determine if you qualify for the order of nondisclosure. If the court determines that you qualify for the order, the court will issue the order if you have paid the $28 fee or submitted a statement of inability to pay.

No later than 15 business days after the court issues the order, the clerk will send a copy of the order to DPS. After receiving the order, DPS will seal the criminal history record information that is the subject of the order and forward a copy of the order to the agencies listed in Section 411.075(b), Government Code. See Section 411.075(b) for a complete list of the agencies and entities that DPS must notify.

Instructions for Completing Letter

(1) Please enter the current date.
(2) Please enter the name of the judge that placed you on deferred adjudication.
(3) Please enter the name of the court that placed you on deferred adjudication. Only the court that placed you on deferred adjudication can issue an order of nondisclosure in your case.
(4) Please enter the address of the court that placed you on deferred adjudication.
(5) Please enter the city, state, and zip code of the court that placed you on deferred adjudication.
(6) Please enter the Criminal Cause Number of your case. This should be on the order that placed you on deferred adjudication.
(7) Please enter your name as shown on the order of deferred adjudication.
(8) Please enter your current legal name. This name may differ if your name has changed.
(9) Please enter either "guilty" or "nolo contendere" as shown on the order that placed you on deferred adjudication under Plea to Offense.
(10) Please enter the offense shown on the order that placed you on deferred adjudication under Offense.
(11) Please enter the date your deferred adjudication began as shown on the order.
(12) Please enter the date your deferred adjudication ended as shown on the order.
(13) Please circle "have" if you will be attaching a copy of the order that placed you on deferred adjudication or "have not" if you are not attaching a copy of the order.
(14) Please enter the date that you received a discharge and dismissal from the court.
(15) Please circle "have" if you will be attaching a copy of the discharge and dismissal or "have not" if you are not attaching a copy of the discharge and dismissal.
(16) Please sign above the line.
(17) Please PRINT your name.
(18) Please enter your mailing address.
(19) Please enter your city, state and zip code.
(20) Please enter your telephone number.

Letter Requesting an Order of Nondisclosure under Section 411.072, Government Code

_____ (1)

The Honorable _____ (2)

_____ (3)

c/o Court Clerk

_____ (4)

_____ (5)

Re: Criminal Cause No. _____ (6)

_____ (7)

To the Honorable Court,

    I, _____ (8), respectfully request the court to issue an order of nondisclosure under Section 411.072, Government Code, in the above-referenced case.

    I entered a plea of _____ (9) to the offense of _____, (10) and this court placed me on deferred adjudication. My term of deferred adjudication began on _____ (11) and ended on _____ (12). I **have/ have not** (13) attached a copy of the Order of Deferred Adjudication in my case. On _____, (14) I received a discharge and dismissal from the court. I **have/have not** (15) attached a copy of the discharge and dismissal.

    I believe that I am entitled to an order of nondisclosure under Section 411.072 for the following reasons:

    1. I was placed on deferred adjudication for a misdemeanor other than

one under Penal Code Chapter 20 (kidnapping, unlawful restraint, or smuggling of persons), 21 (sexual offenses), 22 (assaultive offenses), 25 (offenses against the family), 42 (disorderly conduct and related offenses), 43 (public indecency offenses), 46 (weapons offenses), or 71 (organized crime offenses);

2. Aside from the criminal offense reflected above, I have not been previously convicted of or placed on deferred adjudication for any offense other than a traffic offense punishable by fine only;

3. This court did not enter an affirmative finding that it is not in the best interest of justice for me to receive an automatic order of nondisclosure for the offense for which the order of nondisclosure is requested;

4. I received a discharge and dismissal under Article 42A.111, Code of Criminal Procedure, (formerly, Section 5(c), Article 42.12, Code of Criminal Procedure) on or after September 1, 2017; and

5. I meet the requirements of Section 411.074, Government Code, because:
   a. Including the offense for which the order of nondisclosure is requested, I have never been convicted of or placed on deferred adjudication for any of the following offenses:
      (i) an offense requiring registration as a sex offender under Chapter 62, Code of Criminal Procedure;
      (ii) an offense under Texas Penal Code Section 20.04 (aggravated kidnapping);
      (iii) an offense under any of the following Texas Penal Code Sections:
         - 19.02 (murder);
         - 19.03 (capital murder);
         - 20A.02 (trafficking of persons);
         - 20A.03 (continuous trafficking of persons);
         - 22.04 (injury to a child, elderly individual, or disabled individual);
         - 22.041 (abandoning or endangering a child);
         - 25.07 (violation of court orders or conditions of bond in a family violence, sexual assault or abuse, stalking, or trafficking case);
         - 25.072 (repeated violation of certain court orders or conditions of bond in family violence, sexual assault or abuse, stalking, or trafficking case); or
         - 42.072 (stalking); or
      (iv) any offense involving family violence, as defined by Section

71.004, Family Code;

b. This court has not made an affirmative finding that the offense for which I am requesting an order of nondisclosure involved family violence, as defined by Section 71.004, Family Code; and

c. I was not convicted of or placed on deferred adjudication for any offense other than a traffic offense punishable by fine only during the 180 days following my placement on deferred adjudication.

Based on this information, I respectfully request the court to find that I have met the requirements of Sections 411.072 and 411.074, Government Code, and to issue an order of nondisclosure for the criminal offense referenced in the Criminal Cause Number above.

Sincerely,

_____ (16)

_____ (17)

_____ (18)

_____ (19)

_____ (20)

Cause No. _____

In the Matter of § In the

§ _____

_____ § _____ County, Texas

Order of Nondisclosure Under Section 411.072

On this the _____, day of _____, 20__, the Court reviewed the evidence before it to determine if Petitioner is eligible for an order of nondisclosure under Section 411.072, Government Code.

The Court

 ☐ conducted a hearing.

 ☐ did not conduct a hearing.

After reviewing the evidence made available to the Court, the Court FINDS that:

- On or about _____, Petitioner was placed on deferred adjudication community supervision (hereinafter "deferred adjudication") for the offense of _____ in Criminal Case No. _____;

- Petitioner was placed on deferred adjudication for a misdemeanor other than a misdemeanor under Chapter 20, 21, 22, 25, 42, 43, 46, or 71, Penal Code;

- Petitioner received a discharge and dismissal on or after September 1, 2017;

- An affirmative finding under Article 42A.105(f), Code of Criminal Procedure, indicating that it is not in the best interest of justice for Petitioner to receive an automatic order of nondisclosure was not filed in the papers of the Petitioner's case;

- Petitioner has never been previously convicted of or placed on deferred adjudication for another offense other than a traffic offense punishable by fine only;

- Petitioner satisfies the requirements of Section 411.074, Government Code, as follows:

    o During the 180-day waiting period, Petitioner was not convicted of or placed on deferred adjudication for any offense other than a traffic offense punishable by fine only;

    o The Petitioner was not convicted of or placed on deferred adjudication for and has not been previously convicted of or placed on any other deferred adjudication for:
        - an offense requiring registration as a sex offender under Chapter 62, Code of Criminal Procedure;
        - an offense under Section 20.04, Penal Code, regardless of whether the offense is a reportable conviction or adjudication for purposes of Chapter 62, Code of Criminal Procedure;
        - an offense under Section 19.02, 19.03, 20A.02, 20A.03, 22.04, 22.041, 25.07, 25.072, or 42.072, Penal Code; or
        - any other offense involving family violence, as defined by Section 71.004, Family Code; and

    o The Court did not make an affirmative finding that the offense for which the order of nondisclosure is requested involved family violence, as defined by Section 71.004, Family Code; and

- A minimum of 180 days has passed since the Petitioner's placement on deferred adjudication.

Accordingly, **IT IS HEREBY ORDERED** that criminal justice agencies are prohibited from disclosing to the public criminal history record information related to the offense of _____ for which Petitioner was placed on deferred adjudication on _____, 20____ in Criminal Cause No. _____ in ☐ District Court ☐ County Court ☐ County Court at Law No. _____ in _____County, Texas.

IT IS FURTHER ORDERED that the criminal history record information pertaining to the arrest and prosecution of Petitioner for the offense of _____, as reflected in Criminal Cause No. _____, shall be sealed and disclosed by the court only to individuals or agencies listed in Section 411.076(a), Government Code.

IT IS FURTHER ORDERED that no later than the 15th business day after the date this order issues, the clerk of the court (hereinafter "clerk") shall send all relevant criminal history record information contained in this order or a copy of this order to the Crime Records Service of the Texas Department of Public Safety (hereinafter "DPS") by certified mail (return receipt requested) or secure electronic mail, electronic transmission, or facsimile transmission, in accordance with Section 411.075(a), Government Code.

IT IS FURTHER ORDERED that no later than 10 business days after receiving the relevant criminal history record information contained in this order or a copy of this order from the clerk, DPS shall seal the criminal history record information that is the subject of this order and forward the information or copy of the order to all state and federal agencies listed in 411.075(b), Government Code, by certified mail (return receipt requested) or secure electronic mail, electronic transmission, or facsimile transmission, in accordance with Section 411.075(b), Government Code.

IT IS FURTHER ORDERED that an agency or entity shall seal any criminal history record information maintained by that agency or entity that is the subject of this order no later than 30 business days after the date the agency or entity receives the relevant criminal history record information contained in this order or a copy of this order from DPS or a clerk, in accordance with Section 411.075(d), Government Code.

IT IS FURTHER ORDERED that the clerk shall seal all court records containing information that is the subject of this order as soon as practicable after the date the clerk sends a copy of this order or all relevant criminal history record information contained in this order to DPS, in accordance with Section 411.076(b), Government Code.

Signed on _____.

By _____
Judge Presiding

_____
Court/County

Office of Court Administration

Instructions for Completing the Model Petition for Order of Nondisclosure Under Section 411.0725

BEFORE BEGINNING MAKE SURE YOU ARE USING THE CORRECT PETITION. THIS PETITION AND INSTRUCTIONS ARE FOR PERSONS SEEKING AN ORDER OF NONDISCLOSURE UNDER SECTION 411.0725, GOVERNMENT CODE. DO NOT ATTEMPT TO COMPLETE A PETITION FOR AN ORDER OF NONDISCLOSURE WITHOUT FIRST REVIEWING THE NONDISCLOSURE OVERVIEW TO DETERMINE IF YOU ARE ELIGIBLE FOR AN ORDER OF NONDISCLOSURE AND TO IDENTIFY THE CORRECT FORMS TO USE. THE NONDISCLOSURE OVERVIEW IS AVAILABLE AT THIS LINK: http://www.txcourts.gov/rules-forms/orders-of-nondisclosure.

TO BE ELIGIBLE TO USE THIS PETITION, THE FOLLOWING STATEMENTS MUST BE TRUE:

1. You are not eligible to receive an order of nondisclosure under Section 411.072.
2. You were placed on deferred adjudication for the offense for which the order of nondisclosure is requested.
3. You received a discharge and dismissal of the offense for which you are requesting an order of nondisclosure.
4. You satisfy the requirements of Section 411.074, Government Code.
5. You have waited the applicable waiting period before filing this petition.

Instructions for Completing the Petition

(1) Please leave this line blank. This is not the number of your criminal case. A civil case will be created when you file the petition. The clerk of the court (hereinafter "clerk") will enter a new cause number in this space.

(2) Please enter the name of the court in which you are filing this petition. You must file this petition in the court that placed you on deferred adjudication (hereinafter "deferred adjudication"). The name of the court is displayed at the top of the order that placed you on deferred adjudication.

(3) Please enter your name as it appears on the order of deferred adjudication.

(4) Please enter the name of the county in which the court that placed you on deferred adjudication is situated. This will be the same county displayed on the judgment or order of deferred adjudication in your case.

(5) Please enter your name as you did in (3) above.

(6) Please enter the offense as it appears on the order that placed you on deferred adjudication under Offense. This information should be on the judgment in your case as well.

(7) Please circle "misdemeanor" if the offense for which you are requesting an order of nondisclosure is a misdemeanor or "felony" if the offense is a felony. The judgment and order of deferred adjudication should indicate whether the offense was a misdemeanor or felony.

(8) Please enter the criminal cause number as it appears on the judgment or order that placed you on deferred adjudication. Look for *Case or Cause No.* on either document.

(9) Please enter the date your deferred adjudication began. This date should be on the order of deferred adjudication.

(10) Please enter the date your deferred adjudication ended. This date should be on the court's order that discharged and dismissed the proceedings against you.

(11) Please circle "is" if you are attaching a copy of the judgment or order that placed you on deferred adjudication. Attaching a copy of the court's order may expedite the process for obtaining an order of nondisclosure, but it is not required. Please circle "is not" if you are not attaching a copy of the judgment or order that placed you on deferred adjudication.

(12) Please circle "is" if you are attaching a copy of the discharge and dismissal. Please circle "is not" if you are not attaching a copy of the discharge and dismissal.

(13) Please enter the date as it appears on the discharge and dismissal.

(14) Please review the four statements lettered A through D and place a check mark or an "x" on the line before each statement that is true in your case.

There may be more than one that applies in your case. Be sure to review all four statements.

(15) If you placed a check mark or "x" on the line in front of statement D, please circle "is" if you are attaching a list of your prior convictions and deferred adjudications, or circle "is not" if you are not attaching a list of your prior convictions and deferred adjudications.

(16) Review the three statements and place a check mark or an "x" on the line before the statement that applies to your case. Only one of the options will apply to you. If the offense for which you are requesting an order of nondisclosure is a felony, check the line in front of the first statement. If you check this statement, you must wait five years after your discharge and dismissal before you can file a petition for an order of nondisclosure). If the offense for which you are requesting an order of nondisclosure is a misdemeanor under Chapter 20, 21, 22, 25, 42, 43, or 46 of the Penal Code, place your mark in front of the second statement. If you check this statement, you must wait two years after your discharge and dismissal before you can file a petition for an order of nondisclosure. If your offense is not one under any of the chapters mentioned above, please place a mark in front of the third statement. If you check the third statement, you can file a petition for an order of nondisclosure on or after the date of your discharge and dismissal.

(17) There is a filing fee associated with filing a petition for order of nondisclosure under Section 411.0725. The filing fee is the amount of the court's regular civil filing fee plus an additional $28. Typically, the total filing fee is about $280. However, the amount varies from county to county. You must contact the clerk of the court in which you are filing the petition to obtain the correct amount of the total filing fee. **NOTE**: You should not have to pay the clerk to serve the petition on the attorney for the state (hereinafter "prosecutor"), Department of Public Safety (hereinafter "DPS"), or any other agency or entity, including any law enforcement entity. The statute requires the court, clerk, and DPS to notify the other parties of interest. See Sections 411.0745(e), 411.075(a) and 411.075(b), Government Code, respectively.

As a general rule, you must pay the filing fee in order to file the petition. However, you may be eligible to file a Statement of Inability to Afford Payment of Court Costs in lieu of paying the filing fee. The statement is described in Rule 145 of the Texas Rules of Civil Procedure. You may view Rule 145 online at http://www.txcourts.gov/media/1435952/trcp-all-updated-with-amendments-effective-912016.pdf. You can click here for the form: http://www.txcourts.gov/media/1435953/statement-final-version.pdf.

Please place a check mark or an "x" on the line before the statement that applies to you. Mark or check the line in front of the first statement, if you are paying the filing fee. If you are submitting a **Statement of Inability to Afford Payment of Court Costs** instead, place a check mark or an "x" near the second statement.

(18) Please sign above the line. If you are filing this petition electronically, you may enter "/s/" followed by your typewritten name.

(19) Please PRINT your name.

(20) Please enter your mailing address.

(21) Please enter your city, state and zip code.

(22) Please enter your telephone number.

Process after You Complete the Petition

Assuming you are eligible for an order of nondisclosure under Section 411.0725, the process for obtaining an order under this section is as follows:

First, be sure to wait the requisite time before filing the petition, and check with the clerk to obtain the total amount of the fee (including the $28 fee) that you will have to pay when you file the petition, unless you are submitting a *Statement of Inability to Afford Payment of Court Costs*. Next, be sure to complete the right petition according to the instructions, and after you have done so, print both the petition and the *Order of Nondisclosure*. In most courts, you will have to submit a proposed order with your petition when you file it. The judge will complete the order, if the judge grants your request.

After you file the petition, the clerk will send it to the court and the court will notify the prosecutor. Again, you should not have to pay the clerk to serve notice on the prosecutor or any other party.

The court does not have to hold a hearing, unless the prosecutor requests one.

If a hearing is scheduled, you will be notified. If a hearing is held, the court may ask questions to determine whether you satisfy the requirements of Sections 411.0725 and 411.074. If the court finds that you satisfy the requirements of those sections and that issuance of the order of nondisclosure is in the best interest of justice, the court should grant your request.

If the court does not hold a hearing, the court will review your petition to determine whether an order of nondisclosure shall issue. The court must find that you satisfy the requirements of Sections 411.0725 and 411.074 and that issuance of the order of nondisclosure is in the best interest of justice before the court may grant your request.

The court or prosecutor will have access to your criminal history record information and will use it to determine if you are eligible for an order of nondisclosure.

If the court grants the order of nondisclosure, the clerk will send a copy of the order to DPS. Then, no later than 10 business days after receiving the copy of the order, DPS will seal the part of your criminal history record information that is the subject of the order and forward the order to the agencies listed in Section 411.075(b), Government Code. *See* Section 411.075(b) for a complete list of agencies and entities that DPS must notify.

Cause No. _____
(1)

In the Matter of § In the

§ _____
(2)
_____ § _____ County, Texas
(3) (4)

Petition for Order of Nondisclosure Under Section 411.0725

_____ (5) (hereinafter "Petitioner") respectfully petitions this court for an order of nondisclosure under Section 411.0725, Government Code, for the offense detailed in the following paragraph.

1. The Underlying Order and Order of Discharge and Dismissal

Petitioner was convicted of the offense of _____ (6), a misdemeanor / felony (7) in Criminal Cause No. _____ (8) in this court.

Petitioner was placed on deferred adjudication community supervision (hereinafter "deferred adjudication") under Article 42A.101, Code of Criminal Procedure (formerly, Section 5, Article 42.12). The term of Petitioner's deferred adjudication began on _____ (9) and ended on _____ (10). A copy of the judgment or order placing Petitioner on deferred adjudication **is / is not** (11) attached to this petition.

Page **1** of **6**

OCA MODEL PETITION FOR ORDER OF NONDISCLOSURE UNDER 411.0725, GOVERNMENT CODE

DECEMBER 2017

The court did not proceed to an adjudication of guilt. Instead, the court discharged and dismissed the proceedings against Petitioner. A copy of the discharge and dismissal **is / is not** ₍₁₂₎ attached to this petition. The discharge and dismissal occurred on _____ ₍₁₃₎.

2. Petitioner Satisfies the Requirements of Section 411.0725, Gov't Code

Petitioner satisfies the requirements of Section 411.0725, Government Code, in that Petitioner **is not eligible** for an automatic order of nondisclosure under Section 411.072 because (check all that apply): ₍₁₄₎

_____ A. The misdemeanor offense for which the order of nondisclosure is requested falls under one of the following chapters of the Penal Code:
- 20 (kidnapping, unlawful restraint, smuggling of persons),
- 21 (sexual offenses),
- 22 (assaultive offenses),
- 25 (offenses against the family),
- 42 (disorderly conduct and related offenses),
- 43 (public indecency offenses),
- 46 (weapons offenses), or
- 71 (organized crime offenses).

_____ B. The court found that it is not in the best interest of justice that Petitioner receive an automatic order of nondisclosure under Section 411.072 and filed a statement of that finding with the papers of Petitioner's case.

_____ C. The offense for which the order of nondisclosure is requested is a felony.

_____ D. Petitioner has been previously convicted of or placed on deferred adjudication for an offense other than a traffic offense punishable by fine only. (A list of offenses and dates of Petitioner's previous convictions and deferred adjudications **is/ is not** ₍₁₅₎ attached to the petition.)

____ E. Petitioner received a discharge and dismissal prior to September 1, 2017.

Petitioner also satisfies the requirements of Section 411.0725 in that Petitioner has received a discharge and dismissal for the offense for which the order of nondisclosure is requested.

Finally, Petitioner satisfies the requirements of Section 411.0725 in that Petitioner has waited the requisite time, as indicated below, before filing this petition.(16)

_____ On or after the fifth anniversary of the discharge and dismissal if Petitioner's offense is a felony

_____ On or after the second anniversary of the discharge and dismissal if Petitioner's offense is a misdemeanor under Chapter 20, 21, 22, 25, 42, 43, or 46 of the Penal Code)

_____ On or after the discharge and dismissal if Petitioner's offense is a misdemeanor other than a misdemeanor under Chapter 20, 21, 22, 25, 42, 43, or 46 of the Penal Code)

3. Petitioner Satisfies the Requirements of Section 411.074, Gov't Code

Petitioner satisfies the requirements of Section 411.074 of the Government Code because:

- During the period after the court placed Petitioner on deferred adjudication, and during any applicable waiting period following discharge and dismissal (see Section 2 above), Petitioner was not convicted of or placed on deferred adjudication for any offense other than a traffic offense punishable by fine only;

- Petitioner was not and has not ever been convicted of or placed on deferred adjudication for any of the offenses listed below:
    (A) an offense requiring registration as a sex offender under Chapter 62, Code of Criminal Procedure;
    (B) an offense under Section 20.04, Texas Penal Code (aggravated kidnapping);
    (C) an offense under any of the following Texas Penal Code Sections:
        - 19.02 (murder);
        - 19.03 (capital murder);
        - 20A.02 (trafficking of persons);
        - 20A.03 (continuous trafficking of persons);
        - 22.04 (injury to a child, elderly individual, or disabled individual);
        - 22.041 (abandoning or endangering a child);
        - 25.07 (violation of court orders or conditions of bond in a family violence, sexual assault or abuse, stalking, or trafficking case);
        - 25.072 (repeated violation of certain court orders or conditions of bond in family violence, sexual assault or abuse, stalking, or trafficking case); or
        - 42.072 (stalking); or
    (D) any other offense involving family violence, as defined by Section 71.004, Family Code; and

- The court has not made an affirmative finding that the offense for which the order of nondisclosure is requested involved family violence, as defined by Section 71.004, Family Code.

4. Petitioner is Entitled to File a Petition for an Order of Nondisclosure Under Section 411.0725, Gov't Code

A person is entitled to file a petition for an order of nondisclosure under Section 411.0725, Government Code, if the person:

- Was placed on deferred adjudication for a qualifying misdemeanor or felony offense;
- Is not eligible to receive an order of nondisclosure under Section 411.072, Government Code;
- Has received a discharge and dismissal from the court;
- Has waited the requisite time before filing a petition for an order of nondisclosure; and
- Has met the requirements of Section 411.074 of the Government Code.

5. Issuance of an Order of Nondisclosure is in the Best Interest of Justice

The issuance of an order of nondisclosure is in the best interest of justice.

6. The Fee to File the Petition has been Paid or Otherwise Satisfied

The fee to file this petition is the total amount of the fee required to file a civil petition and $28.00, or a petitioner may submit a *Statement of Inability to Afford Payment of Court Costs* in lieu of paying the filing fee. Petitioner has included (17)

_____ the required filing fee.

_____ a *Statement of Inability to Afford Payment of Court Costs* in lieu of the required filing fee.

7. Prayer for Relief

Petitioner respectfully prays that the court grant Petitioner's request for an order of nondisclosure prohibiting criminal justice agencies from disclosing to the public criminal history record information related to the offense specified in this petition.

Respectfully submitted,

_____
(18)

_____
(19)

_____
(20)

_____
(21)

_____
(22)

Cause No. _____

In the Matter of § In the

§ _____

_____ § _____ County, Texas

Order of Nondisclosure

On this the _____, day of _____, 20__, the Court considered Petitioner's Petition for Order of Nondisclosure.

The State was given notice of the petition and an opportunity to request a hearing. The State

☐ requested a hearing.
☐ did not request a hearing.

The Court
☐ conducted a hearing on _____, 20___.

☐ did not conduct a hearing.

After consideration and a hearing, if a hearing was held as indicated above, the Court **FINDS** that Petitioner is entitled to file a petition for an order of nondisclosure under the section of the Government Code indicated below and that issuance of an order of nondisclosure is in the best interest of justice.

☐ Texas Government Code Section 411.0725
☐ Texas Government Code Section 411.073
☐ Texas Government Code Section 411.0735

Accordingly, **IT IS HEREBY ORDERED** that criminal justice agencies are prohibited from disclosing to the public criminal history record information related to the offense of _____ in Criminal Cause No. _____ in _____County, Texas.

IT IS FURTHER ORDERED that the criminal history record information pertaining to the arrest and prosecution of Petitioner for the above-referenced offense, as reflected in the above-referenced criminal cause number, shall be sealed and disclosed only to those individuals and agencies listed in Section 411.076(a), Government Code.

IT IS FURTHER ORDERED that no later than the 15th business day after the date that this order issues, the clerk of the court (hereinafter "clerk") shall send all relevant criminal history record information contained in this order or a copy of this order to the Crime Records Service of the Texas Department of Public Safety (hereinafter "DPS") by certified mail (return receipt requested) or secure electronic mail, electronic transmission, or facsimile transmission, in accordance with Section 411.075(a), Government Code.

IT IS FURTHER ORDERED that no later than 10 business days after receipt of relevant criminal history record information contained in this order or a copy of this order from the clerk, DPS shall seal the criminal history record information that is the subject of this order and forward the information or a copy of the order to the state and federal agencies listed in Section 411.075(b), Government Code, by certified mail (return receipt requested), secure electronic mail, electronic transmission, or facsimile transmission, in accordance with Section 411.075(b), Government Code.

IT IS FURTHER ORDERED that an agency or entity shall seal any criminal history record information maintained by that agency or entity that is the subject of this order no later than 30 business days after the date that the agency or entity received relevant criminal history record information contained in this order or a copy of this order from DPS or a clerk, in accordance with Section 411.075(d), Government Code.

IT IS FURTHER ORDERED that the clerk shall seal all court records containing information that is the subject of this order as soon as practicable after the date that the clerk sends a copy of this order or all relevant criminal history record information contained in this order to DPS, in accordance with Section 411.076(b), Government Code.

Signed on _____.

_____
Judge Presiding

_____
Court/County

Office of Court Administration

Instructions for Completing the Model Petition for Order of Nondisclosure Under Section 411.0727

BEFORE BEGINNING MAKE SURE YOU ARE USING THE CORRECT PETITION. THIS PETITION AND INSTRUCTIONS ARE FOR PERSONS REQUESTING AN ORDER OF NONDISCLOSURE UNDER SECTION 411.0727, GOVERNMENT CODE. DO NOT ATTEMPT TO COMPLETE A PETITION FOR AN ORDER OF NONDISCLOSURE WITHOUT FIRST REVIEWING THE NONDISCLOSURE OVERVIEW TO DETERMINE IF YOU ARE ELIGIBLE FOR AN ORDER OF NONDISCLOSURE AND TO IDENTIFY THE CORRECT FORM TO USE. THE NONDISCLOSURE OVERVIEW IS AVAILABLE AT THIS LINK: http://www.txcourts.gov/rules-forms/orders-of-nondisclosure.

TO BE ELIGIBLE TO USE THIS FORM EACH OF THE FOLLOWING STATEMENTS MUST BE TRUE:

1. YOU SUCCESSFULLY COMPLETED A VETERANS TREATMENT COURT PROGRAM FOR THE OFFENSE FOR WHICH THE ORDER OF NONDISCLOSURE IS REQUESTED.
2. YOU DID NOT ENTER THE VETERANS TREATMENT COURT PROGRAM AS THE RESULT OF BEING CONVICTED OF AN OFFENSE INVOLVING THE OPERATION OF A MOTOR VEHICLE WHILE INTOXICATED.
3. YOU HAVE NOT BEEN PREVIOUSLY CONVICTED OF AN OFFENSE LISTED IN ARTICLE 42A.054 (a), CODE OF CRIMINAL PROCEDURE, OR OF A SEXUALLY VIOLENT OFFENSE, AS DEFINED BY ARTICLE 62.001, CODE OF CRIMINAL PROCEDURE.
4. YOU WERE NOT CONVICTED OF A FELONY OFFENSE DURING THE TWO-YEAR PERIOD FOLLOWING YOUR SUCESSFUL COMPLETION OF THE VETERANS TREATMENT COURT PROGRAM.
5. A MINIMUM OF TWO YEARS HAS PASSED SINCE YOUR SUCCESSFUL COMPLETION OF THE VETERANS TREATMENT COURT PROGRAM.

IF THE FIVE STATEMENTS ABOVE ARE NOT TRUE, THIS IS NOT THE CORRECT PETITION AND INSTRUCTIONS FOR YOU. YOU MAY BE ELIGIBLE FOR AN ORDER OF NONDISCLOSURE UNDER ANOTHER SECTION OF THE GOVERNMENT CODE. YOU SHOULD RETURN TO THE NONDISCLOSURE OVERVIEW TO DETERMINE IF

YOU ARE ELIGIBLE FOR AN ORDER OF NONDISCLOSURE UNDER ANOTHER SECTION.

Additional Requirements

You are **not eligible** for an order of nondisclosure under Section 411.0727, or any other section, if:

- you were or have ever been convicted of or placed on deferred adjudication community supervision (hereinafter "deferred adjudication") for any of the offenses listed below:
    (i)   an offense requiring registration as a sex offender under Chapter 62, Code of Criminal Procedure;
    (ii) an offense under Texas Penal Code Section 20.04 (aggravated kidnapping);
    (iii) an offense under any of the following sections of the Texas Penal Code:
        - 19.02 (murder);
        - 19.03 (capital murder);
        - 20A.02 (trafficking of persons);
        - 20A.03 (continuous trafficking of persons);
        - 22.04 (injury to a child, elderly individual, or disabled individual);
        - 22.041 (abandoning or endangering a child);
        - 25.07 (violation of court orders or conditions of bond in a family violence, sexual assault or abuse, stalking, or trafficking case);
        - 25.072 (repeated violation of certain court orders or conditions of bond in family violence, sexual assault or abuse, stalking, or trafficking case); or
        - 42.072 (stalking); or
    (iv) any other offense involving family violence, as defined by Section 71.004, Family Code;
- the court made an affirmative finding that your offense, the one for which you are requesting an order of nondisclosure, involved family violence, as defined by Section 71.004, Family Code; or
- if, during the period after the court pronounced the sentence, or placed you on deferred adjudication for the offense for which the order of nondisclosure is requested, and during the two-year

waiting period following your successful completion of the veterans treatment court program, you were convicted of or placed on deferred adjudication for any offense other than a traffic offense punishable by fine only.

Instructions for Completing Petition

(1) Please leave this line blank. This is not the number of your criminal case. A civil case will be created when you file the petition. The clerk of the court (hereinafter "clerk") will enter a new cause number in this space.

(2) Please enter the name of the court in which you are filing this petition. You must file this petition in the court that dismissed your case or placed you on probation or deferred adjudication. The name of the court is shown on the top of the order that dismissed your case or placed you on probation or deferred adjudication.

(3) Please enter your name as it appears in the order that dismissed your case or placed you on probation or deferred adjudication.

(4) Please enter the name of the county in which the court that dismissed your case or placed you on probation or deferred adjudication is located.

(5) Please enter your name as you did in (3) above.

(6) Please enter the name of the offense for which the order of nondisclosure is requested. This is the same offense shown on the dismissal, order placing you on probation or deferred adjudication, or judgment in the case for which the order of nondisclosure is requested.

(7) Please enter the criminal cause number shown on the order that dismissed your case or placed you on probation or deferred adjudication. Look for *Case No.* on that order.

(8) Please enter the date on which you successfully completed the veterans treatment court program.

(9) Please circle "**is**" if you are attaching proof of your successful completion of the veterans treatment court program. Although attaching proof of

successful completion of the veterans treatment court program may expedite the process for obtaining an order of nondisclosure, it is not required. Please circle "**is not**" if you are not attaching proof.

(10) Please enter the date that the veterans treatment court determined that a dismissal of your case is in the best interest of justice. [**Note**: In some counties, the district or county court may also serve as the veterans treatment court.]

(11) Please circle "**is**" if you are attaching a copy of the veterans treatment court's order determining that a dismissal is in the best interest of justice. Please circle "**is not**" if you are not attaching a copy of the order. Attaching a copy of the order may expedite the process, but it is not required.

(12) There is a filing fee associated with the filing of a petition for an order of nondisclosure under Section 411.0727. The filing fee is the amount of the court's regular civil filing fee plus an additional $28.00. Typically, the total filing fee is about $280.00. However, the amount varies from county to county. Please contact the clerk for the court in which you are filing the petition to obtain the total amount of the fee required. **NOTE**: You should not have to pay the clerk to serve the petition on the attorney for the state (hereinafter "prosecutor"), Department of Public Safety (hereinafter "DPS"), or any other agency or entity, including any law enforcement entity. The statute requires the court, clerk, and DPS to notify the other parties of interest. See Sections 411.0745(e), 411.075(a) and 411.075(b), Government Code, respectively.

> *As a general rule, you must pay the filing fee in order to file the petition. However, you may be eligible to file a Statement of Inability to Afford Payment of Court Costs in lieu of paying the filing fee. The statement is described in Rule 145 of the Texas Rules of Civil Procedure. You may read Rule 145 online at http://www.txcourts.gov/media/1435952/trcp-all-updated-with-amendments-effective-912016.pdf. You can click here for the* **Statement of Inability to Afford Payment of Court Costs** *form: http://www.txcourts.gov/media/1435953/statement-final-version.pdf.*

Please place a check mark or an "x" on the line in front of the first statement, if you are paying the filing fee. If you are submitting a **Statement** of Inability to Afford Payment of Court Costs, place a check mark or an "x" on the line in front of the second statement.

(13) Please sign above the line. If you are filing this petition electronically, you may enter "/s/" followed by your typewritten name.

(14) Please PRINT your name.

(15) Please enter your mailing address.

(16) Please enter your city, state and zip code.

(17) Please enter your telephone number.

Process After You Complete the Petition

If you are eligible for an order of nondisclosure under Section 411.0727, the process for obtaining an order under this section is as follows:

First, check in advance with the clerk's office to obtain the total amount of the fee (including the $28 fee) to file a petition for an order of nondisclosure, unless you are submitting a *Statement of Inability to Afford Payment of Court Costs* in lieu of paying the fee. Next, be sure to complete the *correct* petition according to the instructions, and after you have done so, print both the petition and the *Order of Nondisclosure under Section 411.0727*. In most courts, you will have to submit a proposed order with your petition. The judge will complete the order, if the judge grants your request.

You must file the petition in the court that placed you in the veterans treatment court program, not in the veterans treatment court, unless the court that placed you in the veterans treatment court program also serves as the veterans treatment court.

After you file the petition, the clerk will send it to the court and the court will notify the prosecutor. Again, you should not have to pay the clerk to serve notice on the prosecutor or any other party.

A hearing on the petition is not required if the prosecutor does not request a hearing.

If a hearing is scheduled, the court or the clerk will notify you. If there is a hearing, the court may ask questions to establish whether you satisfy the requirements of Sections 411.074 and 411.0727. After the hearing, if the court determines that you are entitled to file the petition and issuance of the order of nondisclosure is in the best interest of justice, the court should grant your request for the order.

If the court does not hold a hearing, the judge will review your petition to determine whether you satisfy the requirements of the statutes and whether issuance of the order of nondisclosure is in the best interest of justice. If the court determines that you are entitled to file the petition and issuance of the order is in the best interest of justice, the court should grant your request for the order.

The court and/or prosecutor will have access to your criminal history record information and will use it to determine if you are entitled to file the petition.

If the court grants the order of nondisclosure, not later than 15 business days after the order issues, the clerk will send a copy of the order to DPS. Then, not later than 10 business days after DPS receives the order, DPS will seal the criminal history record information that is the subject of the order and forward the order to the state and federal agencies listed in Section 411.075(b), Government Code. See Section 411.075(b) for a complete list of agencies and entities that DPS must notify.

Cause No. _____
(1)

In the Matter of § In the

§ _____
(2)
_____ § _____ County, Texas
(3) (4)

Petition for Order of Nondisclosure Under Section 411.0727

_____(5) ("Petitioner") respectfully petitions this court for an order of nondisclosure under Section 411.0727, Government Code, for the offense detailed below.

1. **The Underlying Order**

    Petitioner was charged, convicted, or placed on deferred adjudication for the offense of _____ (6) in Criminal Cause No. _____ (7). As a result of that offense, Petitioner entered a veterans treatment court program under Chapter 124 of the Government Code, or former law, and successfully completed that program on _____, 20____ (8). Proof of Petitioner's completion of the program **is / is not** (9) attached.

    Pursuant to Section 124.001(b), Government Code, on _____, 20____ (10), the veterans treatment court determined that a dismissal of Petitioner's case is in the best interest of justice. A copy of the veterans treatment court's order **is / is not** (11) attached.

2. **Petitioner Satisfies the Requirements of Sec. 411.0727, Government Code**

    Petitioner satisfies the requirements of Sec. 411.0727 of the Government Code in that Petitioner:
    - Has successfully completed the veterans treatment court program;

OCA MODEL PETITION FOR ORDER OF DISCLOSURE UNDER 411.0727, GOVERNMENT CODE DECEMBER 2017

- Did not enter into the veterans treatment court program because of a conviction of an offense involving the operation of a motor vehicle while intoxicated;
- Has never been previously convicted of any of the offenses listed in Article 42A.054(a), Code of Criminal Procedure, which includes the following:
    - Section 15.03, Penal Code (Criminal Solicitation), if the offense is punishable as a first degree felony;
    - Section 19.02, Penal Code (Murder);
    - Section 19.03, Penal Code (Capital Murder);
    - Section 20.04, Penal Code (Aggravated Kidnapping);
    - Section 20A.02, Penal Code (Trafficking of Persons);
    - Section 21.11(a)(1), Penal Code (Indecency with a Child);
    - Section 22.011, Penal Code (Sexual Assault);
    - Section 22.021, Penal Code (Aggravated Sexual Assault)
    - Section 22.04(a)(1), Penal Code (Injury to a Child, Elderly Individual, or Disabled Individual), if the offense is punishable as a first degree felony and the victim of the offense is a child;
    - Section 29.03, Penal Code (Aggravated Robbery);
    - Section 30.02, Penal Code (Burglary), if the offense is punishable as a first degree felony under Subsection (d) of that section and the actor committed the offense with the intent to commit a felony under Section 21.02 (Continuous Sexual Abuse of Young Child or Children), 21.11 (Indecency With a Child), 22.011 (Sexual Assault), 22.021 (Aggravated Sexual Assault), or 25.02 (Prohibited Sexual Conduct) of the Penal Code;
    - Section 43.05, Penal Code (Compelling Prostitution);
    - Section 43.25, Penal Code (Sexual Performance by a Child); and
    - Chapter 481, Health and Safety Code (Texas Controlled Substances Act), for which punishment is increased under Section 481.140 of that Code (Use of Child in Commission of Offense) because of the use or attempted use of a child in the commission of the offense, or under Section 481.134(c), (d), (e), or (f) of that Code (Drug-free Zones) because of a previous conviction of an offense for which punishment was increased under any of those subsections;
- Has never been previously convicted of a sexually violent offense, as defined by Article 62.001, Code of Criminal Procedure;
- Was not convicted of a felony during the two years following Petitioner's successful completion of the veterans treatment court program; and
- Has waited a minimum of two years following Petitioner's successful completion of the veterans treatment court program before filing this petition.

3. Petitioner Satisfies the Requirements of Sec. 411.074, Government Code

Petitioner satisfies the requirements of Sec. 411.074 of the Government Code in that:

- During the period after the court pronounced the sentence or placed Petitioner on deferred adjudication for the offense for which the order of nondisclosure is requested, and during the two-year waiting period following Petitioner's successful completion of the veterans treatment court program, Petitioner was not convicted of or placed on deferred adjudication for any offense other than a traffic offense punishable by fine only;

- Petitioner was not and has not ever been convicted of or placed on deferred adjudication for any of the following offenses:
  - (A) An offense requiring registration as a sex offender under Chapter 62, Code of Criminal Procedure;
  - (B) an offense under Texas Penal Code Section 20.04 (Aggravated Kidnapping);
  - (C) An offense under any of the following sections of the Texas Penal Code:
    - 19.02 (Murder);
    - 19.03 (Capital Murder);
    - 20A.02 (Trafficking of Persons);
    - 20A.03 (Continuous Trafficking of Persons);
    - 22.04 (Injury to a Child, Elderly Individual, or Disabled Individual);
    - 22.041 (Abandoning or Endangering a Child);
    - 25.07 (Violation of Court Orders or Conditions of Bond in a Family Violence, Sexual Assault or Abuse, Stalking, or Trafficking Case);
    - 25.072 (Repeated Violation of Certain Court Orders or Conditions of Bond in Family Violence, Sexual Assault or Abuse, Stalking, or Trafficking Case);
    - 42.072 (Stalking); and
  - (D) Any other offense involving family violence, as defined by Section 71.004, Family Code; and

- The court has not made an affirmative finding that the offense for which the order of nondisclosure is requested involved family violence, as defined by Section 71.004, Family Code.

4. Petitioner is Entitled to File a Petition for an Order of Nondisclosure

Petitioner is entitled to file this petition because Petitioner has satisfied the requirements to do so. A person is entitled to file a petition under Section 411.0727, Government Code, if the person:

- Successfully completes a veterans treatment court program established under Chapter 124, Government Code, or former law, for the offense for which the order of nondisclosure is requested;
- Satisfies the requirements of Section 411.074, Government Code, including: not having been convicted of or placed on deferred adjudication for any offense other than a traffic offense punishable by fine only during the period after the court pronounced the sentence or placed the person on probation or deferred adjudication, and during the two-year waiting period following the person's successful completion of the veterans treatment court program; not having received an affirmative finding by the court that the offense for which the order of nondisclosure is requested involved family violence, as defined by Section 71.004, Family Code; and never having been convicted of or placed on deferred adjudication for an offense listed in Section 411.074(b), Government Code;
- Has never been previously convicted of an offense listed in Article 42A.054(a), Code of Criminal Procedure, or a sexually violent offense, as defined by Article 62.001, Code of Criminal Procedure;
- Was not convicted of a felony offense during the two-year period following the person's successful completion of the veterans treatment court program; and
- Did not enter the veterans treatment court program as the result of a conviction of an offense involving the operation of a motor vehicle while intoxicated.

5. Issuance of an Order of Nondisclosure is in the Best Interest of Justice

The issuance of an order of nondisclosure is in the best interest of justice.

6. The Fee to File the Petition has been Paid or Otherwise Satisfied

The fee to file this petition is the total amount of the fee required to file a civil petition and $28.00, or a petitioner may submit a *Statement of Inability to Afford Payment of Court Costs* in lieu of paying any fee. Petitioner has included (12)

_____ the required filing fee.

_____ a *Statement of Inability to Afford Payment of Court Costs* in lieu of the required fee.

7. Prayer for Relief

Petitioner respectfully prays that the court grant Petitioner's request for an order of nondisclosure under Section 411.0727, Government Code.

Respectfully submitted,

_____
(13)

_____
(14)

_____
(15)

_____
(16)

_____
(17)

Cause No. _____

In the Matter of	§	In the
	§	_____
_____	§	_____ County, Texas

Order of Nondisclosure Under Section 411.0727

On this the _____, day of _____, 20_____, the Court considered Petitioner's Petition for an Order of Nondisclosure under Section 411.0727, Government Code.

The State was given notice of the petition and an opportunity to request a hearing. The State

☐ requested a hearing.

☐ did not request a hearing.

The Court

☐ conducted a hearing on _____, _____.

☐ did not conduct a hearing.

After consideration and a hearing, if a hearing was held as indicated above, the Court **FINDS** that Petitioner entered the veterans treatment court program for the offense(s) of _____, as charged in Criminal Cause No. _____. The Court **FURTHER FINDS** that Petitioner's entrance into the veterans treatment court program did not arise as the result of a conviction for an offense involving the operation of a motor vehicle while intoxicated.

The Court **FURTHER FINDS** that Petitioner is entitled to file the petition and that issuance of the order of nondisclosure is in the best interest of justice.

Accordingly, **IT IS HEREBY ORDERED** that criminal justice agencies are prohibited from disclosing to the public criminal history record information related to the offense for which Petitioner entered the veterans treatment court program.

IT IS FURTHER ORDERED that the criminal history record information pertaining to the arrest and prosecution of Petitioner for the above-referenced offense(s) shall be sealed and disclosed by the court only to individuals and agencies listed in Section 411.076(a), Government Code.

IT IS FURTHER ORDERED that no later than the 15th business day after the date that this order issues, the clerk of the court (hereinafter "clerk") shall send all relevant criminal history record information contained in this order or a copy of this order to the Crime Records Service of the Texas Department of Public Safety (hereinafter "DPS") by certified mail (return receipt requested) or secure electronic mail, electronic transmission, or facsimile transmission, in accordance with Section 411.075(a), Government Code.

IT IS FURTHER ORDERED that no later than 10 business days after receipt of the relevant criminal history record information contained in this order or a copy of this order from the clerk, DPS shall seal the criminal history record information that is the subject of this order and forward the information or copy of the order to all state and federal agencies listed in Section 411.075(b), Government Code, by certified mail (return receipt requested) or secure electronic mail, electronic transmission, or facsimile transmission, in accordance with Section 411.075(b), Government Code.

IT IS FURTHER ORDERED that an agency or entity shall seal any criminal history record information maintained by that agency or entity that is the subject of this order no later than 30 business days after the date the agency or entity receives the relevant criminal history record information contained in this order or a copy of this order from DPS or a clerk, in accordance with Section 411.075(d), Government Code.

IT IS FURTHER ORDERED that the clerk shall seal all court records containing information that is the subject of this order as soon as practicable after the date the clerk sends a copy of this order or all relevant criminal history record information contained in this order to DPS, in accordance with Section 411.076(b), Government Code.

Signed on _____.

_____
Judge Presiding

_____
Court/County

Office of Court Administration

Instructions for Completing the Model Petition for Order of Nondisclosure Under Section 411.0728

BEFORE BEGINNING MAKE SURE YOU ARE USING THE CORRECT PETITION. THIS PETITION AND INSTRUCTIONS ARE FOR PERSONS REQUESTING AN ORDER OF NONDISCLOSURE UNDER SECTION 411.0728, GOVERNMENT CODE, ONLY. DO NOT ATTEMPT TO COMPLETE A PETITION FOR AN ORDER OF NONDISCLOSURE WITHOUT FIRST REVIEWING THE NONDISCLOSURE OVERVIEW TO DETERMINE IF YOU ARE ELIGIBLE FOR AN ORDER OF NONDISCLOSURE AND TO IDENTIFY THE CORRECT FORMS TO USE. THE NONDISCLOSURE OVERVIEW IS AVAILABLE AT THIS LINK: http://www.txcourts.gov/rules-forms/orders-of-nondisclosure.

TO BE ELIGIBLE TO USE THIS FORM YOU MUST BE ABLE TO ANSWER YES TO EACH OF THE FOLLOWING QUESTIONS:

1. IS THE OFFENSE FOR WHICH THE ORDER OF NONDISCLOSURE IS REQUESTED AN OFFENSE LISTED UNDER SECTION 411.0728(a)(1):
   - SECTION 43.02, PENAL CODE, PROSTITUTION;
   - SECTION 43.03(a)(2), PENAL CODE, PROMOTION OF PROSTITUTION AS A CLASS A MISDEMEANOR;
   - SECTION 31.03, PENAL CODE, THEFT AS A CLASS C OR B MISDEMEANOR;
   - SECTION 481.120, HEALTH AND SAFETY CODE, DELIVERY OF MARIHUANA AS A CLASS B MISDEMEANOR; OR
   - SECTION 481, 121, HEALTH AND SAFETY CODE, POSSESSION OF MARIHUANA AS A CLASS B MISDEMEANOR?
2. WHEN YOU COMMITTED THE OFFENSE FOR WHICH THE ORDER OF NONDISCLOSURE IS REQUESTED WERE YOU A VICTIM OF TRAFFICKING OF PERSONS?
3. WERE YOU PLACED ON PROBATION AFTER YOUR CONVICTION?

4. WAS YOUR CONVICTION SUBSEQUENTLY SET ASIDE PURSUANT TO ARTICLE 42A.701, CODE OF CRIMINAL PROCEDURE (REDUCTION OR TERMINATION OF COMMUNITY SUPERVISION PERIOD)?
5. IF THE COURT GRANTS YOUR REQUEST, WILL THIS BE THE FIRST TIME THAT YOU RECEIVE AN ORDER OF NONDISCLOSURE UNDER SECTION 411.0728?

IF YOU CANNOT ANSWER YES TO THE FIVE QUESTIONS ABOVE, THIS IS NOT THE CORRECT PETITION FOR YOU.

You may be eligible for an order of nondisclosure under another section of the Government Code. You should return to the nondisclosure overview to determine if you are eligible for an order of nondisclosure under another section and to identify the correct form to use.

NOTE: In order to be eligible for an order of nondisclosure under Section 411.0728, the order setting aside your conviction must have occurred **on or after September 1, 2015,** if you were convicted of prostitution under Section 43.02, Penal Code, or **on or after September 1, 2017,** if you were convicted of any other offense under Section 411.0728(a)(1).

Additional Requirements

You are **not eligible** for an order of nondisclosure under Sec. 411.0728, or any other section, if:
- You were or have ever been convicted of or placed on deferred adjudication community supervision (hereinafter "deferred adjudication") for any of the offenses listed below:
    (i) an offense requiring registration as a sex offender under Chapter 62, Code of Criminal Procedure;
    (ii) an offense under Texas Penal Code Section 20.04 (aggravated kidnapping);
    (iii) an offense under any of the following Texas Penal Code Sections:
    - 19.02 (murder);
    - 19.03 (capital murder);
    - 20A.02 (trafficking of persons);
    - 20A.03 (continuous trafficking of persons);

- o 22.04 (injury to a child, elderly individual, or disabled individual);
- o 22.041 (abandoning or endangering a child);
- o 25.07 (violation of court orders or conditions of bond in a family violence, sexual assault or abuse, stalking, or trafficking case);
- o 25.072 (repeated violation of certain court orders or conditions of bond in family violence, sexual assault or abuse, stalking, or trafficking case); or
- o 42.072 (stalking); or

(iv) any other offense involving family violence, as defined by Section 71.004, Family Code;

- The court made an affirmative finding that your offense, the one for which you are requesting an order of nondisclosure, involved family violence, as defined by Section 71.004, Family Code; or
- If, during the period after the court placed you on probation and until the date that your conviction was set aside, you were convicted of or placed on deferred adjudication for any offense other than a traffic offense punishable by fine only.

Instructions for Completing Petition

(1) Please leave this line blank. This is not the number of your criminal case. A civil case will be created when you file the petition. The clerk of the court (hereinafter "clerk") will enter a new cause number in this space.

(2) Please enter the name of the court in which you are filing this petition. You must file this petition in the court that placed you on probation. The name of the court is shown on the top of the order that placed you on probation.

(3) Please enter your name as it appears in the order that placed you on probation.

(4) Please enter the name of the county in which the court that placed you on probation is situated. This will be the same county as shown on your order.

(5) Please enter your name as you did in (3) above.

(6) Place an "X" or check mark next to the offense for which you were convicted. The order that placed you on probation or the judgment in your case will reflect the offense of your conviction.

(7) Please enter the criminal cause number shown on the order that placed you on probation. Look for *Case No.* on that order.

(8) Please enter the date that the court placed you on probation.

(9) Please circle "is" if you are attaching a copy of the court's order or document showing that you were placed on probation following your conviction. Attaching a copy of the court's order or document may expedite the process for obtaining an order of nondisclosure, but it is not required. Please circle "is not" if you are not attaching a copy of the court's order or document.

(10) Please circle "is" if you are attaching a copy of the court's order that set aside your conviction. Circle "is not" if you are not attaching a copy of the order.

(11) Please place an "X" or check mark next to the offenses that apply to you.

(12) There is a filing fee associated with filing of a petition for an order of nondisclosure under Section 411.0728. The filing fee is the amount of the court's regular civil filing fee plus an additional $28.00. Typically, the total filing fee is about $280.00. However, the amount varies from county to county. Please contact the clerk for the court in which you are filing the petition to obtain the total amount of the fee required. **NOTE:** You should not have to pay the clerk to serve the petition on the attorney for the state (hereinafter "prosecutor"), Department of Public Safety (hereinafter "DPS"), or any other agency or entity, including any law enforcement entity. The statute requires the court, clerk, and DPS to notify the other parties of interest. See Sections 411.0745(e), 411.075(a) and 411.075(b), Government Code, respectively.

> *As a general rule, you must pay the filing fee in order to file the petition. However, you may be eligible to file a Statement of Inability to Afford Payment of Court Costs in lieu of paying the filing fee. The statement is described in Rule 145 of the*

Texas Rules of Civil Procedure. You may view Rule 145 online at http://www.txcourts.gov/media/1435952/trcp-all-updated-with-amendments-effective-912016.pdf. You can click here for the **Statement of Inability to Afford Payment of Court Costs**: *http://www.txcourts.gov/media/1435953/statement-final-version.pdf.*

Please place a check mark or an "x" on the line in front of the first statement, if you are paying the filing fee. If you are submitting a **Statement of Inability to Afford Payment of Court Costs**, place a check mark or an "x" on the line in front of the second statement.

(13) Please sign above the line. If you are filing this petition electronically, you may enter "/s/" followed by your typewritten name.

(14) Please PRINT your name.

(15) Please enter your mailing address.

(16) Please enter your city, state and zip code.

(17) Please enter your telephone number.

Process after You Complete the Petition

If you are eligible for an order of nondisclosure under Section 411.0728, the process for obtaining an order of nondisclosure under this section is as follows:

First, check in advance with the clerk's office to obtain the total amount of the fee (including the $28 fee), unless you are submitting a *Statement of Inability to Afford Payment of Court Costs* in lieu of paying the fee. Next, be sure to complete the correct petition according to the instructions, and after you have done so, print both the petition and the *Order of Nondisclosure under Section 411.0728*. In most courts, you will have to submit a proposed order with your petition. The judge will complete the order, if the judge grants your request.

After you file the petition, the clerk will send it to the court and the court will notify the prosecutor. Again, you should not have to pay the clerk to serve notice on the prosecutor or any other party.

A hearing on the petition is not required if the prosecutor does not request a hearing.

If a hearing is scheduled, the court or the clerk will notify you. If there is a hearing, the court may ask questions to establish whether you satisfy the requirements of Sections 411.074 and 411.0728. After the hearing, if the court finds that you are entitled to file the petition and that issuance of the order of nondisclosure is in the best interest of justice, the court should grant your request for the order.

If the court does not hold a hearing, the judge will review your petition to determine whether you satisfy the requirements of the statutes and whether issuance of the order of nondisclosure is in the best interest of justice. If the court determines that you are entitled to file the petition and issuance of the order is in the best interest of justice, the court should grant your request for the order.

The court and/or prosecutor will have access to your criminal history record information and will use it to determine if you are entitled to file the petition.

If the court grants the order of nondisclosure, no later than 15 business days after the order issues, the clerk will send a copy of the order to DPS. Then, no later than 10 business days after DPS receives the copy of the order, DPS will seal the criminal history record information that is the subject of the order and forward the order to the state and federal agencies listed in Section 411.075(b), Government Code. See Section 411.075(b) for a complete list of agencies and entities that DPS must notify.

Cause No. _____
(1)

In the Matter of § In the

§

§ _____
(2)
_____ § _____ County, Texas
(3) (4)

Petition for Order of Nondisclosure Under Section 411.0728

_____ (5) ("Petitioner") respectfully petitions this court for an order of nondisclosure under Section 411.0728, Government Code, for the offense detailed below.

1. **The Underlying Order**

    Petitioner was convicted of the offense indicated below (6) and placed on community supervision (hereinafter "probation") under Chapter 42A (formerly Article 42.12), Code of Criminal Procedure, following that conviction in Criminal Cause No. _____ (7) by this court on _____, _____. (8)

    ____ **Prostitution** (felony or misdemeanor)
    ____ **Promotion of Prostitution** (Class A misdemeanor only)
    ____ **Delivery or Possession of Marihuana** (Class B misdemeanor only)
    ____ **Theft** (Class C and B misdemeanors only)

    A copy of the order or document showing that Petitioner was placed on probation **is / is not** (9) attached to this petition.

    Petitioner's conviction was subsequently set aside by the court under Article 42A.701 (formerly Article 42.12, §20(a)), Code of Criminal Procedure. A copy of the order setting aside the conviction **is / is not** (10) attached to this petition.

2. **Petitioner Satisfies the Requirements of Sec. 411.0728, Government Code**

    Petitioner satisfies the requirements of Section 411.0728 of the Government Code in that:

- Petitioner was placed on probation after conviction for an offense under:(11)
  ____ Section 481.120 (Delivery of Marihuana), Health and Safety Code, that was punishable under subsection (b)(1) of that section as a Class B misdemeanor;
  ____ Section 481.121 (Possession of Marihuana), Health and Safety Code, that was punishable under subsection (b)(1) of that section as a Class B misdemeanor;
  ____ Section 31.03 (Theft), Penal Code, that was punishable under subsection (e) (1) or (2) of the section as a Class C or B misdemeanor;
  ____ Section 43.02 (Prostitution), Penal Code; or
  ____ Section 43.03(a)(2) (Promotion of Prostitution), Penal Code, that was punishable as a Class A misdemeanor;
- Petitioner committed the above-mentioned offense solely as a victim of trafficking of persons;
- Petitioner's conviction was set aside **on or after September 1, 2017**, but if Petitioner's conviction was for the offense of prostitution, Petitioner's conviction was set aside **on or after September 1, 2015**;
- Petitioner has not previously received an order of nondisclosure under Section 411.0728; and
- Petitioner satisfies the requirements of Section 411.074, Government Code.

3. Petitioner Satisfies the Requirements of Sec. 411.074, Government Code

Petitioner satisfies the requirements of Section 411.074 of the Government Code in that:

- During the period after the court placed Petitioner on probation and until the date that Petitioner's conviction was set aside, Petitioner was not convicted of or placed on deferred adjudication for any offense other than a traffic offense punishable by fine only;

- Petitioner was not and has not ever been previously convicted of or placed on deferred adjudication for any of the following offenses:
    (A) an offense requiring registration as a sex offender under Chapter 62, Code of Criminal Procedure;
    (B) an offense under Texas Penal Code Section 20.04 (Aggravated Kidnapping);
    (C) an offense under any of the following sections of the Texas Penal Code:
      - 19.02 (Murder);
      - 19.03 (Capital Murder);
      - 20A.02 (Trafficking of Persons);

- 20A.03 (Continuous Trafficking of Persons);
- 22.04 (Injury to a Child, Elderly Individual, or Disabled Individual);
- 22.041 (Abandoning or Endangering a Child);
- 25.07 (Violation of Court Orders or Conditions of Bond in a Family Violence, Sexual Assault or Abuse, Stalking, or Trafficking Case);
- 25.072 (Repeated Violation of Certain Court Orders or Conditions of Bond in Family Violence, Sexual Assault or Abuse, Stalking, or Trafficking Case);
- 42.072 (Stalking); and

(D) any other offense involving family violence, as defined by Section 71.004, Family Code; and

- The court has not made an affirmative finding that Petitioner's offense involved family violence, as defined by Section 71.004, Family Code.

4. Petitioner is Entitled to File a Petition for an Order of Nondisclosure

Petitioner is entitled to file this petition because Petitioner has satisfied the requirements to do so. A person is entitled to file a petition for an order of nondisclosure under Section 411.0728, Government Code, if:

- the person seeks an order of nondisclosure for an offense listed under Section 411.0728(a), Government Code;
- the person was placed on probation after conviction for that offense;
- the person's conviction was set aside on or after September 1, 2015 (for prostitution offenses), or on or after September 1, 2017 (for all other offenses);
- the person committed the offense solely as a victim of trafficking of persons;
- the person has not previously received an order of nondisclosure under Section 411.0728, Government Code, and the person asserts this as a fact in his or her petition; and
- the person satisfies the requirements of Section 411.074, Government Code, including: during the period after the person was placed on probation and until the date that the person's conviction was set aside, not having been convicted of or placed on deferred adjudication for any offense other than a traffic offense punishable by fine only; not having received an affirmative finding by the court that the person's offense involved family violence, as defined by Section 71.004, Family Code; and never having been

convicted of or placed on deferred adjudication for an offense listed in Section 411.074(b), Government Code.

5. Issuance of an Order of Nondisclosure is in the Best Interest of Justice

The issuance of an order of nondisclosure is in the best of justice.

6. The Fee to File the Petition has been Paid or Otherwise Satisfied

The fee to file this petition is the total amount of the fee required to file a civil petition and $28.00, or a petitioner may submit a *Statement of Inability to Afford Payment of Court Costs* in lieu of paying any fee. Petitioner has included (12)

_____ the required filing fee.

_____ a *Statement of Inability to Afford Payment of Court Costs* in lieu of the required fee.

7. Prayer for Relief

Petitioner respectfully prays that the court grant Petitioner's request for an order of nondisclosure under Section 411.0728, Government Code.

Respectfully submitted,

_____
(13)

_____
(14)

_____
(15)

_____
(16)

_____
(17)

Cause No. _____

In the Matter of § In the

§ _____

_____ § _____ County, Texas

<u>Order of Nondisclosure</u>
<u>Under Section 411.0728</u>
<u>(Victims of Trafficking of Persons)</u>

On this the _____, day of _____, 20_____, the Court considered Petitioner's petition for an order of nondisclosure under Section 411.0728, Government Code.

The State was given notice of the petition and an opportunity to request a hearing. The State

☐ requested a hearing.

☐ did not request a hearing.

The Court

☐ conducted a hearing on _____, _____.

☐ did not conduct a hearing.

After consideration and a hearing, if a hearing was held as indicated above, the Court **FINDS** that Petitioner has not previously received an order of nondisclosure under Section 411.0728, Government Code and that Petitioner committed the offense in Criminal Cause No. _____ solely as a victim of trafficking of persons. The Court **FURTHER FINDS** that issuance of an order of nondisclosure is in the best interest of justice.

Accordingly, **IT IS HEREBY ORDERED** that criminal justice agencies are prohibited from disclosing to the public criminal history record information related to the offense of _____ for which Petitioner was placed on community supervision (hereinafter "probation") on_____, 20_____ in the above-referenced criminal cause number.

IT IS FURTHER ORDERED that the criminal history record information pertaining to the arrest and prosecution of Petitioner for the offense of Prostitution, as charged in the above-referenced criminal cause number, shall be sealed and disclosed by the court only to individuals and agencies listed in Section 411.076(a), Government Code.

IT IS FURTHER ORDERED that no later than the 15th business day after the date that this order issues, the clerk of the court (hereinafter "clerk") shall send all relevant criminal history record information contained in this order or a copy of this order to the Crime Records Service of the Texas Department of Public Safety (hereinafter "DPS") by certified mail (return receipt requested) or secure electronic mail, electronic transmission, or facsimile transmission, in accordance with Section 411.075(a), Government Code.

IT IS FURTHER ORDERED that no later than 10 business days after receipt of the relevant criminal history record information contained in this order or a copy of this order from the clerk, DPS shall seal the criminal history record information that is the subject of this order and forward the information or copy of the order to all state and federal agencies listed in Section 411.075(b), Government Code, by certified mail (return receipt requested) or secure electronic mail, electronic transmission, or facsimile transmission, in accordance with Section 411.075(b), Government Code.

IT IS FURTHER ORDERED that an agency or entity shall seal any criminal history record information maintained by that agency or entity that is the subject of this order no later than 30 business days after the date that the agency or entity received relevant criminal history record information contained in this order or a copy of this order from DPS or a clerk, in accordance with Section 411.075(d), Government Code.

IT IS FURTHER ORDERED that the clerk shall seal all court records containing information that is the subject of this order as soon as practicable after the date that the clerk sends a copy of this order or all relevant criminal history record information contained in this order to DPS, in accordance with Section 411.076(b), Government Code.

Signed on _____.

_____
Judge Presiding

_____
Court/County

Office of Court Administration

Instructions for Completing the Model Petition for Order of Nondisclosure Under Section 411.073

BEFORE BEGINNING MAKE SURE YOU ARE USING THE CORRECT PETITION. THIS PETITION AND INSTRUCTIONS ARE FOR PERSONS SEEKING AN ORDER OF NONDISCLOSURE UNDER SECTION 411.073, GOVERNMENT CODE. DO NOT ATTEMPT TO COMPLETE A PETITION FOR AN ORDER OF NONDISCLOSURE WITHOUT FIRST REVIEWING THE NONDISCLOSURE OVERVIEW TO DETERMINE IF YOU ARE ELIGIBLE FOR AN ORDER OF NONDISCLOSURE AND TO IDENTIFY THE CORRECT FORMS TO USE. THE NONDISCLOSURE OVERVIEW IS AVAILABLE AT: http://www.txcourts.gov/rules-forms/orders-of-nondisclosure.

TO BE ELIGIBLE TO USE THIS PETITION YOU MUST BE ABLE TO ANSWER YES TO EACH OF THE FOLLOWING QUESTIONS:

1. WERE YOU CONVICTED OF A MISDEMEANOR OTHER THAN A MISDEMEANOR UNDER SECTION 106.041, ALCOHOL BEVERAGE CODE, SECTION 49.04, 49.05, 49.06, OR 49.065, PENAL CODE, OR CHAPTER 71, PENAL CODE?
2. WERE YOU PLACED ON PROBATION FOLLOWING YOUR CONVICTION FOR THE MISDEMEANOR OFFENSE?
3. DID YOU COMPLETE THAT PROBATION, INCLUDING ANY TERM OF CONFINEMENT IMPOSED AND PAYMENT OF ALL FINES, COSTS, AND RESTITUTION, IF ANY?
4. ASIDE FROM THE MISDEMEANOR CONVICTION, IT IS TRUE THAT YOU HAVE NEVER BEEN PREVIOUSLY CONVICTED OF OR PLACED ON DEFERRED ADJUDICATION FOR ANOTHER OFFENSE OTHER THAN A TRAFFIC OFFENSE PUNISHABLE BY FINE ONLY?
5. DO YOU SATISY THE BASIC ELIGIBLITY REQUIREMENTS OF SECTION 411.074, GOVERNMENT CODE? (PLEASE SEE THE NONDISCLOSURE OVERVIEW FOR THESE REQUIREMENTS.)
6. HAVE YOU SATISFIED THE REQUIRED WAITING PERIOD BEFORE FILING THIS PETITION? (THE NONDISCLOSURE OVERVIEW HELPED YOU TO DETERMINE THE APPLICABLE WAITING PERIOD FOR YOUR OFFENSE.)

IF YOU CANNOT ANSWER YES TO THE SIX QUESTIONS ABOVE, THIS IS NOT THE CORRECT PETITION FOR YOU.

You may be eligible for an order of nondisclosure under another section of the Government Code. You should return to the nondisclosure overview to determine if you are eligible for an order of nondisclosure under another section and to identify the correct form to use.

Instructions for Completing Petition

(1) Please leave this line blank. This is not the number of your criminal case. A civil case will be created when you file the petition. The clerk of the court (hereinafter "clerk") will enter a new cause number in this space.

(2) Please enter the name of the court in which you are filing this petition. You must file this petition in the court that placed you on community supervision (hereinafter "probation"). The name of the court is shown on the top of the order that placed you on probation.

(3) Please enter your name as it appears in the order that placed you on probation.

(4) Please enter the name of the county in which the court that placed you on probation is situated. This will be the same county as shown on your order.

(5) Please enter your name as you did in (3) above.

(6) Please enter the name of the offense for which you were convicted. The name of the offense is on the judgment or order that placed you on probation under Offense.

(7) Please enter the criminal cause number as shown on the court's order that placed you on probation. Look for *Case No.* on that order.

(8) Please enter the date of your conviction for the offense for which the order of nondisclosure is requested.

(9) Please enter the date that you were placed on probation. This should be on the order or document that placed you on probation.

(10) Please enter the date that you completed probation.

(11) Please circle "is" if you are attaching a copy of the document or order showing that the court placed you on probation and, if applicable, sentenced you to a period of confinement. Attaching a copy of the document or order may expedite the process for obtaining an order of nondisclosure, but it is not required. Please circle "is not" if you are not attaching a copy of the document or order.

(12) Please circle "is" if you are attaching a copy of the court's order showing that you completed probation and any period of confinement, if you were ordered confined. Attaching a copy of the court's order may expedite the process for obtaining an order of nondisclosure, but it is not required. Please circle "is not" if you are not attaching a copy of the court's order. The jail that released you may have given you a document that shows the date you were released from confinement.

(13) Place a check mark or an "x" on the line in front of the statement that applies to your case. If the offense for which you are requesting an order of nondisclosure is a misdemeanor under Chapter 20, 21, 22, 25, 42, 43, or 46 of the Penal Code, place your mark in front of the first statement. (If you checked this statement, you must wait two years from the date of completing your probation to file a petition for nondisclosure.) If your offense is not under one of the Chapters listed in the prior sentence, then place a mark in front of the second statement. (If you have checked the second statement, you can file a petition for an order of nondisclosure on or after the date you complete your term of probation.)

(14) There is a filing fee associated with filing a petition for order of nondisclosure under Section 411.073. The filing fee is the amount of the court's regular civil filing fee plus an additional $28. Typically, the total filing fee is about $280. However, the amount varies from county to county. Please contact the clerk for the court in which you are filing the petition to obtain the correct amount of the total filing fee. **NOTE**: You do not have to pay the clerk to serve the petition on the attorney for the state (hereinafter "prosecutor"), Department of Public Safety (hereinafter "DPS"), or any other agency or entity, including any law enforcement entity. The

statute requires the court, clerk, and DPS to notify the other parties of interest. See Sections 411.0745(e), 411.075(a) and 411.075(b), Government Code, respectively.

> *As a general rule, you must pay the filing fee in order to file the petition. However, you may be eligible to file a **Statement of Inability to Afford Payment of Court Costs** in lieu of paying the filing fee. The statement is described in Rule 145 of the Texas Rules of Civil Procedure. You may view Rule 145 online at http://www.txcourts.gov/media/1435952/trcp-all-updated-with-amendments-effective-912016.pdf. You can click here for the form: http://www.txcourts.gov/media/1435953/statement-final-version.pdf.*

Please place a check mark or an "x" on the line before the statement that applies to you. Place a check mark or "x" in front of the first statement, if you are paying the filing fee. If you are submitting a **Statement of Inability to Afford Payment of Court Costs** instead, place a check mark or an "x" in front of the second statement.

(15) Please sign above the line. If you are filing this petition electronically, you may enter "/s/" followed by your typewritten name.

(16) Please PRINT your name.

(17) Please enter your mailing address.

(18) Please enter your city, state and zip code.

(19) Please enter your telephone number.

Process After You Complete the Petition

If you are eligible for an order of nondisclosure under Section 411.073, the process for obtaining an order under this section is as follows:

First, make sure that you satisfy the waiting period requirement before filing your petition, and check in advance with the clerk's office to obtain the total amount of the fee (including the $28 fee) to file a petition for an order of nondisclosure, unless you are submitting a *Statement of Inability to Afford Payment of Court Costs* in lieu of paying the fee. Next, be sure to complete the correct petition according to the instructions, and after you have done so, print both the petition and the *Order of Nondisclosure*. In most courts, you will have to submit a proposed order with your petition when you file it. The judge will complete the order, if the judge grants your request.

After you file the petition, the clerk will send it to the court, and the court will notify the prosecutor. Again, you should not have to pay the clerk to serve notice on the prosecutor or any other party.

A hearing on the petition is not required if the prosecutor does not request a hearing.

If a hearing is scheduled, the court or the clerk will notify you. If there is a hearing, the court may ask questions to establish whether you satisfy the requirements of Sections 411.074 and 411.073. After the hearing, if the court finds that you satisfy the requirements of the statutes and that issuance of the order of nondisclosure is in the best interest of justice, the court should grant your request for the order.

If the court does not hold a hearing, the judge will review your petition to determine whether you satisfy the requirements of the statutes and whether issuance of the order of nondisclosure is in the best interest of justice. If the court finds that you have satisfied the requirements of the law and that the issuance of the order is in the best interest of justice, the court should grant your request for the order.

The court and/or prosecutor will have access to your criminal history record information and will use it to determine if you are eligible to file the petition.

If the court grants the order of nondisclosure, no later than 15 business days after the order issues, the clerk will send a copy of the order to DPS. Then, no later than 10 business days after DPS receives the copy of the order, DPS will seal any criminal history record information that is the subject of the order and forward the order to the state and federal agencies listed in 411.075(b), Government Code. See Section 411.075(b) for a complete list of agencies and entities that DPS must notify.

Cause No. _____
(1)

In the Matter of   §   In the

                          §   _____
                                           (2)
_____   §   _____ County, Texas
         (3)   (4)

Petition for Order of Nondisclosure Under Section 411.073

_____ (5) ("Petitioner") respectfully petitions the court for an order of nondisclosure under Section 411.073, Government Code, for the offense detailed below.

1. The Underlying Order and Completion of Community Supervision

Petitioner was convicted of the misdemeanor offense of _____ (6) in Criminal Cause No. _____ (7) in this court on _____, _____. (8)

Following the conviction, Petitioner was placed on community supervision (hereinafter "probation") on _____, _____. (9) Petitioner's probation was not revoked. Petitioner completed probation, including any term of confinement imposed and payment of all fines, costs, and restitution, if any, on _____, _____. (10)

A copy of the document or order showing that Petitioner was placed on probation **is / is not** (11) attached. The order or document showing that Petitioner completed

OCA MODEL PETITION FOR ORDER OF NONDISCLOSURE
UNDER SECTION 411.073, GOVERNMENT CODE

DECEMBER 2017

probation, including any term of confinement imposed and payment of all fines, costs, and restitution, if any, **is / is not** attached. (12)

2. Petitioner Satisfies the Requirements of Section 411.073, Government Code

Petitioner satisfies the requirements of Section 411.073, Government Code, in that:

- Petitioner's offense is a misdemeanor other than a misdemeanor under:
    - §106.041, Alcoholic Beverage Code (Driving/Operating Watercraft Under the Influence of Alcohol By Minor),
    - §49.04, Penal Code (Driving While Intoxicated),
    - §49.05, Penal Code (Flying While Intoxicated),
    - §49.06, Penal Code (Boating While Intoxicated),
    - §49.065, Penal Code (Assembling or Operating an Amusement Ride While Intoxicated), or
    - Chapter 71, Penal Code (Organized Crime);
- Following conviction for the offense, Petitioner was placed on probation under a provision of Chapter 42A (formerly Article 42.12), Code of Criminal Procedure, other than Subchapter C (formerly Section 5 of Article 42.12) of that chapter;
- Petitioner completed the period of probation, including any term of confinement imposed and payment of all fines, costs, and restitution, if any, and was not revoked;
- Petitioner has never been previously convicted of or placed on deferred adjudication community supervision (hereinafter "deferred adjudication") for another offense other than a traffic offense punishable by fine only;
- Petitioner has waited the requisite time, as indicated below, before filing this petition. (13)

_____ On or after the second anniversary of the date that Petitioner completed probation, if Petitioner's offense was a misdemeanor under Chapter 20, 21, 22, 25, 42, 43, or 46, Penal Code

_____ On or after the date that Petitioner completed probation, if Petitioner's offense was **not** a misdemeanor under Chapter 20, 21, 22, 25, 42, 43, or 46, Penal Code); and

- Petitioner satisfies the requirements of Section 411.074, Government Code.

3. Petitioner Satisfies the Requirements of Section 411.074, Gov't Code

Petitioner satisfies the requirements of Section 411.074, Government Code, in that:

- During the period after the court placed Petitioner on probation, and during any applicable waiting period (as indicated in Section 2 above) after completion of the probation, Petitioner was not convicted of or placed on deferred adjudication for any offense other than a traffic offense punishable by fine only;

- Petitioner was not and has not ever been previously convicted of or placed on deferred adjudication for any of the following:

    (A) an offense requiring registration as a sex offender under Chapter 62, Code of Criminal Procedure;

    (B) an offense under Texas Penal Code Section 20.04 (aggravated kidnapping);

    (C) an offense under any of the following sections of the Texas Penal Code:
    - 19.02 (murder);
    - 19.03 (capital murder);
    - 20A.02 (trafficking of persons);
    - 20A.03 (continuous trafficking of persons);

- 22.04 (injury to a child, elderly individual, or disabled individual);
- 22.041 (abandoning or endangering a child);
- 25.07 (violation of court orders or conditions of bond in a family violence, sexual assault or abuse, stalking, or trafficking case);
- 25.072 (repeated violation of certain court orders or conditions of bond in family violence, sexual assault or abuse, stalking, or trafficking case); or
- 42.072 (stalking); or

(D) any other offense involving family violence, as defined by Section 71.004, Family Code; and

- The court has not made an affirmative finding that Petitioner's offense involved family violence, as defined by Section 71.004, Family Code.

4. Petitioner is Entitled to File a Petition for an Order of Nondisclosure

Petitioner is entitled to file this petition because Petitioner has satisfied the requirements to do so. A person is entitled to file a petition for an order of nondisclosure under Section 411.073, Government Code, if the person:

- was convicted of a misdemeanor other than a misdemeanor listed in Sections 411.073(a) and 411.074(b), Government Code;
- was placed on probation following the conviction;
- completed the period of probation (the probation was not revoked), including any term of confinement imposed and payment of all fines, costs, and restitution, if any;
- has never been previously convicted of or placed on deferred adjudication for another offense other than a traffic offense punishable by fine only;
- has waited the requisite time before filing a petition for an order of nondisclosure under Section 411.073, Government Code;

- has satisfied the requirements of Section 411.074, Government Code, including: not having been convicted of or placed on deferred adjudication for any offense other than a traffic offense punishable by fine only, during the period after the person was placed on probation and during any applicable waiting period following the completion of that probation; not having received an affirmative finding by the court that the offense for which the order of nondisclosure is requested involved family violence, as defined by Sec. 71.004, Family Code; and never having been convicted of or placed on deferred adjudication for an offense listed in Section 411.074(b), Government Code.

5. Issuance of an Order of Nondisclosure is in the Best Interest of Justice

The issuance of an order of nondisclosure is in the best interest of justice.

6. The Fee to File the Petition has been Paid or Otherwise Satisfied

The fee to file this petition is the total amount of the fee required to file a civil petition and $28.00, or a petitioner may submit a *Statement of Inability to Afford Payment of Court Costs* in lieu of paying any fees. Petitioner has included: (14)

_____ the required filing fee; or

_____ a *Statement of Inability to Afford Payment of Court Costs* in lieu of the required fee.

7. Prayer for Relief

Petitioner respectfully prays that the court grant Petitioner's request for an order of nondisclosure under Section 411.073, Government Code.

Respectfully submitted,

_____
(15)

_____
(16)

_____
(17)

_____
(18)

_____
(19)

Cause No. _____

In the Matter of § In the

§ _____

_____ § _____ County, Texas

Order of Nondisclosure

On this the _____, day of _____, 20__, the Court considered Petitioner's Petition for Order of Nondisclosure.

The State was given notice of the petition and an opportunity to request a hearing. The State
- ☐ requested a hearing.
- ☐ did not request a hearing.

The Court
- ☐ conducted a hearing on _____, 20___.
- ☐ did not conduct a hearing.

After consideration and a hearing, if a hearing was held as indicated above, the Court **FINDS** that Petitioner is entitled to file a petition for an order of nondisclosure under the section of the Government Code indicated below and that issuance of an order of nondisclosure is in the best interest of justice.

- ☐ Texas Government Code Section 411.0725
- ☐ Texas Government Code Section 411.073
- ☐ Texas Government Code Section 411.0735

Accordingly, **IT IS HEREBY ORDERED** that criminal justice agencies are prohibited from disclosing to the public criminal history record information related to the offense of _____ in Criminal Cause No. _____ in _____County, Texas.

IT IS FURTHER ORDERED that the criminal history record information pertaining to the arrest and prosecution of Petitioner for the above-referenced offense, as reflected in the above-referenced criminal cause number, shall be sealed and disclosed only to those individuals and agencies listed in Section 411.076(a), Government Code.

IT IS FURTHER ORDERED that no later than the 15th business day after the date that this order issues, the clerk of the court (hereinafter "clerk") shall send all relevant criminal history record information contained in this order or a copy of this order to the Crime Records Service of the Texas Department of Public Safety (hereinafter "DPS") by certified mail (return receipt requested) or secure electronic mail, electronic transmission, or facsimile transmission, in accordance with Section 411.075(a), Government Code.

IT IS FURTHER ORDERED that no later than 10 business days after receipt of relevant criminal history record information contained in this order or a copy of this order from the clerk, DPS shall seal the criminal history record information that is the subject of this order and forward the information or a copy of the order to the state and federal agencies listed in Section 411.075(b), Government Code, by certified mail (return receipt requested), secure electronic mail, electronic transmission, or facsimile transmission, in accordance with Section 411.075(b), Government Code.

IT IS FURTHER ORDERED that an agency or entity shall seal any criminal history record information maintained by that agency or entity that is the subject of this order no later than 30 business days after the date that the agency or entity received relevant criminal history record information contained in this order or a copy of this order from DPS or a clerk, in accordance with Section 411.075(d), Government Code.

IT IS FURTHER ORDERED that the clerk shall seal all court records containing information that is the subject of this order as soon as practicable after the date that the clerk sends a copy of this order or all relevant criminal history record information contained in this order to DPS, in accordance with Section 411.076(b), Government Code.

Signed on _____.

_____
Judge Presiding

_____
Court/County

Office of Court Administration

Instructions for Completing the Model Petition for Order of Nondisclosure Under Section 411.0731

BEFORE BEGINNING MAKE SURE YOU ARE USING THE CORRECT MODEL PETITION. THIS PETITION AND INSTRUCTIONS ARE FOR PERSONS REQUESTING AN ORDER OF NONDISCLOSURE UNDER SECTION 411.0731, GOVERNMENT CODE. DO NOT ATTEMPT TO COMPLETE A PETITION FOR AN ORDER OF NONDISCLOSURE WITHOUT FIRST REVIEWING THE NONDISCLOSURE OVERVIEW TO DETERMINE IF YOU ARE ELIGIBLE FOR AN ORDER OF NONDISCLOSURE AND TO IDENTIFY THE CORRECT FORM TO USE. THE NONDISCLOSURE OVERVIEW IS AVAILABLE AT THIS LINK: http://www.txcourts.gov/rules-forms/orders-of-nondisclosure.

TO BE ELIGIBLE TO USE THIS PETITION THE FOLLOWING STATEMENTS MUST BE TRUE.

1. YOU WERE CONVICTED OF A CLASS B MISDEMEANOR OFFENSE OF DRIVING WHILE INTOXICATED MISDEMEANOR UNDER SECTION 49.04, PENAL CODE. [If your conviction was for a Class A misdemeanor under Section 49.04, you are not eligible for an order of nondisclosure under Section 411.0731.]
2. YOU WERE PLACED ON COMMUNITY SUPERVISION ("PROBATION") FOLLOWING YOUR CONVICTION, INCLUDING ANY FORM OF PROBATION THAT REQUIRED YOU TO SERVE A TERM OF CONFINEMENT.
3. YOUR ALCOHOL CONCENTRATION LEVEL WAS BELOW 0.15.
4. YOU COMPLETED YOUR TERM OF PROBATION, INCLUDING SERVING ANY TERM OF CONFINEMENT IMPOSED AND PAYING ALL FINES, COSTS, AND RESTITUTION, IF ANY. [If your probation was revoked, you are not eligible for an order of nondisclosure under Section 411.0731.]
5. YOU ARE A FIRST TIME OFFENDER IN THAT YOU HAVE NOT BEEN PREVIOUSLY CONVICTED OF OR PLACED ON DEFERRED ADJUDICATION COMMUNITY SUPERVISION ("DEFERRED ADJUDICTION") FOR ANOTHER OFFENSE OTHER THAN A TRAFFIC OFFENSE PUNISHABLE BY FINE ONLY.
6. THE REQUISITE TIME BEFORE FILING A PETITION FOR AN ORDER OF NONDISCLOSURE UNDER SECTION 411.0731 HAS PASSED. [The waiting period is two or five years following completion of your probation, depending on your circumstances. If you do not know the required

waiting period, you should return to the nondisclosure overview to determine the required waiting period.]

IF THE STATEMENTS ABOVE ARE NOT TRUE, THIS IS NOT THE CORRECT PETITION FOR YOU.

You may be eligible to file a petition for an order of nondisclosure under Section 411.0736, Government Code. You should return to the nondisclosure overview to determine if you are eligible to file a petition for an order of nondisclosure under Section 411.0736.

Additional Requirements

1. You are **not eligible** for an order of nondisclosure under Section 411.0731, or any other section, if you were or have ever been convicted of or placed on deferred adjudication community supervision (hereinafter "deferred adjudication") for any of the offenses listed below:

    (i) an offense requiring registration as a sex offender under Chapter 62, Code of Criminal Procedure;

    (ii) an offense under Section 20.04, Texas Penal Code, (aggravated kidnapping);

    (iii) an offense under any of the following sections of the Texas Penal Code:
    - 19.02 (murder);
    - 19.03 (capital murder);
    - 20A.02 (trafficking of persons);
    - 20A.03 (continuous trafficking of persons);
    - 22.04 (injury to a child, elderly individual, or disabled individual);
    - 22.041 (abandoning or endangering a child);
    - 25.07 (violation of court orders or conditions of bond in a family violence, sexual assault or abuse, stalking, or trafficking case);
    - 25.072 (repeated violation of certain court orders or conditions of bond in family violence, sexual assault or abuse, stalking, or trafficking case); or
    - 42.072 (stalking); or

(iv) any other offense involving family violence, as defined by Section 71.004, Family Code.

2. You are **not eligible** for an order of nondisclosure under Section 411.0731 if, during the period after the court placed you on probation, and during any applicable waiting period, you were convicted of or placed on deferred adjudication for any offense other than a traffic offense punishable by fine only.

3. You are **not eligible** for an order of nondisclosure under Section 411.0731 if the court made an affirmative finding that your offense involved family violence.

Instructions for Completing Petition

(1) Please leave this line blank. This is not the cause number in your criminal case. A civil case will be created when you file your petition. The clerk of the court (hereinafter "clerk") will enter a new cause number in this space.

(2) Please enter the name of the court in which you are filing this petition. You must file this petition in the court that placed you on probation. The name of the court is shown on the top of the order or judgment that placed you on probation.

(3) Please enter your name as it appears on the order or judgment that placed you on probation.

(4) Please enter the name of the county in which the court that placed you on probation is located.

(5) Please enter your name as you did in (3) above.

(6) Please enter the criminal cause number shown on an order or judgment in your DWI case. Look for *Case* or *Cause No.* on that order or judgment.

(7) Please enter the date that you were convicted of driving while intoxicated.

(8) Please enter the date that you were placed on probation.

(9) **You must attach evidence that shows you are entitled to file this petition.** This means that you must prove to the court that you were convicted and placed on probation for a Class B misdemeanor DWI offense under Section 49.04, Penal Code.

(10) Please enter the date that you completed probation in your DWI case.

(11) **You must attach evidence that shows you are entitled to file this petition.** This means that you must prove to the court that you completed probation, including any term of confinement imposed and payment of all fines, costs, and restitution, if any. You can attach a copy of your discharge and/or dismissal, jail documents, and any receipts or other proof of payment.

(12) Please place a check mark or an "x" on the line next to the statement that reflects the waiting period that applies to you.

(13) There is a filing fee associated with filing a petition for order of nondisclosure under Section 411.0731. The filing fee is the amount of the court's regular civil filing fee plus an additional $28.00. Typically, the total filing fee is about $280.00. However, the amount varies from county to county. Please contact the clerk for the court in which you are filing the petition to obtain the correct amount of the total filing fee. **NOTE:** You should not have to pay the clerk to serve the petition on the attorney for the state (hereinafter "prosecutor"), Department of Public Safety (hereinafter "DPS"), or any other agency or entity, including any law enforcement entity. The statute requires the court, clerk, and DPS to notify the other parties of interest. See Sections 411.0745(e), 411.075(a) and 411.075(b), Government Code, respectively.

> *As a general rule, you must pay the filing fee in order to file the petition. However, you may be eligible to file a Statement of Inability to Afford Payment of Court Costs in lieu of paying the filing fee. The statement is described in Rule 145 of the Texas Rules of Civil Procedure. You may read Rule 145 online at http://www.txcourts.gov/media/1435952/trcp-all-updated-with-amendments-effective-912016.pdf. You can click here for the* **Statement of Inability to Afford Payment of Court Costs** *form: http://www.txcourts.gov/media/1435953/statement-final-version.pdf.*

Please place a check mark or an "x" on the line in front of the first statement, if you are paying the filing fee. If you are submitting a **Statement of Inability to Afford Payment of Court Costs**, place a check mark or an "x" on the line in front of the second statement.

(14) Please sign above the line. If you are filing this petition electronically, you may enter "/s/" followed by your typewritten name.

(15) Please PRINT your name.

(16) Please enter your mailing address.

(17) Please enter your city, state and zip code.

(18) Please enter your telephone number.

Process after You Complete the Petition

If you are eligible for an order of nondisclosure under Section 411.0731, the process for obtaining an order of nondisclosure under that section is as follows:

First, check in advance with the clerk's office to obtain the total amount of the fee (including the $28 fee) required to file a petition for an order of nondisclosure, unless you are submitting a *Statement of Inability to Afford Payment of Court Costs*. Next, be sure to complete the correct petition according to the instructions above, and after you have done so, print both the petition and the *Order of Nondisclosure under Section 411.0731.* In most courts, you will have to submit a proposed order when you file your petition. The judge will complete the order, if the judge grants your request.

You must file the petition in the court that placed you on probation.

After you file the petition, the clerk will send it to the court, and the court will notify the prosecutor. Again, you should not have to pay the clerk to serve notice of your petition on the prosecutor or any other party.

A hearing on the petition is not required if the prosecutor does not request a hearing.

If a hearing is scheduled, the court or the clerk will notify you. If there is a hearing, the court may ask questions to establish whether you satisfy the requirements of Sections 411.074 and 411.0731. After the hearing, if the court determines that you satisfy the requirements of the statutes and that issuance of the order of nondisclosure is in the best interest of justice, the court should grant your request for the order of nondisclosure.

If the court does not hold a hearing, the judge will review your petition to determine whether you satisfy the requirements of the statutes and whether issuance of the order of nondisclosure is in the best interest of justice. If the court finds that you have satisfied the requirements of the law and that the issuance of the order is in the best interest of justice, the court should grant your request for the order of nondisclosure.

Under no circumstances will the court grant an order of nondisclosure, if the prosecutor or attorney representing the state proves by sufficient evidence that your commission of the DWI offense resulted in an accident involving another person, including a passenger in your motor vehicle.

The court and/or prosecutor will have access to your criminal history record information and will use it to determine if you are eligible to file the petition.

If the court grants the order of nondisclosure, no later than 15 business days after the order issues, the clerk will send a copy of the order to DPS. Then, no later than 10 business days after DPS receives the order, DPS will seal the criminal history record information that is the subject of the order and forward a copy of the order to the state and federal agencies listed in Section 411.075(b), Government Code. See Section 411.075(b) for a complete list of the agencies and entities that DPS must notify.

Cause No. _____
(1)

In the Matter of § In the

§ _____
(2)

_____ § _____ County, Texas
(3) (4)

Petition for Order of Nondisclosure Under Section 411.0731

_____ (5) ("Petitioner") respectfully petitions the court for an order of nondisclosure under Section 411.0731, Government Code, for the offense detailed below.

1. **The Underlying Order**

    Petitioner was convicted of an offense under Section 49.04 (Driving While Intoxicated), Penal Code, other than an offense punishable as a Class A misdemeanor under that section, in Criminal Cause No. _____ (6) in this court on _____, _____. (7) Following the conviction, Petitioner was placed on community supervision (hereinafter "probation") under Chapter 42A (formerly Article 42.12), Code of Criminal Procedure, on _____, _____. (8) Evidence that Petitioner was convicted and placed on probation **is** attached. (9)

    Petitioner's probation was not revoked. Petitioner completed probation, including any term of confinement imposed and payment of all fines, costs, and restitution, if any, on _____, 20_____. (10) Evidence that Petitioner completed probation, including evidence that Petitioner completed any term of confinement imposed and payment of all fines, costs, and restitution, if any, **is** attached. (11)

2. **Petitioner Satisfies the Requirements of Section 411.0731, Government Code**

    Petitioner satisfies the requirements of Section 411.0731, Government Code, in that:

- Petitioner was convicted of an offense under Section 49.04 (Driving While Intoxicated), Penal Code, other than an offense punishable as a Class A misdemeanor under that section;
- Petitioner's alcohol concentration level was less than 0.15 at the time an analysis of the petitioner's blood, breath, or urine was performed;
- Petitioner was placed on probation following Petitioner's conviction, including a probation that required Petitioner to serve a term of confinement as a condition of probation or before being placed on probation;
- Petitioner's probation was not revoked;
- Petitioner completed Petitioner's period of probation, including any term of confinement imposed and payment of all fines, costs, and restitution, if any;
- Petitioner satisfies the requirements of Section 411.074, Government Code;
- Petitioner has never been previously convicted of or placed on deferred adjudication community supervision ("deferred adjudication") for another offense other than a traffic offense punishable by fine only;
- Petitioner waited the requisite time, as indicated below, before filing this petition. (12)

    _____ Two years after completing probation (if Petitioner successfully complied with a condition of probation that, for a period of not less than six months, restricted Petitioner's use of a motor vehicle to a motor vehicle equipped with an ignition interlock device, then must wait)

    _____ Five years after completing probation (if the court that placed Petitioner on probation **did not** restrict Petitioner's use of a motor vehicle to a motor vehicle equipped with an ignition interlock device, or restricted Petitioner's use of a motor vehicle to a motor vehicle equipped with an ignition interlock device for a period of less than six months); and
- Petitioner's petition includes evidence that Petitioner is entitled to file this petition.

3. Petitioner Satisfies the Requirements of Sec. 411.074, Government Code

Petitioner satisfies the requirements of Section 411.074, Government Code, in that:

- During the period after the court placed Petitioner on probation, and during the applicable waiting period, as indicated above, Petitioner was not convicted of or placed on deferred adjudication for any offense other than a traffic offense punishable by fine only;

- Petitioner was not and has not ever been convicted of or placed on deferred adjudication for any of the following:

(A) an offense requiring registration as a sex offender under Chapter 62, Code of Criminal Procedure;

(B) an offense under Texas Penal Code Section 20.04 (Aggravated Kidnapping);

(C) an offense under any of the following Texas Penal Code Sections:

- 19.02 (Murder);
- 19.03 (Capital Murder);
- 20A.02 (Trafficking of Persons);
- 20A.03 (Continuous Trafficking of Persons);
- 22.04 (Injury to a Child, Elderly Individual, or Disabled Individual);
- 22.041 (Abandoning or Endangering a Child);
- 25.07 (Violation of Court Orders or Conditions of Bond in a Family Violence, Sexual Assault or Abuse, Stalking, or Trafficking Case);
- 25.072 (Repeated Violation of Certain Court Orders or Conditions of Bond in Family Violence, Sexual Assault or Abuse, Stalking, or Trafficking Case); or
- 42.072 (Stalking); or

(D) any other offense involving family violence, as defined by Section 71.004, Family Code; and

- The court has not made an affirmative finding that Petitioner's offense involved family violence, as defined by Section 71.004, Family Code.

4. Petitioner is Entitled to File a Petition for an Order of Nondisclosure

Petitioner is entitled to file this petition because Petitioner has satisfied the requirements to do so. A person is entitled to file a petition for an order of nondisclosure under Section 411.0731, Government Code, if the person:

- Was convicted of an offense under Section 49.04 (Driving While Intoxicated), Penal Code, other than an offense punishable as a Class A misdemeanor under that section;
- Had an alcohol concentration level that was less than 0.15 at the time an analysis of the person's blood, breath, or urine was performed;
- Was placed on probation under Chapter 42A, Code of Criminal Procedure (formerly, Article 42.12) following his or her conviction;
- Did not have his or her probation revoked;
- Completed the period of probation, including any term of confinement imposed and payment of all fines, costs, and restitution, if any;
- Has satisfied the requirements of Section 411.074, Government Code, including:
  - not having been convicted of or placed on deferred adjudication for any offense other than a traffic offense punishable by fine only, during the period after the person was placed on probation and during any applicable waiting period;
  - not having ever been convicted of or placed on deferred adjudication for any of the offenses listed below:
    - an offense requiring registration as a sex offender under Chapter 62, Code of Criminal Procedure;
    - an offense under Texas Penal Code Section 20.04 (Aggravated Kidnapping);
    - an offense under any of the following Texas Penal Code Sections:
      - 19.02 (Murder);

- 19.03 (Capital Murder);
- 20A.02 (Trafficking of Persons);
- 20A.03 (Continuous Trafficking of Persons);
- 22.04 (Injury to a Child, Elderly Individual, or Disabled Individual);
- 22.041 (Abandoning or Endangering a Child);
- 25.07 (Violation of Court Orders or Conditions of Bond in a Family Violence, Sexual Assault or Abuse, Stalking, or Trafficking Case);
- 25.072 (Repeated Violation of Certain Court Orders or Conditions of Bond in Family Violence, Sexual Assault or Abuse, Stalking, or Trafficking Case); or
- 42.072 (Stalking); or
- any other offense involving family violence, as defined by Section 71.004, Family Code; and
  - not having received an affirmative finding by the court that the offense for which the order of nondisclosure is requested involved family violence, as defined by Section 71.004, Family Code;
- Has not been previously convicted of or placed on deferred adjudication for another offense other than a traffic offense punishable by fine only;
- Has waited the requisite time (see applicable waiting period indicated above) before filing a petition for an order of nondisclosure under Section 411.0731, Government Code; and
- Has included in his or her petition evidence that shows the person is entitled to file a petition for an order of nondisclosure under Section 411.0731, Government Code.

5. Issuance of an Order of Nondisclosure is in the Best Interest of Justice

The issuance of an order of nondisclosure is in the best of justice.

6. The Fee to File the Petition has been Paid or Otherwise Satisfied

The fee to file this petition is the total amount of the fee required to file a civil petition and $28.00, or a petitioner may submit a *Statement of Inability to Afford Payment of Court Costs* in lieu of paying any fees. Petitioner has included (13)

_____ the required filing fee.

_____ a *Statement of Inability to Afford Payment of Court Costs* in lieu of the required fee.

7. Prayer for Relief

Petitioner respectfully prays that the court grant Petitioner's request for an order of nondisclosure under Section 411.0731, Government Code.

Respectfully submitted,

_____
(14)

_____
(15)

_____
(16)

_____
(17)

_____
(18)

Cause No. _____

In the Matter of § In the

§ _____

_____ § _____ County, Texas

Order of Nondisclosure Under Section 411.0731

On this the _____, day of _____, 20____, the Court considered Petitioner's petition for an order of nondisclosure under Section 411.0731, Government Code.

The State was given notice of the petition and an opportunity to request a hearing. The State

☐ requested a hearing.

☐ did not request a hearing.

The Court

☐ conducted a hearing on _____, _____.

☐ did not conduct a hearing.

Petitioner was convicted and placed on probation for an offense under Section 49.04 (Driving While Intoxicated), Penal Code, other than an offense punishable as a Class A misdemeanor under that section, in Criminal Cause No. _____, in this court.

After consideration and a hearing, if a hearing was held as indicated above, the Court **FINDS** that Petitioner is entitled to file a petition and satisfies the requirements for an order of nondisclosure under Section 411.0731, Government Code. The Court **FURTHER FINDS** that issuance of an order of nondisclosure is in the best interest of justice.

The Court **FURTHER FINDS** that Petitioner's commission of the above-mentioned offense did not result in a motor vehicle accident involving another person, including a person in Petitioner's vehicle.

The Court did not make an affirmative finding that the offense for which the order of nondisclosure is requested involved family violence, as defined by Section 71.004, Family Code.

Accordingly, **IT IS HEREBY ORDERED** that criminal justice agencies are prohibited from disclosing to the public criminal history record information related to the above-mentioned offense.

IT IS FURTHER ORDERED that the criminal history record information pertaining to the arrest and prosecution of Petitioner for the above-mentioned offense shall be sealed and disclosed by the court only to individuals or agencies listed in Section 411.076(a), Government Code.

IT IS FURTHER ORDERED that no later than the 15th business day after the date that this order issues, the clerk of the court (hereinafter "clerk") shall send all relevant criminal history record information contained in this order or a copy of this order to the Crime Records Service of the Texas Department of Public Safety (hereinafter "DPS") by certified mail, return receipt requested, or secure electronic mail, electronic transmission, or facsimile transmission, in accordance with Section 411.075(a), Government Code.

IT IS FURTHER ORDERED that no later than 10 business days after receipt of the relevant criminal history record information contained in this order or a copy of this order from the clerk, DPS shall seal the criminal history record information that is the subject of this order and forward the information or copy of this order to the state and federal agencies listed in 411.075(b), Government Code, in accordance with Section 411.075(b).

IT IS FURTHER ORDERED that an agency or entity shall seal any criminal history record information maintained by that agency or entity that is the subject of this order no later than 30 business days after the date the agency or entity received the relevant criminal history record information contained in this order or a copy of this order from DPS or a clerk, in accordance with Section 411.075(d), Government Code.

IT IS FURTHER ORDERED that the clerk shall seal all court records containing information that is the subject of this order as soon as practicable after the date the clerk sends a copy of this order or all relevant criminal history record information contained in this order to DPS, in accordance with Section 411.076(b), Government Code.

Signed on _____, 20_____.

_____
Judge Presiding

_____
Court/County

Office of Court Administration

Instructions for Completing the Model Petition for Order of Nondisclosure Under Section 411.0735

BEFORE BEGINNING MAKE SURE YOU ARE USING THE CORRECT PETITION. THIS PETITION AND INSTRUCTIONS ARE FOR PERSONS REQUESTING AN ORDER OF NONDISCLOSURE UNDER SECTION 411.0735, GOVERNMENT CODE. DO NOT ATTEMPT TO COMPLETE A PETITION FOR AN ORDER OF NONDISCLOSURE WITHOUT FIRST REVIEWING THE NONDISCLOSURE OVERVIEW TO DETERMINE IF YOU ARE ELIGIBLE FOR AN ORDER OF NONDISCLOSURE AND TO IDENTIFY THE CORRECT FORM TO USE. THE NONDISCLOSURE OVERVIEW IS AVAILABLE AT THIS LINK: http://www.txcourts.gov/rules-forms/orders-of-nondisclosure.

TO BE ELIGIBLE TO USE THIS FORM THE FOLLOWING STATEMENTS MUST BE TRUE:

1. YOU WERE CONVICTED OF A MISDEMEANOR OTHER THAN A MISDEMEANOR UNDER **SECTION 106.041**, ALCOHOLIC BEVERAGE CODE, **SECTION 49.04**, PENAL CODE, **SECTION 49.05**, PENAL CODE, **SECTION 49.06**, PENAL CODE, **SECTION 49.065**, PENAL CODE, OR **CHAPTER 71**, PENAL CODE.
2. YOU ARE NOT ELIGIBLE FOR AN ORDER OF NONDISCLOSURE UNDER SECTION 411.073, GOVERNMENT CODE.
3. YOU COMPLETED THE SENTENCE IN YOUR CASE, INCLUDING ANY TERM OF CONFINEMENT IMPOSED AND PAYMENT OF ALL FINES, COSTS, AND RESTITUTION, IF ANY.
4. YOU HAVE NOT BEEN PREVIOUSLY CONVICTED OF OR PLACED ON DEFERRED ADJUDICATION FOR ANY OTHER OFFENSE OTHER THAN A TRAFFIC OFFENSE PUNISHABLE BY FINE ONLY.
5. YOUR MISDEMEANOR CONVICTION **WAS NOT** FOR AN OFFENSE THAT IS VIOLENT OR SEXUAL IN NATURE, OTHER THAN AN OFFENSE UNDER SECTION 22.01, PENAL CODE (ASSAULT).
6. YOU HAVE WAITED THE REQUIRED TIME (SEE THE DISCUSSION OF WAITING PERIOD REQUIRED UNDER 411.0735 IN THE NONDISCLOSURE OVERVIEW)

BEFORE FILING A PETITION FOR AN ORDER OF NONDISCLOSURE UNDER SECTION 411.0735.

IF THE SIX STATEMENTS ABOVE ARE NOT TRUE, THIS IS NOT THE CORRECT PETITION FOR YOU. You may be eligible to file a petition for an order of nondisclosure under another section of the Government Code. You should return to the nondisclosure overview to determine if you are eligible to file a petition for an order of nondisclosure under another section.

Additional Requirements

1. You are **not eligible** for an order of nondisclosure under Sec. 411.0735, or any other section, if you were or have ever been convicted of or placed on deferred adjudication community supervision (hereinafter "deferred adjudication") for any of the offenses listed below:
    - (i) An offense requiring registration as a sex offender under Chapter 62, Code of Criminal Procedure;
    - (ii) An offense under Texas Penal Code Section 20.04 (aggravated kidnapping);
    - (iii) An offense under any of the following Texas Penal Code Sections:
        - 19.02 (murder);
        - 19.03 (capital murder);
        - 20A.02 (trafficking of persons);
        - 20A.03 (continuous trafficking of persons);
        - 22.04 (injury to a child, elderly individual, or disabled individual);
        - 22.041 (abandoning or endangering a child);
        - 25.07 (violation of court orders or conditions of bond in a family violence, sexual assault or abuse, stalking, or trafficking case);
        - 25.072 (repeated violation of certain court orders or conditions of bond in family violence, sexual assault or abuse, stalking, or trafficking case); or
        - 42.072 (stalking); or
    - (iv) Any other offense involving family violence, as defined by Section 71.004, Family Code.

2. You are **not eligible** for an order of nondisclosure under Section 411.0735 if, during the period after the court pronounced the sentence in your case, and during any applicable waiting period, you were convicted of or placed on deferred adjudication for any offense other than a traffic offense punishable by fine only.

3. You are **not eligible** for an order of nondisclosure under Sec. 411.0735 if the court made an affirmative finding that the misdemeanor for which the order of nondisclosure is requested involved family violence, as defined by Section 71.004, Family Code.

Instructions for Completing Petition

(1) Please leave this blank. This is not the number of your criminal case. A civil case will be created when you file the petition. The clerk of the court (hereinafter "clerk") will enter a new cause number in this space.

(2) Please enter the name of the court in which you are filing this petition. You must file this petition in the court that convicted you of the misdemeanor for which you are requesting an order of nondisclosure. The name of the court is shown on the top of the court's judgment or order that sentenced you.

(3) Please enter your name as shown on the court's order or judgment that sentenced you.

(4) Please enter the name of the county in which the court that sentenced you is situated. This will be the same county as shown on the court's order or judgment that sentenced you.

(5) Please enter your name as you did in (3) above.

(6) Please enter the name of the offense as shown on the court's order or judgment that sentenced you.

(7) Please enter the criminal cause number as shown on the court's order or judgment that sentenced you. Look for *Case No.* on that order or judgment.

(8) Please enter the date on which you were convicted.

(9) Please enter the terms of your sentence.

(10) Please enter the date that you completed your sentence. This should be the date that you were released from jail or discharged from probation or deferred adjudication, and paid all fines, costs, and restitution imposed by the court.

(11) Please circle "is" if you are attaching a copy of the court's order or judgment that sentenced you. Attaching a copy of the Court's order or judgment may expedite the process of obtaining an order of nondisclosure, but it is not required. Please circle "is not" if you are not attaching a copy of the court's order or judgment. **NOTE**: You are eligible to file a Petition for Nondisclosure under Section 411.0735 on or after the date that you completed your sentence, if you were convicted of a misdemeanor punishable by fine only, or on or after the second anniversary of the date that you completed your sentence, if you were convicted of a misdemeanor other than a misdemeanor punishable by fine only.

(12) Please circle "is" if you are attaching evidence showing that you completed your sentence, including evidence that you completed any term of confinement imposed and paid all the fines, costs, and restitution imposed in your case. Attaching a copy of the evidence may speed up obtaining an order of nondisclosure, but it is not required. Please circle "is not" if you are not attaching a copy of evidence showing that you completed your sentence. Such evidence may include a copy of your release or discharge paper. The jail that released you may have given you several documents when you were released. Check those documents to see if any reflects your release date. If any does, you may submit a copy of that document. If you were placed on probation or deferred adjudication, you may submit a copy of the document discharging you from probation or deferred adjudication. If you were ordered to pay a fine, costs, or restitution, you may attach proof of final payment. Do not worry if you do not have a document to attach. However, please remember that you cannot file a petition for nondisclosure until: (1) you have completed your sentence; and (2) at least two years have passed since you completed your sentence, unless you were convicted of an offense punishable by fine only.

(13) There is a filing fee associated with filing a petition for an order of nondisclosure under Section 411.0735. The filing fee is the amount of the court's regular civil filing fee plus an additional $28. Typically, the total filing fee is about $280. However, the amount varies from county to county. Please contact the clerk for the court in which you are filing the petition to obtain the correct amount of the total filing fee. **NOTE**: You should not have to pay the clerk to serve the petition on the attorney for the state (hereinafter "prosecutor"), Department of Public Safety (hereinafter "DPS"), or any other agency or entity, including any law enforcement entity. The statute requires the court, clerk, and DPS to notify the other parties of interest. See Sections 411.0745(e), 411.075(a) and 411.075(b), Government Code, respectively.

> *As a general rule, you must pay the filing fee in order to file this petition. However, you may be eligible to file a **Statement of Inability to Afford Payment of Court Costs** in lieu of paying the filing fee. The statement is described in Rule 145 of the Texas Rules of Civil Procedure 145. You may view Rule 145 online at http://www.txcourts.gov/media/1435952/trcp-all-updated-with-amendments-effective-912016.pdf. You can click here for the form: http://www.txcourts.gov/media/1435953/statement-final-version.pdf.*

Please place a check mark or an "x" on the line before the statement that applies to you. Place a check mark or "x" in front of the first statement, if you are paying the filing fee. If you are submitting a **Statement of Inability to Afford Payment of Court Costs** instead, place a check mark or an "x" in front of the second statement.

(14) Please sign above the line. If you are filing this petition electronically, you may enter "/s/" followed by your typewritten name.

(15) Please PRINT your name.

(16) Please enter your mailing address.

(17) Please enter your city, state and zip code.

(18) Please enter your telephone number.

Process after You Complete the PETITION

If you are eligible for an order of nondisclosure under Section 411.0735, the process for obtaining an order under that section is as follows:

First, be sure to wait the requisite time before filing the petition, and check in advance with the clerk's office to obtain the total amount of the fee (including the $28 fee) required to file a petition for an order of nondisclosure, unless you are submitting a *Statement of Inability to Afford Payment of Court Costs* in lieu of paying the fee. Next, be sure to complete the correct petition according to the instructions above, and after you have done so, print both the petition and the *Order of Nondisclosure*. In most courts, you will have to submit a proposed order with the petition when you file it. The judge will complete the order, if the judge grants your request.

You must file the petition in the court that sentenced you.

After you file the petition, the clerk will send it to the court and the court will notify the prosecutor. Again, you should not have to pay the clerk to serve notice on the prosecutor or any other party.

A hearing on the petition is not required if the prosecutor does not request a hearing.

If a hearing is scheduled, the court or clerk will notify you. If there is a hearing, the court may ask questions to establish whether you satisfy the requirements of Sections 411.074 and 411.0735, Government Code. After the hearing, if the court determines that you satisfy the requirements of the statutes and that issuance of the order of nondisclosure is in the best interest of justice, the court should grant your request for the order.

If the court does not hold a hearing, the judge will review your petition to determine whether you satisfy the requirements of the statutes and whether issuance of the order of nondisclosure is in the best interest of justice. If the court finds that you have satisfied the requirements of the statutes and that the issuance of the order is in the best interest of justice, the court should grant your request for the order.

The court and/or prosecutor will have access to your criminal history record information and will use it to determine if you are eligible to file the petition.

If the court grants the order of nondisclosure, no later than 15 business days after the order issues, the clerk will send a copy of the order to DPS. Then, no later than 10 business days after DPS receives the order, DPS will seal the criminal history record information that is the subject of the order and forward a copy of the order to the state and federal agencies listed in 411.075(b), Government Code. See Section 411.075(b) for a complete list of agencies and entities that DPS must notify.

Cause No. _____
₍₁₎

In the Matter of § In the

§

§ _____ ₍₂₎

_____ § _____ County, Texas
₍₃₎ ₍₄₎

Petition for Order of Nondisclosure Under Section 411.0735

_____ ₍₅₎ ("Petitioner") respectfully petitions this court for an order of nondisclosure under Section 411.0735, Government Code, for the offense detailed below.

1. The Underlying Order and Completion of Period of Confinement

Petitioner was convicted of the misdemeanor offense of _____ ₍₆₎ in Criminal Cause No. _____ ₍₇₎ in this court on _____, _____, _____. ₍₈₎

Following the conviction, Petitioner was sentenced to _____ ₍₉₎. Petitioner completed the sentence on _____, _____ ₍₁₀₎. A copy of the court's judgment or document showing Petitioner's sentence **is / is not** ₍₁₁₎ attached. Evidence of Petitioner's completion on the sentence, including any term of confinement imposed and payment of all fines, costs, and restitution, if any, **is / is not** ₍₁₂₎ attached.

2. Petitioner Satisfies the Requirements of Section 411.0735, Government Code

Petitioner satisfies the requirement under Section 411.0735, Government Code, in that:

- Petitioner is not eligible for an order of nondisclosure under Section 411.073, Government Code.

OCA MODEL PETITION FOR ORDER OF NONDISCLOSURE
UNDER SECTION 411.0735, GOVERNMENT CODE

DECEMBER 2017

- Petitioner was convicted of a misdemeanor other than a misdemeanor under any of the following:
    - Sec. 106.041, Alcoholic Beverage Code (Driving/Operating Watercraft Under the Influence of Alcohol By Minor),
    - Sec. 49.04, Penal Code (Driving While Intoxicated),
    - Sec. 49.05, Penal Code (Flying While Intoxicated),
    - Sec. 49.06, Penal Code (Boating While Intoxicated),
    - Sec. 49.065, Penal Code (Assembling or Operating an Amusement Ride While Intoxicated), or
    - Chapter 71, Penal Code (Organized Crimes);
- Petitioner completed the sentence in the misdemeanor case, including any term of confinement imposed and payment of all fines, costs, and restitution, if any;
- Petitioner satisfies the basic eligibility requirements of Section 411.074, Government Code;
- Petitioner has never been previously convicted of or placed on deferred adjudication for another offense other than a traffic offense punishable by fine only;
- The offense for which the order of nondisclosure is requested is not violent or sexual in nature. Per Section 411.0735(c-1), Government Code, this requirement does not include an assault under Section 22.01, Penal Code; and
- Petitioner has waited the requisite time before filing this petition. If Petitioner's offense is punishable by fine only, Petitioner may file this petition on or after the date that Petitioner completed the sentence in the case. Otherwise, Petitioner must wait 2 years after completing the sentence in his or her case before filing this petition.

3. **Petitioner Satisfies the Requirements of Section 411.074, Government Code**

Petitioner satisfies the requirements of Section 411.074, Government Code, in that:

- During the period after the court pronounced the sentence for the offense for which the order of nondisclosure is requested, and during the two-year period following Petitioner's completion of the sentence, if the misdemeanor was a Class A or B misdemeanor, Petitioner was not convicted of or placed on deferred adjudication for any offense other than a traffic offense punishable by fine only. If the offense was a misdemeanor punishable by fine only, there is no waiting period.

- Petitioner was not and has not ever been convicted of or placed on deferred adjudication for any of the offenses listed below:
    (A) an offense requiring registration as a sex offender under Chapter 62, Code of Criminal Procedure;
    (B) an offense under Texas Penal Code Section 20.04 (aggravated kidnapping);
    (C) an offense under any of the following sections of the Texas Penal Code:
        - 19.02 (murder);
        - 19.03 (capital murder);
        - 20A.02 (trafficking of persons);
        - 20A.03 (continuous trafficking of persons);
        - 22.04 (injury to a child, elderly individual, or disabled individual);
        - 22.041 (abandoning or endangering a child);
        - 25.07 (violation of court orders or conditions of bond in a family violence, sexual assault or abuse, stalking, or trafficking case);
        - 25.072 (repeated violation of certain court orders or conditions of bond in family violence, sexual assault or abuse, stalking, or trafficking case); or
        - 42.072 (stalking); or
    (D) any other offense involving family violence, as defined by Section 71.004, Family Code; and
- The court did not make an affirmative finding that the offense for which the order of nondisclosure is requested involved family violence, as defined by Section 71.004, Family Code.

4. Petitioner is Entitled to File a Petition for an Order of Nondisclosure

Petitioner is entitled to file this petition because Petitioner has satisfied each of the requirements necessary to do so. A person is entitled to file a petition for an order of nondisclosure under Section 411.0735, Government Code, if the person:

- Was convicted and sentenced for a misdemeanor other than a misdemeanor listed under Section 411.0735(a)(1), Government Code, which includes the following:
    - Sec. 106.041, Alcoholic Beverage Code (Driving/Operating Watercraft Under the Influence of Alcohol By Minor),
    - Sec. 49.04, Penal Code (Driving While Intoxicated),
    - Sec. 49.05, Penal Code (Flying While Intoxicated),
    - Sec. 49.06, Penal Code (Boating While Intoxicated),
    - Sec. 49.065, Penal Code (Assembling or Operating an Amusement Ride While Intoxicated), or
    - Chapter 71, Penal Code (Organized Crimes);
- Is not eligible for an order of nondisclosure under Section 411.073, Government Code;
- Completed the sentence in the case, including any term of confinement imposed and payment of all fines, costs, and restitution, if any;
- Has never been previously convicted of or placed on deferred adjudication for another offense other than a traffic offense punishable by fine only;
- Has satisfied the requirements of Section 411.074, Government Code, including: not receiving a conviction or deferred adjudication for any offense other than a traffic offense punishable by fine only, during the period after the court pronounced the sentence for the misdemeanor, and during any applicable waiting period; not having ever been convicted of or placed on deferred adjudication for an offense listed in 411.074(b); and not having received an affirmative finding by the court that the misdemeanor for which the order of nondisclosure is requested involved family violence as defined by Section 71.004, Family Code; and
- Has waited the requisite time before filing a petition for an order of nondisclosure under Section 411.0735, Government Code.

5. Issuance of an Order of Nondisclosure is in the Best Interest of Justice

The issuance of an order of nondisclosure is in the best interest of justice.

6. The Fee to File the Petition has been Paid or Otherwise Satisfied

The fee to file this petition is the total amount of the fee required to file a civil petition and $28.00, or a petitioner may submit a *Statement of Inability to Afford Payment of Court Costs* in lieu of paying any fee. Petitioner has included (13)

_____ the required filing fee.

_____ a *Statement of Inability to Afford Payment of Court Costs* in lieu of the required fee.

7. Prayer for Relief

Petitioner respectfully prays that the court grant Petitioner's request for an order of nondisclosure under Section 411.0735, Government Code.

Respectfully submitted,

_____
(14)

_____
(15)

_____
(16)

_____
(17)

_____
(18)

Cause No. _____

In the Matter of   §   In the

§   _____

_____ §   _____ County, Texas

Order of Nondisclosure

On this the _____, day of _____, 20__, the Court considered Petitioner's Petition for Order of Nondisclosure.

The State was given notice of the petition and an opportunity to request a hearing. The State

☐ requested a hearing.

☐ did not request a hearing.

The Court

☐ conducted a hearing on _____, 20___.

☐ did not conduct a hearing.

After consideration and a hearing, if a hearing was held as indicated above, the Court **FINDS** that Petitioner is entitled to file a petition for an order of nondisclosure under the section of the Government Code indicated below and that issuance of an order of nondisclosure is in the best interest of justice.

☐ Texas Government Code Section 411.0725
☐ Texas Government Code Section 411.073
☐ Texas Government Code Section 411.0735

Accordingly, **IT IS HEREBY ORDERED** that criminal justice agencies are prohibited from disclosing to the public criminal history record information related to the offense of _____ in Criminal Cause No. _____ in _____County, Texas.

IT IS FURTHER ORDERED that the criminal history record information pertaining to the arrest and prosecution of Petitioner for the above-referenced offense, as reflected in the above-referenced criminal cause number, shall be sealed and disclosed only to those individuals and agencies listed in Section 411.076(a), Government Code.

IT IS FURTHER ORDERED that no later than the 15th business day after the date that this order issues, the clerk of the court (hereinafter "clerk") shall send all relevant criminal history record information contained in this order or a copy of this order to the Crime Records Service of the Texas Department of Public Safety (hereinafter "DPS") by certified mail (return receipt requested) or secure electronic mail, electronic transmission, or facsimile transmission, in accordance with Section 411.075(a), Government Code.

IT IS FURTHER ORDERED that no later than 10 business days after receipt of relevant criminal history record information contained in this order or a copy of this order from the clerk, DPS shall seal the criminal history record information that is the subject of this order and forward the information or a copy of the order to the state and federal agencies listed in Section 411.075(b), Government Code, by certified mail (return receipt requested), secure electronic mail, electronic transmission, or facsimile transmission, in accordance with Section 411.075(b), Government Code.

IT IS FURTHER ORDERED that an agency or entity shall seal any criminal history record information maintained by that agency or entity that is the subject of this order no later than 30 business days after the date that the agency or entity received relevant criminal history record information contained in this order or a copy of this order from DPS or a clerk, in accordance with Section 411.075(d), Government Code.

IT IS FURTHER ORDERED that the clerk shall seal all court records containing information that is the subject of this order as soon as practicable after the date that the clerk sends a copy of this order or all relevant criminal history record information contained in this order to DPS, in accordance with Section 411.076(b), Government Code.

Signed on _____.

_____
Judge Presiding

_____
Court/County

Office of Court Administration

Instructions for Completing the Model Petition for Order of Nondisclosure Under Section 411.0736

BEFORE BEGINNING MAKE SURE YOU ARE USING THE CORRECT MODEL PETITION. THIS PETITION AND INSTRUCTIONS ARE FOR PERSONS REQUESTING AN ORDER OF NONDISCLOSURE UNDER SECTION 411.0736, GOVERNMENT CODE. DO NOT ATTEMPT TO COMPLETE A PETITION FOR AN ORDER OF NONDISCLOSURE WITHOUT FIRST REVIEWING THE NONDISCLOSURE OVERVIEW TO DETERMINE IF YOU ARE ELIGIBLE FOR AN ORDER OF NONDISCLOSURE AND TO IDENTIFY THE CORRECT FORM TO USE. THE NONDISCLOSURE OVERVIEW IS AVAILABLE AT THIS LINK: http://www.txcourts.gov/rules-forms/orders-of-nondisclosure.

TO BE ELIGIBLE TO USE THIS PETITION THE FOLLOWING STATEMENTS MUST BE TRUE.

1. YOU WERE CONVICTED OF A <u>CLASS B MISDEMEANOR</u> OFFENSE OF DRIVING WHILE INTOXICATED UNDER SECTION 49.04, PENAL CODE. [If your conviction was for a Class A misdemeanor under Section 49.04, you are not eligible for an order of nondisclosure under Section 411.0731.]
2. YOUR ALCOHOL CONCENTRATION LEVEL WAS BELOW 0.15.
3. YOU ARE NOT ELIGIBLE FOR AN ORDER OF NONDISCLOSURE UNDER SECTION 411.0731, GOVERNMENT CODE.
4. YOU COMPLETED YOUR SENTENCE, INCLUDING ANY TERM OF CONFINEMENT IMPOSED AND PAYMENT OF ALL FINES, COSTS, AND RESTITUTION, IF ANY.
5. YOU ARE A FIRST TIME OFFENDER IN THAT YOU HAVE NOT BEEN PREVIOUSLY CONVICTED OF OR PLACED ON DEFERRED ADJUDICATION COMMUNITY SUPERVISION ("DEFERRED ADJUDICTION") FOR ANOTHER OFFENSE OTHER THAN A TRAFFIC OFFENSE PUNISHABLE BY FINE ONLY.
6. THE REQUISITE TIME BEFORE FILING A PETITION FOR AN ORDER OF NONDISCLOSURE UNDER 411.0736, GOVERNMENT CODE, HAS PASSED. [The waiting period is three or five years following completion of your sentence, depending on your circumstances. If you do not know the required waiting period, you should return to the nondisclosure overview to determine the required waiting period.]

IF THE STATEMENTS ABOVE ARE NOT TRUE, THIS IS NOT THE CORRECT PETITION FOR YOU.

Additional Requirements

1. You are **not eligible** for an order of nondisclosure under Section 411.0736, or any other section, if you were or have ever been convicted of or placed on deferred adjudication community supervision (hereinafter "deferred adjudication") for any of the offenses listed below:
    (i) an offense requiring registration as a sex offender under Chapter 62, Code of Criminal Procedure;
    (ii) an offense under Section 20.04, Texas Penal Code, (aggravated kidnapping);
    (iii) an offense under any of the following sections of the Texas Penal Code:
    - 19.02 (murder);
    - 19.03 (capital murder);
    - 20A.02 (trafficking of persons);
    - 20A.03 (continuous trafficking of persons);
    - 22.04 (injury to a child, elderly individual, or disabled individual);
    - 22.041 (abandoning or endangering a child);
    - 25.07 (violation of court orders or conditions of bond in a family violence, sexual assault or abuse, stalking, or trafficking case);
    - 25.072 (repeated violation of certain court orders or conditions of bond in family violence, sexual assault or abuse, stalking, or trafficking case); or
    - 42.072 (stalking); or
    (iv) any other offense involving family violence, as defined by Section 71.004, Family Code.

2. You are **not eligible** to file a petition for an order of nondisclosure under Section 411.0736 if, during the period after the court pronounced the sentence in your case and during any applicable waiting period, you were convicted of or placed on deferred adjudication for any offense other than a traffic offense punishable by fine only.

3. You are **not eligible** for an order of nondisclosure under Sec. 411.0736 if the court made an affirmative finding that your offense involved family violence.

Instructions for Completing Petition

(1) Please leave this line blank. This is not the cause number in your criminal case. A civil case will be created when you file the petition. The clerk of the court (hereinafter "clerk") will enter a new cause number in this space.

(2) Please enter the name of the court in which you are filing this petition. You must file this petition in the court that sentenced you. The name of the court is shown on the top of the order or judgment in your DWI case.

(3) Please enter your name as it appears on the order or judgment in your DWI case.

(4) Please enter the name of the county in which the court that sentenced you is located.

(5) Please enter your name as you did in (3) above.

(6) Please enter the criminal cause number shown on an order or judgment in your DWI case. Look for *Case* or *Cause No.* on that order or judgment.

(7) Please enter the date of your conviction in the DWI case. This date should be on the order or judgment in your DWI case.

(8) **You must attach evidence that shows you are entitled to file this petition.** This means that you must prove to the court that you were convicted and sentenced for a Class B misdemeanor DWI offense under Section 49.04, Penal Code.

(9) Please enter the date that you completed the sentence in your DWI case.

(10) **You must attach evidence that shows you are entitled to file this petition.** This means that you must prove to the court that you completed the sentence in your DWI case, including any term of confinement imposed and payment of all fines, costs, and restitution, if any. You may attach documents

from the jail that discharged you and receipts or other proof of payment of any fine, costs, and restitution imposed. The judgment will show if a fine or restitution was imposed. If you were ordered to pay a fine, court costs, or restitution, the county clerk may be able to provide proof or a receipt of your payments.

(11) Please place a check mark or an "x" on the line next to the statement that reflects the waiting period that applies to you.

(12) There is a filing fee associated with filing a petition for order of nondisclosure under Section 411.0736. The filing fee is the amount of the court's regular civil filing fee plus an additional $28.00. Typically, the total filing fee is about $280.00. However, the amount varies from county to county. Please contact the clerk for the court in which you are filing the petition to obtain the correct amount of the total filing fee. **NOTE**: You should not have to pay the clerk to serve the petition on the attorney for the state (hereinafter "prosecutor"), Department of Public Safety (hereinafter "DPS"), or any other agency or entity, including any law enforcement entity. The statute requires the court, clerk, and DPS to notify the other parties of interest. See Sections 411.0745(e), 411.075(a) and 411.075(b), Government Code, respectively.

> *As a general rule, you must pay the filing fee in order to file the petition. However, you may be eligible to file a Statement of Inability to Afford Payment of Court Costs in lieu of paying the filing fee. The statement is described in Rule 145 of the Texas Rules of Civil Procedure. You may read Rule 145 online at http://www.txcourts.gov/media/1435952/trcp-all-updated-with-amendments-effective-912016.pdf. You can click here for* **the Statement of Inability to Afford Payment of Court Costs** *form: http://www.txcourts.gov/media/1435953/statement-final-version.pdf.*

Please place a check mark or an "x" on the line in front of the first statement, if you are paying the filing fee. If you are submitting a **Statement of Inability to Afford Payment of Court Costs**, place a check mark or an "x" on the line in front of the second statement.

(13) Please sign above the line. If you are filing this petition electronically, you may enter "/s/" followed by your typewritten name.

(14) Please PRINT your name.

(15) Please enter your mailing address.

(16) Please enter your city, state and zip code.

(17) Please enter your telephone number.

Process after You Complete the Petition

If you are eligible for an order of nondisclosure under Section 411.0736, the process for obtaining an order of nondisclosure under that section is as follows:

First, check in advance with the clerk's office to obtain the total amount of the fee (including the $28 fee) to file a petition for an order of nondisclosure, unless you are submitting a *Statement of Inability to Afford Payment of Court Costs*. Next, be sure to complete the correct petition according to the instructions above, and after you have done so, print both the petition and the *Order of Nondisclosure under Section 411.0736*. In most courts, you will have to submit a proposed order when you file the petition. The judge will complete the order, if the judge grants your request.

You must file the petition in the court that sentenced you.

After you file the petition, the clerk will send it to the court, and the court will notify the prosecutor. Again, you should not have to pay the clerk to serve notice of your petition on the prosecutor or any other party.

A hearing on the petition is not required if the prosecutor does not request a hearing.

If a hearing is scheduled, the court or the clerk will notify you. If there is a hearing, the court may ask questions to establish whether you satisfy the requirements of Sections 411.074 and 411.0736. After the hearing, if the court finds that you have satisfied the requirements of the statutes and that issuance of the order of nondisclosure is in the best interest of justice, the court should grant your request for the order of nondisclosure.

If the court does not hold a hearing, the judge will review your petition to determine whether you have satisfied the requirements of the statutes and whether issuance of the order of nondisclosure is in the best interest of justice. If the court finds that you have satisfied the requirements of the law and that the issuance of the order is in the best interest of justice, the court should grant your request for the order of nondisclosure.

Under no circumstances will the court grant an order of nondisclosure, if the prosecutor or attorney representing the state proves by sufficient evidence that your commission of the DWI offense resulted in an accident involving another person, including a passenger in your motor vehicle.

The court and/or prosecutor will have access to your criminal history record information and will use it to determine if you are eligible to file the petition.

If the court grants the order of nondisclosure, no later than 15 business days after the order issues, the clerk will send a copy of the order to DPS. Then, no later than 10 business days after DPS receives the order, DPS will seal the criminal history record information that is the subject of the order and forward the order to the state and federal agencies listed in Section 411.075(b), Government Code. See Section 411.075(b) for a complete list of the agencies and entities that DPS must notify.

Cause No. _____
(1)

In the Matter of § In the
 § _____
 (2)
_____ § _____ County, Texas
(3) (4)

Petition for Order of Nondisclosure Under Section 411.0736

_____ (5) ("Petitioner") respectfully petitions this court for an order of nondisclosure under Section 411.0736, Government Code, for the offense detailed below.

1. The Underlying Order

Petitioner was convicted of an offense under Section 49.04 (Driving While Intoxicated), Penal Code, other than an offense punishable as a Class A misdemeanor under that section, in this court in Criminal Cause No. _____ (6) on _____, ____. (7) Petitioner was subsequently sentenced for that offense. Evidence that Petitioner was convicted and sentenced is attached. (8)

Petitioner completed the sentence on _____, 20___. (9) Evidence that Petitioner completed the sentence, including evidence that Petitioner completed any term of confinement imposed and payment of all fines, costs, and restitution, if any, is attached. (10)

2. Petitioner Satisfies the Requirements of Sec. 411.0736, Government Code

Petitioner satisfies the requirements of Section 411.0736 of the Government Code in that:

- Petitioner was convicted of an offense under Section 49.04 (Driving While Intoxicated), Penal Code, other than an offense punishable as a Class A misdemeanor under that section;
- Petitioner's alcohol concentration level was less than 0.15 at the time an analysis of the petitioner's blood, breath, or urine was performed;
- Petitioner is not eligible for an order of nondisclosure under Section 411.0731, Government Code;
- Petitioner completed Petitioner's sentence, including any term of confinement imposed and payment of all fines, costs, and restitution, if any;
- Petitioner satisfies the requirements of Section 411.074, Government Code;
- Petitioner has never been previously convicted of or placed on deferred adjudication community supervision ("deferred adjudication") for another offense other than a traffic offense punishable by fine only;
- Petitioner has waited the requisite time before filing this petition: [11]
    _____ Three years after completing the sentence (if Petitioner successfully complied with a condition of the sentence that, for a period of not less than six months, restricted Petitioner's use of a motor vehicle to a motor vehicle equipped with an ignition interlock device); or
    _____ Five years after completing the sentence (if the court that sentenced Petitioner **did not** restrict Petitioner's use of a motor vehicle to a motor vehicle equipped with an ignition interlock device, or restricted Petitioner's use of a motor vehicle to a motor vehicle equipped with an ignition interlock device, but such restriction was for a period of less than six months); and
- Petitioner's petition includes evidence that Petitioner is entitled to file this petition.

3. Petitioner Satisfies the Requirements of Sec. 411.074, Government Code

Petitioner satisfies the requirements of Section 411.074, Government Code, in that:

- During the period after the court pronounced the sentence in Petitioner's DWI case, and during the applicable waiting period, as indicated above, Petitioner was not convicted of or placed on deferred adjudication for any offense other than a traffic offense punishable by fine only;

- Petitioner was not and has not ever been convicted of or placed on deferred adjudication for any of the following:
    - (A) An offense requiring registration as a sex offender under Chapter 62, Code of Criminal Procedure;
    - (B) An offense under Texas Penal Code Section 20.04 (Aggravated Kidnapping);
    - (C) An offense under any of the following Texas Penal Code Sections:
        - 19.02 (Murder);
        - 19.03 (Capital Murder);
        - 20A.02 (Trafficking of Persons);
        - 20A.03 (Continuous Trafficking of Persons);
        - 22.04 (Injury to a Child, Elderly Individual, or Disabled Individual);
        - 22.041 (Abandoning or Endangering a Child);
        - 25.07 (Violation of Court Orders or Conditions of Bond in a Family Violence, Sexual Assault or Abuse, Stalking, or Trafficking Case);
        - 25.072 (Repeated Violation of Certain Court Orders or Conditions of Bond in Family Violence, Sexual Assault or Abuse, Stalking, or Trafficking Case); or
        - 42.072 (Stalking); or
    - (D) Any other offense involving family violence, as defined by Section 71.004, Family Code; and

- The court has not made an affirmative finding that Petitioner's offense involved family violence, as defined by Section 71.004, Family Code.

4. **Petitioner is Entitled to File a Petition for an Order of Nondisclosure**

Petitioner is entitled to file a petition because Petitioner has satisfied the requirements to do so. A person is entitled to file a petition for an order of nondisclosure under Section 411.0736, Government Code, if the person:

- Was convicted and sentenced for an offense under Section 49.04 (Driving While Intoxicated), Penal Code, other than an offense punishable as a Class A misdemeanor under that section;
- Had an alcohol concentration level that was less than 0.15 at the time an analysis of the petitioner's blood, breath, or urine was performed;
- Is not eligible for an order of nondisclosure under Section 411.0731, Government Code;
- Completed the sentence imposed, including any term of confinement imposed and payment of all fines, costs, and restitution, if any;
- Has satisfied the requirements of Section 411.074, Government Code, including:
  - Not having been convicted of or placed on deferred adjudication for any other offense other than a traffic offense punishable by fine only, during the period after the court pronounced the sentence for the person's DWI offense, and during any applicable waiting period;
  - Not having ever been convicted of or placed on deferred adjudication for any of the offenses listed below:
    - An offense requiring registration as a sex offender under Chapter 62, Code of Criminal Procedure;
    - An offense under Texas Penal Code Section 20.04 (Aggravated Kidnapping);
    - An offense under any of the following Texas Penal Code Sections:
      - 19.02 (Murder);
      - 19.03 (Capital Murder);
      - 20A.02 (Trafficking of Persons);
      - 20A.03 (Continuous Trafficking of Persons);
      - 22.04 (Injury to a Child, Elderly Individual, or Disabled Individual);
      - 22.041 (Abandoning or Endangering a Child);
      - 25.07 (Violation of Court Orders or Conditions of Bond in a Family Violence, Sexual Assault or Abuse, Stalking, or Trafficking Case);
      - 25.072 (Repeated Violation of Certain Court Orders or Conditions of Bond in Family Violence, Sexual Assault or Abuse, Stalking, or Trafficking Case); or

- 42.072 (Stalking); or
  - Any other offense involving family violence, as defined by Section 71.004, Family Code; and
    - Not having received an affirmative finding by the court that the offense for which the order of nondisclosure is requested involved family violence, as defined by Section 71.004, Family Code;
- Has not been previously convicted of or placed on deferred adjudication for another offense other than a traffic offense punishable by fine only;
- Has waited the requisite time (see applicable waiting period indicated above) before filing a petition for an order of nondisclosure; and
- Has included in his or her petition evidence that shows the person is entitled to file a petition for an order of nondisclosure under Section 411.0736, Government Code.

5. Issuance of an Order of Nondisclosure is in the Best Interest of Justice

The issuance of an order of nondisclosure is in the best of justice.

6. The Fee to File the Petition has been Paid or Otherwise Satisfied

The fee to file this petition is the total amount of the fee required to file a civil petition and $28.00, or a petitioner may submit a *Statement of Inability to Afford Payment of Court Costs* in lieu of paying any fees. Petitioner has included

(12)

_____ the required filing fee.

_____ a *Statement of Inability to Afford Payment of Court Costs* in lieu of the required fee.

7. Prayer for Relief

Petitioner respectfully prays that the court grant Petitioner's request for an order of nondisclosure under Section 411.0736, Government Code.

Respectfully submitted,

_____
(13)
_____
(14)
_____
(15)
_____
(16)
_____
(17)

Cause No. _____

In the Matter of § In the

§ _____

_____ § _____ County, Texas

Order of Nondisclosure Under Section 411.0736

On this the _____, day of _____, 20____, the Court considered Petitioner's petition for an order of nondisclosure under Section 411.0736, Government Code.

The State was given notice of the petition and an opportunity to request a hearing. The State

☐ requested a hearing.

☐ did not request a hearing.

The Court

☐ conducted a hearing on _____, _____.

☐ did not conduct a hearing.

Petitioner was convicted and sentenced for an offense under Section 49.04 (Driving While Intoxicated), Penal Code, other than an offense punishable as a Class A misdemeanor under that section, in Criminal Cause No. _____, in this court.

After consideration and a hearing, if a hearing was held as indicated above, the Court **FINDS** that Petitioner is entitled to file a petition and has satisfied the requirements for an order of nondisclosure under Section 411.0736, Government Code. The Court **FURTHER FINDS** that issuance of an order of nondisclosure is in the best interest of justice.

The Court **FURTHER FINDS** that Petitioner's commission of the above-mentioned offense did not result in a motor vehicle accident involving another person, including a person in Petitioner's vehicle.

The Court did not make an affirmative finding that the offense for which the order of nondisclosure is requested involved family violence, as defined by Section 71.004, Family Code.

Accordingly, **IT IS HEREBY ORDERED** that criminal justice agencies are prohibited from disclosing to the public criminal history record information related to the above-mentioned offense.

IT IS FURTHER ORDERED that the criminal history record information pertaining to the arrest and prosecution of Petitioner for the above-mentioned offense shall be sealed and disclosed by the court only to individuals or agencies listed in Section 411.076(a), Government Code.

IT IS FURTHER ORDERED that no later than the 15th business day after the date that this order issues, the clerk of the court (hereinafter "clerk") shall send all relevant criminal history record information contained in this order or a copy of this order to the Crime Records Service of the Texas Department of Public Safety (hereinafter "DPS") by certified mail (return receipt requested) or secure electronic mail, electronic transmission, or facsimile transmission, in accordance with Section 411.075(a), Government Code.

IT IS FURTHER ORDERED that no later than 10 business days after receipt of the relevant criminal history record information contained in this order or a copy of this order from the clerk, DPS shall seal the criminal history record information that is the subject of this order and forward the information or copy of this order to the state and federal agencies listed in 411.075(b), Government Code, in accordance with Section 411.075(b).

IT IS FURTHER ORDERED that an agency or entity shall seal any criminal history record information maintained by that agency or entity that is the subject of this order no later than 30 business days after the date the agency or entity received the relevant criminal history record information contained in this order or a copy of this order from DPS or a clerk, in accordance with Section 411.075(d), Government Code.

IT IS FURTHER ORDERED that the clerk shall seal all court records containing information that is the subject of this order as soon as practicable after the date the clerk sends a copy of this order or all relevant criminal history record information contained in this order to DPS, in accordance with Section 411.076(b), Government Code.

Signed on _____, 20_____.

_____
Judge Presiding

_____
Court/County

APPENDIX L

Texas Length of Duty to Register Compared to the Minimum Required Registration Period Under Federal Law (34 USC § 20911)

June 2019

Texas Code of Criminal Procedure Chapter 62, Subchapter I. Early Termination of Certain Persons' Obligation to Register.

Art. 62.402. Determination of Minimum Required Registration Period

(a) The department by rule shall determine the minimum required registration period under federal law for each reportable conviction or adjudication under this chapter.

(b) After determining the minimum required registration period for each reportable conviction or adjudication under Subsection (a), the department shall compile and publish a list of reportable convictions or adjudications for which a person must register under this chapter for a period that exceeds the minimum required registration period under federal law.

(c) To the extent possible, the department shall periodically verify with the United States Department of Justice's Office of Sex Offender Sentencing, Monitoring, Apprehending, Registering, and Tracking or another appropriate federal agency or office the accuracy of the list of reportable convictions or adjudications described by Subsection (b).

Under Art. 62.403(b), a person with a single reportable adjudication or conviction may apply to the Council on Sex Offender Treatment for an individual risk assessment. Therefore, a second reportable offense that makes the Texas registration period longer than the Federal requirement would not be eligible for deregistration because there is no longer just a single reportable offense. [i.e. §§ 20.02, or 21.11(a)(2)]

Art. 62.404 allows a registrant who has requested and received an individual risk assessment to file with the trial court that sentenced the person for the reportable conviction or adjudication a motion for early termination of the person's obligation to register.

Texas Statute	Texas Offense	Length of Duty to Register in Texas	Length of Duty to Register under SORNA
	Not a single offense OR Federal registration requirement is LONGER or EQUAL TO the Texas registration requirement, so NOT ELIGIBLE to apply for deregistration under CCP 62.403(b)	A single offense AND Federal registration requirement is SHORTER than the Texas registration requirement, so ELIGIBLE to apply for deregistration under CCP 62.403(b)	
§ 20.02	Unlawful Restraint with an affirmative finding that the victim was under 17	Adult conviction, non-parent offender 1st reportable conviction	Post-10	Tier I
		Adult conviction, non-parent offender 2nd reportable conviction	Lifetime	Tier I
		Attempt/conspiracy/solicitation	Post-10	Tier I
		Committed by a parent	Same as above, depending on circumstances	No duty to register
§ 20.03	Kidnapping with an affirmative finding that victim was under 17	Adult conviction, non-parent offender 1st reportable conviction	Post-10	Tier III
		Adult conviction, non-parent offender 2nd reportable conviction	Lifetime	Lifetime
		Attempt/conspiracy/solicitation	Post-10	Tier III
			Lifetime	Lifetime
		Committed by a parent	Same as above, depending on circumstances	No duty to register

353

Texas Length of Duty to Register Compared to the Minimum Required Registration Period Under Federal Law (34 USC § 20911)

June 2019

Texas Statute	Texas Offense		Length of Duty to Register in Texas	Length of Duty to Register under SORNA
			Not a single offense OR Federal registration requirement is LONGER or EQUAL TO the Texas registration requirement, so NOT ELIGIBLE to apply for deregistration under CCP 62.403(b)	A single offense AND Federal registration requirement is SHORTER than the Texas registration requirement, so ELIGIBLE to apply for deregistration under CCP 62.403(b)
§ 20.04	Aggravated Kidnapping with an affirmative finding that victim was under 17	Adult conviction, non-parent offender	Post-10	Tier III Lifetime
		Adult conviction, 1st repeatable conviction	Lifetime	Tier III Lifetime
		Adult conviction, non-parent offender 2nd repeatable conviction	Lifetime	Tier III Lifetime
		Attempt/conspiracy/solicitation	Post-10	Tier III Lifetime
		Committed by a parent	Same as above, depending on circumstances	No duty to register
§ 20.04(a)(4)	Aggravated Kidnapping with the intent to violate or abuse victim sexually	Adult conviction	Lifetime	Tier III Lifetime
		Attempt/conspiracy/solicitation	Post-10	Tier III Lifetime
§ 20A.02(a)(3) or (a)(4)	Trafficking of Adults	Adult conviction	Lifetime	Tier I 15 years
		Attempt/conspiracy/solicitation	Post-10	Tier I 15 years
§ 20A.02(a)(7) or (a)(8)	Trafficking of Children	Adult conviction	Lifetime	Tier II 25 years
		Attempt/conspiracy/solicitation	Post-10	Tier II 25 years
§ 20A.03	Continuous Trafficking of Persons (if victims are 18 or older)	Adult conviction	Lifetime	Tier I 15 years
		Attempt/conspiracy/solicitation	Post-10	Tier I 15 years
§ 20A.03	Continuous Trafficking of Persons (if victims are under 18)	Adult conviction	Lifetime	Tier II 25 years
		Attempt/conspiracy/solicitation	Post-10	Tier II 25 years

Texas Length of Duty to Register Compared to the Minimum Required Registration Period Under Federal Law (34 USC § 20911)

June 2019

Texas Statute	Texas Offense	Length of Duty to Register in Texas		Length of Duty to Register under SORNA
Note: a single offense OR Federal registration requirement is LONGER or EQUAL to the Texas registration requirement, so NOT ELIGIBLE to apply for deregistration under CCP 62.403(b)				A single offense AND Federal registration requirement is SHORTER than the Texas registration requirement, so ELIGIBLE to apply for deregistration under CCP 62.403(b)
§ 25.02	Prohibited Sexual Conduct	Adult conviction	Lifetime	Tier III
		Attempt/conspiracy/solicitation	Post-10	Tier III
				Lifetime
§ 30.02(d)	Burglary of a Habitation with Intent to Commit Sex Offense	Adult conviction	Lifetime	Tier III
		Attempt/conspiracy/solicitation	Post-10	Tier III
				Lifetime
§ 33.021	Online Solicitation of a Minor	Post-10		Tier II 25 years
§ 43.02(c-1)(3)	Prostitution with a person younger than 18	Post-10		Tier II 25 years
§ 43.05(a)(1)	Compelling Prostitution of an Adult over 18 and Attempt/conspiracy/solicitation	Post-10		No duty to register
§ 43.05(a)(2)	Compelling Prostitution Victim under 18	Adult conviction	Lifetime	Tier II 25 years
		Attempt/conspiracy/solicitation	Post-10	Tier II 25 years
§ 43.23(h)	Obscenity (if adult conviction and victim under age 18)	Lifetime		Tier II 25 years *if the victim is visually depicted in representations described under § 43.21(a)(1)(B) of the Texas Penal Code
§ 43.25	Sexual Performance by a Child	Adult conviction	Lifetime	Tier II 25 years
		Attempt/conspiracy/solicitation	Post-10	Tier II 25 years
§ 43.26(a)	Possession of Child Pornography	Adult conviction	Lifetime	Tier I 15 years
		Attempt/conspiracy/solicitation	Post-10	Tier I 15 years

Texas Length of Duty to Register Compared to the Minimum Required Registration Period Under Federal Law (34 USC § 20911)

June 2019

Texas Statute	Texas Offense	Length of Duty to Register in Texas		Length of Duty to Register under SORNA
		Not a single offense OR Federal registration requirement is LONGER or EQUAL to the Texas registration requirement, so NOT ELIGIBLE to apply for deregistration under CCP 62.403(b)		*A single offense AND Federal registration requirement is SHORTER than the Texas registration requirement, so ELIGIBLE to apply for deregistration under CCP 62.403(b)*
§ 21.02	Continuous Sexual Abuse of Young Child or Children	Adult conviction (victim under 13)	Lifetime	Tier III Lifetime
		Adult conviction (victim age 13-17)	Lifetime	Tier II 25 years
		Attempt/conspiracy/solicitation	Post-10	Tier III Lifetime or Tier II 25 years
§ 21.08	Indecent Exposure	2 or more violations and the 2nd violation is NOT a deferred adjudication	Post-10	No duty to register
§ 21.09	Bestiality and Attempt/conspiracy/solicitation	Post-10		Tier I 15 years
§ 21.11(a)(1)	Indecency with a Child by Contact	Adult conviction (victim age 13-17)	Lifetime	Tier II 25 years
		Adult conviction (victim under 13)	Lifetime	Tier III Lifetime
		Attempt/conspiracy/solicitation	Post-10	Tier III Lifetime or Tier II 25 years
§ 21.11(a)(2)	Indecency with a Child by Exposure	1 conviction	Post-10	Tier I 15 years
		2 or more convictions	Lifetime	Tier I 15 years
		Attempt/conspiracy/solicitation	Post-10	Tier I 15 years
§ 22.011	Sexual Assault	Adult conviction	Lifetime	Tier III Lifetime
		Attempt/conspiracy/solicitation	Post-10	Tier III Lifetime
		Adult conviction if exception under 34 U.S. 20911(5)(c) applies	Lifetime	No duty to register
§ 22.021	Aggravated Sexual Assault	Adult conviction	Lifetime	Tier III Lifetime
		Attempt/conspiracy/solicitation	Post-10	Tier III Lifetime

Texas Length of Duty to Register Compared to the Minimum Required Registration Period Under Federal Law (34 USC § 20911)

June 2019

Texas Statute	Texas Offense	Length of Duty to Register in Texas			Length of Duty to Register under SORNA
§ 43.26(e)	Promotion of Child Pornography	Not a single offense OR Federal registration requirement is LONGER or EQUAL to the Texas registration requirement, so NOT ELIGIBLE to apply for deregistration under CCP 62.4030)			A single offense AND Federal registration requirement is SHORTER than the Texas registration requirement, so ELIGIBLE to apply for deregistration under CCP 62.4030)
		Adult conviction		Lifetime	Tier II 25 years
		Attempt/conspiracy/solicitation		Post-10	Tier II 25 years
	Juveniles under 14 at the time of offense	Adjudication of delinquent conduct for any of the above offenses		Post-10	No duty to register
	Juveniles 14 or older at the time of offense	Adjudication of delinquent conduct for any of the above Tier I or II offenses		Post-10	No duty to register
	Juveniles 14 or older at the time of offense	Adjudication of delinquent conduct for any of the above Tier III offenses		Post-10	Lifetime

References:

https://texreg.sos.state.tx.us/public/readtac$ext.TacPage?sl=R&app=9&p_dir=&p_rloc=&p_tloc=&p_ploc=&pg=1&p_tac=&ti=37&pt=1&ch=37&rl=3

Texas Administrative Code
TITLE 37   PUBLIC SAFETY AND CORRECTIONS
PART 1   TEXAS DEPARTMENT OF PUBLIC SAFETY
CHAPTER 37   SEX OFFENDER REGISTRATION
RULE §37.3   Minimum Required Registration Period

Texas Public Sex Offender Registry
HOMEPAGE   SEX OFFENDER REGISTRY
TIERED OFFENSES   TEXAS OFFENSES TIERED UNDER THE FEDERAL ADAM WALSH ACT

https://records.txdps.state.tx.us/SexOffenderRegistry/sor-public/SORNA.pdf

APPENDIX M

MC: ME
Bar Code Area
FS#:
Central File Maintenance
P.O. BOX 12048
AUSTIN, TX 78711-2048

CHILD SUPPORT DIVISION

Date:

OAG Case Number:

<u>Vea Español al Otro Lado</u>

Important

Dear

Please read this page. It describes your responsibilities if you choose to authorize another party to receive case information on your behalf or obtain assistance from a private collection agency or private attorney. Below are some of the conditions that must be met for us to properly work the child support case. Failure to follow these guidelines may result in our taking appropriate action as permitted by federal regulations.

- All case information provided to a third party must be used for child support purposes only.
- All requests for information must be answered within the time frame specified.
- All payments must go through the Texas Child Support Disbursement Unit before being distributed to a private collection agency or private attorney.
- Any changes in arrears must be approved by our office.
- Non-cash child support must be approved by our office.
- We must be provided with timely notice of each order, writ or lien entered in the case by your representative.

To authorize the release of information and/or child support payments to another party, complete the enclosed form.

Please return the completed form to:

Office of the Attorney General
Central File Maintenance
P.O. BOX 12048
Austin, TX 78711-2048

If you have any questions, please call 1-800-252-8014.

June 2016

1A004e

MC: _____   Attorney General Case #: _____

AUTHORIZATION FOR RELEASE OF INFORMATION OR PAYMENTS

Print your current name: _____

Other names you have used: _____

Name of the other party in the case: _____

Names of all children on this case: _____

OAG Case Number *(10 digit number included in OAG correspondence about this case)*: _____

Phone number where you can be contacted: (____) _____

☐ home ☐ work ☐ cell ☐ relative or friend

You do not have to redirect your payments in order to release information or records. The two choices provided below are independent of each other.

By submitting this completed, signed, and dated form, I authorize and request the Office of the Attorney General (OAG) to do the following: *(You must place your **initials** next to each item that applies.)*

Release information or records on my case
(OAG number given above)

This person is (check one)   Initials: _____
    ☐ my attorney
    ☐ a private collection agency
    ☐ a representative that I am designating.

Name: _____   Phone Number: _____

Address: _____   City, State: _____ Zip Code: _____

OR

Send any payments on my case *(OAG number given above)* to the
person I am naming below. I understand that this may delay my
receiving my payment. I also understand that this revokes any direct
deposit authorization that I have already given to the Office of the
Attorney General.   Initials: _____

This person is (check one)
    ☐ my attorney
    ☐ a private collection agency
    ☐ a representative that I am designating.

Name: _____   Phone Number: _____

Address: _____   City, State: _____ Zip Code: _____

I understand that this authorization automatically expires if the case is closed. I may choose to revoke this authorization at any time by submitting a completed, signed, and dated Revocation of Authorization for Release of Information or Payments.

I understand that the Office of the Attorney General of Texas is not responsible for disputes between the listed party and me as a result of this arrangement. *(Please note the date of your signature is required.)*

_____   _____
Signature   Date *(required)*

_____
Address

_____
City, State, ZIP

June 2016   1A004e

APPENDIX N

CHILD SUPPORT

Information for Incarcerated Parents and Parents Returning to the Community

CHILD SUPPORT ■ ESTABLISHING PATERNITY ■ VISITATION ■ DNA TESTING ■ RESOURCES

TABLE OF CONTENTS

OAG services .... page 1

FAQ .... page 2

Contact Information .... page 6

Definitions .... page 7

Inquiry Form .... back page

THE TEXAS OFFICE OF THE ATTORNEY GENERAL (OAG)

believes that children need love and support from both parents.

While you are incarcerated, do everything you can to show your children you love them, care about them and support them.

This booklet answers common questions that parents have about how to handle their child support case while they are incarcerated and what to do when they are released. The booklet also includes definitions of child support and legal terms. Terms in **boldface type** are defined in the definitions section starting on page 7.

The OAG welcomes questions from parents about their Texas child support cases. Please review the following two lists to see what information and services we can and cannot provide while you are incarcerated.

THE OAG CAN PROVIDE:

1. Basic information about your **child support** case
2. The terms of the **order** (such as monthly child support payments and total arrears owed)
3. A review of your case to see if you are eligible for a **child support modification** (upon your request)
4. The address and phone number of the child support office handling your case
5. Information on how to establish **paternity** for your child if you weren't married to the other parent when the child was born
6. The state of Texas Child Support Guidelines (how the child support amount is calculated by state law)
7. In some cases, we may be able to forward one letter for your child to the **custodial parent**, if you do not know the custodial parent's address, and you have an open child support case. The custodial parent will be given whatever contact information you include in the letter.

THE OAG CANNOT:

1. Change custody or enforce visitation
2. File a Termination of Parental Rights petition
3. Give you the address of your children or the other parent
4. Perform DNA testing if you signed an Acknowledgment of Paternity (AOP), or if there is an existing child support order
5. Answer questions other than child support inquiries
6. Obtain information from the court if you do not have a case with the OAG

7. Transport you to court for a hearing or request a bench warrant on your behalf
8. Lift a bench warrant
9. Stop the interest on your arrears
10. Provide legal advice or an attorney

FREQUENTLY ASKED QUESTIONS ABOUT PATERNITY

What does paternity mean?
Paternity means legal determination of fatherhood.

For Married Parents...
When a baby is born to married parents, Texas law automatically recognizes the husband as the father. Married couples do not do anything to establish paternity.

For Unmarried Parents...
When a baby is born to parents who are not married to each other, Texas law does NOT automatically recognize the biological father as a legal parent. Biological fathers must establish paternity to become legal parents and gain legal rights to their children.

How can the paternity of a child be established?
When the mother and father agree, they can voluntarily establish paternity by signing an Acknowledgment of Paternity (AOP). An AOP establishes the father's legal relationship with the child when it is filed with the Texas Vital Statistics Unit (VSU).

How does a father's name get on his child's birth certificate?
Once paternity is established, the father's name can go on the birth certificate. If an AOP is signed at the hospital when a child is born, the father's name is automatically added to the birth certificate. If paternity is established after leaving the hospital, either through a court order or by signing an AOP, the Texas VSU has a process to request that the father's name be added to the birth certificate.

What if the incarcerated parent wants to sign the AOP?
If the incarcerated parent and the other parent both agree that they want to sign an AOP, the parent who is not incarcerated can contact staff at the local child support office, or call (866) 255-2006.

What are the legal benefits of establishing paternity?
Establishing paternity has many benefits for children and parents. The most important benefit for children is knowing that they have a father who wants to be in their life. Once paternity is established, the **legal father** has all the parental rights and responsibilities of a father who was married to the mother. Also, the legal father may be listed on the child's birth certificate, giving the child a sense of identity. Establishing paternity also gives children, if eligible, the opportunity to receive Social Security, military and health insurance benefits from both the mother and the father.

How do you change the child's last name to the father's last name?
If paternity is established for a very young child through the completion and filing of an AOP, a name change may be possible through a process with the VSU. If paternity is being established through the court, parents can ask the court to change a child's

last name to the legal father's last name when the paternity order is finalized. Otherwise, parents may submit a separate petition (request) to the court to change the child's name.

What if I change my mind after I sign the AOP?

It can be very difficult for an incarcerated parent to rescind or challenge an AOP.

Depending on the situation, a person may be able to follow a very specific and time-sensitive process to **rescind** (take back) the AOP or challenge the AOP in court. If you have been recently released and wish to find out more about how to rescind or challenge an AOP, visit texaslawhelp.org, click [Families and Kids] and then click [Paternity].

What if I'm not sure who is the biological father of the child?

If either parent has a doubt about who is the child's biological father, neither should sign an AOP. Parents should get a genetic test to confirm who is the biological father before signing an AOP. Once parents get the results of the genetic test, they may then complete an AOP or go to court to establish the biological father as the legal father of the child.

In many instances, if paternity has not already been established, genetic testing may be provided at no cost by opening a child support case with the Office of the Attorney General. The OAG will not provide genetic testing to parents who have already established paternity through a court order or by completing an AOP. Parents who can access genetic testing through an accredited private lab or over-the-counter kit from a pharmacy may be able to identify the biological father without opening a child support case.

FREQUENTLY ASKED QUESTIONS ABOUT CHILD SUPPORT

Can I open a case with the Office of the Attorney General?

The OAG accepts applications from mothers, fathers and other individuals who request services. OAG attorneys represent the state of Texas in providing child support services and do not represent either parent in the case.

We think of ourselves as still being together as a couple, so why do I have a child support case?

A child support case was opened because the other parent and your children do not live with you. If the custodial parent (CP) applies for Temporary Assistance for Needy Families (TANF) or Medicaid, the state may proceed with a child support case even when the CP does not want child support.

What should I do if I have a child support case when I enter prison?

If you have a child support case, provide the office that is handling your case with your current address. By doing this, you will receive monthly updates that show how much you have paid and how much you owe in past-due support. If you want to try to lower your monthly child support payment, send in the form on page 9 of this booklet, or contact your local child support office and ask for a **review and adjustment packet**.

Remember: If you are able to send in all or some of your child support payments, send them through the State Disbursement Unit. Do not send child support payments directly to the other parent.

If I am in prison, I cannot work. Why doesn't my child support order change automatically?

The OAG cannot automatically change your child support, only the court that has jurisdiction in your case can change the amount of child support you are required to pay. The court will consider changing the child support amount after the correct legal papers are filed. The court also must allow the other parent to present evidence that can affect the court decision.

How can my child support order be changed?

If you want the court to change your child support order while you are in prison, legal papers must be filed in court. One way to see if the court will change your order is by completing the OAG's Incarcerated Noncustodial Parent Affidavit of Income/Assets form and returning it to our office. You may be asked to provide financial information and a notarized statement that can be given to the court for evidence. The completed forms do not guarantee that your child support will change, but they will help the court make a decision. You also can hire a private attorney to file papers with the court.

Remember that the amount you owe doesn't change until the court makes a ruling. Also, interest is added to child support that goes unpaid while you are in prison. If you are able to pay any child support while you are incarcerated, it will help you and your child.

What happens to my child support payments while I'm in prison?

If you are the custodial parent and you do not contact the OAG, payments will continue to be sent through the payment method you selected: by direct deposit to a bank account or debit card, or by mail to the address previously provided. The OAG will continue to send your child support payments to you unless a **court order** redirects them to another person. For example, the court may order that payments go to the person with physical custody of your children while you are incarcerated.

While I'm in prison, can the child support I receive go to the person who is taking care of my children? If so, what should I do?

Yes, your child support can go to the person caring for your children. There are two ways to redirect child support to a child's caregiver. One way is by completing an "Authorization for Release of Information and Payment" and returning it to the OAG. Include the name of the person who is to receive the payments.

A second way to redirect payments is for the person with physical custody of the children to apply for child support services. Then, the OAG will seek a child support order to redirect the child support payments to that person. Caregivers must provide proof that the children live with them before the OAG can file a legal motion to redirect child support. Examples of proof include children's school or daycare records, or an affidavit of possession.

Where can I get help with my child support or information about my child support case?

If you are incarcerated, the law library is a good place to start. The law librarian can give you the "Child Support Inquiry Form for Incarcerated Parents." **All requests for information about child support or your child** support case must be made on this form. Please allow 60-90 days for a response.

FREQUENTLY ASKED QUESTIONS ABOUT CUSTODY AND VISITATION

Does the OAG handle custody and visitation problems?
The Office of the Attorney General is not authorized to handle custody or visitation disputes. After incarceration, the Access and Visitation Hotline can provide parenting time (visitation) resources that may help reunite and resume parenting time with your children. The hotline number is (866) 292-4636. The hotline is answered in English and Spanish, Monday-Friday, 1–7 p.m.

Are fathers treated differently from mothers in child support matters?
No. Texas laws about support, custody and visitation do not mention the parent's gender. Texas law focuses on the best interest of the child.

What should I do if I believe my child is being abused?
Call the Department of Family and Protective Services at (800) 252-5400. If you do not have access to a phone, ask someone else to make the call for you.

FREQUENTLY ASKED QUESTIONS UPON RELEASE FROM INCARCERATION

Most people need time to get on their feet after leaving prison. The OAG may be able to temporarily delay certain enforcement actions when parents provide evidence that they are looking for a job and making some child support payments. It's important to make an appointment with a child support office upon release from prison. Request a review of your court order when you return to work, or if you reunite with your child's other parent.

Are there any services available to help me get a job so I can pay my child support?
You can go to the Texas Workforce Commission's local workforce development board for job search help, skills training and employment support services. You also may dial 211 or search the Internet for referrals to educational, literacy or parenting classes, or referrals to substance abuse counseling. In some cases, the court may order a noncustodial parent who is behind on child support payments to take part in one or more of these services.

What can I do about my child support case once I am released from prison?

- Contact the child support office handling your case and provide your new phone number, address and employment information. If you are living in transitional housing, let the office know how much of your **income** is deducted to cover the expense. Remember that the more information you provide, the easier it is for the child support office to make informed decisions about your case.

- Pay child support regularly while you are looking for work. Even if you can't pay the full amount, pay what you can.

- Stay in touch with the child support office handling your case about your job search efforts, and find employment before an enforcement action is taken.

- Notify the child support office as soon as you get a job, so that the office can send an order to your employer to automatically deduct child support from your pay check and send it to the Texas State Disbursement Unit.

- Request referrals for parenting classes, job help or other social services.

My child support order was modified during my incarceration. Now that I am out, will my monthly payment change?

If your child support order was lowered while you were in prison, the court will consider your release from prison as a reason it can change your child support order. After your release from prison, the amount you pay in child support will likely increase to reflect your actual earnings or your earning capacity.

Do I have to go to court to get my child support modified when I get out of prison?

Not always; in some cases you may be eligible for the **Child Support Review Process (CSRP)**, which is one way to handle legal issues on your child support case without going to court. In CSRP, both parents are given the opportunity to meet with a child support officer at a local child support office to establish a legal order. Ask at the child support office if you are eligible.

How does the court decide how much child support I will pay?

Texas law sets the following general guidelines for child support payments. The percentage is applied to the net resources of the noncustodial parent.

- 20% for one child
- 25% for two children
- 30% for three children
- 35% for four children
- 40% for five children
- Not less than 40% for six or more children

Special rules apply if you have children in more than one household.

I have remarried, and my spouse makes a very good living. Will the child support office take my child support out of my spouse's earnings? Will my spouse's income be counted when my child support amount is calculated?

No. Child support cannot be taken out of a spouse's check or earnings. A new spouse's income will not be added to your net resources when calculating the amount of child support to be paid.

I have children with different mothers. How will the court determine the amount of child support that I pay?

When you have children in different households, the court uses a multiple household formula to determine the amount of support you must pay. It is important that you let the judge or child support review officer know that you are legally responsible to support other children who have a different mother.

CONTACT INFORMATION FOR USE AFTER INCARCERATION

BY U. S. MAIL

Office of the Attorney General
Child Support Division
P. O. Box 12017
Austin, TX 78711-2017

ON THE INTERNET

website: www.texasattorneygeneral.gov
email: child.support@texasattorneygeneral.gov

BY TELEPHONE

Customer Service Centers (800) 252-8014
Paternity Opportunity Program (866) 255-2006

24-HOUR PAYMENT AND CASE STATUS INFORMATION

(800) 252-8014

FOR THE DEAF AND HARD-OF-HEARING

1-800-Relay-TX
(800) 735-2989

CHILD SUPPORT DEFINITIONS:

Accredited private lab – A lab accredited by the American Association of Blood Banks to perform genetic testing to determine whether a man is the biological father of a child

Accrual – Sum of child support payments that are due or overdue

Amend the birth certificate – A special request made to the Texas Vital Statistics Unit that allows parents to change information on a child's birth certificate

Arrearage – Past due, unpaid child support owed by the noncustodial parent

Acknowledgment of Paternity (AOP) – A document that unmarried parents can voluntarily sign to establish legal paternity for their child without going to court. The form does not establish child support or resolve custody and visitation.

Case – A collection of people associated with a particular child support order, court hearing, and/or request for IV-D services. This typically includes: a custodial parent (CP), one or more children, a noncustodial parent (NCP) and/or presumed father (PF). Every child support case has a unique Case ID number

Case ID – Unique identification number assigned to a child support case

Child support modification – A court ordered change to a child support order, which can include your child support payment amount being lowered or raised

Child support – Financial support paid by a parent to help support a child or children of whom they do not have custody

Child Support Review Process (CSRP) – OAG expedited administrative actions to establish, modify, and enforce child support and medical support obligations, to determine parentage, or to take any other actions authorized under Title IV-D of the Social Security Act

Court order – A legally binding document issued by a court of law. A court order related to child support can dictate how often, how much, and/or what kind of support a noncustodial parent must pay and how long he or she must pay

Custodial parent (CP) – The person who has primary care, custody and control of the child, also referred to as the obligee

Dependent – A child who is under the care of someone else. Most children are dependents. The child ceases to be a dependent when he or she reaches the age of 18, as determined by state law, but depending on the state's provisions, may remain eligible for child support for a period after he or she turns 18 years of age

Default judgment – A judgment entered when a person fails to respond to a legal action or fails to appear in court even though the person was notified of the legal action and court date

Genetic testing (DNA testing) – Analysis of inherited factors to determine whether a man is a child's biological father

Guidelines – A standard method for setting child support amounts based on the income of the parent(s) and other factors determined by state law

Income – Any periodic form of payment to an individual, regardless of source, including wages, salaries, commissions, bonuses, worker's compensation, disability, pension, or retirement program payments and interest

Legal father – A man who is recognized by law as the male parent of a child

Material and substantial change – A serious and meaningful change, something that makes enough of a difference to the family's situation that it justifies a review of the child support order

Monthly support obligation – The amount of money a noncustodial parent is required to pay per month

Net resources – Income and earnings minus allowable deductions, such as federal taxes

Noncustodial parent (NCP) – The parent who does not have primary care, custody and control of the child, also referred to as the obligor

OAG – Office of the Attorney General

Obligated – A term meaning that a noncustodial parent (NCP) is required to meet the financial terms of a court or administrative order

Obligation – Amount of money to be paid as support by a noncustodial parent (NCP). It can take the form of financial support for the child, medical support or spousal support. An obligation is recurring and ongoing. It is not a one-time debt

Order – Direction of a magistrate, judge or properly empowered administrative officer

Paternity – Legal determination of fatherhood

Rescind – To cancel, refers to a change of mind after signing an Acknowledgment of Paternity (AOP)

Review and adjustment packet – A Texas Child Support Division forms packet. The packet may be automatically sent once every three years while the child support case is open, or may be sent when a parent requests a review of the child support obligation, and includes questions about each parent's financial and family situation

Visitation provisions – Language in a court order that says when a parent has parenting time (visitation) with the child(ren) listed on the court order

NOTES

INQUIRY FORM FOR INCARCERATED PARENTS

Read the section below carefully before completing this form. If you have multiple cases, use one form for each case. (Photocopies are acceptable).

(Please print)

NAME (Last, first, middle): _____ INMATE#: _____

FACILITY NAME: _____

FACILITY ADDRESS: _____ CITY/ZIP CODE: _____

SOCIAL SECURITY NUMBER: _____

ATTORNEY GENERAL CASE NUMBER: _____

COURT CAUSE NUMBER & COUNTY OF JURISDICTION: _____

OTHER PARENT'S NAME: _____

NAME OF CHILD(REN): _____

DATE OF ENTRY: _____ DATE OF RELEASE: _____

PLEASE CHECK **ONLY** THE LINES YOU WANT US TO RESPOND TO:

____ I would like the address and phone number of the child support office handling my case.

____ I have a child support case, and I am requesting that it be reviewed to see if I qualify for a lower monthly child support payment.

____ I was not married to the mother/father of my child _____ (child's name) and would like to establish paternity (legal fatherhood) for this child.

NOTE: Requests for information not listed above will not be answered. State and federal law limits the release of certain information on child support cases.

SIGNATURE _____ DATE _____

MAIL TO:

Office of the Attorney General

Child Support Division

Mail Code 038

P. O. Box 12017

Austin, TX 78711-2017

CHILD SUPPORT DIVISION

Dear Parent:

Re: Your Request for Review

Thank you for your inquiry regarding a review of your child support order. Please sign this form and return it with the completed Child Support Review Questionnaire to the child support office that is handling your case. You can find the address by calling 1-800-252-8014, or selecting "Child Support Interactive" from the child support section of the Attorney General's Web site at www.texasattorneygeneral.gov.

Name:	Social Security #:	OAG Case #:

I request the Child Support Division of the Office of the Attorney General to conduct a review of my child support order. I understand the following:

- The attorneys of the Office of the Attorney General represent the State of Texas. They will provide me with child support services, but do not represent me or any other individual.
- A review addresses only child support and medical support.
- The non-custodial parent may be required to provide medical insurance for the child(ren).
- A review of a child support order will determine if the order complies with the Texas child support guidelines.
- A request for a review may be withdrawn by the requestor.

Please list the reason you are requesting a review:

_____   _____
Signature   Date Signed

Within three weeks of receiving all of the necessary information from you, we will determine if a review of your child support order is appropriate and we will notify you of our decision. If it is determined that a review should be conducted, the other party named in your child support order will be asked to complete a questionnaire. Thank you for your cooperation.

Office of the Attorney General
Child Support Division

November 2014   *An Equal Employment Opportunity Employer · Printed on Recycled Paper*   Form 3L015ac-online

CHILD SUPPORT REVIEW QUESTIONNAIRE

INSTRUCTIONS

Please type, print, or write clearly. Answer all questions as completely and accurately as you can. Please return the completed form along with copies of your income tax returns for the past two years, and your two most recent pay stubs. If you do not have these items, please send us your W-2 Forms for the past two years.

Date:	OAG Case Number:

INFORMATION ABOUT YOU (Please Print All Information)
Important Safety Information

If you have concerns about your child(ren)'s safety, there are some protections available in the child support process.

Do you have concerns about any of the following?
- the other parent or other individuals having access to your physical contact information?
- negotiating in person with the other parent?
- contact with the other parent during exchange of the child(ren) for visitation?

☐ Yes ☐ No   If yes, please explain. _____

Do you have a protective order, police report, or other supporting document? ☐ Yes ☐ No   **If possible attach a copy of any documentation.**
If you answered YES to either of the previous questions, you will be sent an Affidavit of Nondisclosure.

Name (Last, First, Middle)	Social Security No.	Date of Birth	Relationship to Child(ren)	
Address: Street Address	Apt. #	City	State	Zip Code
Home Telephone No.	Work Telephone No.	Do you have custody of the child(ren)? ☐ YES ☐ NO		
Employer		Employer's Telephone No.		
Employer Address: Street Address		City	State	Zip Code

INFORMATION ABOUT THE OTHER PARTY

Name (Last, First, Middle)	Social Security No.	Date of Birth	Relationship to Child(ren)	
Address: Street Address	Apt. #	City	State	Zip Code
Current Employer		Employer's Telephone No. (	Home Telephone No.	
Employer Address: Street Address		City	State	Zip Code

INFORMATION ABOUT THE CHILD(REN) (List only your children with the other party named above.)

Name (Last, First, Middle)	Sex	Social Security Number	Date of Birth	Place of Birth

NOVEMBER 2014   PAGE 1   FORM 3F002E

FINANCIAL INFORMATION

YOUR GROSS (before any deductions) MONTHLY INCOME FROM:	CURRENT INFORMATION AMOUNT	INFORMATION AT TIME OF LAST SUPPORT ORDER AMOUNT
Salary and Wages (including commissions, bonuses, and overtime)		
Self-Employment		
Pensions and Retirement		
Social Security Benefits		
Unemployment Benefits		
Disability and Workers' Compensation Benefits		
Dividends and Interest		
Net Rentals		
Other (specify):		
TOTAL MONTHLY INCOME		

YOUR MONTHLY DEDUCTIONS FOR:	CURRENT INFORMATION AMOUNT	INFORMATION AT TIME OF LAST SUPPORT ORDER AMOUNT
Union Dues		
Health Insurance You Pay For Your Child(ren) On This Order		

Insurance Company	Policy Number	Child(ren) Covered		
	TOTAL MONTHLY DEDUCTIONS			

YOUR ASSETS:	CURRENT INFORMATION AMOUNT	INFORMATION AT TIME OF LAST SUPPORT ORDER AMOUNT
Cash On Hand		
Money in Checking Accounts		
Money in Savings Accounts		
Money in Any Other Accounts		
Retirement or Pension Funds		
Life Insurance Cash Value		
Stocks, Bonds, or Other Investment Securities		
Real Estate		
Other Assets (please specify)		
TOTAL VALUE OF ALL ASSETS		

CHILDREN:	CURRENT INFORMATION NUMBER	INFORMATION AT TIME OF LAST SUPPORT ORDER NUMBER
Children you are legally obligated to support either in you home or by court order.		

Read the statements below. Check the box next to those you believe are true, and explain why.

☐ The other parent's income has substantially (check one) ☐ increased ☐ decreased since the date of the current child support order.

By how much? $ _____ per _____

Explain why

Do you have any other children, not already mentioned in this questionnaire, **who currently live with you?**
☐ Yes ☐ No   If "yes", complete the box below. Do **not** include stepchildren.

Name (Last, First, Middle)	Sex	Social Security #	Date of Birth	Place of Birth

Do you have any other children, not already mentioned in this questionnaire, **whom you are legally obligated to support?**
☐ Yes ☐ No   If "yes", complete the box below.   Please attach copies of your court orders, if available.

Name (Last, First, Middle)	Sex	Social Security #	Date of Birth	Place of Birth

Is there any other information we should consider that has not been covered in this questionnaire? For example, Special needs of the children subject to this order.

Explain

By my signature below, I certify that the information provided by me in this form is true and correct to the best of my knowledge.

Texas Government Code ● 559 gives you the right to review and request correction of information on this form.

_____   _____
Signature   Date Signed

APPENDIX P
SAMPLE PETITION AND ORDER FOR MODIFICATION OF CHILD SUPPORT

Note: These forms are intended only as an example and guide for drafting. Please seek the assistance of an attorney.

Cause No: _____

IN THE INTEREST OF	§	IN THE _____ JUDICIAL DISTRICT
1. _____	§	COURT OF
2. _____		
CHILDREN	§	_____ COUNTY, TEXAS

Petition to Modify Parent-Child Relationship

DISCOVERY LEVEL

Discovery in this case is intended to be conducted under level 1 of rule 190 of the Texas Rules of Civil Procedure.

OBJECTION TO ASSIGNMENT OF CASE TO ASSOCIATE JUDGE

Petitioner objects to the assignment of this matter to an associate judge for a trial on the merits or presiding at a jury trial.

PETITIONER AND ORDER TO BE MODIFIED

This suit to modify a prior order is brought by _____, Petitioner, who is _____ years of age and resides at _____. Petitioner is the [mother or father] and non-custodial parent of the child and has standing to bring this suit. The requested modification will be in the best interest of the child.

The order to be modified is entitled *Order in Suit Affecting Parent Child Relationship* and was rendered on _____ [date].

JURISDICTION

This Court has continuing, exclusive jurisdiction of this suit.

CHILD

The following child(ren) is/are the subject of this suit:

Name:
Sex:
Birth date:

Name:
Sex:
Birth date:

PARTIES AFFECTED

The names and addresses of each party whose rights, privileges, duties, or powers may be affected by this motion are:

Name:
Address:
Relationship:

Process should be served at that address.

CHILD'S PROPERTY

There has been no change of consequence in the status of the child's property since the prior order was rendered.

SUPPORT

The circumstances of the child or a person affected by the order have materially and substantially changed since the rendition of the order to be modified, and the support payments previously ordered should be reevaluated. The support payments previously ordered are not in substantial compliance with the guidelines in chapter 154 of the Texas Family Code. Petitioner requests that the court re-evaluates the previous support order to accommodate Petitioner's current financial status. Petitioner requests that any decrease be made retroactive. The requested modification is in the best interest of the child(ren).

PRAYER

Petitioner prays that citation and notice issue as required by law and that the Court enter its orders in accordance with the allegations contained in this petition.

Petitioner prays for general relief.

Respectfully submitted,

_____
[ATTORNEY OR PETITIONER PRO SE]
ADDRESS
PHONE NUMBER

Certificate of Service

I certify that a true copy of the above was served on each attorney of record or party in accordance with the Texas Rules of Civil Procedure on _____.

_____
[ATTORNEY OR PETITIONER PRO SE]

Cause No: _____

IN THE INTEREST OF	§	IN THE _____ JUDICIAL DISTRICT
1. _____	§	COURT OF
2. _____		
CHILDREN	§	_____ COUNTY, TEXAS

ORDER IN SUIT TO MODIFY PARENT-CHILD RELATIONSHIP – CHILD SUPPORT

On _____ the Court heard this case.

Appearances

Petitioner, _____, appeared in person and announced ready for trial.

Respondent, _____, appeared in person and announced ready for trial.

Jurisdiction

The Court, after examining the record and the evidence and argument of counsel, finds that it has jurisdiction of this case and of all the parties and that no other court has continuing, exclusive jurisdiction of this case. All persons entitled to citation were properly cited.

Jury

A jury was waived, and all questions of fact and of law were submitted to the Court.

Record

The making of a record of testimony was waived by the parties with the consent of the Court.

Children

The Court finds that the following children are the subject of this suit:

Name:
Sex:
Birth date:

Name:
Sex:
Birth date:

Findings

The Court finds that the material allegations in the petition to modify are true and that the requested modification is in the best interest of the children. IT IS ORDERED that the requested modification is GRANTED in the best interest of the children.

Child Support

IT IS ORDERED that _____ is obligated to pay and shall pay to _____ child support of _____ dollars ($_____) per month, with the first payment being due and payable on _____ and a like payment being due and payable on the _____ day of each month thereafter until the first month following the date of the earliest occurrence of one of the events specified below:

1. any child reaches the age of eighteen years or graduates from high school, whichever occurs later;
2. any child marries;
3. any child dies;
4. the parent-child relationship is terminated based on genetic testing that excludes the obligor as the child's genetic father;
5. the child enlists in the armed forces of the United States and begins active service as defined by section 101 of title 10 of the United States Code; or
6. any child's disabilities are otherwise removed for general purposes.

Payment

IT IS ORDERED that all payments shall be made through the state disbursement unit at Texas Child Support Disbursement Unit, P.O. Box 659791, San Antonio, Texas 78265-9791, and thereafter promptly remitted to _____ for the support of the children.

Required Information

The information required for each party by section 105.006(a) of the Texas Family Code is as follows:

Name: _____
Social Security number: XXX-XX- X_____
TX Driver's license number: _____
Current residence address: _____
Mailing address: _____
Telephone _____
Name of employer: _____
Address of employment: _____

Name: _____
Social Security number: XXX-XX- X_____
TX Driver's license number: _____
Current residence address: _____
Mailing address: _____
Telephone: _____
Name of employer: _____
Address of employment: _____

Costs

IT IS ORDERED that costs of court are to be borne by the party who incurred them.

Relief Not Granted

IT IS ORDERED that all relief requested in this case and not expressly granted is denied. All other terms of the prior orders not specifically modified in this order shall remain in full force and effect.

SIGNED on _____.

_____
JUDGE PRESIDING

APPENDIX Q

———————————————
County of Residence

Fold on line and seal before mailing

BUSINESS REPLY MAIL
FIRST-CLASS MAIL   PERMIT NO. 4511   AUSTIN, TX

POSTAGE WILL BE PAID BY ADDRESSEE

NO POSTAGE
NECESSARY
IF MAILED
IN THE
UNITED STATES

SECRETARY OF STATE
ELECTIONS DIVISION
PO BOX 12887
AUSTIN TX 78711-9972

Fold on line and seal before mailing

Qualifications

- You must register to vote in the county in which you reside.
- You must be a citizen of the United States.
- You must be at least 17 years and 10 months old to register, and you must be 18 years of age by Election Day.
- You must not be finally convicted of a felony, or if you are a felon, you must have completed all of your punishment, including any term of incarceration, parole, supervision, period of probation, or you must have received a pardon.
- You must not have been determined by a final judgment of a court exercising probate jurisdiction to be totally mentally incapacitated or partially mentally incapacitated without the right to vote.

Filling out the Application

- Review the application carefully, fill it out, sign and date it and mail it to the voter registrar in your county or drop it by the Voter Registrar's office.

- All voters who register to vote in Texas must provide a Texas driver's license number or personal identification number issued by the Texas Department of Public Safety. If you don't have such a number, simply provide the last four digits of your social security number. If you don't have a social security number, you need to state that fact.
- Your voter registration will become effective 30 days after it is received or on your 18th birthday, whichever is later. Your registration must be effective on or before an election day in order to vote in that election.
- If you move to another county, you must re-register in the county of your new residence.

Please visit the Texas Secretary of State website, www.sos.state.tx.us, and for additional election information visit **www.votetexas.gov**.

Este formulario está disponible en español. Favor de llamar a su registrador de votantes local para conseguir una versión en español.

Texas Voter Registration Application

Prescribed by the Office of the Secretary of State VR30.2016E.13

For Official Use Only

Please complete sections by printing LEGIBLY. If you have any questions about how to fill out this application, please call your local voter registrar.

1 These Questions Must Be Completed Before Proceeding (Check one)

☐ New Application ☐ Change of Address, Name, or Other Information ☐ Request for a Replacement Card

Are you a United States Citizen?	☐ Yes	☐ No
Will you be 18 years of age on or before election day?	☐ Yes	☐ No

If you checked 'No' in response to either of the above, do not complete this form.

Are you interested in serving as an election worker?	☐ Yes	☐ No

2
Last Name Include Suffix if any (Jr, Sr, III)	First Name	Middle Name (if any)	Former Name (if any)

3
Residence Address: Street Address and Apartment Number. If none, describe where you live. (Do not include P.O. Box, Rural Rt. or Business Address)	City	TEXAS
	County	Zip Code

4
Mailing Address: Street Address and Apartment Number. (If mail cannot be delivered to your residence address.)	City	State
		Zip Code

5 City and County of Former Residence in Texas

6 Date of Birth: (mm/dd/yyyy) ☐☐/☐☐/☐☐☐☐

7 Gender (Optional) ☐ Male ☐ Female

8 Telephone Number (Optional) Include Area Code (☐☐☐)☐☐☐-☐☐☐☐

9 Texas Driver's License No. or Texas Personal I.D. No. (Issued by the Department of Public Safety)
☐☐☐☐☐☐☐☐

If no Texas Driver's License or Personal Identification, give last 4 digits of your Social Security Number
XXX-XX-☐☐☐☐

☐ I have not been issued a Texas Driver's License/Personal Identification Number or Social Security Number.

10
I understand that giving false information to procure a voter registration is perjury, and a crime under state and federal law. Conviction of this crime may result in imprisonment up to 180 days, a fine up to $2,000, or both. Please read all <u>three</u> statements to affirm before signing.

- I am a resident of this county and a U.S. citizen;
- I have not been finally convicted of a felony, or if a felon, I have completed all of my punishment including any term of incarceration, parole, supervision, period of probation, or I have been pardoned; and
- I have not been determined by a final judgment of a court exercising probate jurisdiction to be totally mentally incapacitated or partially mentally incapacitated without the right to vote.

X _____ Date ___/___/___

Signature of Applicant or Agent and Relationship to Applicant or Printed Name of Applicant if Signed by Witness and Date.

APPENDIX R

Request for Status Information Letter

VERIFY: I am <u>not</u> registered with the Selective Service System and requesting a Status Information Letter. I am now 26 years old or older and was born after December 31, 1959.

NOTE: No action will be taken on this request unless ALL <u>REQUIRED</u> information / documentation with an asterisk (*) are received (where applicable). KEEP a copy of all documents and correspondence submitted.

Section 1:

* Name _____
           * First Name   * Middle Name   * Last Name

List any other names used _____
                                     Include any multiple last names

* Current Mailing Address _____
                                       * Street Address

_____
        * City   * State   * Zip Code

* Social Security Number _____

* Date of Birth _____
                * Month / * Day / * Year

Daytime Telephone Number _____

E-mail Address _____

Section 2:

MILITARY:

    List dates of active duty service: _____ to _____

    List dates of reserve duty service: _____ to _____

    List dates of military school service: _____ to _____

    Military school attended: _____

    * Attach copy of DD 214 (or DD Form 4 if still on active duty)

☐ INCARCERATED   ☐ INSTITUTIONALIZED   ☐ HOSPITALIZED   ☐ HOME CONFINED

    * List dates during which you were incarcerated, institutionalized, hospitalized, or confined to a home. For multiple dates, list all:

    _____ to _____ , _____ to _____ , _____ to _____

* Attach proof of each instance.

NON-CITIZEN / UNDOCUMENTED IMMIGRANT:

　* Date you entered the United States for the first time: _____
　　　　　　　　　　　　　　　　　　　　　　　　　　　　　　　* Month / * Day / * Year

　* USCIS (formerly INS) status at time of entry: _____

　* REQUIRED: List all immigrant status(es) held since entering the country, and give dates:
　　(Attach separate sheet if necessary)

　　_____ to _____   USCIS Status _____
　　_____ to _____   USCIS Status _____
　　_____ to _____   USCIS Status _____
　　_____ to _____   USCIS Status _____

　* Attach copies of supporting documentation (see the included INSTRUCTIONS for details)

TRANSGENDER:

　At birth my gender was: _____
　*Attach copy of original birth certificate or similar documentation. If name on form is different from name on birth certificate due to name change, please include court order or other name change documentation.

* REASON WHY YOU FAILED TO REGISTER WITH SELECTIVE SERVICE UPON REACHING AGE 18 AND BEFORE REACHING AGE 26:

_____
_____
_____
_____

Section 3:

IMPORTANT NOTE: No action can be taken until we receive ALL required information / documentation with an asterisk (*) are received. You should retain a copy of all documents and correspondence submitted to us.

Print, sign and date, and mail this letter to the address below, together with ALL copies of required documents and all other supporting information you may wish to include.

_____   _____
　　　　　* Signature   　　　　　* Date

　　　　　　　　　　　Selective Service System
　　　　　　　　　　　ATTN: SIL
　　　　　　　　　　　PO Box 94638
　　　　　　　　　　　Palatine, IL 60094-4638

INSTRUCTIONS

For filling out the "Request for Status Information Letter"

SECTION 1:

- Name (**required**): you must provide your complete name, and any other names you have ever used. If you have more than one last name, you must provide both names.

- Address (**required**): you must include your complete mailing address. Forms received without a mailing address will not be processed.

- Social Security Number (**required, if you have one**): If you have a social security number, you must provide it. Also, if you have ever used a different social security number, provide it as well.

- Date of Birth (**required**): This form is only for men born after December 31, 1959, who are 26 years old or older. You must provide your complete date of birth.

- Daytime Telephone Number: If possible, provide a telephone number where you can be reached during the day, in case we need to contact you.

- Email Address: If possible, provide your email address in case we need to contact you.

SECTION 2: (Requires dates and supporting documentation)

This section is for explaining and documenting why you did not register with Selective Service. This section consists of five different parts. You must complete and submit documentation for any and all parts that apply to you.

Military:
To obtain proof of military service (DD-214, Official Military Personnel File) write to: National Personnel Records Center, GSA, Military Personnel Records Center, 9700 Page Blvd., St. Louis, MO, 63132. Or visit http://www.archives.gov/veterans/military-service-records

Incarcerated, institutionalized, hospitalized, or home confined:
For each instance, provide type of confinement, dates of confinement, and supporting documentation.

Non-Citizen / Non-Immigrants:
If you entered the United States for the first time after your 26th birthday, you must provide documentation to support your claim. Valid documentation includes: entry stamp in your passport, I-94 with entry stamp on it. If you entered the United States illegally after your 26th birthday, you must provide proof that you were not living in the United States from age 18 to age 26. **Please note**: your Resident Alien Card (Green Card) is not proof of entry to the United States.

If you entered the United States as a valid non-immigrant, and remained in that status to your 26th birthday, you must provide documentation to support your claim. For example, if you entered the United States as an F-1 student, and remained in that status until your 26th birthday, you would need to provide documentation indicating that you were admitted on an F-1 visa and attended school full-time as required. (Acceptable documents for this situation include copies of your I-20s or a letter from the school you attended indicating your full time attendance as a non-immigrant). The same thing applies for all non-immigrant statuses. You must explain, if at any point, you violated the terms of your visa, or overstayed your visa and became an undocumented immigrant.

You should provide as much information as possible. We will use the information you provide to determine your registration status. A list of documents to provide can be found at:
https://www.sss.gov/Portals/0/PDFs/DocumentationList.pdf

<u>Transgender:</u>
For individuals who have had a gender change. You must indicate what sex you were at birth, and attach documentation which indicates this as well. If your name has changed, please provide court orders or other name change documentation.

<u>Reason why you failed to register with Selective Service upon reaching age 18 and before reaching age 26</u>:
Provide a written explanation for not registering with Selective Service.

SECTION 3:

Sign and date the letter (**required**). Return this letter to the address listed with copies of supporting documents, showing proof and anything else you may wish to include. IMPORTANT: <u>Do not send original documents</u>, as they will not be returned. **You should retain a copy of all documents and correspondence submitted.**

HELPFUL INFORMATION

- This form is designed to be printed for use, and cannot be submitted online. After printing, complete the form, attach **ALL** supporting documentation, and mail to: Selective Service System, ATTN: SIL, PO Box 94638, Palatine, IL 60094-4638.

- <u>This form is for use only by men born after December 31, 1959</u>, who are not registered and are now 26 years old or older.

- This form is <u>not</u> a registration form, and by submitting it, you will not be registered.

- If you feel that you have already registered, verify your registration on our website (**www.sss.gov**), or call our Registration Information Office at (847) 688-6888 to obtain your Selective Service registration number.

- We will issue a Status Information Letter based on the information you provide. This letter will clarify your status with Selective Service. **KEEP your status information letter from Selective Service in your permanent files for future reference.**

- If you are being denied a right, benefit, or privilege because you are not registered, submit a <u>copy</u> of your status information letter from Selective Service and a separate letter in which you explain in the best of your ability the reasons surrounding your failure to register, to the agency administering the right, benefit, or privilege. That agency will make the final determination regarding your eligibility. The Selective Service System does not determine your eligibility for any right, benefit, or privilege.

Remember to KEEP your original Status Information Letter in your permanent files.

July 20, 2015

Made in the USA
Coppell, TX
27 August 2022